Body Battlegrounds

Body Battlegrounds

Transgressions, Tensions, and Transformations

*Edited by Chris Bobel
and Samantha Kwan*

Vanderbilt University Press
Nashville

Library of Congress Cataloging-in-Publication Data
Names: Bobel, Chris, 1963– editor. | Kwan, Samantha, 1971– editor.
Title: Body battlegrounds: transgressions, tensions, and transformations /
edited by Chris Bobel and Samantha Kwan.
Description: Nashville, TN: Vanderbilt University Press, [2019] | Includes
bibliographical references and index. |
Identifiers: LCCN 2018027236 (print) | LCCN 2018044292 (ebook) | ISBN
9780826522351 (ebook) | ISBN 9780826522337 (cloth:) | ISBN
9780826522344 (pbk.)
Subjects: LCSH: Human body—Social aspects. | Manners and customs. |
Women—Psychology. | Sexual minorities—Psychology.
Classification: LCC HM636 (ebook) | LCC HM636.B5837 2019 (print) | DDC
306.4/613—dc23
LC record available at lccn.loc.gov/2018027236

ISBN 978-0-8265-2233-7 (hardcover)
ISBN 978-0-8265-2234-4 (paperback)
ISBN 978-0-8265-2235-1 (ebook)

For Leela, Jan, Matthew, James, Lucy, Saartje, Fiona, Francecca, Nabra, Rick, and Tilly

Contents

Acknowledgments

Ours is a project that depended on countless generous, smart, creative people to bring to fruition.

We begin with our editor Michael Ames, whose belief in the aim of the book and wise advice on nearly every detail served as our rudder in sometimes-rocky seas. And next, we thank the wonderful Joell Smith-Borne, who handled the editorial process with the perfect combination of eagle eyes, efficiency, and equanimity.

We were fortunate to have the handiwork of skilled and good-natured Taylor Burns who prepared the manuscript for peer review and Camille Nelson who expertly prepared the index. We deeply appreciate Meika Loe and the two anonymous reviewers who provided tremendously helpful feedback that strengthened the book. We are also grateful to Fanni Farago for her assistance supporting and supplementing our marketing efforts.

We tapped many people to help us spread word of the book. Some went out of their way to connect us with potential contributors, shining a light on the value of intellectual community (and email!). Among these good people are Abigail Brooks, Connie Chow, Michael Cottingham, Abby Ferber, Robb Hernandez, Afshan Jafar, Simi Linton, Sharon Oselin, CJ Pascoe, Abigail Saguy, Mary Nell Trautner, and Anne Zelek.

A special thanks goes out to talented Jax Gonzalez who designed our Call for Contributors flyer and the incredibly creative Elina Tuomi for sharing her beautiful artwork with us as possible cover images.

We also thank Breanne Fahs, who not only contributed a chapter, but also generously allowed us to "pinch" the title of her chapter as the title of the entire collection.

Body Battlegrounds

Introduction

Chris Bobel and Samantha Kwan

Bodies are messy. Everybody knows this, and yet we, culturally speaking, go to great lengths to conceal this basic human truth. Bodies come in an innumerable array of shapes, sizes, skin tones, and physical capacities. Everybody knows this, too, and yet we, culturally speaking, uphold a pretty narrow notion of what makes a good one, an attractive one, a desirable one. This is because every culture has an abundance of rules circumscribing what bodies should or should not do or look like. There are norms about body hair, giving birth, and treating medical diseases. There are even norms about what should happen to our bodies when we die.

Norms are complex and varied. While some are institutionalized—such as public-indecency laws that regulate women's right to expose their breasts in public—others are subtle and threaded throughout media discourses and everyday talk. There are no formal prohibitions stating that gay men cannot be fat and desirable, or that boys cannot participate in baton twirling. However, the reactions to these embodiments suggest some compelling unwritten rules.

Norms are also contingent upon time and place. A young *hijabi* observes that she has lost her teachers' smiles after 9/11. She is the same *hijabi* who chats comfortably with her peers at an urban college but is then subject to a physical and verbal assault in a parking lot outside a Walmart.

Norms exert tremendous pressure on us to conform. Of course, ideologies and practices of age, class, gender, sexuality, race, ethnicity, and ability intersect to inform expectations around accepted cultural standards. Nevertheless, to state the obvious, norms normalize. They are embedded in institutions, structures, and discourses, creating social relations of power that exert a near-magnetic force on us. These social relations can produce bodies that are disciplined and docile (Foucault 1995). Ultimately, we self-regulate. As Bartky remarks about women's compliance with narrowly defined beauty norms, "no one is marched off for electrolysis at gunpoint" (1988, 75). At times we knowingly comply. A gay man, well aware of the norms of gender in the northeast Bronx, decides it's easier to go outside passing as straight. By wearing loose fitting clothes and downplaying anything that might allow others to code his sexuality as gay, he'll avoid the verbal harassment he often experiences walking down the street. Other times, we are less conscious of our compliance. For example, as part of their morning routines, many women put on makeup. They give little consideration as to how this taken-for-granted act reinforces "emphasized femininity," a form of femininity defined around subordination and the accommodation of the interests of men (Connell 1987). Self-regulation persists even when it works against self-interest; scholarship exposes how beauty practices are harmful to girls' and women's physical health and mental well-being (Jeffreys 2015). Indeed, there is a robust literature exploring how norms of embodiment flatten diversity, resulting in often-damaging consequences.

In many ways, compliance is often easier than resistance. When we play by the rules, life is a little less complicated in a way—our well-being, as well as our sense of self and our place in the social order, is less likely to be threatened. Blending in often means feeling secure, and potentially reaping social and material benefits. The typical male college student might not look like Dwayne Johnson or Chris Hemsworth, two of *People* magazine's recent sexiest men alive. Yet, an ideal of masculinity—hegemonic masculinity[1]—underlies the student's efforts to exude confidence, exhibit courage, and embody physical strength. He begins a high protein diet, takes creatine, and spends several nights a week lifting weights. He hopes by doing so, he will impress his peers. His efforts will likely be rewarded. A body hierarchy privileges individuals who exhibit embodied capital (Bourdieu 1984; Wacquant 1995), and plenty of empirical studies document the social and economic advantages of conforming to dominant physical attractiveness norms (Rhode 2010). Meanwhile, individuals who do not conform are penalized and subject to bias, discrimination, and prejudice (Diedrichs and Puhl 2016; Rhode 2010).

Body as Battleground

Yet individuals don't always play by the rules. Where power manifests, there is resistance (Foucault 1990). Despite the cultural and social forces that constrain agency, individuals challenge cultural embodiment norms. At an academic conference, an autistic student uses her body to protest the longstanding history of behavioral experts predicting less optimal outcomes for individuals with autism. Mormon women openly flaunt the modesty standards of the Church of Jesus Christ of Latter-Day Saints by obtaining tattoos and posing nude online. These acts of opposition, however big or small, disrupt and challenge normative scripts about the body.

Simply put, the body is a battleground. On this battleground, individuals fight for recognition of their authentic selves, their autonomy, their full potential. They attempt to reconfigure normative practices and processes, fighting to redefine narrow scripts.

We humbly borrow this battleground metaphor from the US women's movement. In 1989, feminist artist Barbara Kruger designed a now iconic flier for a pro-choice rally in Washington, DC. It featured a photo of a woman's face, split in half, photo and photo negative. The text, in bright red, reads, "Your Body is a Battleground." The words became a rallying cry for pro-choice activists (Caldwell 2016). Indeed, there is a rich tradition of feminists leading the way in examinations of resistance and the body. For example, feminist scholars have deconstructed controlling images of Black women and, using an intersectional lens, have exposed how structures of sexism, classism, and racism combine to marginalize Black bodies (e.g., Collins 2009; Craig 2002; Crenshaw 1991; hooks 1981), the bodies of Latinas and Asian Americans (e.g., Guzmán and Valdivia 2004; Kaw 1993), and the bodies of women of color more generally (e.g., Silliman et al. 2016). Butler's (1990) foundational work destabilizing gender and sexuality has also paved the wave for queer voices to illuminate sexist, heteronormative, and cisnormative assumptions in everyday life (Bornstein and Bergman 2010; Schilt and Westbrook 2009).[2] Similarly, feminist scholars of intersexuality have destabilized the sex binary, challenging the medical management of naturally occurring diversity in sex development (Davis 2015; Preves 2003).[3]

Defining Embodied Resistance

While there are competing discourses about the body that arise in any situation, dominant discourses deem certain acts proper, desirable, and culturally acceptable. At the heart of these body battles are agents exhibiting *embodied resistance,* which we define as acts, be they material or discursive, that oppose hegemonic norms, customs, and conventions about the body in a given context.

Acts of embodied resistance involve risk. Risks can be psychological and involve identity conflict and mental anguish. For instance, a girl's decision to get dreadlocks may seem like a trivial one. After all, it's just hair, right? Now consider she's an immigrant in a new country where dreadlocks are associated with rebellion and smoking weed. Moreover, none of her friends have dreadlocks; the only woman she knows with them is Whoopi Goldberg. And in her view, Whoopi isn't exactly known as a sex symbol. The decision to get her hair loc'd becomes one about fitting in, feeling beautiful, and expressing herself. Similarly, presenting an authentic self may be especially important to a teacher who identifies as nonbinary and transmasculine. When this educator unapologetically shows up for class, they signify to the next generation that the students themselves don't have to replicate the gender status quo. It can be safe to show one's true self.

Notably, in modernity, the body and self are particularly entwined. We live in a "somatic society" where "major political and moral problems are expressed through the conduit of the human body" (Turner 1996, 6). Individuals undergo "body projects," manipulating and reconstructing their bodies to align with their sense of self. As Shilling describes, the body is a "process of becoming; a *project* which should be worked at and accomplished as part of an individual's self-identity" (2003, 4).

Battleground risks can also be physical and involve violent threats to one's personal security. Challenges to gender norms are especially dangerous because social norms hold individuals accountable to their sex categories (West and Zimmerman 1987). We are expected to exhibit and embody the roles ascribed to our sex categories, namely masculine or feminine. Heteronormativity and cisnormativity further reinforce restrictive scripts and embodiments of gender and sexuality. Because some believe, contra a social constructionist perspective, that these scripts are essentially rooted in nature and biologically determined (see DeLamater and Hyde 1998), violations of gender and sexuality norms are deemed especially egregious and thus subject to violent patrol, physically and symbolically. This is observed in the marginalization of transgender and nonbinary individuals, along with their high rates of interpersonal violence (Human Rights Campaign Foundation 2016).

Rules of Engagement in Risky Spaces

There is some debate about whether individuals must *intentionally* resist norms for an act to constitute resistance. Some acts do not necessarily entail intentional resistance, yet they nevertheless challenge body norms. Consider an athlete in a wheelchair or a woman who refuses breast reconstruction after mastectomy. Is the simple act of leaving one's home an affront to norms that construct wheelchair users as immobile and weak, or the norm that a woman should have voluptuous breasts to signify her sexuality and femininity? Does the daily public presence of these individuals not potentially disrupt dominant expectations, even if they are simply going about their everyday lives without trying to make a political statement?

Similarly, some acts of embodied resistance are more publicly recognizable than others. On the one hand, some acts explicitly challenge oppressive ideologies. For example, a fat activist produces a podcast that defies the pervasive ideal perpetuated by mainstream media that only thin bodies can be beautiful and live full and satisfying lives. On the other hand, some forms of embodied resistance are subtler, quieter, and perhaps not even recognizable by observers. Growing up using various skin-lightening concoctions, a South Asian woman chooses to embrace her brown skin, even though others may be ignorant of her daily fight against the beauty norm of fair skin.

Upon these body battlegrounds, warriors use an arsenal of weapons. A menstrual activist employs a camera when she photographs the vivid ribbons of her menstrual blood moving through water, rescripting the shameful and abject into complex and beautiful art. A teenage girl turns to the internet to seek an assessment of her appearance. She stares into the camera and earnestly asks: "Am I pretty or ugly?" Another girl parodies this same YouTube trend by smearing lipstick around her mouth and under her nose. Dousing herself in perfume, she coughs comically and laughs wildly.

Battles can be fought alone, but they can also be part of collective action. When individuals unite in their shared resistance and strive toward social change, they find community and validation. A group of women challenge draconian welfare reform through public protest, donning wedding dresses and making up their faces to simulate the effects of battery. Their resistance fortifies the movement for women's economic empowerment. Grieving loved ones refuse the for-profit funeral industry by caring for their deceased loved ones in their own homes. Their choice is part of the burgeoning home death movement. Fat men gather for a lighthearted weekend. Their ostensibly silly games and contests are part of the very serious body acceptance movement.

Embodied resistance, then, is a movement toward equality and empowerment. Each resistant act, no matter how small, plays a role in destabilizing social patterns. Or does it? Body norms, after all, only seem natural and entrenched because they are reified through repetition. Rule breaking counteracts taken-for-granted expectations. Ultimately, embodied resistance manifests anywhere along a continuum of agency-in-action. The things that unite acts that defy bodily norms in any given context are people's attempts at self-valuation through reclamation of power and agency and/or through rebellion against the hegemony of social customs that limit individuality.

But not all agentic acts are the same. It is crucial that, as we study resistance, we are ever mindful that sometimes it comes with unanticipated compliance. Take for instance Barber's (2016) study of the social interactions in men's grooming salons that reveal how patrons manage to, perhaps counterintuitively, buttress their privileged social locations as white, straight, professional men. As Hays (1994) asserts, there are multiple types of agency. Structurally reproductive agency, as the name suggests, involves choices that fail to destabilize extant social structures that undergird everyday life, while structurally transformative agency involves acts that inspire social change.

When might rule violators actually motivate stricter adherence to social norms, even when their intent is transgressive? We encourage readers of *Body Battlegrounds* to consider what kinds of agency power certain moments of resistance. Are they actually disrupting or reinforcing of the status quo, or are they suspended somewhere in between? This brings us to a fundamental question. What is the impact of embodied resistance? Does each moment of opposition pave the way to a world where we celebrate the body in its many unique manifestations, or does norm violation strengthen the norms themselves? When radical doulas celebrate the pregnant body, how might they risk essentializing gender and sexuality? When boys and young men participate in competitive twirling, how does their challenge to gender stereotypes rely on valorized definitions of masculinity? It is our hope that this collection of research and narrative may bring some clarity to the vexing tensions between resistance and reification.

Transgressions, Tensions, and Transformations

Our desire to understand the complexities of embodied resistance began in 2011 when we coedited *Embodied Resistance: Challenging the Norms, Breaking the Rules*. We hoped to feed the flourishing scholarship that seeks to understand transgression. We, both professors who teach courses in body studies, craved a collection of empirical research and first person narratives that captured the diversity of "talking back" to oppressive standards of bodies in a variety of social contexts. We were invested in raising the profile of resistance, helping this emerging literature shed light on the complexities of embodiment, and imagining the displacement of norms for genuine self-expression. And we were pleased to learn of the book's favorable reception, especially among students.

But as with many projects, we knew we were not done. As such, we curated *Body Battlegrounds: Transgressions, Tensions, and Transformations*. We gathered all new material to continue the project of exploring resistance at the site of the human body. No doubt many things have changed since 2011, both in the academy and beyond, that make the study of embodied resistance still—perhaps even more—relevant and important. Not only has new innovative research and writing emerged since we published *Embodied Resistance*, but the political and social climate has changed quite dramatically. We live in a time when biomedicalization is on the rise while reproductive rights are eroding. We live in a time when white supremacists feel authorized to publicly spew their hate, and Islamophobia and anti-immigrant sentiment is encoded into policy. But we also live in a time when new tools of resistance are available. Black Lives Matter, the March for Women's Lives, and youth-led movements focused on immigration rights and stricter gun control are each shining examples of how activists can harness the power of social media to connect people who share anger, frustration, and vision for a more just world. These changes inspired us to gather the best new work that describes and analyzes resistance during a historical moment that calls for models of fighting back.

The Plan of the Book

In *Body Battlegrounds*, our goal is another theoretically and empirically engaging, highly readable collection of scholarly, activist, and personal writing. We did not intentionally limit our choices to qualitative research, but we again found that the research that provided the most textured, nuanced, and intimate insights relied on textual analyses, in-depth interviewing, and participant observation.

We also did not exhaust the range of topics possible and acknowledge the paucity of research and narratives in certain areas. The research and stories herein are mostly situated in the contemporary United States. And while many of our pieces explore gender and some use a rich intersectional lens, we had hoped to include more content that addresses other axes of identity and experience, including race, ethnicity, class, sexuality, disability, religiosity, age, and beyond. This leads us to echo our 2011 challenge to readers to fill these gaps with their own work. We invite everyone who encounters this book to generate knowledge that more fully captures the tremendous diversity of what it means to deviate from the norms of embodiment, particularly though an intersectional lens. We encourage our readers to join us in shaping a robust literature the plumbs the depths of this fascinating and ever-evolving topic.

Body Battlegrounds is organized as four visually rich, interrelated parts. Part I, "Going 'Natural,'" celebrates the unaltered. We place scare quotes around the word *natural* here to avoid essentializing the body and to signal that even notions of the natural are socially constructed. In this section, pieces explore refusals to body interventions such as shaving, dieting, or skin lightening, and the consequences of these choices. Two of our pieces analyze movements that resist the loss of control of life's major transitions, literally from birth to death. Part II, "Representing Resistance," investigates various articulations—often explicitly visual and/or public—that creatively confront somatic norms. In Part III, "Creating Community, Disrupting Assumptions," the units of analyses are groups or individuals who identify with groups typically misunderstood and often maligned, such as Muslims or the Deaf. Finally, the research and narratives in Part IV, "Transforming Institutions and Ideologies," centers on resistance that at some level engages institutional change, even if subtly or through the acts of one bold individual. Schools, sporting events, and the doctor's office are all sites ripe for rewriting the norms of embodiment, as our authors demonstrate.

Each section is anchored by concepts central to the study of resistance to the somatic norm. We, of course, acknowledge the limits of such an exercise, as many of the concepts are not constrained to these tidy sections. Indeed, we are well aware of the hazards (and ironies) of oversimplifying for the purposes of categorization in a collection about the perils and promise of not fitting in. Thus, we expect and indeed encourage our readers, in the spirit of the book's main theme, to *resist* our categorizations.

The thirteen research-based chapters are written with the student in mind—accessible, theoretically and methodologically transparent, and rich with the voices of the actors at the center of inquiry. We also include sixteen personal narratives that capture the respective section's main themes and "drive home" the often very intimate issues this emergent literature probes. We hope these short pieces will launch dynamic classroom discussions and students will participate with their own experiences and analysis of these themes.

Body Battlegrounds thus invites readers to enter the lives of these norm challengers and rule breakers. Throughout we engage the many questions that resistance manifests—a deliberate inquiry that moves us closer to something more than a deeper understanding of bodies that refuse to fit into too-small spaces. This exploration enables a more complex appreciation of the social meanings of *all* of our bodies and builds the foundation for a more just society. In that spirit, we close with a few lines of Sonya Renee Taylor's powerful poem that—in its entirety—serves as our afterword.

Forget all you have been told.
Resistance is an everyday act,
the work of excavating each tiny artifact
of the oppressor that lives in you.
Your call to be a balm to every self-inflicted wound
is how movements are birthed.

NOTES

1. Hegemonic masculinity is a dominant construction of masculinity that creates behavioral expectations for boys and men; it subordinates other expressions of masculinity and legitimizes men's subordination of women. See Connell (2005) and Connell and Messerschmidt (2005).
2. Heteronormativity is the assumption that heterosexuality is the "normal" and preferred sexual orientation. Cisnormativity is the assumption that all, or almost all, individuals are cisgender. Cisgender is the designation for people whose gender identity corresponds with the sex they were assigned at birth. See Warner (1999) and Schilt and Westbrook (2009).
3. Intersex is an "umbrella term that refers to people who have one or more of a range of variations in sex characteristics that fall outside of traditional conceptions of male or female bodies" (interACT 20179).

REFERENCES

Barber, Kristen. 2016. *Styling Masculinity: Gender, Class, and Inequality in the Men's Grooming Industry*. New Brunswick, NJ: Rutgers University Press.

Bartky, Sandra Lee. 1988. "Foucault, Femininity, and the Modernization of Patriarchal Power." In *Feminism and Foucault: Reflections on Resistance*, edited by Irene Diamond and Lee Quinby, 61–86. Boston: Northeastern University Press.

Bornstein, Kate, and S. Bear Bergman. 2010. *Gender Outlaws: The Next Generation*. Berkeley, CA: Seal Press.

Bourdieu, Pierre. 1984. *Distinction: A Social Critique of the Judgment of Taste*. Cambridge, MA: Harvard University Press.

Butler, Judith. 1990. *Gender Trouble: Feminism and the Subversion of Identity*. New York: Routledge.

Caldwell, Ellen. 2016. "The History of 'Your Body is a Battleground.'" *JSTOR Daily*, July 15. *daily.jstor.org/the-history-your-body-is-a-battleground*.

Collins, Patricia Hill. 2009. *Black Feminist Thought: Knowledge, Consciousness, and the Politics of Empowerment*. New York: Routledge.

Connell, R. W. 1987. *Gender and Power: Society, the Person and Sexual Politics*. Cambridge: Polity.

———. 2005. *Masculinities*, 2nd ed. Berkeley: University of California Press.

Connell, R. W., and James Messerschmidt. 2005. "Hegemonic Masculinity: Rethinking the Concept." *Gender and Society* 19, no. 6: 829–859.

Craig, Maxine. 2002. *Ain't I a Beauty Queen?: Black Women, Beauty, and the Politics of Race.* New York: Oxford University Press.

Crenshaw, Kimberlé. 1991. "Mapping the Margins: Intersectionality, Identity Politics, and Violence against Women of Color." *Stanford Law Review* 43, no. 6: 1241–99.

Davis, Georgiann. 2015. *Contesting Intersex: The Dubious Diagnosis.* New York: New York University Press.

DeLamater, John D., and Janet Shibley Hyde. 1998. "Essentialism vs. Social Constructionism in the Study of Human Sexuality." *Journal of Sex Research* 35, no. 1: 10–18.

Diedrichs, Phillippa C., and Rebecca Puhl. 2016. "Weight Bias: Prejudice and Discrimination toward Overweight and Obese People." In *The Cambridge Handbook of the Psychology of Prejudice*, edited by Chris G. Sibley and Fiona Kate Barlow, 392–412. Cambridge, UK: Cambridge University Press.

Foucault, Michel. 1990. *The History of Sexuality. Volume 1: An Introduction.* New York: Vintage Books.

———. 1995. *Discipline and Punish: The Birth of the Prison.* New York: Vintage Books.

Guzmán, Isabel Molina, and Angharad N. Valdivia. 2004. "Brain, Brow, and Booty: Latina Iconicity in US Popular Culture." *Communication Review* 7, no. 2: 205–21.

Hays, Sharon. 1994. "Structure and Agency and the Sticky Problem of Culture." *Sociological Theory* 12, no. 1: 57–72.

hooks, bell. 1981. *Ain't I a Woman: Black Women and Feminism.* Boston, MA: South End Press.

Human Rights Campaign Foundation. 2016. *A Matter of Life and Death: Fatal Violence against Transgender People in America 2016.* Washington, DC: Human Rights Campaign Foundation.

interACT. 2017. *INTERSEX 101: Everything You Want to Know!* Sudbury, MA: interACT. *interactadvocates.org/wp-content/uploads/2017/03/INTERSEX101.pdf.*

Jeffreys, Sheila. 2015. *Beauty and Misogyny: Harmful Cultural Practices in the West*, 2nd ed. New York: Routledge.

Kaw, Eugenia. 1993. "Medicalization of Racial Features: Asian American Women and Cosmetic Surgery." *Medical Anthropology Quarterly* 7, no. 1: 74–89.

Preves, Sharon E. 2003. *Intersex and Identity: The Contested Self.* Piscataway, NJ: Rutgers University Press.

Rhode, Deborah L. 2010. *The Beauty Bias: The Injustice of Appearance in Life and Law.* New York: Oxford University Press.

Schilt, Kristen, and Laurel Westbrook. 2009. "Doing Gender, Doing Heteronormativity: 'Gender Normals,' Transgender People, and the Social Maintenance of Heterosexuality." *Gender & Society* 23, no. 4: 440–64.

Shilling, Chris. 2003. *The Body and Social Theory*, 2nd ed. London: SAGE Publications.

Silliman, Jael Miriam, Marlene Gerber Fried, Loretta J. Ross, and Elena Gutiérrez. 2016. *Undivided Rights: Women of Color Organize for Reproductive Justice*, 2nd ed. Chicago: Haymarket Books.

Turner, Bryan S. 1996. *The Body and Society*, 2nd ed. London: SAGE Publications.

Wacquant, Loïc J. D. 1995. "Pugs at Work: Bodily Capital and Bodily Labour among Professional Boxers." *Body & Society* 1, no. 1: 65–93.

Warner, Michael. 1999. *The Trouble with Normal: Sex, Politics, and the Ethics of Queer Life.* New York: Free Press.

West, Candace, and Don H. Zimmerman. 1987. "Doing Gender." *Gender & Society* 1, no. 2: 125–51.

PART I
Going "Natural"

1

Body Hair Battlegrounds

The Consequences, Reverberations, and Promises of Women Growing Their Leg, Pubic, and Underarm Hair

Breanne Fahs

Dangerously Crazy about Body Hair

I often remark to students and colleagues alike that hair is "crazy making." Perhaps because we spend such an enormous amount of time managing and containing our hair—making sure it does not get too unruly or wild; trimming and shaving and plucking it into submission; cutting, dyeing, waxing, and styling our hair—it becomes impossible to truly assess how strongly we cling to ideas about "proper" and attractive hair and, by association, "proper" femininity and masculinity. Hair brings out deeply personal notions of morality, cleanliness, beauty, attractiveness, and status. In my career as a woman and gender studies professor and a practicing clinical psychologist, I have spent a rather large amount of time thinking about, studying, exploring, and provoking others to experiment with their body hair. This has offered me many insights into "doing gender" but has often come at great cost to me both professionally (as many have labeled this work as too "trivial" or "silly") and personally (as my work on hair has inspired others to act in irrational ways toward me). And yet, each time that these reactions unfold, and each time the *price* of the work becomes clear, I feel renewed inspiration about the importance of these body hair battlegrounds.

In her now-seminal essay, "Thinking Sex," Gayle Rubin (1984) said about the necessity of thinking seriously about sexuality, "To some, sexuality may seem to be an unimportant topic, a frivolous diversion from the more critical problems of poverty, war, disease, racism, famine, or nuclear annihilation. But it is precisely at times such as these, when we live with the possibility of unthinkable destruction, that people are likely to become dangerously crazy about sexuality. . . . Disputes over sexual behavior often become vehicles for displacing social anxieties, and discharging their attendant emotional intensity" (267). In this chapter, I argue that hair, too, makes us dangerously crazy, wildly incapable of direct and self-reflexive conversation, infused with the most panicky and anxiety-ridden sense of danger. Like Rubin, I argue that feminist scholars should approach the study of hair with the most seriousness we can muster, seeing it as a vehicle for social control, displaced anxiety, intense emotional energy, and cultural distress. Hair is at once a marker of social class and "respectability," a highly racialized site of inequality and difference (particularly for African American women), a deeply gendered signifier of beauty and gender (non)conformity, and a form of artistic and cultural expression; it is messy and complex and always-already laden with stories about power.

This chapter extends my earlier work on a pedagogical exercise about body hair (Fahs and Delgado 2011; Fahs 2011, 2012, 2013, 2014), in which I outlined the ways that female college students characterized the temporary experience of growing out their body hair, by revisiting the question: *What do women's overt body hair rebellions provoke in others?* Drawing from an extra credit assignment I give to students that asks them to engage in nonnormative body hair behavior (women grow hair on their legs, underarms, and pubis while men shave hair from these areas) and write about the experience, I revisit the question of what this assignment teaches students and the sorts of things that they learn from challenging traditional gender roles. Instead of only looking at the specific individual experiences of students in my courses who have chosen to grow out their body hair, in this chapter I also examine the ongoing public media attention (most intense in 2014) that this assignment received in the (mostly conservative) news media. In order to imagine what women's body hair rebellions have provoked—both individually, collectively, and, now, culturally—I first trace the most recent literature on body hair, including an examination of my own work on women's body hair rebellions. I then examine the chaotic experiencing of watching my work "go viral"—often with negative consequences for me and this work—as an example of why hair deserves the utmost attention in times of social stress, and why body hair rebellions matter. I conclude the chapter by looking at four recent semesters of women's studies students who participated in this assignment and lay out some of the more interesting patterns of their reports on the experience.

Recent Literature on Body Hair

Despite accusations that research on body hair is "trivial" and that contemporary women live in a "postfeminist" society that gives them freedom to do whatever they want with their bodies, several scholars have continued to research women's relationship to body hair removal and its meanings. In *Plucked* (2015), a large-scale examination of the cultural practices of hair removal, Rebecca Herzig argued that hair removal for women shifted from a "mutilation" practice (largely disdained in mainstream culture) to a mandate for women (where hairy women were seen as politically extreme, sexually deviant, or mentally ill). Herzig's work, by outlining the forces that have driven this recent mandate for women to remove body hair, offers a major contribution to the task of "taking seriously" women's body hair decisions.

Looking to the quantitative literature on body hair, studies show that over 91.5 percent of women in the United States regularly remove their leg hair and 93 percent regularly remove underarm hair (Tiggemann and Kenyon 1998). A recent Australian study found that approximately 96 percent of women regularly removed their leg and underarm hair, 60 percent removed at least some pubic hair, and 48 percent removed all pubic hair (Tiggemann and Hodgson 2008). One UK study found that over 99 percent of women reported removing body hair at some point in their lives (Toerien, Wilkinson, and Choi 2005) and a study of Australian women found that 98 percent of women were removing both leg and underarm hair (Tiggemann and Lewis 2004). In all, these estimates across Western cultures emphasize extremely high rates of body hair removal for women.

Much of the recent social science research on body hair has focused on women's removal of pubic hair, with a variety of recent studies looking at the increase in women's beliefs that hairless genitals symbolize cleanliness, sexiness, choice, and normativity (Braun, Tricklebank and Clarke 2013; Riddell, Varto and Hodgson 2010; Smolak and Murnen 2011). A cross-sectional study of low-income Hispanic, Black, and white women found that pubic hair grooming was more common among white, younger, under- or "normal"-weight participants, those making over $30,000 per year, and those having five or more lifetime sexual partners, though all demographics reported high rates of pubic hair grooming (DeMaria and Berenson 2013). In a Canadian sample, approximately half of women shaved their bikini line and 30 percent removed all pubic hair, with most citing appearance in a bathing suit, attractiveness, and cleanliness as the reasons (Riddell, Varto, and Hodgson 2010). A US sample also found high rates of pubic hair removal across demographics (Herbenick et al. 2013). Women reported far more removal of pubic hair than did men, and cited reasons of sexiness and feeling "normal" as the primary reasons they removed hair; these reasons correlated with feelings of self-objectification and self-surveillance (Smolak and Murnen 2011). Further, women cared more about removing their pubic hair than men did about removing their own, citing sexual impacts as one of their concerns (Braun, Tricklebank, and Clarke 2013).

In my previous work, starting with the publication of my first piece on body hair rebellions back in the 2011 *Embodied Resistance* collection, I found that women of color faced harsher penalties for growing body hair, both because they typically had darker hair but also because they faced pressures from family around respectability (Fahs and Delgado 2011). In my first journal article on the body hair assignment, I also found that women faced clear heteronormative patrolling messages and had to contend with fear of hate crimes, fear of being "outed" as lesbian, and homophobic reactions to their body hair (Fahs 2011). Following the publication of these two studies, I published three other journal articles on different aspects of women rebelling against the hairlessness norm: one that outlined the trajectory of the body hair extra credit assignment (Fahs 2012), one about men's experiences shaving body hair (in which men masculinized the experience and rebelled by, for example, shaving their legs with a buck knife) (Fahs 2013), and one where I compared women's imagined experiences with growing body hair to their actual experiences (revealing that actual body hair growth inspired a variety of people in women's lives to control, comment upon, and show disgust about body hair, while imagining such growth mostly resulted in women saying it was "no big deal" and that they had "personal choice") (Fahs 2014). Each of these studies further emphasized how embodied resistance through body hair growth came at great personal cost to women, in part by revealing networks of people—partners, family members, co-workers, and friends—invested in controlling women's bodies.

While not much scholarly attention has focused on how women might use body hair to rebel against gender norms, popular media stories have sometimes framed body hair as a prominent public act of rebellion for women (celebrity or otherwise) who have grown tired of body policing and constraints. Consider how hippie women in the 1960s who challenged norms of shaving were criticized (see Weitz 2001). Links between fashion and rebellion—the body as a social text that reflects the social mores, values, and identity politics of the day (Craig 2002)—also apply to body hair. With pornography glorifying women's hairless vulvas (Vannier, Currie and O'Sullivan 2014) and magazines emphasizing that women will have "great sex" if they remove their body hair (Ménard and Kleinplatz 2008), women who rebel against body hair norms face steep pressures to conform to sociocultural norms of "appropriate" hair growth. Despite this, a variety of celebrities have espoused body hair growth as a public rebellion, including Miley Cyrus, Sarah Silverman, Scout Willis, Penélope Cruz, Madonna, Gaby Hoffman, Juliette Lewis, Drew Barrymore, Julia Roberts, and Mo'nique (Butler 2015). Dyeing armpit hair has also received attention, with debates online about whether it represents symbolic rebellion, narcissistic calls for attention, or the latest fashionable statement (Holley 2014; Newman 2015). Young women who identified as "eco-grrrls" also sometimes used body hair growth as the ultimate political act of rejecting gender norms (Fry and Lousley 2001). Thus, body hair is emerging as a key player in gendered rebellions of the body, with new iterations of body hair rebellions appearing each year.

Body Hair Gone Wild (or Viral)

The body hair assignment has continued to grow and evolve—with students rebelling in new ways, recruiting others to join them in doing the project, confronting new challenges (workplaces, expressions of femininity), and redefining gender roles—and this has meant the assignment has gotten new kinds of attention from the public sphere when I share the results in journals, conferences, and media outlets. One of the great pedagogical strengths of the assignment is its ability to rapidly ignite conversations about body hair among women and their "social networks." Hair has much salience in people's lives and represents an easy access point for tougher discussions around hegemonic masculinity, social control, compulsory heterosexuality, and intersectionality. People *love* to talk about body hair; it somehow is just provocative enough that conversation is allowable about the subject, while still being taboo enough that debates, strong feelings, defiant actions, and healthy banter can easily ensue. As a sex researcher, I have published on a variety of topics I wish people would talk more about—for example, the rapid growth in numbers of teenage girls having unprotected anal sex with teenage boys, or the specific sorts of power imbalances that exist in "mainstream" pornography these days—but it seems that none of my work has inspired more conversation and media attention than body hair. This may reflect how people have to choose and manage aspects of their hair every day: shaving, plucking, waxing, grooming, washing, styling, presenting, controlling, etc. Hair is wholly relatable because everyone deals with it in their lives. (Sexuality, on the other hand, can alienate certain audiences fairly quickly and has fewer nearly universal "entry points" into conversation.)

While feminist researchers often worry their work goes unread or they do not engage enough in the public sphere as public intellectuals, my unanticipated jump into the media spotlight proved to be a harrowing experience that underscored the difficulty of having such exposure. In the summer of 2014, I had just published my most recent piece on body hair in *Psychology of Women Quarterly*, a respected journal that publishes mostly empirical psychological pieces about women and gender. In June, my university

(Arizona State University) had published a short online story about the body hair assignment and how I had won the Mary Roth Walsh teaching award from the American Psychological Association for designing the assignment. This short online article got picked up by a conservative journalism student (and member of the red-baiting Campus Reform organization) who sent it to some ultra-conservative media outlets like the *Drudge Report* and Fox News. Soon, stories about the body hair assignment had "gone viral," with over one thousand news outlets running "stories" about the body hair assignment within weeks. The story morphed in fascinating ways with a number of false details circulating wildly: I routinely "checked" students' pubic hair; I was running a Communist training camp; I was giving enormous amounts of extra credit; I was handing out A grades for armpit hair (notably, leg hair disappeared from most of these stories and armpit hair loomed large); and I was "ruining America" by giving this "pointless" assignment. I learned quickly that nearly every major media outlet that ran the story had not researched a single original detail. Instead, they reprinted (and reprinted and reprinted) the same quotes, ideas, and information as the original story, often selectively leaving out information about the potential value of the assignment, without bothering to fact check or even to gather new pieces of information.

Soon, the hate mail started pouring in. Hundreds of emails were sent to me, the university, the Dean, and my program about my body hair assignment. Angry parents wrote the school. Outraged conservatives—I later learned from our security team that these were individual letters sent from all over the country—sent hotheaded, vitriolic letters calling me every profane name imaginable (of course centering on sexual identity, gender, fatness, and, in some cases, race). Fox News speculated on national television about my own body hair practices and "analyzed" my eyebrows for clues. Rush Limbaugh talked about the assignment to his listeners. Eventually, emails started to arrive that outlined for me in vivid detail how I should die. People posted comments about bringing guns to my university or "shitting" on my desk. These various grotesque forms of hatred bombarded my life (and prompted an immediate security evaluation from the campus police). I had to get emergency training in speaking (or not) to the media, and I underwent a further security evaluation by local police for monitoring my home. My emails were reviewed by a team of experts (it compounds the assault on your dignity when hateful things about your body and your imagined identities circulate to the higher-ups at your place of work), and I consoled myself by clinging to the occasional message of support sent from fellow psychologists, sociologists, and the beloved menstrual mafia. Body hair had gone wild, or at least it seemed that way. Such a serious attempt to silence an extra credit assignment about body hair may even signify the success of that assignment, given that counter-movements are most vitriolic when traditional foundations are challenged (Staggenborg and Taylor 2005).

I recount these events not to again dive headlong into the "drama" of that situation but to emphasize the importance of embodied resistance. Such resistance is not merely abstract, theoretical, irrelevant, or pointless; resistance based in the body is fundamental to the understanding of how power operates, how power is deployed, and how people can resist power. Body-hair-gone-viral shows a deep insecurity about the status of gender and the maintenance of gender roles today. And while I understand that people emailing me and telling me I should die because of this body hair assignment could be a form of cultural hyperbole, exaggeration, or "insanity"—something I should brush off as worthless and insignificant—I am not entirely certain I agree. My students' experiences with body hair show a kind of pervasive, now decade-long freak-out about women growing body hair. By combining visceral disgust, conflicts about race and class, confusion about what constitutes rebellion, and various phobias and "-isms" (homophobia, sexism, racism, and transphobia, in particular), body hair is, I think, of paramount importance. The hatred of women for rebelling *is real*. The hatred toward me for assigning this *is real*. The hatred toward gender rebels, punks, and freaks *is real*.

The Body Hair Experiment Revisited

Despite this backlash, the assignment continues in full force. I still ask students to engage in nonnormative body hair behavior for a period of ten weeks, to keep a journal about their feelings, and to write a short paper about their experiences at the end of the semester. Since 2008, I have done this assignment nearly every semester in a variety of courses: Critical Perspectives on Sexuality; Gender, Bodies, and Health; Trash, Freaks, and SCUM; and Race, Class, and Gender.

Each semester differs, and each group has its own dynamic unique to those students. That said, with remarkable consistency students have reported learning a lot from this assignment about the networks in their own personal lives that control, comment upon, limit, punish, or restrict their bodily choices. Many students prior to this assignment imagine that they have nearly unlimited choices with their bodies; after doing this assignment, their viewpoints on the patrolling of gender norms vastly changes. (They also, of course, often feel far more rebellious and brave about asserting their right to their own bodily choices, which sometimes means they break up with boyfriends who admonished their body hair, or they rebel against co-workers or family members who labeled their bodies as "gross" or "disgusting.")

In a review of four recent semesters of the body hair assignment (Spring 2013, Fall 2013, Spring 2015, and Fall 2015), a total of fifty-nine students participated in the assignment (while eight did not). This included eight men and fifty-one women from diverse backgrounds (race, class, sexual identity). All were enrolled in upper-division women and gender studies courses or graduate courses in social justice and human rights (recently my courses have been cross-listed). I found a variety of recent themes—some similar to previous years and some new—in how women experienced this assignment over these three years: (1) awareness of underarm, leg, and pubic hair as *differently* attached to gender and sexuality norms; (2) deeply felt sense that body hair makes them repulsive to others; (3) strong barriers at many workplaces to having body hair; (4) contradictions between growing body hair as a rebellion and women's body hair being seen as "sexy"; (5) body hair as a way to explore trans identities; and (6) women of color feeling that white (especially blond) women cannot understand their body hair experiences (a racial consciousness gap). Note: in the descriptions below, all names have been changed to protect students' identities and demographic information was offered voluntarily by participants on their consent forms.

Different Body Regions, Different Meanings

During the last four semesters of the body hair assignment, students have indicated that they attach different meanings to their legs, underarms, and pubic hair. Typically, legs have represented the site with the most freedom and flexibility regarding hair. For example, Evelyn (19/Latina/heterosexual) said, "My leg hair wasn't as big of a deal as my armpit hair. I sometimes have let my legs grow out before, but I would *never* do that with my armpit hair." Pubic hair, by contrast, seemed more private compared to armpit hair, as pubic hair was only discussed with partners and elicited no "public" responses. Leila (22/Latina/lesbian) described her relationship with her pubic hair in intensely private terms, noting a reversal in how she expected to feel about growing pubic hair: "Having pubic hair made me realize how uncomfortable I actually felt before when I didn't have it. I felt like a thirteen-year-old girl before and shameful feelings came up. I used to avoid looking at my hairless vulva, so I definitely felt refreshed when I stopped shaving."

Underarm hair has elicited the strongest and most intense reactions both internally (from women reflecting on the assignment) and externally (from people in women's lives who evaluate and judge their hairy bodies). This may connect to its more public status—others can see underarm hair more easily than leg or pubic hair—or it may connect to its status as more abject or more connected to masculinity than other kinds of hair. Cat (22/white/heterosexual) noticed a difference in how her friend reacted to leg and armpit hair: "I have a friend who hates my armpit hair along with everyone else's armpit hair. She refuses to even look at mine. She has seen my hair legs many times and she does not even take a second glance at them at this point, but armpits are apparently a whole other beast." Suzanna (23/Latina/bisexual) felt triumphant when purposefully making others uncomfortable with her armpit hair: "Whenever I was at the grocery store and someone was by me, I made it a point to lift my arm near their face and pretend like I was grabbling something from a top shelf. The face reactions that I got were priceless. One lady literally gasped and left her cart full of stuff in the middle of the aisle as she walked away." This sense that different regions of the body have different meanings attached to gender and sexuality—with armpit hair symbolizing the most defiant and panic-inducing region—shows how meanings of body hair inspired different sorts of reactions in others and carry different symbolic weight.

Hair as Deeply Repulsive

Women often described their body hair as abject, "gross," and deeply repulsive, using language that reflected visceral disgust. This persisted, notably, even while women recognized the inherent value of the assignment. Vivian (26/white/lesbian) said, "I thought I would be fine with this and others would be disgusted. Unfortunately, I found that other people were not as bothered by the body hair as I was. This was a disappointing discovery for me as a feminist. I felt dirty and unkempt. The hair made me feel ugly." Desiree (22/Latina/heterosexual), too, noted that she felt tremendous anxiety about body hair and that she felt repulsive to others: "My body hair gave me anxiety. I had to actively remind myself that it was okay to let the hair grow and that there was absolutely nothing wrong with it. I was tempted to shave it every day. I felt dirty. I avoided sexual acts which required me to remove clothing. I definitely tried to keep my armpits hidden." These internal descriptions of feeling repulsed by body hair reveal the ways that women experienced conflict between how they *should* feel and how they *did* feel.

Reactions of visceral disgust appeared regularly in family and friends' assessments of women's body hair. For example, Amy (25/biracial/heterosexual) noted, "My aunt hated it and pretended to gag." Sally (20/white/heterosexual) had a friend who thought she had gone crazy: "My friend was grossed out but couldn't explain why armpit hair was so appalling for women (which I couldn't either prior to this assignment). I'm also pretty sure she thought I had lost it for a little bit too." Ginger (22/white/bisexual) noted that, "My cousins tried to sneak up on me and sniff me out to 'prove' that I smell worse with body hair than without it. Why are they so obsessed with smelling my dirty laundry and forming cases about body odor and its relationship to body hair?" These visceral versions of repulsion that women heard about and contended with deeply impacted their feelings about body hair and, in some cases, undermined the (at least somewhat) positive feelings they had about growing their own body hair.

Workplace Barriers to Having Body Hair

As increasing numbers of my students have full-time jobs—many of which are in professional settings rather than in minimum-wage and more casual settings—the pressures to equate hairlessness with both femininity and professionalism have increased. Amy (25/biracial/heterosexual) noted that she felt quite self-conscious at work when she wore her normal work attire: "Mostly I felt self-conscious, especially at work, as body hair on women is generally considered unprofessional and I wear a dress almost every day. When I wore short sleeves, I was hyper vigilant to keep my arms at my sides or to watch other people to see if they noticed my hair underarms and what their reactions would be." Ashleigh (23/white/heterosexual) endured her colleagues continually asking, "You're still showering right?" Carrie (26/white/bisexual) described workplace harassment around her body hair: "My boss wanted to discuss it with me every single day. He came up to me and told me how gross it looked, how unprofessional I was for having it, and how disgusting my legs looked in skirts. I tried to reason with him and explain what this assignment was for, but he didn't buy it. Other coworkers supported him in humiliating me in this way. I wanted to be brave but mostly I just felt ashamed of my body." This sense that body hair does not "belong" in the workplace was difficult for women to challenge.

Body Hair as Rebellious Versus Erotic

One unexpected finding of the last several semesters was that some students reported tensions between seeing body hair as a form of rebellion and, for some, feeling disappointed when others saw body hair as "sexy." Ashleigh (23/white/heterosexual) wrote of her boyfriend's reversal of feelings about body hair and how this diminished the feeling of rebellion for her: "I was so happy when he finally conceded that body hair norms for women were wrong and that my body hair was just as normal as his. However, recently he has started to find it sexy. I see a smile on his face when I raise my arms, for example, and that pisses me off because my armpit hair was supposed to be a way for me to subvert gender norms." Lena (21/white/heterosexual) also discovered this reversal from rebellion to eroticism with her boyfriend: "Having body hair made me feel like a feminist warrior. I didn't want my boyfriend to like it. I wanted him to be grossed out. But when he wasn't grossed out, it was because he thought it was 'hot' and not because I was a feminist warrior." This conflict between hair as rebellion and hair as "sexy" showed how body norms can shift in meaning rapidly and in directions women did not want.

Other women described a stronger sense that body hair represented *only* rebellion. Cat (22/white/heterosexual) described her refusal to care about pressures to remove body hair: "I simply do not have the energy to care if my legs are baby smooth when wearing shorts. I cannot be bothered to spend time with men who think they have a say in my armpits. In fact, I just really cannot be bothered with pressure to fit into any gender norm, hair or otherwise." Similarly, Leila (22/Latina/lesbian) felt better about herself while growing body hair, sensing that she gained her partner's approval: "Growing my body hair made me feel good about myself, or at least part of myself again. I felt empowered as a badass feminist again. My partner was excited that I was growing my body hair out. She didn't understand why I shaved in the first place." Finally, Anjelica (21/Latina/lesbian) described growing body hair as a true feminist statement for her: "I am happy that I am able to use my body as a metaphor for protest against patriarchy. We seem to forget that body hair is a natural occurrence, and we only attribute it to certain demographics, cultures, or historical periods. I believe this is our way of alienating or distancing ourselves from body hair in order to negatively criticize it."

Body Hair as a Way to Explore Trans Identities

In the last four semesters of doing the assignment, I also had two trans-identified students who tried the body hair assignment (both female-to-male in transition, both of whom had never grown body hair before). For them, the assignment mapped onto their anticipated transitions and gave them a window into the way that hair and gender overlap. Casey (21/Latina(o)/trans-identified lesbian) described an experience where newly grown body hair helped him to feel more "manly": "We went to Walmart this week and I did get weird stares and some people had a hard time figuring out if I was a girl or a guy. A lady walked by as I reached for something and said, 'excuse me, sir . . .' and took three looks at me, up to down, 'uh, excuse me Miss?' and walked by. I tried to see how many more people would question my gender. . . . It makes me mad in a way because now that I have body hair, people automatically think I'm male. I feel like it's stupid to think that! I mean, I may be a bit androgynous sometimes but having body hair shouldn't put me in the man category right away." Chance (20/white/trans-identified heterosexual) described the body hair assignment as a first step in gauging others' responses to his gender identity: "Growing body hair helped my mom to finally imagine me as a male for the first time. She even started using the male pronouns and my male name when she had resisted that before. She still thought the hair was disgusting but it helped her to see me as a man. My brother liked the hair too and said I 'looked like a dude.'" These students helped to further broaden the potential scope of what the body hair assignment can do in teaching students about how their bodies are policed or controlled by others (and how gender identity and hair are deeply intertwined).

Racial Consciousness Gap

Women of color with dark hair also repeatedly wrote in their papers that white (especially blond) women could not understand them and that white women did not experience the same stigma. This seemed like a layered comment both about the technical

Students at the end of the body hair assignment show their collective strength.
Photograph by Breanne Fahs

differences in body hair but also about the sense of social penalty or punishment. For example, Alma (20/Latina/heterosexual) described her body hair in comparison to the blond women in class as difficult for her in part because she had a long history of being compared to white women: "I have dark hair, so of course I was going to have dark body hair. I felt envious of all the girls who had light body hair. White girls always had blond body hair so even during my childhood, I grew to hate my dark body hair, which made me lack confidence with my body." Sasha (22/African American/heterosexual) also felt that white women did not understand the difficulty of having dark, visible hair for a woman of color: "I listened to the white women in the class complain about their boyfriends and how their boyfriends didn't like their hair, how hard it was to tell their mothers. They don't know anything about hard. Being Black means I always have to worry about others thinking less of me, not just my boyfriend. I wouldn't dare tell my mother that I grew armpit hair. It's not even an option for me like it is for the white women in class." This sense of a racial consciousness gap seemed notable in that women of color wrestled with notions of respectability, stigma, and social punishment differently than did white women.

Notes on Body Hair and Resistance

Looking ahead, I conclude with a few points I want to reiterate to readers of this collection: (1) We must imagine why our own (body) hair matters and what sorts of social meanings it has in our lives. (2) After careful consideration, I have good reason to believe that women can far better see, feel, and understand the networks of social control and policing that exists around their bodies when they use their bodies to engage in nonnormative gender behavior. Simply imagining such resistance is not enough. The body must be utilized for such resistance in order to understand the controlling apparatuses of our families, friends, coworkers, and partners. (3) Beneath the veneer of cultural "encouragement" for women to comply with gender roles and social norms is a kind of cultural terrorism (that is, the enforcement of gender norms and deep hostility and even violence toward those who do not conform) that can emerge randomly and without warning. Taking seriously the potential chaos of such resistances will only make the feminist movement stronger and smarter. (4) Finally, I hope we can continue to use our bodies to defy and rebel against all sorts of norms that restrict, harm, and limit women's movements, options, and possibilities. Whether individually or collectively, the body vividly reveals the intersections of self/culture, control/chaos, person/group, conservative/progressive, and cynicism/hope. These tensions underscore the possibilities of the (hairy) body and the potential in imagining something new.

REFERENCES

Braun, Virginia, Gemma Tricklebank, and Victoria Clarke. 2013. "'It Shouldn't Stick Out From Your Bikini at the Beach': Meaning, Gender, and the Hairy/Hairless Body." *Psychology of Women Quarterly* 37, no. 4: 478–93.
Butler, Meg. 2015. "Do You Let It Grow? Women Who Don't Shave." *Madame Noire*, April 24, 2015. *madamenoire.com/528409/do-you-let-it-grow-celebrity-women-who-dont-shave/5*.
Craig, Maxine. 2002. *Ain't I a Beauty Queen? Black Women, Beauty, and the Politics of Race.* New York: Oxford University Press.
DeMaria, Andrea L., and Abbey B. Berenson. 2013. "Prevalence and Correlates of Pubic Hair Grooming among Low-Income Hispanic, Black, and White Women." *Body Image* 10, no. 2: 226–31.
Fahs, Breanne, and Denise A. Delgado. 2011. "The Specter of Excess: Race, Class, and Gender in Women's Body Hair Narratives." In *Embodied Resistance: Challenging the Norms, Breaking the Rules,* edited by Chris Bobel and Samantha Kwan, 13–25. Nashville, TN: Vanderbilt University Press.
Fahs, Breanne. 2011. "Dreaded 'Otherness': Heteronormative Patrolling in Women's Body Hair Rebellions." *Gender & Society* 25, no. 4: 451–72.

————. 2012. "Breaking Body Hair Boundaries: Classroom Exercises for Challenging Social Constructions of the Body and Sexuality." *Feminism & Psychology* 22, no. 4: 482–506.

————. 2013. "Shaving It All Off: Examining Social Norms of Body Hair among College Men in a Women's Studies Course." *Women's Studies: An Inter-disciplinary Journal* 42, no. 5: 559–77.

————. 2014. "Perilous Patches and Pitstaches: Imagined Versus Lived Experiences of Women's Body Hair Growth." *Psychology of Women Quarterly* 38, no. 2: 167–80.

Fry, Kimberley, and Cheryl Lousley. 2001. "Girls Just Want to Have Fun with Politics: Out of the Contradictions of Popular Culture, Eco-Grrrls Are Rising to Define Feminism, Environmentalism, and Political Action." *Alternatives Journal* 27, no. 2: 24–28.

Herbenick, Debby, Devon Hensel, Nicole K. Smith, Vanessa Schick, Michael Reece, Stephanie A. Sanders, and Dennis J. Fortenberry. 2013. "Pubic Hair Removal and Sexual Behavior: Findings from a Prospective Daily Diary Study of Sexually Active Women in the United States." *Journal of Sexual Medicine* 10, no. 3: 678–85.

Herzig, Rebecca. 2015. *Plucked: A History of Hair Removal.* New York: New York University Press.

Holley, Peter. 2014. "Why Women Are Dyeing Their Armpit Hair." *Washington Post,* December 13, 2014. *www.washingtonpost.com/news/post-nation/wp/2014/12/13/meet-the-woman-who-helped-start-the-dyed-armpit-hair-trend.*

Ménard, A. Dana, and Peggy J. Kleinplatz. 2008. "Twenty-One Moves Guaranteed to Make His Thighs Go Up in Flames: Depictions of 'Great Sex' in Popular Magazines." *Sexuality & Culture* 12, no. 1: 1–20.

Newman, Andrew Adam. 2015. "Women Who Dye Their (Armpit) Hair." *New York Times,* July 14, 2015. *www.nytimes.com/2015/07/16/fashion/women-who-dye-their-armpit-hair.html.*

Riddell, Lenore, Hannah Varto, and Zoë G. Hodgson. 2010. "Smooth Talking: The Phenomenon of Pubic Hair Removal in Women." *Canadian Journal of Human Sexuality* 19, no. 3: 121–30.

Rubin, Gayle. 1984. "Thinking Sex: Notes for a Radical Theory of the Politics of Sexuality." In *Pleasure and Danger: Exploring Female Sexuality*, edited by Carol S. Vance, 267–94. London: Pandora.

Smolak, Linda, and Sarah K. Murnen. 2011. "Gender, Self-Objectification, and Pubic Hair Removal." *Sex Roles* 65, no. 7: 506–17.

Staggenborg, Suzanne, and Verta Taylor. 2005. "Whatever Happened to the Women's Movement?" *Mobilization: An International Quarterly* 10, no. 1: 37–52.

Tiggemann, Marika, and Suzanna Hodgson. 2008. "The Hairlessness Norm Extended: Reasons for and Predictors of Women's Body Hair Removal at Different Body Sites." *Sex Roles* 59, no. 11: 889–97.

Tiggemann, Marika, and Sarah J. Kenyon. 1998. "The Hairlessness Norm: The Removal of Body Hair in Women." *Sex Roles* 39, no. 11-12: 873–75.

Tiggemann, Marika, and Christine Lewis. 2004. "Attitudes toward Women's Body Hair: Relationship with Disgust Sensitivity." *Psychology of Women Quarterly* 28, no. 4: 381–87.

Toerien, Merran, Sue Wilkinson, and Precilla Y. L. Choi. 2005. "Body Hair Removal: The 'Mundane' Production of Normative Femininity." *Sex Roles* 52, no. 5: 399–406.

Vannier, Sarah A., Anna B. Currie, and Lucia F. O'Sullivan. 2014. "Schoolgirls and Soccer Moms: A Content Analysis of Free 'Teen' and 'MILF' Online Pornography." *Journal of Sex Research* 51, no. 3: 253–64.

Weitz, Rose. 2001. "Women and Their Hair: Seeking Power through Resistance and Accommodation." *Gender & Society* 15, no. 5: 667–86.

2

Radical Doulas, Childbirth Activism, and the Politics of Embodiment

Monica Basile

> Asking a naked woman who is in the grip of contractions and feeling vulnerable to stand up to the medical establishment is pretty radical.
>
> —Evelyn Saldana, birth doula

> I have worked with groups that organized around independent media, antiwar activism, globalization, water privatization, and local community building. Ultimately, birth work is the most rewarding and satisfying work that I have done. I appreciate this work because it is obviously very personal and intimate, [. . .] but I also know that it's bigger than the individuals I serve. When women reclaim the right to birth on their own terms, they might feel more empowered to challenge other forms of oppression and discrimination in their lives.
>
> —Megan Tate, birth doula

Childbirth is a bodily experience that is shaped by social, economic, and political forces, and birth doulas bear witness every day to this convergence as they support families through the experience of labor and birth. Doulas seek to provide an important intervention into the uneven distribution of power and authoritative knowledge in the birthing room by placing value and priority on the everyday nonmedical bodily knowledge and experiences of birthing people.[1] Evelyn Saldana's description in the epigraph above outlines a key argument about the politics of doula care: that facilitating a laboring woman's expression of power while she is in a vulnerable, liminal state, and embedded in an institutional setting, is a radical act of resistance.

As Megan Tate points out, however, these acts of resistance have implications beyond the level of individual interactions with the medical system. While much feminist scholarship concerning the politics of birth centralizes the issue of medicalization, my research expands this analysis to better understand the cultural impact of doula care as part of a larger picture of reproductive health and reproductive justice advocacy. I observe that in addition to challenging the medicalization of birth, doulas are seeking to contribute to social justice through working to empower people in multiple facets of their lives, beyond the birthing room.

The radical doula movement is made up of doulas whose work is grounded in explicitly feminist, class conscious, and antiracist politics, and who situate their care practices in terms of larger community organizing and activist projects. I argue that this movement represents a new direction in doula care that forges connections between birthworkers and activists for causes such as LGBTQ rights, abortion rights, prisoners' rights, and economic and racial justice. By reimagining the reach of their work, radical doulas are drawing necessary connections to social justice issues that are often overlooked within the childbirth reform movement, which tends to focus on medicalization as the primary issue. Although some have argued that doulas are not able to create lasting institutional change, I observe that doulas are increasingly claiming identities as activists, and that those who call themselves radical doulas are bringing a distinct politics of embodiment into their birth work.[2]

What Is a Doula?

Doulas are people—usually, but not always, mothers—who are trained and often certified to provide nonmedical physical, emotional, and informational support during pregnancy, childbirth, and/or the postpartum period.[3] The emergence of the modern doula movement is an outgrowth of the women's health movement of the 1970s, which criticized the medicalization of birth in the hospital setting as patriarchal and disempowering to women (Ehrenreich and English 1970; Arms 1975). For example, feminists and scholars have questioned the routine use of practices such as episiotomy, the use of forceps, restricting women to hospital beds for delivery, and invasive monitoring protocols as medically unnecessary and dehumanizing (Davis-Floyd [1992] 2003); Martin 1997; Rothman 1982).

Alongside the grassroots efforts of the women's health movement, feminist anthropologists and sociologists pioneered a body of scholarship concerning birth practices. Barbara Katz Rothman's foundational text *In Labor: Women and Power in the Birthplace* (1982) examined American childbirth practices from a feminist perspective and conceptualized a fundamental difference between two approaches to birth: the medical model, which sees birth as pathological and in need of control, and the holistic model, which espouses the belief that birth is a normal process in need of support. This distinction gave legitimacy to the homebirth and midwifery movements, tied them to feminism, and provided a new and useful set of terms within which to advocate for women-centered birth practices. Informed by both Rothman's analysis and the cross-cultural approach of works such as Brigitte Jordan's *Birth in Four Cultures* ([1978] 1993), Robbie Davis-Floyd (2001) proposed a third, mediating model: the humanistic approach. Humanism, Davis-Floyd explains, originated "as an effort driven by nurses and physicians working within the medical system to reform it from the inside" (S10). As doulas have become a more mainstream element of maternity care in the United States, the "inside" is precisely where they have found themselves.

Doulas began to professionalize in the 1980s as a way to rehumanize the birth experience, recentralize the embodied knowledge of birthing women, and help mothers advocate for their bodily autonomy in institutional birth settings. The popularity of doula care has been growing steadily since then, and there are now thousands of people worldwide who have embraced this profession. DONA International, the oldest and largest doula-certifying organization, reported 12,000 certified doulas in 2016—a significant expansion since the first doula was certified in 1994 ("About DONA International" 2018). While DONA is by far the most widely recognized doula organization, there are many other national and local organizations that train and certify doulas.

Not all doula work is the same. Birth doulas provide assistance during labor and delivery, and postpartum doulas provide care in the period after birth. Some doulas offer support for abortion, adoption, pregnancy loss, and other reproductive experiences. Some practice privately and are paid by individuals for their services, and others work on a volunteer basis, sometimes in formalized hospital-sponsored programs designed to offer doula care to anyone who may want labor support. Still others provide community-based care in programs that are affiliated with clinics, prisons, neighborhood centers, and other agencies and institutions. As the word "doula" has become more mainstream, its meaning has expanded beyond pregnancy and birth; it is also now used to describe those who provide emotional support to the dying and their families. Doulas, as individuals, represent a wide variety of personal backgrounds, political and religious convictions, experiences with birth, and philosophies of care.

A birth doula usually meets with expectant parents several times during pregnancy to discuss their concerns and desires for the upcoming birth. The doula will help the expectant parent(s) to create a list of preferences for the upcoming birth, and will be responsible to "help the woman have a safe and satisfying childbirth as the woman defines it" (Simkin 2016, 1). The birth doula typically sets aside one month of on-call time for each birth—two weeks before and two weeks after the estimated due date. The doula joins the birthing parent (and their partner and/or family) once labor begins and stays with them for the duration of labor and delivery. During labor and birth, the doula performs a variety of tasks, such as helping with comfort measures like relaxation, movement, and positioning; assisting families in gathering information about the course of their labor and their options; and providing emotional reassurance and comfort to the woman and her family. After the birth, the doula helps with initial breastfeeding and bonding and usually makes one or two further visits in the weeks following birth to review the birth and answer questions about postpartum recovery or infant care. Doulas attend births in hospitals, birth centers, and home settings, but practice most frequently in hospitals.

In contrast to midwives, physicians, and nurses, a doula's presence during labor and birth is continuous and uninterrupted and thus represents a continuity of care that is rare in obstetrical settings. Since doulas do not perform clinical tasks of primary health care provision, they are able to focus their attention completely on the mother's emotional, mental, and even spiritual needs, as well as her physical comfort. Clinical research on doula care has been extensive and has repeatedly shown that doula support is associated with lower rates of cesarean deliveries, pain medication usage, induction of labor, forceps and vacuum deliveries, and postpartum depression (Bohren et al. 2017; Hodnett and Osborn 1989; Hofmeyr et al. 1991; Kennell et al. 1991; Klaus et al. 1986; Sosa et al. 1980). There have been no documented drawbacks to doula care.

Doulas are part of a larger childbirth reform movement that includes professionals in related fields, such as childbirth educators and lactation counselors; midwives and physicians; midwifery advocates; and other parents and concerned citizens. Although some of the routine obstetrical practices that were widespread in the 1960s and 1970s, such as episiotomy, have become less common, birth remains highly medicalized in the United States. Childbirth reformers today are particularly concerned with issues such as the cesarean rate in the US, which reached an all-time high of 32.9 percent in 2009 and has only slightly lowered to 32 percent as of 2015 (Martin et al. 2017, 9), These rates far exceed the 10 to 15 percent rate that the World Health Organization suggests is optimal for maternal-fetal health. The WHO cautions that the overuse of cesarean surgery introduces unnecessary and sometimes serious risks to mothers and babies, at significant cost to health care systems (2015). Despite spending more money per capita on health care than any other nation, the United States has comparatively poor outcomes in terms of perinatal, neonatal, and maternal mortality and low birth weight (Sakala and Corry 2008, 3). Black mothers and babies experience even more concerning maternal and perinatal health outcomes, with far higher rates of preterm birth, low birth weight, and infant mortality (Mathews MacDorman, and Thoma 2015). Childbirth reformers advocate for a reversal of this state of affairs, calling for increased use of midwives, doulas, and other alternatives to the mainstream medical model of birth, citing cost-effectiveness and the improved outcomes for mothers and babies associated with these forms of care (Sandall et al. 2016).

In order to gain entry into American birthing rooms, doulas must work to fit into existing hospital structures, dealing with the occasionally conflicting needs of birthing women and hospital staff through complex combinations of negotiation, resistance, and acquiescence (Morton and Clift 2014). Although many doulas undertake their work with the goal of creating change in the culture and practice of birth, they tend to view this change as occurring on an individual basis. A common expression among doulas is "changing the world one birth at a time." Because of the willingness of most doulas to work within the structures of the hospital, some scholars have questioned the effectiveness of doulas as change-makers (Norman 2007; Block 2007). However, my research shows that doulas, in general, tend to see their advocacy role as extremely important. Radical doulas, in particular, see the realms of doula work and social justice activism as fully integrated, and see their intervention as affecting change on both individual and structural levels.

In 2007, Miriam Zoila Perez coined the term "radical doula." She outlines the reasons she began using this term to describe herself:

> This was a designation that I came to assume for myself through an understanding that my beliefs (which seemed to me completely logical and altogether natural) placed me apart from a large part of what I have come to call the "birth activist" community (midwives, doulas, and advocates who work toward changing the standards of care for birthing women in the US). . . . My politics are a seeming contradiction: I'm a doula and I'm a pro-choice abortion advocate. I'm a doula and I'm a lesbian. I'm a doula and I may never have children. I'm a doula and I'm Latina. I'm doula and I'm not entirely comfortable with the gender/sex binary. (2007)

This way of embodying doulahood is a departure from the mainstream "birth activist" community Perez refers to. Although the doula movement has its roots in the feminist health movement, which in many ways defined itself as radical, doulas and doula organizations have generally tended to represent the prototypical doula as feminine, motherly, middle class, white, heteronormative, and often apolitical, in order to conform to cultural codes that signal "professionalism." Perez began publishing a blog and website entitled Radical Doula (*radicaldoula.com*) as a way to connect with those in the doula community who likewise embody these "seeming contradictions," and she has been joined by many others who question the limitations of the mainstream representation of doulas. Her blog regularly featured profiles of other doulas who embrace this designation. Perez has since published a book called *The Radical Doula Guide* (2012), and she writes and speaks as a leader within this growing movement.

I focus this chapter on radical doulas as a subgroup within the doula movement. I argue that those who call themselves radical doulas are bringing a distinct politics of embodiment into their birth work, exemplary of the reproductive justice paradigm that treats social justice activism and birth care as fundamentally intertwined. Stemming from this perspective, radical doulas undertake powerful and productive work that is set apart by four characteristics: an acknowledgement of intersectionality; a prioritization of underserved populations; an emphasis on multiplicity and diversity of identity; and an anti-essentialist view of birthing bodies. As they mobilize these values, radical doulas are poised to transform the doula movement and change the face of childbirth activism.

Methods

My research seeks to understand the doula movement on two levels. First, I am interested in how doulas interact rhetorically with representational practices that shape the meaning of childbirth. Second, I am interested in how doulas see themselves as agents of social change. As an interdisciplinary feminist project, my investigation of the doula movement relies on several methodological approaches including discourse analysis, participant observation, face-to-face ethnographic interviews, and online survey data.[4] I conducted face-to-face interviews with fifteen doulas, and 156 doulas from forty US states and five Canadian provinces completed a detailed online survey that included multiple open-ended questions and elicited richly descriptive responses. All quotes from survey respondents and interviews come from my data and transcripts, collected between 2007 and 2011. The average age of my research participants was thirty-two (oldest sixty-eight, youngest twenty). The vast majority identified as female, four identified as male, and one as genderqueer. I asked interviewees and survey respondents to identify their race/ethnicity as an open-ended question: 84 percent identified as white; 11 percent black; 3 percent Native American/American Indian; 2 percent Hispanic/Latina; 1 percent each as Jewish, White/Hispanic; Asian/Pacific Islander; Afro-Latina, and biracial/mixed-race. The vast majority, 94 percent, had some college education, and 68 percent had college degrees. I assigned pseudonyms to all of my interviewees and survey respondents, except for already public figures. To analyze my data from both surveys and interviews, I collected responses to each of my questions and developed codes from recurring responses. From these codes, significant themes and issues emerged, and these themes and issues structure my arguments.

Like many feminist ethnographers, I see myself as embodied in my research, rather than detached from it (Behar and Gordon 1995; Wolf 1992). Much of my knowledge about doulas and childbirth activism comes from my own experiences over the past twenty years in the childbirth profession, first as a birth doula and childbirth educator, and more recently as a midwife and midwifery advocate. These experiences have allowed me access to the lived realities of birth work and have given me the opportunity to participate in extensive relevant interactions and communications with the general public, families I have served, policy makers, and other activists and childbirth professionals. This research is also informed by my experiences as a young single mother and participant in the third-wave feminist movement. These experiences inform my own shifting embodiment of seemingly contradictory identities and political commitments and shape my engagement with the third-wave politics of the radical doula movement.

Radical Doula Work, Reproductive Justice, and Third-Wave Activism

Radical doulas draw on several perspectives that are characteristic of both the reproductive justice paradigm and third-wave feminism: intersectionality theory, especially as developed by feminists of color; postmodernist and postcolonial feminist theory; and youth culture that celebrates multiplicity and contradiction. These perspectives have contributed fruitfully to the understanding of how bodies come to be discursively and politically positioned through the insistence that categories of race, class, gender, nationality, and sexuality are always intertwined and mutually constitutive of each other. They are also concerned with creating solidarity and alliances in ways that do not erase difference, but avoid investing difference with hierarchical significance (Garrison 2000; Hernandez, Rehman, and Moraga 2002; Walker 1995). Critiques of feminism by scholars, theorists, and activists of color, and by third-wave feminists, "did not seek to undermine the feminist movement, but rather to refigure and enhance it so as to make it more diverse and inclusive" (Mann and Huffman 2005, 57). I argue that radical doulas are acting in the same spirit as they enact new and distinct approaches to birth work.

Intersectionality

The primary political project of the natural childbirth and doula movements of the past several decades has been the demedicalization of birth and the expansion of women's choices in childbirth. However, while the natural childbirth movement has been highly attuned to issues of gendered power imbalances in the birthing room, it has tended to assume a universal "women's experience" of childbirth and has largely ignored issues of race, class, sexuality, and other intersections of social location that can affect how reproductive and birth care is accessed and experienced.

In contrast, the medicalization of birth is not the central concern of radical doulas; rather, they view reproductive experiences, including childbirth, as a key point of intersectionality where larger patterns of privilege, oppression, and resistance converge on a highly personal level. Exemplifying this perspective, Sara Young, a survey respondent in New York said, "Yes [I identify as a radical doula]. I understand the systemic roots of hetero-patriarchy, class oppression, racial oppression, and power dynamics that have a direct effect on the US birth system. I bring this understanding to my doula practice and work to subvert oppression by helping clients to radically trans-form their relationships with their bodies, partners, sexual identities, and families."

This perspective is not a new invention of radical doulas; it is informed by a rich and extensive history of theorizing and organizing by activists of color who point out that that reproductive "choice" does not apply equally to all (Morgen 2002; Nelson 2003; Ross et al. 2017; Silliman et al. 2004). Because social and economic inequality leads to uneven access to reproductive autonomy, a reliance on the rhetoric of "choice" and health care "consumption" inhibits effective advocacy.

For radical doulas, it is important to recognize that birthing choices are part of the spectrum of reproductive rights and are tied to struggles for social justice and hu-man rights. This perspective is encompassed by the term "reproductive justice," which was developed through reproductive rights organizing by women of color in the 1980s and '90s. Loretta Ross, cofounder of SisterSong Women of Color Reproductive Health Collective and foremother of the reproductive justice movement, explains:

> Reproductive justice is in essence an intersectional theory emerging from the experiences of women of color whose multiple communities experience a complex set of reproductive oppressions. It is based on the understanding that the impacts of race, class, gender and sexual identity oppressions are not additive but integrative, producing this paradigm of intersectionality. . . . Reproductive justice is a positive approach that links sexuality, health, and human rights to social justice movements by placing abortion and reproductive health issues in the larger context of the well-being and health of women, families and communities because reproductive justice seamlessly integrates those individual and group human rights particularly important to marginalized communities. We believe that the ability of any woman to determine her own reproductive destiny is directly linked to the conditions in her community and these conditions are not just a matter of individual choice and access. (2011)

A reproductive justice framework clarifies the connections between birth work and advocacy agendas that are often considered unrelated and even contradictory: abor-tion rights, midwifery advocacy, drug policy reform, anti–domestic violence advocacy, health care reform, and prison reform. Radical doulas are highly attuned to these con-nections. They see their work not just as expanding choices "one birth at a time," but as intervening in multiple, intersecting forms of structural oppression.

Prioritizing the Underserved

Because radical doulas see their work as intervening in social injustice, one core value they share is prioritizing the underserved. They tend to be particularly interested in providing care to vulnerable or marginalized populations: those who are low-income, immigrants or refugees, English language learners, racial or ethnic minorities, LGBTQ, or parenting in non-nuclear family structures. For many radical doulas, this interest springs directly from embodied experiences in the birthing room. Doulas bear witness, on a regular basis, to ways in which their clients' medical treatment differs based upon their social location. Survey respondents across the country noted such discrepancies. For example, Jane Halliday in Wisconsin said, "Most striking was the difference in treatment in the hospitals and by nurses for my clients who were women of color, low income, or teenagers, many fitting into all of these categories. I have seen RNs say things to them that are so hurtful and discouraging and would never be said to a private client who was white, well-educated, and over 25."

Similarly, Nancy Rich in New York said, "What I noticed was that the medical establishment took my clients less seriously when they were low-income combined with African-American." Kimberly Greenlee in Washington, DC, echoed this: "Nurses are sometimes pretty rude to teen moms. I hear comments like, 'you should have thought of how painful it was going to be before you went and got pregnant!'" And Norma Jameson in Connecticut observed, "In caring for same sex couples, I find that there are more barriers to communication in the hospital. The non-pregnant mother is not seen as a parent by some caregivers." In situations like these, the politics of the doula's presence and advocacy take on a distinct and crucial significance. In advocating for their clients, doulas are advocating not only for humanizing a particular individual birth experience, but for the humane treatment of a marginalized population.

Rather than practicing under the fee-for-service private doula model, many radical doulas tend to favor volunteering their services or working as part of publicly or privately funded programs, such as community-based, prison, or full-spectrum doula programs. Community-based doulas (CBDs) practice within programs that are designed to "serve communities that have been self-defined as underserved" (Abramson, Breedlove, and Isaacs 2006, 31). The CBD model is derived from the community health worker approach, wherein CBDs are usually members of the same racial, ethnic, and/or socioeconomic background as those they serve. As of 2013, Health Connect One, the leading community-based doula organization in the United States, reported mentoring fifty CBD organizations in eighteen states, with another forty-four organizations in stages of development, serving a diverse range of communities (Health Connect One 2014). The stated goals and accomplishments of community-based doula programs are primarily concerned with reducing health disparities, reducing costs, and creating measurable long-term benefits for disadvantaged women and families. These outcomes may certainly be brought about, in part, through the humanizing influence of the doula, but demedicalization itself tends not to be the primary aim of these programs.

As of 2018, prison doula programs operate actively in five states in the United States.[5] The Rebecca Project, which investigates policies affecting incarcerated mothers and their children, reports that about five percent of women entering prisons and jails are pregnant, and that incarcerated pregnant women lack quality prenatal care (National Women's Law Center 2010, 10). Through prison doula programs, doulas and childbirth educators provide classes and support groups to pregnant women and mothers in prison; they provide direct support during labor and birth; they organize community-awareness and educational events; and they undertake collaborations with allied organizations related to incarcerated mothers' issues. Prison doulas serve people who are extremely socially vulnerable and subject to the most coercive of institutional constraints. For this reason, it becomes even more important for doulas involved with this type of care to be committed to understanding prison issues, social justice, and consensus-model decision making.

Finally, full spectrum doulas provide support not only in childbirth; they also provide the doula model of care to those experiencing abortion, miscarriage, stillbirth, and adoption. In addition to requiring grief support and other forms of emotional care, those experiencing pregnancy losses face bodily experiences and medical treatment options that can be difficult to navigate without the benefit of informational support. Families on both sides of the adoption experience also have specific emotional and educational needs. By drawing connections between birth, abortion, adoption, pregnancy loss, and other reproductive experiences, full spectrum doulas recognize that the needs of pregnant people go far beyond, and are far more complicated than, a reductive polar opposition of pro- and anti-choice.[6]

Emphasis on Multiplicity and Diversity

In addition to the desire to serve those with less socioeconomic privilege, radical doulas seek to make doula care more accessible to greater numbers of people through making connections with nontraditional families. They often do this through their own embodiment of nontraditional identities. This stands in contrast to more mainstream doulas' efforts to promote doula care through seeking acceptance within the medical establishment by embodying "professionalism." As a self-described radical doula, survey participant Hazel Davis in Oregon critiqued the standard of professionalism for doulas: "Internalized sexism shapes our professional standards: wear pearls, smile, don't drink or dance or swear, don't date, don't be sexy or opinionated, don't be butch, don't look or be too young, don't be 'cultural,' don't look or act too common, don't act too smart, be the Pious Heterosexual Archetype of Feminine Purity and Submissiveness. Very limiting."

What Hazel describes is a particular performance of middle-class, white, heterosexual femininity that pervades ideals of professionalism in many spheres of American society. Her analysis, however, raises an important question: Does this professional standard represent a disconnect, if doulas' care is to be a feminist or liberatory project? And does it put limitations on who feels they can be a doula or have a doula? This homogeneity affects how doulas are received in the hospital as well. One doula I spoke with, Diana Crenshaw, told me that as a black woman, she is often not recognized as a doula in the birthing room. "People assume I'm an auntie or a grandmother or another family member," she said. Her experience highlights the racist attitudes that limit the possibility for some doulas of being perceived as professionals to begin with.

In 2010, a group of self-identified radical doulas founded *SQUAT Birth Journal* as a means of representing the diversity of the birthworker community. Its mission statement explains these goals: "We strive to provide a forum where radical, often unheard voices can share their message. . . . We acknowledge the need for the midwifery movement to expand its consciousness, scope of practice, and accessibility. We seek to provide a safe space of expression and community for those who wish to shift current birth culture as an essential part of the midwifery and birth movement" ("Our Mission" 2016, 3).

SQUAT's imagery emphasized racial and cultural diversity, and the publication featured articles on topics such as multicultural birthing traditions, abortion care, and understanding racism and oppression in midwifery. Although *SQUAT* ended its publication in 2016, it represented an important intervention into the politics of the representation of doulas.

Radical doulas critique the racial homogeneity of the doula community as a barrier to a wide range of families receiving care. Wave Azul, who has worked as a doula in several states, said in an interview: "There are not enough doulas of color. And that was true in California, where it was much more diverse than Iowa, and in North Carolina where it was much more diverse than Iowa. There's just something missing there. And I think, in part, that could be related to the whiteness of DONA and the privileges you must have in order to attend training."

One of the weaknesses of doula trainings identified most commonly by those who took my survey was the lack of adequate attention to diversity and racial disparities in the more prominent doula training organizations. The International Center for Traditional Childbearing (ICTC) is notable for working specifically to attend to these issues and to increase racial diversity among birthworkers, and it was clear in my research that many radical doulas actively sought training offered by the ICTC. Also notable is the organization Doula Trainings International (DTI), founded in 2011. A training and certifying organization for "the modern doula," DTI centers diversity and inclusivity and includes a social justice steering committee in its leadership.

The heteronormativity of the mainstream doula community is another limitation that several doulas in my study specifically cited as personally difficult. Ginger Rossi, a survey respondent from Colorado, said, "I cried the first night of doula training, convinced that there was no place for me as a lesbian in the birth world." Although social networking technologies have opened up more opportunities for lesbian, bisexual, trans, and queer-identified doulas to connect with each other, it can be isolating to be surrounded by representations of birth that ignore LGBTQ existence and experience. Jason Epstein, one of the male-identified doulas who responded to my survey, observed, "The birth community seems diverse, community-based, and tends to fight sexist oppression. On the other hand it feels very heterosexist, transphobic, and always refers to birthers, doulas, and others as 'mommas,' 'ladies,' or 'sisters.'"

Jason points out that the community of birthworkers is well aware of problems relating to sexism but has not yet gone beyond essentialist ways of thinking about birth, or extended that political awareness to incorporate language that is inclusive of the LGBTQ community. Jason decided to become a doula because, as he said, "a transgender friend was thinking of becoming pregnant and needed someone who could refer to someone giving birth with male pronouns." The notion of childbirth as separate from femaleness represents a new challenge to the doula profession, but more than one doula I spoke to indicated that there is a need for doulas who are capable of making this leap.

Anti-essentialist Views of the Birthing Body

Many doulas act as allies to the LGBTQ community, even if they do not identify this way themselves. The use of the term "partner" to refer to a pregnant client's significant other has become widespread in the past five to ten years among doulas and other childbirth professionals, as evidenced in literature, websites, and common language usage. But for many radical doulas, who tend to be attuned to the presence of transgender and gender-nonconforming parents, it has also become important to use gender-neutral language to refer to pregnant and birthing people themselves. While this is still making its way into mainstream birth culture, many birthworkers are actively using gender-inclusive terms like "pregnant people" and "birthing parent" rather than "women" or "mothers" in their blogs, websites, conversational language, and publications like *SQUAT Birth Journal*. This shift, however, has not been uncontroversial. In 2015, the Midwives' Alliance of North America revised their core competencies to incorporate gender-inclusive language. This was hailed as a landmark by some and decried as an outrage against femininity by others, including some high-profile and influential midwives.[7]

By using gender-neutral language and recognizing trans and gender-variant experiences of parenthood, radical doulas de-link gender from pregnancy and childbirth—experiences that are generally considered quintessentially female. This move among some doulas represents a radical rethinking of the meaning of sex and gender and a profound challenge to an essentialist, binary gender system. The use of gender-inclusive language in this context mirrors the strategies of the third-wave feminist menstrual activists described by Chris Bobel (2010) who use the term "menstruator" rather "woman," thereby acknowledging that not only women menstruate and also that menstruation is not a part of every woman's experience. Following Bobel's argument, I observe that radical doulas represent a similar third-wave feminist movement, centered on bodily experience but interested in deconstructing essentialist ideas of womanhood and gendered embodiment. As radical menstrual activists view menstruation as "a bodily process that exists not independently of, but in relationship to, the gendered body" (Bobel 2010, 156), so do many radical doulas view childbirth.

Conclusion: Radical Doulas and the Politics of Embodiment

The politics of race, class, gender, and sexuality are fundamentally about bodies: bodies differentially situated within economic and social orders that allow or limit access to health care resources, and within ideological orders that define the very meanings of what constitutes health or disease on both an individual and social level. Angela Davis wrote, "the pursuit of health in body, mind, and spirit weaves in and out of every major struggle women have ever waged in our quest for social, economic, and political emancipation" (1990, 19).

Radical doulas recognize that politicization springs from embodiment and that bodily experience informs action, theory, and praxis. Jessica Lomas, who works with a community-based doula program in Washington, explains: "It's powerful to feel like you are creating change in your own body. If you feel capable in your own skin of growing and birthing and raising a child, then how does that affect our involvement in other social justice issues? Powerfully!"

This attitude reflects the belief that, as doulas help increase their clients' sense of bodily power and integrity, they also help them experience social power and integrity. As one self-described radical doula envisioned, doulas and those they serve are working together as "fellow activists." For radical doulas, the work they do is not simply about helping someone to give birth, or to avoid unnecessary medical interventions; rather, it is about advocating for a wider range of human rights in the context of reproductive experiences.

Through insisting on an intersectional perspective, increasing awareness of the needs and experiences of less privileged women and families, and embodying and celebrating a multiplicity of identities, radical doulas seek to increase access to care for those who may not meet normative ideas of motherhood or femininity and who may not be considered "legitimate mothers" (Solinger 2005). Through challenging some of the doula community's longstanding beliefs and priorities, radical doulas endeavor to make the birth community more diverse, and to make the benefits of doula care more widely available to a broader range of people. Radical doulas see this as an intervention that can improve the reproductive experiences of the people they serve and, in turn, powerfully affect the lives of those people beyond the birthing room. In this way, radical doulas are introducing productive critiques of the childbirth reform movement and making important contributions to ensuring the autonomy, integrity, and dignity of all birthing people.

NOTES

1. For more on authoritative knowledge in the context of birth, see Davis-Floyd and Sargent 1997.
2. This chapter builds on my discussion of reproductive justice doulas in "Reimagining the Birthing Body: Reproductive Justice and New Directions in Doula Care" (Basile 2015).
3. Although the doula profession is overwhelmingly cisgender female dominated, I use the term "people" instead of "women" here to recognize the presence of male, transgender, genderqueer, and non-gender-conforming doulas. Because my project engages with doulas' critiques of gendered ways of understanding birth and birth work, I use gender-specific and gender-neutral language interchangeably.
4. I conducted this research as part of a doctoral dissertation in Gender, Women's and Sexuality Studies at the University of Iowa. I conducted my interviews and online surveys with approval from the Institutional Review Board (IRB# 200903769). For more information see Basile 2012.
5. These are the Birth Attendants in Olympia, Washington; the Minnesota Prison Doula Project (formerly Isis Rising); Motherhood Behind Bars in Georgia; the Baltimore Doula Project in Maryland; and the Alabama Prison Birth Project. The Prison Birth Project in Amherst, Massachusetts, founded in 2008, closed in February 2018.
6. Full spectrum doula programs operate in many cities across the United States, including Seattle, Atlanta, Chicago, Boston, Philadelphia, and Asheville, North Carolina, with their forerunner being the Doula Project, founded in New York City in 2008. The Doula Project's fifty trained doulas have provided services to more than five thousand people in New York City, and the organization has developed a replication model for full spectrum doula programs (The Doula Project, "About Us," *www.doulaproject.net*). For more on the Doula Project and full spectrum doula care, see Mahoney and Mitchell 2016.
7. This discussion is archived on the Midwives Alliance of North America's web site, *mana.org*. "Use of Inclusive Language," 2016, *mana.org/healthcare-policy/use-of-inclusive-language*.

REFERENCES

"About DONA International." 2018. DONA International. *www.dona.org/the-dona-advantage/about*.

Abramson, Rachel, Ginger Breedlove, and Beth Isaacs. 2006. *The Community-Based Doula: Supporting Families Before, During, and After Childbirth*. Washington, DC: Zero to Three Press.

Arms, Suzanne. 1975. *Immaculate Deception: A New Look at Women and Childbirth in America.* Boston: Houghton Mifflin.

Basile, Monica. 2012. *Reproductive Justice and Childbirth Reform: Doulas as Agents of Social Change.* PhD diss., University of Iowa.

_____. 2015. "Reimagining the Birthing Body: Reproductive Justice and New Directions in Doula Care." In *Doulas and Intimate Labour: Boundaries, Bodies and Birth,* edited by Angela Castañeda and Julie Searcy. Ontario, CA: Demeter Press.

Behar, Ruth, and Deborah A. Gordon, eds. 1995. *Women Writing Culture.* Berkeley: University of California Press.

Block, Jennifer. 2007. *Pushed: The Painful Truth about Childbirth and Modern Maternity Care.* Cambridge, MA: Da Capo Press.

Bobel, Chris. 2010. *New Blood: Third Wave Feminism and the Politics of Menstruation.* New Brunswick, NJ: Rutgers University Press.

Bohren, Meghan A., G. Justus Hofmeyr, Carol Sakala, Reiko K. Fukuzawa, and Anna Cuthbert. 2017. "Continuous Support for Women During Childbirth." (Cochrane Review). In *The Cochrane Database of Systematic Reviews*, no. 7. Art. no.: CD003766. doi: 10.1002/14651858.CD003766.pub6.

Davis, Angela. 1990. "Sick and Tired of Being Sick and Tired: The Politics of Black Women's Health." In *The Black Women's Health Book: Speaking for Ourselves*, edited by Evelyn C. White, 18–26. Seattle: Seal Press.

Davis-Floyd, Robbie. (1992) 2003. *Birth as an American Rite of Passage.* Berkeley: University of California Press.

_____. 2001. "The Technocratic, Humanistic, and Holistic Models of Birth." *International Journal of Gynecology and Obstetrics* 75 (suppl. 1): S5–S23.

Davis-Floyd, Robbie, and Carolyn Sargent, eds. 1997. *Childbirth and Authoritative Knowledge: Cross-Cultural Perspectives.* Berkeley: University of California Press.

Ehrenreich, Barbara, and Deirdre English. 1970. *Witches, Midwives and Nurses.* New York: Feminist Press.

Garrison, E. K. 2000. "U.S. Feminism-Grrrl Style! Youth (Sub)Cultures and the Technologies of the Third Wave." *Feminist Studies* 26 (1): 141–70.

Health Connect One. 2013. "Community-Based Doula Replication." Chicago: Health Connect One. *www.healthconnectone.org/wp-content/uploads/bsk-pdf-manager/CBD_Program_Replication_and_History_Nov_2013_20.pdf.*

Hernandez, Daisy, Bushra Rehman, and Cherrie Moraga, eds. 2002. *Colonize This! Young Women of Color on Today's Feminism.* Berkeley: Seal Press.

Hodnett, Ellen D., and Richard Osborn. 1989. "Effects of Continuous Intrapartum Professional Support on Childbirth Outcomes." *Research in Nursing and Health* 12: 289–97. doi: 10.1002/nur.4770120504.

Hofmeyr, G. Justus, V. Cheryl Nikodem, Wendy-Lynne Wolman, Beverly E. Chalmers, and Tami Kramer. 1991. "Companionship to Modify the Clinical Birth Environment: Effects on Progress and Perceptions of Labour and Breast Feeding." *British Journal of Obstetrics and Gynecology* 98: 756–64.

Jordan, Brigitte. (1978) 1993. *Birth in Four Cultures: A Cross-Cultural Investigation of Childbirth in Yucatan, Holland, Sweden, and the United States.* Prospect Heights, IL: Waveland Press.

Kennell, John H., Marshall Klaus, Susan McGrath, Steven Robertson, and Clark Hinkley. 1991. "Continuous Emotional Support during Labor in a U.S. Hospital." *Journal of the American Medical Association* 265: 2197–201.

Klaus, Marshall H., John H. Kennell, S. S. Robertson, and Roberto Sosa. 1986. "Effects of

Social Support during Parturition on Maternal and Infant Morbidity." *British Medical Journal* 293: 585–87.

Mahoney, Mary, and Lauren Mitchell. 2016. *The Doulas: Radical Care for Pregnant People.* New York: Feminist Press.

Mann, Susan Archer, and Douglas J. Huffman. 2005. "The Decentering of Second Wave Feminism and the Rise of the Third Wave." *Science & Society* 69, no. 1: 56–91.

Martin, Emily. 1997. *The Woman in the Body: A Cultural Analysis of Reproduction.* Boston: Beacon Press.

Martin, Joyce A., Brady E. Hamilton, Michelle J. K. Osterman, Anne K. Driscoll, and T. J. Mathews. 2017. "Births: Final Data for 2015." *National Vital Statistics Reports* 66, no. 1. Hyattsville, MD: National Center for Health Statistics. *www.cdc.gov/nchs/data/nvsr/ nvsr66/nvsr66_01.pdf.*

Mathews, T. J., M. F. MacDorman, and M. E. Thoma. 2015. "Infant Mortality Statistics from the 2013 Period Linked Birth/Infant Death Data Set." *National Vital Statistics Reports* 64, no. 9. Hyattsville, MD: National Center for Health Statistics. *www.cdc.gov/ nchs/data/nvsr/nvsr64/nvsr64_09.pdf.*

Morgen, Sandra. 2002. *Into Our Own Hands: The Women's Health Movement in the United States, 1969–1990.* New Brunswick: Rutgers University Press.

Morton, Christine, and Elayne Clift. 2014. *Birth Ambassadors: Doulas and the Re-emergence of Woman-Supported Birth in America.* Amarillo, TX: Praeclarus Press.

Nelson, Jennifer. 2003. *Women of Color and the Reproductive Rights Movement.* New York: New York University Press.

Norman, Bari Meltzer, and Barbara Katz Rothman. 2007. "The New Arrival: Labor Doulas and the Fragmentation of Midwifery and Caregiving." In *Laboring On: Birth in Transition in the United States*, edited by Wendy Simonds, Barbara Katz Rothman, and Bari Meltzer Norman, 251–82. New York: Routledge.

"Our Mission." 2016. *SQUAT Birth Journal*, no. 22: 3.

Perez, Miriam. 2007. "On Being a Radical Doula." *Feministing*, February 20, 2007. *feministing .com/2007/02/20/on_being_a_radical_doula_1.*

———. 2012. "*The Radical Doula Guide: A Political Primer for Full Spectrum Pregnancy and Childbirth Support.*" Self-published.

Rebecca Project for Human Rights and National Women's Law Center. 2010. *Mothers behind Bars: A State-by-State Report Card and Analysis of Federal Policies on Conditions of Confinement for Pregnant and Parenting Women and the Effect on Their Children.* Washington, DC: National Women's Law Center. *www.nwlc.org/sites/default/files/pdfs/ mothersbehindbars2010.pdf.*

Rothman, Barbara Katz. 1982. *In Labor: Women and Power in the Birthplace.* New York: W. W. Norton.

Ross, Loretta. 2011. "Understanding Reproductive Justice." Trust Black Women. *www.trust blackwomen.org/our-work/what-is-reproductive-justice/9-what-is-reproductive-justice.*

Ross, Loretta, Lynn Roberts, Erika Derkas, Whitney Peoples, and Pamela Bridgewater Toure. 2017. *Radical Reproductive Justice.* New York: Feminist Press.

Sakala, Carol, and Maureen P. Corry. 2008. *Evidence-Based Maternity Care: What It Is and What It Can Achieve.* New York: Milbank Memorial Fund.

Sandall, J., H. Soltani, S. Gates, A. Shennan, and D. Devane. 2016. "Midwife-Led Continuity Models of Care Compared with Other Models of Care for Women during Pregnancy, Birth, and Early Parenting." *Cochrane Database of Systematic Reviews*, issue 4, art. no. CD004667. doi: 10.1002/14651858.CD004667.pub5.

Silliman, Jael, Marlene Gerber Fried, Loretta Ross, and Elena Gutierrez, 2004. *Undivided*

Rights: Women of Color Organize for Reproductive Justice. Cambridge, MA: South End Press.

Simkin, Penny. 2016. "Position Paper: The Birth Doula's Role in Maternity Care." Chicago: DONA International. *www.dona.org/wp-content/uploads/2018/03/DONA-Birth-Position -Paper-FINAL.pdf*.

Solinger, Rickie. 2005. *Pregnancy and Power: A Short History of Reproductive Politics in America*. New York: New York University Press.

Sosa, R., J. H. Kennell, S. Robertson, and J. Urrutia. 1980. "The Effect of a Supportive Companion on Perinatal Problems, Length of Labor and Mother-Infant Interaction." *New England Journal of Medicine* 303: 597–600.

World Health Organization. 2015. "*WHO Statement on Caesarean Rates*." WHO/RHR/ 15.02. Geneva: World Health Organization *apps.who.int/iris/bitstream/10665/161442/1/ WHO_RHR_15.02_eng.pdf*.

Walker, Rebecca, ed. 1995. *To Be Real: Telling the Truth and Changing the Face of Feminism*. New York: Anchor Books.

Wolf, Margery. 1992. *A Thrice-Told Tale: Feminism, Postmodernism, and Ethnographic Responsibility*. Palo Alto, CA: Stanford University Press.

3

Caring for the Corpse

Embodied Transgression and Transformation in Home Funeral Advocacy

Anne Esacove

He was laying in the bed, but he had the most beautiful jacket on and there were these heart-shaped stones placed along his heart and there was an eagle feather across his waist. [They] had just done a beautiful job of . . . decorating his body. . . . So, I just sat there for about a half hour and I talked to him and put my hands on his body. Did some breathing, a few prayers, and then left. Wow, I'm really feeling this emotionally. And, I don't even know what the emotion is. It was just being close to a body, remains, so fresh from death with no barrier of embalming, and sitting there alone with him. That's his remains. He's gone.

Betty's description of sitting vigil with her newly deceased neighbor closely mirrors many home funeral stories I heard from advocates, paraprofessionals, and everyday people during the course of my research exploring the natural death movement: the beauty of the decorated body, the profound emotional experience of being close to an unembalmed corpse, and, most important, the ability to come to accept the death in your own time.[1] As with many of us living in the contemporary United States, Betty had never before seen an unembalmed body, much less sat alone with a corpse. Home funeral advocates aim to make this experience commonplace by encouraging and assisting families to care for their own dead. The National Home Funeral Alliance (NHFA) defines a home funeral as "when a loved one is cared for at home or sacred space after death" (Webster 2017) largely by family and friends. Care for the dead can be as small a gesture as wiping the face with a warm cloth at the hospital before the body is removed or as involved as preparing, maintaining, transporting, and burying the dead over the course of a three-day vigil. Linda, a movement leader, summed up the most consistently expressed themes about home funerals in this way: "The crux of home funeral, really, is just not being afraid of all of it. Keeping it under the family's control, the family's responsibility, and the family's privilege of continuing [to care] for that loved one."

While the actual practice of caring for the dead at home is quite rare in the United States (one movement leader estimates only .01 percent of deaths), home funerals have garnered increasing attention. For example, in the nine years after it was established, the NHFA grew from fewer than fifty people to more than one thousand members (NHFA 2016). Home funerals have also received high-profile media attention with pieces in the *New York Times*, *Huffington Post*, and *National Public Radio*, as well a number of local newspapers and radio shows.

A self-proclaimed social justice movement, home funeral advocates aim to normalize death—making it an ordinary part of life rather than something to be feared and avoided. They work to resist a problem they call "death denial" by breaking down barriers between the living and the dead and protecting the rights of families. Caring for the corpse is said to be key to this transformation—if we reclaim the care of the dead, we can fully embrace life and contribute to a kinder, healthier, and more sustainable society.

In this chapter, I examine the cultural assumptions and idealizations that motivate people to question and recreate well-established funeral practices (Roe 1994; Tilly 2002). As the corpse is central to the home funeral worldview, it is also at the center of this analysis. Home funeral advocates bring into view (figuratively and literally) one of the most feared and hidden of bodies—the corpse. In doing so, they challenge deeply held cultural beliefs, breach body taboos, and disrupt the institutional authority of the funeral industry. They also attempt to transform the dead body from an object of fear into something to be revered. But, as my analysis will show, these transgressions are facilitated by traditional notions of gender and sexuality and a simplification and homogenization of death care practices across time and place, particularly the practices of groups of people (assumed) to have ongoing traditions of caring for their own dead.

Methods

To explore the cultural assumptions and practices of home funeral advocates, I interviewed forty-two home funeral guides, movement leaders, and others who have participated in a home funeral. The in-depth, semi-structured interviews were conducted on the telephone and lasted, on average, sixty-five minutes (ranging from 38 to 130 minutes). My questions included how they came to participate in the movement and/or an actual home funeral, exactly what happens at a home funeral, who participates in the care of the corpse, and the goals of the movement. The informants were recruited through notices on home-funeral-related electronic mailing lists and in the NHFA newsletter, referrals from people who were interviewed, and by directly contacting key movement leaders whom I identified through an internet search and referrals.

The informants reflect three levels of involvement in home funeral advocacy. Leaders are involved in efforts to create and disseminate (through organizational boards, national trainings, documentaries, and books) the movement's worldview and objectives. Guides work in their communities to provide home funeral awareness education and assist families in caring for their dead at home. Participants are people who have attended a home funeral. Their involvement ranged from simply attending a vigil to preparing and maintaining the body. Quotes from the informants are cited by a pseudonym followed by a letter indicating their level of involvement: L for leaders, G for guides, and P for participants.

Reflecting what is acknowledged by advocates to be the composition of the home funeral movement, the interview sample is overwhelmingly middle-aged, white women with the financial means to do the largely unpaid work of supporting and advocating for home funerals.[2] Most are either retired or have an occupation that provides their livelihood and is flexible enough to allow them to pursue their "passion." Many of the informants link home funeral advocacy to the natural birth movement of the 1970s or the "baby boomer" generation more generally—an identity primarily used to denote an attitude of "not just going along with the status quo" (Debra-L) and doing "things out of the box" (Sharon-G), rather than a specific age range.

I analyzed verbatim transcripts of the interviews using a combination of inductively and deductively derived codes (Strauss and Corbin 1990). Each transcript was coded using a total of fifty code categories. The codes most pertinent to this analysis include body, gender, conventional industry, social justice, and practicalities of home funerals.[3] Patterns within and among the distinct codes were examined and models of connections were created. I then used the websites of key movement organizations and leaders and participant observation at movement events as secondary data to provide an external check on my analysis.

Death Denial: Diagnosing a Wide Array of Social Problems

Home funeral advocates identify a systemic problem in need of remedy: Restrictive laws and policies, coupled with cultural practices, create numerous barriers between the living and the body of dead. These barriers include limited visiting hours, caskets that are placed too high for children to view the dead, receiving lines that allow for only a moment with the deceased, and the increasing use of direct cremation.[4] Of particular concern to advocates are misconceptions among the public that it is legally mandated that a licensed funeral director be involved in the care and disposition of the dead (a myth that is perpetuated by the funeral industry).

Embalming and the use of body bags to "whisk away" the dead are the most frequently discussed barriers, and the ones that provoke the most passionate and heartfelt critiques. This description of a parent being taken away in a body bag is representative of experiences shared during the interviews, many of which included tears: "I just cannot tell you how horrible it was to see my mom go off in a body bag. You know? I just can't talk about it" (Sharon-G). In this case, as with most references, the body bag represents the "whisking away" (Cynthia-G, Mary-L, Lisa-L, Nancy-L) of the deceased before the family is ready, knowing that they likely will "never see the body again" (Sandra-L). As such, the body bag represents a primary barrier to connecting to the dead. Further, both the speed at which the body is removed and the body bag itself are seen as unnecessary practices designed to ease the work of funeral industry staff.

Of course, not all bodies are whisked away never to be seen again. Embalming is one of the mainstays of the conventional funeral director (Laderman 2003; Mitford 1998). Home funeral advocates universally reject the procedure as unnatural, unnecessary, and detrimental to connecting to death. Rather than the image of a beautifully embalmed body said by the industry to assist in the grieving process (Laderman 2003; Mitford 1998), embalmed bodies are described in the interviews as scary, weird, unreal, sanitizing, like a lax dog, doll-like, and a mockery of the dead. One leader described his first experience of seeing "a dead person in the funeral context" and thus embalmed this way: "It was almost science fiction. It was like an alien and it scared the shit out of me. It really disturbed me. It was not anything at all like the grandmother that I thought I knew" (Michael-L).

As with this informant, people are most disturbed that their love ones did not look like themselves. They would "rather remember them as they were"—"I think one of the things that I found in the funeral home is the person doesn't really look like themselves, you know? They've been plastered with makeup [even] if they never wore makeup a day in their lives. They just look a little fake and I would rather remember them as they were" (Barbara-G).

The absence of corpses in their natural state either due to cremation or embalming is said by informants to contribute to a society-wide disconnection from death; out of sight, out of mind. As one leader explained, "Death is not integrated into our being" (Lisa-L). As a result, there is widespread fear in the United States of dead bodies, and fear and denial of death itself, with a handful of notable exceptions discussed below. Death denial, advocates claim, contributes to a wide range of social ills. Not surprisingly, one of the most commonly discussed effects of death denial is "unresolved grief" which is said to be endemic to conventional funeral practices, as represented in a quote from a leader who suggests that substance abuse and domestic violence are linked to unresolved grief: "I do think that a significant portion of the population in this country is walking around with unresolved grief, and really complicated grief, and really destructive grief. I think that you could even think about drug abuse, drinking, and domestic violence" (Debra-L).

Most informants' critiques of conventional after-death care, and the resulting death denial, are more far-reaching than unresolved grief. Home funeral advocates link denial and fear of death to a wide range of modern societal ills. Fear of death is said to be a primary cause of the overuse of medical care, which leads to unnecessary suffering at the end of life. Advocates also believe that when death is not integrated into life, individuals and society do not value life. This is said to contribute to suicide, wars, and environmental degradation. In a perverse irony, according to this logic, in our desperate need to run from and defy death, we destroy ourselves, our society, and the planet.

Regardless of the specific details of their personal experiences with death, home funeral advocates all agree that there is a profound problem with the conventional ways in which US society cares for our dead. Dead bodies are whisked away as soon after death as possible, and hidden from view and touch. They are then either molded by embalming into unnatural, mock versions of the living, or immediately cremated. For advocates, though, the corpse is not only a source of psychological distress and social ills. The dead body is also a transformative object that offers a path toward a deeper connection to an authentic self and to life more broadly.

Welcoming the Dead Back into Our Lives: Prescription for Change

Experiencing the transition of the dead body "unadorned with formaldehyde and make up and wax" (Mary-L) is said to be the key to accepting the death of a person, reconnecting to death more generally and, in the most profound cases, creating deeper connections to others. Quoting one of the "grandmothers" of the movement, this leader eloquently describes the visceral experience of integrating death "into our being":

> You integrate with all your senses. When you care for the body yourself, you're able to take it in through all of your senses that the person has died, and that will help you. It's not just hearing the news and seeing the body from a distance or not at all. You can smell, you can touch, you can hear that they're not breathing. You can take it in viscerally. They're not breathing anymore. Their body is cold. Their body is stiff and this is what death looks like and it's that great mystery. (Mary-L)

While there are a few stories of people who are not able to enter the room with the body, the interviews are replete with stories of people crossing "the doorway of fear" and having "that fear just dissolve" (Dianne-L). This is the case in this story told by a guide in which a woman overcomes her fear to eventually sit by the side of her daughter-in-law:

> In one case, a beautiful [woman] passed away from cancer and her husband's mother came up from [her hometown]. [She] was petrified to be in the house even, but ended up gradually, gradually, walking down the hallway, step by step, with me by her side—and just letting her stop and feel what she was feeling—and gradually, gradually getting to the room and seeing the beauty in there with all the candles and how beautiful she was laid out with silks and flowers, and all the people just being so loving around her. She was eventually sitting by her side, putting her hand on [her daughter-in-law's] heart and just crying and saying how much she meant to her. It was just so beautiful, not only for her to get to experience that, but for her son to get to see her overcome all of those beliefs that sucked her in and just be really connected. So, [home funerals have] just incredible potential for the deepest possible healing. (Susan-G)

Most importantly, the acceptance of a death is said to be a process. Conventional funeral practices are traumatic because the removal and transformation of the body (either by embalming or cremation) is too abrupt. People need to spend time with the dead body so they can successfully make a transition, as described by a guide who cared for a parent at home: "It was just amazing to have [three days] to sort of say goodbye to this body, which truly was now a dead body. There was none of my mother there. It was clear that her spirit was gone and that she was on the other side, and so I felt like I really gave her a good departure and something that eased her crossing and eased the family's crossing" (Patricia-G).

People who participate in caring for their dead are more than spectators. They prepare and maintain the corpse and can bring the dead body to its final disposition. This includes cleaning and drying the body to remove bacteria and any fluids that have been released, dressing the body (including a diaper or other absorbent pad), moving the body to a table or into a casket for the vigil, and keeping the body cool with dry ice or Techni Ice. In some cases, families transport the body to the crematorium or burial ground; a few even build the casket themselves or dig and fill the grave.

Caring for the dead involves physically touching the corpse. According to advocates, this touch is profoundly important and transformative. Even the smallest acts of care, such as putting a veil over the face of the deceased (Pamela-L) or wiping their hand with a cloth (Dianne-L), are said to have a profound healing effect. It is the touch of one body to another that makes these acts transformative. A leader explains the importance of touch for letting go of fear of the dead:

> Touch is just so important. I mean, we can see, we can smell, we can try to understand things, but nothing teaches us like touch does. I know that feeling of reaching out to your loved one and touching them in death and not feeling warmth, no movement. A real understanding. That's always really interesting . . . that moment when you touch someone and you have a little bit of fear, or a lot of fear—some people have tremendous fear about doing it. Then they do touch and then they can't stop. They keep rubbing and they just go, "Wow." You know, it's just an amazing moment. So very powerful. (Linda-L)

In most cases, informants provide detailed accounts of "ritual" washing: anointing with fragrant essential oils, adorning the body with beads, religious icons, or flowers, and making the deceased look beautiful. Missing from the numerous detailed descriptions of caring for the dead in the interviews are the practicalities of dealing with what is, when mentioned at all, euphemistically referred to as the "ick factor" (Donna-G). A more forthright leader with many years of experience caring for dead bodies described body care this way: "It involves a lot of bodily fluids and shit and vomit and blood and, you know, it's gross and smells." Reflecting on the silences in the interviews, she went on to say, "that's the ugly side that people don't really want to talk about" (Carol-L).

There is universal agreement among informants that normalizing death includes working out grief in a "very practical kind of way" (Teresa-L), such as walking the dog, labeling casserole dishes, and making coffee. Many of the home funeral–related tasks discussed in the interviews are likely familiar to anyone who has sat Shiva or attended a wake. It is the presence of the natural dead body at a home funeral that is said to make these practical tasks distinct and uniquely healing. Blurring the line between the sacred and profane (Durkheim [1912] 1995), for advocates the power of the home funeral is that it brings the sacred (i.e., the corpse) into the mundane domestic lives of families. A profound transformation is said to occur when we welcome the dead body back into our everyday lives.

One of the most experienced leaders described how death "becomes a natural part of the life cycle" and is "integrated" for families when life and death co-exist in the same space: "There may be times where they're wailing or crying, but there's also lots of times where they're laughing and just being at home in their home. The teenagers just doing what the teenagers do. The kids are at the computer playing games . . . everybody's life is going on. It becomes a natural part of the life cycle and that gets us beyond [our] fears" (Kimberly-L).

Home funeral participants express similar experiences of normalcy and death being part of life:

> The death felt so natural all the way. The dying, because we were home and I was very much a part of his dying and then I was very much a part of the after death. All the way through. There was a role. It was never taken away from me. And so, when it was over, I really felt like I never left life because the death was part of the

life. Of living. So, I never felt like I had to re-enter my life because that was all *in* my life. (Lori-P)

Welcoming the dead back into our lives is said to have far-reaching and widespread effects. Most immediately, there is healthier grief and a smaller financial burden for family and friends of the deceased. Almost every advocate interviewed also described, unsolicited by me, social benefits of reconnecting to death. The sensory experience of death is said to create a deep, viseral understanding of the frailty and fleetingness of life. At the same time, it dissipates the deep-seated fear of death that is said to be so problematic. It is the balance of these two realizations—that life is fleeting and death is not to be feared—that is said to change people deeply. This leader explained that normalizing death was a "push back" against the privatization and individualization of contempory life, and that it rebuilds a "collective capacity" to support one another:

> I would say there's sort of the reclaiming of the time or rebuilding the capacity to where death was a normalized part of life, and not privatized, not trivialized, not commercialized. I think there's that empowerment piece of it's not necessary to walk into a private room labeled "therapy" in order to engage around one of life's fundamental facets, which is that we die, and that we grieve. So, I think much of this is also under the heading of how do we show up for each other, and it's a push back against not only the privatized, but also the individualized nature of contemporary life. (Kathleen-L)

Other informants echo this sentiment, saying that connecting to one's own mortality "makes life more enriched" (Kathy-L), and gives purpose and meaning to our lives. These realizations help people connect to what is said to be a more authentic self and shift people away from consumption and other self-focused activities to a greater connection with other people, humanity, and "spirit." Reconnecting to death is also said to have potentially profound effects on society. In some cases, informants broadly predicted a more healthy society, while in others a larger shift is imagined: "Long range, human-scale wise, I guess I would see sort of a shifting into a more evolutionary process. I can't even imagine if we shifted our consciousness enough so that we had a peaceful society. Peaceful and loving and kind society. I think [home funerals are] a step in that direction. Actually I do. I think it's a step toward that" (Julie-L). This leader is not alone in her prediction that reconnecting to death would have "an impact on absolutely everything in the culture" (Laura-L).

Advocates are willing to do the largely unpaid work of promoting and facilitating home funerals because they deeply believe in the transformative power of caring for one's own dead. Yet, they explain, it takes courage to do this work, as it entails transgressing against a monolithic industry and decades of cultural norms.

Bodily Transgressions: Explanations and Silences

Home funeral advocates see themselves as part of a social justice struggle to protect the rights of families to ensure that they have a choice when it comes to caring for their dead. The courage it takes to do this work is a common theme in the interviews and in discussions observed at advocate events. It takes courage for families to make a choice "in opposition to the general flow . . . the dominant culture" (Brenda-L) and enter the unknown, since most families have never experienced a home funeral before holding one themselves. Advocates also need courage to do their work, which at times includes acting on behalf of families in direct confrontation with institutional authorities, including coroners who will not release the body to the family, unscrupulous funeral directors, and, in one case, a police officer investigating reports of "a dead body" in the house. The overwhelming power attributed to the funeral industry makes even a conversation between members of the movement and conventional funeral directors worthy of comment and commendation. This is particularly apparent at advocate events where it is very common for participants to remark on the courage of others when they interact with funeral professionals, even tangentially. Advocates spoke often about working under the specter of the funeral industry, fearful to make even a small mistake that would be used by industry lobbyists to outlaw all family involvement in caring for the dead. One leader described the "pioneering" work of advocates and families as rebuilding a path that has always been here but is currently choked with weeds: "Everyone that has had a home funeral is doing that and everybody who's gone through the trainings is doing that. They're all pioneers. So, they have the courage. It takes courage to look into the face of death and to be willing to say, 'Yeah, we need something much more relevant. Much more meaningful to people. Much more healing for people'" (Kimberly-L).

While there is reason to question how precarious the work of advocates actually is, home funerals themselves are truly transgressive. Family and friends who care for their dead contest normative and commodified approaches to after-death care in the United States. In doing so, they challenge our deeply conflicted relationship with death and disrupt the authority of science and medicine by defying conventional wisdom that established mortuary practices (particularly embalming) protect the public's health and support healthy grieving (Halfmann 2012; Mitford 1998; Seymour 1999).

The preparation of the corpse also breaches a number of body taboos. Interestingly, these transgressions, which are at the center of the home funeral, are hardly ever mentioned in any of my sources of data. Children wash the breasts and genitals of their parents. Friends and distant relatives wipe blood, feces, and other purging fluids from the deceased's body. Yet there are only two moments in the interviews when someone expressed hesitation about touching a dead body because of the intimacy of the care. The first was a woman who wants a home funeral for herself but does not want her husband to "be a part of the intimate part that, you know, he doesn't want to be a part of" (Donna-G). The other was a story, shared in response to a direct question about this issue, concerning a daughter and a husband caring for their mother/wife: "They had started with her face and arms and chest and then they got down to the . . . to the genital area and the daughter looked at her father or stepfather and said, 'Um, maybe you'd like to. . . . Maybe you'd like to wash this. I think you're probably more comfortable with this part'" (Kimberly-L).

For the most part, informants do not mention the intimate aspects of caring for the corpse. When they do talk about this kind of care, they do so very factually; they just see their friends' and family members' naked bodies, wipe their genitals and anuses, and diaper the dead.

In the descriptions of caring for the dead, informants did hint as to why intimate touch is not marked or considered problematic. My analysis exposes three key strategies used by advocates to "patch" the breach of modesty taboos that is required when caring for a dead body (O'Brien 2011). The first of the commonly used strategies is to desexualize the corpse. This is often accomplished by equating the body of the dead with a baby's body, as with this leader: "When it comes to intimate care that might have felt awkward, very awkward, while they were alive, actually becomes almost nothing. It's different. When they're alive, the last thing I could think about doing was wiping my dad's butt. But, when he died, it was just . . . it was like caring for a baby" (Linda-L).

Mirroring a number of other informants, Linda went on to suggest social conventions "just kind of float away" when one participates in this "loving act": "We don't think twice about cleaning up babies, and if you keep that in the forefront of your mind as you're caring for that body, it doesn't matter who it was, what your relationship to it was, it's still a very loving act. . . . That whole social convention that we are concerned with, privacy issues, and all that kind of stuff just kind of float away" (Linda-L).

In other cases, the dead body is specifically referred to as sexless, as with this leader who shared a story about her brother's transformation after the death of their mother. Before their mother's death, her brother explicitly said, "I'm not washing her naked body. I'm not going to see my mother's naked body." But, after the death she told me: "[my brother is] grabbing a washcloth and washing a leg, and he didn't leave the room." She went on to explain that the body becomes "sexless" after death, and touching the genitals of the dead is no different than touching any other body part (Kathy-L).

The second commonly used strategy for explaining people's ease with and willingness to touch the body of the dead is to naturalize the care of the corpse. Not only is caring for one's own dead said to occur "all over the world" (Karen-L), it was also repeatedly said to be "intuitive" (Mary-L, Lisa-L, Carol-L) and "in our DNA" (Cheryl-L, Liz-L, Kathy-L) as in this quote: "The most technical thing there is to do is how to move a body without injuring yourself. The rest of it is completely natural" (David-G).

Home care of the dead is also naturalized by linking it to groups of people who are seen as being removed from the forces of modern society, including "indigenous" people, the Amish, *chevrot kadisha* Orthodox Jewish communities, and children who, in particular, are said to "gravitate toward" (Lisa-L) the dead. This is often accomplished by oversimplifying, homogenizing, and (at times) exoticizing death care rituals across time and place. For example, the wide diversity of "indigenous cultures" are overwhelmingly collapsed into a single idealized representation of being "in touch with cycles of nature" (Susan-G), and Jewish funeral practices are most commonly represented by orthodox religious traditions, largely ignoring the practices of reformed and conservative Judaism, which more closely align with conventional funeral practices. More generally, one movement leader described preparing the body at a contemporary home funeral as "like we've done for thousands of years—millions of years probably—in every other culture in the world" (Lisa-L).

Finally, informants create a natural division of labor for after-death care that further explains the acceptability of intimate body touch. While there are a handful of examples of men preparing the corpse, men's "natural" labor was largely said to be to build the casket, move the prepared body, and make coffee. These responsibilities are attributed to men's superior strength and natural inclination to "do" rather than talk (Connie-G; Ronald-G). Women, on the other hand, are said to naturally gravitate to caring or emotional work, which includes cleaning and dressing the dead body: "Well, women kind of generally tend to be the caregivers, more naturally, and so I can see them being more willing to change the clothes or do things like that than men" (Dianne-L).[5] Women's labor was further naturalized by a very common link made by informants between natural after-death care and natural/home births. This gendered division of labor was frequently discussed in both the interviews— "In my family, the men, of course, went right out and built the coffin . . . probably throughout history, it's been women who have done that care [of the body]" (Jean-G)—and in movement materials: "Historically in America, after-death care was considered the exclusive duty of women. Meanwhile, the men built the casket, dug the grave and transported the body" (HFCMPG 2009, 13).

Cultural Assumptions and Idealizations

Home funeral advocacy is one component of a collection of alternative death-related activities that have arisen in response to the conventional death industry in the United States. Home funeral advocates offer the corpse as a transformative object with pro-found healing powers for individuals and society. Witnessing the natural changes that happen to bodies after death and, more importantly, physically caring for the corpse is said to provide a visceral connection to the mystery of death, the cycle of life, and humanity. People who care for their own dead "bring more authenticity into their lives" (Brenda-L), and are said to contribute to a healthier, kinder, and more sustainable society.

Although home funerals are transgressive in many ways, the image of the ideal home funeral offered by advocates and many of the practices they discuss, in fact, support conservative notions of gender and sexuality. Advocates argue for inherent gendered traits. Men build coffins and move the corpse, while women care for the body. This naturalizes gendered divisions of labor and erases women's very physical labor of caring for the corpse by labeling it caring/emotional work. This not only re-inforces problematic gender dichotomies, it also places more responsibility on women than men for caring for the dead, essentially extending women's work from the womb to the grave.

Rather than challenging bodily norms, the strategies used to comfortably breach modesty taboos actually reinforce those very taboos. Desexualization of adult corpses through infantilization reinforces the sexualization of (live) adult bodies; an adult's breasts and genitals can only be touched nonsexually by another adult in limited cir-cumstances. These include when that person was in an intimate relationship with the deceased before death (e.g., a spouse) or if the person is a professional (such as a nurse) or paraprofessional (e.g., home funeral guide). Intertwining conventional no-tions of gender and of sexuality, women are imagined to be more naturally able than men to touch other bodies in a nonsexual way. This reinforces the notion that women themselves are less sexual than men. In cases when the adult body is not desexualized, caring for the dead body is hyper-naturalized— "in our DNA." Given that women are said to overwhelmingly be the ones who care for the dead body, this often-repeated generic claim is actually a gendered claim: caring for the dead is in *women's* DNA. These normative notions of gender and sexuality help to patch the transgression of modesty taboos that is required when caring for a dead body by equating caring for the corpse with acts that are familiar and comfortable; most commonly, replacing the hegemonic image of women lovingly caring for their children with one of women lovingly caring for their dead.

More broadly, the descriptions of home funerals shared by informants reflect an implicit idealized (well-resourced) small town community where family and friends are able to step out of their daily lives for a three-day vigil, people live in privately owned homes large enough to accommodate a vigil, and official offices are easily reachable and navigable. While a discussion of the problematic racial and religious dimensions of home funeral advocacy is beyond the scope of this chapter, it is important to note that advocates are largely silent about the historic and cultural forces that make large, expensive, professionally managed funerals the fulfillment of moral demands and a marker of social inclusion.

After dozens of interviews with advocates, I believe that the narrow, conservative notions of gender and sexuality and the classed dimensions of home funeral advocacy are not intentional. Advocates are not calling for a regressive return to conservative practices and roles. Rather, the privileged social positions of most advocates, coupled with what appears to be a close-knit home funeral community, narrow the range of possible configurations they can imagine for caring for the dead and the barriers to offering that care. They also likely overestimate the degree to which families want to be involved in caring for the corpse. This limits the resonance of their advocacy beyond a narrow population. As a result, while advocates shift the corpse from an object to be feared to one to be revered and expand options for what the experience of death can be, they do so far more narrowly than they imagine.

NOTES

Data collection was supported by a grant from The Fund for the Advancement of the Discipline supported by the American Sociological Association and the National Science Foundation.

1. All quotes from individuals, including the epigraph for this essay, come from research interviews I conducted between September 2014 and December 2015. All names are pseudonyms.
2. Three of the forty-two informants are men.
3. Advocates refer to the professionalized and increasingly corporatized funeral practices that are commonplace in the United States as "conventional" and reclaim "traditional" for family-guided after-death care.
4. In direct cremation, the corpse is cremated soon after death and before a funeral service is held.
5. A few informants clarified that women's "natural" caregiving is a social artifact. A larger number of informants essentialized the gendered division of labor, stating it as a fact without the need for explanation.

REFERENCES

Durkheim, Emile. (1912) 1995. *The Elementary Forms of Religious Life*. New York: Free Press.

Halfmann, Drew. 2012. "Recognizing Medicalization and Demedicalization: Discourses, Practices and Identities." *Health* 16, no. 2: 186–207.

HFCMPG (Home Funeral Committee Manual Publishing Group). 2009. *Undertaken with Love: A Home Funeral Guide for Congregations and Communities*. The Home Funeral Manual Publishing Group. Self-published, Lulu.

Laderman, Gary. 2003. *Rest in Peace: A Cultural History of Death and the Funeral Home in Twentieth-Century America*. New York: Oxford University Press.

Mitford, Jessica. 1998. *The American Way of Death Revisited*. New York: Vintage Books.

NHFA (National Home Funeral Alliance). 2016. "NHFA membership reaches 1000!" *National Home Funeral Alliance Newsletter* (January).

O'Brien, Jodi. 2011. "Building and Breaching Reality." In *The Production of Reality: Essays and Readings on Social Interaction*, 5th ed., edited by Jodi O'Brien, 338–58. Thousand Oaks, CA: Sage Publications.

Roe, Emery. 1994. *Narrative Policy Analysis: Theory and Practice*. Durham, NC: Duke University Press.

Seymour, Jane Elizabeth. 1999. "Revisiting Medicalisation and 'Natural' Death." *Social Science & Medicine* 49, no. 5: 691–704.

Struass, Anselm, and Juliet Corbin. 1990. *Basics of Qualitative Research: Grounded Theory Procedures and Techniques*. Newberry Park, CA: SAGE.

Tilly, Charles. 2002. *Stories, Identities and Political Change*. Lanham, MD: Rowman and Littlefield.

Webster, Lee. 2017. "Why Families Come First: From 'Families First: Home Funerals and the National Home Funeral Alliance.'" National Home Funeral Alliance. *www.homefuneralalliance.org/why-families-come-first.html*.

Deconstructing Reconstructing

Challenging Medical Advice Following Mastectomy

Joanna Rankin

My experience with cancer began when I was thirty-three years old. I was a PhD candidate, far from home, with a nine-month-old son, my first. After I found a large lump in my right breast, I was diagnosed with locally advanced breast cancer. Within a few days my whole life turned upside down. In addition to the emotional distress that I experienced, my body and my identity began to change. Whereas the previous week I had been a student, a researcher, a mother, and a wife, I was suddenly, first and foremost, a patient. The experience of becoming a patient, along with the attempt to move out of that role, was a more complex passage than I had anticipated.

During my treatment I experienced a host of physical changes. My hair fell out; I lost my eyebrows and lashes; my fingernails and toenails fell out; and my eyes watered constantly. I gained weight; my veins bruised and collapsed; and my tired face grew round and puffy. Following chemotherapy I had bilateral mastectomies with immediate reconstruction. I underwent several weeks of radiation, as well as ongoing hormonal therapy that I continue to date. Each of these treatments moved me further from my "natural," and thus assumed "healthy," and feminine body. They led to hair loss, weight gain, breast amputation, and swollen limbs (resulting from lymphedema). I faced head-on the loss of feminine beauty, perceived by many as one of the most difficult aspects of breast cancer for women.[1]

In recent decades the increased incidence of advanced breast cancer resulting in mastectomy in young women has brought these issues to the forefront, especially in the discussion of reconstructive surgery.[2] While my course of treatment was intended primarily to remove the cancer, it also revolved strongly around the recovery and maintenance of an acceptable feminized body image. A well-meaning medical team regularly offered makeup and beauty tips and referrals to workshops on subjects such as how to tie headscarves in clever ways. I was encouraged from the point of diagnosis to have immediate reconstructive surgery in order to avoid what I was told would be the psychologically trying experience of waking up from a mastectomy without breasts. I heeded this expert advice during a time of weakness and confusion; I had implant surgery, the most common reconstructive procedure, at the same time as my mastectomies.[3] This involved implanting tissue expanders beneath my pectoral muscles that were injected with saline on a weekly basis in order to stretch the muscles enough to eventually insert an implant behind them. Following a radical mastectomy, there is not adequate tissue to hold an implant in place as there would be for someone undergoing cosmetic implant surgeries. This procedure, intended to increase my well-being and self-confidence, worked to achieve the opposite.

To date, I have had five breast surgeries. I attended weekly visits to the plastic surgeon who both squeezed infected fluid from my stitches and injected saline into ports in my breasts; I also had cadaver tissue sewn into my chest. For over a year I had a string of infections that involved a period of daily visits to a wound clinic, surgical drains, a barrage of powerful antibiotics, multiple visits to emergency rooms, hospital stays for intravenous antibiotics, emergency surgery, a broken rib, an apparently rare complication that could have occurred during surgery or tissue expansion, and, more generally, a year of pain and unhappiness. My body, turned over to "experts," was physically brutalized, and I lost myself in my newly medicalized form. While I had been warned of the potential of complications associated with this procedure, I was unprepared for the severity and duration of these complications. I knew that that up to 35 percent of implant reconstructions result in infection;[4] I did not anticipate the types of complications: skin necrosis, cellulitis, chronic wounds, and life-threatening sepsis. I later learned that 46 percent of immediate reconstructive implant surgeries result in major complications such as those I faced.[5]

About six weeks into a new job, I was required to have emergency surgery to remove one of my implants. The prosthetic breast had become dangerously infected one week after I had completed a six-month round of antibiotics. I was hospitalized immediately and had surgery the following morning. Subsequent to this, I requested that the other implant, which had also been infected on a regular basis, be removed. This was done shortly thereafter, ending a period of almost two years of my life that had been dominated by my breasts.

While I had experienced pressure from surgeons to keep my remaining implant and to try, once again, to "fix" the one that had been removed, the ongoing encouragement to erase my scars and correct my imperfect body, along with the impact of my journey, compelled me to resist this medical advice. At both emotional and physical levels, I needed to decline another surgery, one that would have involved taking muscle from my back to build new breasts followed by a thirteen-week recovery period. I instead chose to embrace and empower myself through an alternate bodily form outside of the role of patient that had so defined me throughout my cancer experience.

While it has taken me a significant amount of time to be able to look at, to touch, or to allow my surgically marked chest to be touched, to reconceive it as my own has been the most challenging task. To move away from seeing my altered body as something ugly, scarred, and deviant has required me to resignify this corporeal space on my own terms. When I started to explore images of women who had had tattoos following mastectomies, I was struck by the pictures of faces smiling, bodies proudly on display. The sense of confidence and well-being that I had been promised through reconstruction seemed evident in these images. The images presented bodies that were altered by surgery but that were also transformed by the women's choice to tattoo.

Three years after my mastectomies and two years after my final surgery, I chose to tattoo my chest, not to cover my scars but to salvage this part of my body and shed

The author and her tattoo,
"Scars and Swallows."
Photograph by Joanna Rankin

the role of patient. Both the act of marking my own body and the adornment itself have been important aspects of my journey.

Being tattooed, experiencing pain that was intentionally chosen rather than medically required, was a freeing experience. To bare my scarred chest to a stranger, who was not a medical professional, without shame or judgement, gave me the confidence to no longer fear the stares I anticipated whenever my chest was exposed. My pain was my own, my fear was my own, my body was, once again, my *own*.

Where I had formerly disguised my chest with scarves and high-necked shirts, I am now, without prosthetics, without nipples, ornamented with two large and unapologetic swallows that I wear with pride. Traditionally symbolic of a sailor's safe return from a journey, for me the swallows mark not only the successful end of my journey with cancer, but also the affirmation of my identity as something new, fluid, consciously chosen, and celebrated. By rejecting the conformity that came with reconstruction and choosing instead to mark my own body, I have also reclaimed this space as my own. Rather than the normal/abnormal binary, I now celebrate my atypical body that resulted from my small but personally impactful act of resistance. The ability to embrace my bodily difference has offered me a refreshing and much-needed challenge to entrenched standards of female beauty that accompany breast reconstruction. It also serves as a reminder that no one need experience unnecessary surgery or discomfort in order to achieve the "wellness" and self-confidence promised by reconstructive options.

NOTES

1. Amy K. Alderman, Edwin G. Wilkens, Hyungjin Myra Kim, and Julie C. Lowery, "Complications in Post-Mastectomy Breast Reconstruction: Two Year Results of the Michigan Breast Reconstruction Outcome Study," *Plastic and Reconstructive Surgery* 109, no. 7 (2002): 2265.
2. Rebecca H. Johnson, Franklin L. Chien, and Archie Bleyer, "Incidence of Breast Cancer with Distant Involvement among Women in the United States, 1976–2009," *Journal of the American Medical Association* 309, no. 8 (2013): 800.
3. Adrian S. H. Ooi and David H. Song, "Reducing Infection Risk in Implant-Based Breast-Reconstruction Surgery: Challenges and Solutions," *Breast Cancer: Targets and Therapy* 8 (2016): 161, doi.org/10.2147/BCTT.S97764.
4. Ooi and Song, 161.
5. Alderman et al., "Complications in Post-Mastectomy," 2268.

My Ten-Year Dreadlock Journey

Why I Love the "Kink" in My Hair . . . Today

Cheryl Thompson

When I was a child, every message I received—not just from mainstream media but from black media too—was that straight hair equaled beauty. All of my favorite black celebrities at the time—from Janet Jackson to Oprah Winfrey—had straightened hair. Whoopi Goldberg was the only black woman I knew of with natural hair. She had dreadlocks, but she was never talked about in terms of beauty so I had no reason, at a young age, to desire dreadlocks. Why would I want a hairstyle that no one else seemed to want? Like most girls my age—I was thirteen at the time—my main focus was to look "cute" and *only* girls with straightened hair were ever called cute.

So when I turned fourteen, getting a relaxer seemed like the most logical thing to do. I was not alone. My peers relaxed their hair too. After all, we were at a pivotal age. We had just started high school, we had just started our menstrual cycles, and we were on our way to *becoming* women. Nothing signaled that transition from childhood to womanhood more than long, straight, flowing hair. I don't think I wanted to be "white," which is one of the criticisms young black women often face when they straighten their hair. I think I wanted to be beautiful, or at least what I thought was beautiful.

I vividly remember the day my mom took me and my twin sister into the black hair salon to have the chemical product applied professionally. While the chemical hurt more than I had anticipated, I felt a sense of sadness over the loss of my hair's natural texture but also excitement that I now had hair that swung from side to side like everyone else. My mother is from a generation of black women who used a "hot comb" to straighten their hair, also known as thermal straightening. She had never used a chemical hair straightener, i.e., relaxer, before, and it wasn't her first choice for us. But we begged and begged her to get us one because all the other black girls were doing it, and, in some cases, had already done so years before we did. So relaxing my hair was like joining a special club.

Throughout my twenties, my hair was a hot mess. It was constantly breaking and thinning because chemical relaxers are very harsh on the hair follicle even with oils and sprays. Relaxers have even been linked to health problems such as an increased risk of uterine fibroids. I kept up these destructive routines while working at a corporate job and then at a small firm. And then I landed a job where I could work from home. This shift enabled me to dare to finally embrace my natural hair.

It was 2007, and I had turned thirty just seven months prior. I walked into a professional natural hair studio in Toronto and "loc'd" my hair. While I could have worn my hair in an Afro, which has, historically, been a politicized hairstyle, I wanted dreadlocks because they spoke not only to my cultural heritage as a Jamaican-Canadian but also to a deeper, embodied spirit of resistance. While I am not a Rasta, I have always respected the politics behind the religion and the idea that we should embrace who we are in the midst of a society or culture that does not always do so.

My Jamaican parents immigrated to Canada in the 1960s. Outwardly they neither denigrated dreadlocks nor celebrated the hairstyle. But they did associate it with rebellion against society and with drugs (specifically, smoking weed)—two things immigrants trying to assimilate into a new country tend to avoid! Some people still associate dreadlocks with Jamaican reggae singer Bob Marley or with Rastafari, the religious movement that grew out of the Caribbean island that is commonly associated with smoking marijuana, wearing dreadlocks, and a belief that Ras Tafari, the black man who was crowned Haile Selassie I, Emperor of Ethiopia in 1930, is the Second Advent of God. Today, most people with dreadlocks are not a Rasta or Jamaican. In my case, however, the latter happens to be true.

So for me, the decision to "dread" my hair was a major life decision that could have brought about negative consequences both inside and outside of my family. Thankfully, my two sisters had already transitioned to dreadlocks; by the time I made up my mind to do so as well, there was little my parents could do and they embraced the hairstyle and made the process less stressful for me.

Several years ago I was in Las Vegas on vacation. While there, I could not help but notice the absence of black women wearing dreadlocks like me. For four days, it felt as if I was the only black woman in Nevada not wearing a weave![1] It was the first time I was acutely aware that dreadlocks are not as common as I had thought they were. In Toronto, where I live, people have been wearing dreadlocks since the 1980s, when the style became part of a natural way of life, an alternative to using a relaxer or wearing a weave.

I have ultimately learned three things over the course of my ten-year dreadlock journey. First, it is really important to never pass judgement on others who still use relaxers or wear weaves. Everyone must go on their own hair journey. Second, my journey has taught me to love who I am and to recognize that we can set our own standards of beauty; we don't have to adhere to the standard that circulates in the media. Third, one's past behavior does not always determine one's future behavior. I spent most of my childhood and adulthood looking outward at models, celebrities, and women and girls at school for direction on how I should wear my hair, when the truth is, those same people were probably doing the very same thing.

Now that I have worn dreadlocks for ten years, I look back at my fourteen-year-old self and wonder what I was thinking. The reality is, I wasn't thinking at all—I just wanted to belong. I have come a long way since those days, and I honor the transformation of my hair. Today, I love the "kink" in my hair because it tells the story of my *being* and *becoming*.

NOTES

1. A hair weave is a hairstyle created by weaving pieces of human hair or synthetic hair into one's natural hair to increase its length, texture, or thickness.

Living My Full Life

Rejecting Weight Loss as an Imperative for Recovery from Binge Eating Disorder

Christina Fisanick

After suffering for over twenty-eight years with binge eating disorder (BED), I finally entered recovery a few months before I turned forty. It took a major shift in mindset to arrive at the point where I not only accepted that I have an eating disorder, but that dieting—another diet—would not be the cure. In fact, my motivation for seeking help had nothing to do with my weight but everything to do with what was happening in my head and heart. I was living half of a life. Not because I was obese, but because obsessive thoughts and behaviors around food kept me from being truly engaged in the world.

The night before I entered recovery from BED, I sat alone on the living room floor, my husband and son asleep upstairs. I was making and eating large bowls of butter cream frosting. With a pound of sugar and a half a pound of butter in each batch, I was trying to fix something that hurt so badly that I wanted to escape it. I watched *The Notebook* there in the dark, just me and my bowl of icing tinted robin's egg blue. Each time Noah cried, I cried. I realized that I was crying for me and not him. I was crying for all of the times I had used food as an escape. I was crying for how much I was hurting inside. My pain had nothing at all to do with my weight, but absolutely everything to do with being unable to cope with life without a spoon in my mouth.

The next morning, I took the online screening for binge eating disorder on the website for the National Eating Disorder Association (NEDA). It confirmed that I have an eating disorder. I emailed a NEDA Navigator, who helped me find a therapist, and I officially entered recovery. My therapist was and remains a wonderful, loving source of support, but she and I agreed I should seek other avenues of support as well, and I was surprised by what I found. Despite a growing body of scholarship demonstrating that chronic dieting is one of the contributors to the development of BED and that an emphasis on weight loss and body image delays recovery, the majority of recovery programs encourage and applaud weight loss. In fact, when I went to see my family doctor about BED, he said, "Look, it doesn't matter how you lose weight, but you just need to do it." He then offered me diet pills, which I rejected.

I fought and continue to fight the rule that my recovery from BED must be defined by my dress size. Isn't that the way women's success is always measured? I can tell you that I have been in the depths of BED thin and in the depths of it fat. My weight has never been an indication of my mental well-being. Given that BED is a mental illness, it stands to reason that mental fitness is a far more accurate measure of successful recovery than my weight in pounds and inches. Spending the day focusing on the events at hand and not on my next meal is a mark of good recovery. Eating mindfully and joyfully until I feel satisfied is an example of good recovery. Both can be accomplished at any weight.

Beyond that, I couldn't help but see this message about dieting and weight loss to be yet another way to control women's bodies and to reiterate the tired old message that women must take up as little space as possible. For me, though, recovery was about finally taking up space, becoming fully and completely who I am. If weight loss was part of my journey, then so be it, but I absolutely refused to go back to the days when the number on the bathroom scale dictated my mood for the day—for good or ill. I refused to believe that, despite all of my incredible improvements through recovery, none of it was valid unless I achieved some type of pre-approved "healthy weight."

For the first time in my adult life, I took a stand for myself. I wanted more than anything to stop eating compulsively, not because I was fat but because I felt so bad on the inside. In one bite, I believed I was protecting myself from a world that was rejecting me, when in reality I was abusing myself for being the kind of person that would invite the world's rejection. I ate compulsively to cope with those feelings, creating a vicious cycle that makes recovering from BED so difficult. By the time I sought help, I refused to define recovery by a notch on my belt loop. Instead, I found well-being in serving others, meditating, doing yoga, writing, talking, singing, dancing, and overall in enjoying my body just as it is, not as it might someday become. I know my body better than ever. I know my own curves and dips and angles. I know if I am hungry. I know if I am sad. I know if I am happy.

When I was seeking thinness, I was not seeking my body or myself. I was looking for someone else's body—an imaginary thing floating just out of reach. It turns out, my own body, just as it is, is enough. Recovering from BED has brought sanity into my life. I am no longer food and weight obsessed, but I do struggle to push back those old thoughts from time to time. While I am no longer living in tomorrow where all of my problems will be solved in some kind of normal-weight utopia, I do have moments of body loathing. Instead of binge eating to cope with these emotions, though, I turn to honoring my body through swimming laps and meditating. Even on the hardest days, I try my best to be grateful I am alive and well in this body, my body, myself.

Pretty Brown

Encounters with My Skin Color

Praveena Lakshmanan

I grew up in a traditional and conservative family that moved, in pursuit of better opportunities, from rural life in Kerala, the southernmost state in India, to Mumbai, a megacity located in Western India. Whether it was living in Mumbai or spending summer breaks in Kerala, I was well protected from the harsh realities of both city and rural life. As a girl raised a Hindu-Brahmin in the city of Mumbai, I had to adhere continuously to certain unspoken norms such as cleansing my face with honey and lemon at least twice a day, avoiding long hours in the sun, dressing well, and looking pretty. Taking care of my appearance, especially working to lighten my skin tone, became second nature to me; it seemed like I always understood these expectations. Sandalwood paste (made from sandalwood powder, almond powder, and milk), turmeric powder mixed with saffron and rose water, and other similar concoctions regularly found a home in the bathroom, both in Mumbai and Kerala. Applying these home-made skin lighteners to my face was a daily ritual, and a common practice among girls and women in many Hindu-Brahmin families in the South. I was little aware of the implications of these rituals then, and I diligently followed without questioning them for years.

It was not until my early twenties when I interacted with new peer groups outside of home and other familiar environments that I began to understand the politics of skin color. The repetitive reminders about how blessed I was to have light skin broadcasted only one message: You are beautiful because you are fair. The privilege was all mine!

I remember clearly advising a student in my office in Mumbai. Sitting across from me at the table, he awkwardly stared at me. I tried to focus on reviewing his work.

"You need to work more on this paragraph here," I said. I sensed he wasn't paying attention. I looked at him and decided to confront him.

"Is something wrong?" I asked.

"No," he replied. "Well, actually, it's a bit personal," he continued. "Are you from the South?"

"The South?" I asked.

"Your name is Praveena Lakshmanan, right?" He pointed to the ID that hung around my neck.

"Yeah," I replied with amusement.

"So . . . how come you are so fair? You do not look like you are from the South." I could not help but notice his smile. In his mind, he seemed to believe had offered me a compliment.

Awkwardly, I attempted to end the conversation "Well, I guess I need to ask my parents about it." Why was I awkward to the point of being rude? As I look back, perhaps it was the flagrant comment but more likely I felt objectified. The feeling of being looked at and stared at.

I knew he was alluding to the popular stereotype that individuals from southern India are dark-skinned, but I was surprised he had brought it up. My father's name, Lakshmanan, gave away that I was not from Mumbai and had roots elsewhere. While I was accustomed to hearing "positive" things about my skin color, this was the first time my identity had been questioned because of my complexion. I was too fair to belong, to have my roots in southern India.

Did I understand all the implications of his question at that time? Probably not to their fullest. I had much to learn, experience, realize, resist, and reject as I moved back and forth across national borders.

A few years after that incident, I moved to the United States, an immigrant and a woman in her mid-twenties. As my location shifted, so did my perceptions about my complexion. I also started to notice a change in other people's comprehension of my skin color. The privilege of being fair seemed to have vanished overnight. My skin color forced me into a lower strata in my adopted homeland. About eight to ten months before leaving India, I had given up using any skin-lightening products because of the sheer amount of time and effort they required. While I had initially enjoyed the attention my fair skin brought from family, friends and strangers in India, I soon grew tired of the superficiality of it all. Also, the anger of being judged on skin color, which I discerned had always existed even if beneath the surface of my emotions, slowly took over any sense of joy. Nevertheless, in the United States, I saw myself drawn to the products again as a way to fit in. And there were many more options available here. Never had I imagined spending so much time and money caring for my skin color. And yet, truth be told, most of the products made little difference.

My interaction with the South Asian diaspora added another layer of issues. "Fair" was still the operative theme in some of these circles, and my specific skin tone relative to other South Asian immigrants was of most interest. For example, one acquaintance, an Indian American woman, said to me, "Hamein tumara gehuhasa complexion bahut pasand hai, aaj kal sabka nahi hota." (I like the wheatish complexion that you have; not everyone has it these days.) In the Indian diaspora, my particular shade of brown was constantly evaluated. It was a lot to deal with—I was no longer privileged as I was back in India. The saving grace was a temporary relief—with folks, specifically younger second generation Indian Americans and white Americans, who thought I had a natural tan. Other times, I was that perfect shade of brown. I was caught in a state of constant confusion, so I sought external validation.

And it all came to a head a couple of years later.

I returned to India during the summer for a friend's wedding. At the event, my mother's friend approached me, looked me up and down, and said, "What have you done to yourself?"

I was confused. So I naturally asked, "Why? What's happened to me?"

She held my chin and pushed my face up to the light. With a smile, she said, "What happened to our beautiful girl? You've gotten so dark!" Another friend of my mother standing near us chimed in. She suggested I use a skin-lightening product called Fair and Lovely. My mother, who was right next to me during this exchange, defensively retorted, "Oh, she swims." I smiled uncomfortably.

I had reached a tipping point. On the way back home, I snapped at my mother. I told her how disappointed I was. I had so many questions. Is dark the opposite of beautiful? I asked her, "Did they actually think I am less beautiful because I have gotten a shade darker? Or are they just conditioned to believe that? Are a whole lot of us conditioned to believe that?"

Fair and Lovely. Does the name not say it all?

But as I vocalized my frustrations, I realized that I was now able to rationalize and contextualize what had happened to me. My complexion had become a defining characteristic of my being. I was tired of the emotional work and of spending the time and money necessary to maintain this identity. I was tired of constantly responding to questions about my skin color. I was tired of forcing a smile, no matter how tired, disgusted, or uncomfortable I felt in response to comments I received. I was tired of my parents protecting me when the shade of my skin changed. Through it all, I was beginning to realize that by constantly trying to meet cultural standards, I was disguising myself—the true me. I had spent little time focusing on things that actually mattered, such as being confident in my own skin—things that were not skin deep.

I have come a long way from feeling insecure about my skin tone. Over the years, I have realized that there are complex skin-color systems in every society. Being brown has contested meanings in different contexts. Sometimes individuals belonging to different cultures have a tendency to unknowingly internalize many things, such as associating fair skin with beauty. We carry our implicit biases wherever we go.

Overtime I have taken a more active role by resisting, speaking up, and pushing for active discourse on the subject of colorism in a global context. It is liberating, and I feel stronger and more confident. On the personal front, I have decided to be "healthy, brown, and lovely." I have discarded the skin-lightening products. I will swim more and spend time in the sun.

I refuse to be judged based on my skin color.

PART II
Representing Resistance

4

Blood as Resistance

Photography as Contemporary Menstrual Activism

Shayda Kafai

When first thinking through this topic, I returned to my own body's memories. I remembered how in the fifth grade, after watching that obligatory, grainy film about puberty, I was given a small plastic bag. When I opened it, I found scented maxi pads. I remembered the discreetness of the opaque bag and the covert messages it communicated: my new bodily transition must be hidden at all costs. I also remembered sitting in class in seventh grade sweating with cramps. I shifted in my seat, feeling my full, bulky pad. I was too terrified to stand up, afraid I had stained my jeans, that the small mark, the color of ox blood and shame, would be revealed. I hold these stories with me as I write and think about menstruation and its enduring companion: secrecy.

In *Under Wraps: A History of Menstrual Hygiene Technology*, Sharra Vostral (2008) explores the menstrual product industry and how the technology of menstrual hygiene products can help a menstruator pass as a modest "non-bleeder" (2).[1] Vostral argues that menstrual product technology such as tampons and maxi pads enable menstruators to engage in the "politics of passing" (3). These technologies allow us to move past the stereotype of the hysterical, dysfunctional, bleeding menstruator. They help us keep our cycles hidden. The first Kotex tampons in 1930, for example, were named Fibs, a name suggesting that menstruating was humiliating and that a menstruator should, instead, fib (Houppert 1999, 14). Although this history of concealment aims to maintain one's purity and chastity, concepts so rigorously associated with femininity (Houppert 1999, 69), it also bonds menstruation with shame. One need only recall the shower scene from the 1976 film or the 2013 remake of *Carrie* to remember the overwhelming disgust and humiliation that arises from a publicized awareness of menstruation. With euphemisms like *the curse*, *the crimson wave*, and *shark week*, it is no wonder that menstruators are taught to view their menstrual cycle as a bodily function that terrorizes their lives.

This chapter is rooted in menstrual activism, the feminist movement of the late twentieth century that seeks to unsettle the rhetoric that menstruation is necessarily shameful and taboo (Bobel 2010). Specifically, it explores a dimension of contemporary menstrual activism: the art-making of menstrual activists Jen Lewis and Rupi Kaur. Although nearly fifty years have passed since the first time menses were used in art-making, menstrual art still instigates social change and challenges the regressive ways we culturally view menstruation and menstruators.

The Connotations of Menstruation

Before exploring menstrual activism, we must first discover why in both Western and non-Western societies, we view menstruation with such negative connotations. Bobel (2010) argues that androcentrism as an institution frames the social construction of menstruation: "Leaky, liquid, flowing menstruation . . . is constructed as a shameful form of pollution that must be contained . . . [it] is constituted as a problem in need of a solution" (31). In this framing, a woman's body becomes unwieldy and in need of control. Kissling (2006) expands this argument by exploring French feminist Simone de Beauvoir's reading of menstruation and woman as Other (3). In her seminal text *The Second Sex* (1949), de Beauvoir argues that "menstrual periods inspire horror in adolescent girls because they thrust them into an inferior and damaged category" (329). Here, the woman is Other, a positionality that is antithetical to man, the Subject (Kissling 2006, 6). This argument speaks to the ways we view menses, essential femininity, and the menstrual cycle more generally. Menstruation goes beyond biology and becomes "a cultural event" (2).

It is our culture's use and maintenance of gender dualities, the Other and the Subject, that perpetuates menstruation as taboo. In a nineteenth- and early twentieth-century context, menstrual blood imbued a woman with transformative, though mostly negative, abilities (Whelan 1975, 106). For example, in 1878 a member of the British Medical Association asked his colleagues whether a woman's menses had properties to cure ham. In France, menstruating women were not allowed into sugar refineries for fear that their menses would blacken the sugar, while in Mexico menstruating women were kept away from silver mines as they were thought to "disappear" the silver from metal (Novak 1921, 5). These historic examples reveal menses, and by extension women, to be toxic, a perception suggesting not only that menstruation is gendered, but further that its connotations stigmatize women (Johnston-Robledo and Chrisler 2013, 13).

Menstrual Activism and a History of Menstrual Art-Making

Menstrual activism began in the 1970s with the rise of women's health movements.[2] Its goal is to "reject the construction of menstruation as a problem in need of a solution" (Bobel 2010, 7). Menstrual activists offer a radical alternative to the menstrual status quo of shame, silence, and secrecy; they strive toward body positivity (Johnston-Robledo and Chrisler 2013; de Beauvoir [1949] 2009). For Bobel (2010), integral to tracing the historical lineage of menstrual activism and the menstrual product industry is problematizing the belief that women and *only* women menstruate. She reminds readers that some transgender men and gender-nonconforming people menstruate, and that not *all* women menstruate, including some athletes and post-menopausal women (11). Critical to Bobel's analysis of menstrual activism, then, is a de-conflation of sex and gender.

Bobel identifies two branches in the genealogy of menstrual activism: feminist spiritualists and radical menstruation activists. The former includes "activists who work to reclaim menstruation as a healthy, spiritual, empowering, and even pleasurable experience for women" (66). Rooted in second wave feminism and 1970s communal and ritual work around menstruation, this branch is built on woman-centric "self-actualization," or the belief that cultivating a self-transformative view of menstruation is possible and nourishing (66).[3] Because feminist spiritualists focus on individualized and essentialized notions of femininity, their work does not typically reach beyond their own communities (66).

Radical menstruation activists, also known as radical menstruators or menarchists, on the other hand, are informed by queer and nonbinary politics (100). Viewing menstruation through an intersectional lens, the goal of menarchists is to make visible the "ways heteronormative patriarchal institutions have justified their power and control over menstruating bodies" (Patterson 2014, 105). This branch of menstrual activists aims to reveal the social constructions of menstruation while also troubling its institutionalized framings. In order to challenge the stigmatic myths ascribed onto menstruation, menarchists look to third-wave feminism and the DIY thrust of the punk movement (Bobel 2010, 104). By engaging in a socially hypercritical punk aesthetic, these radical activists empower others to "take control" of their cycles and, consequently, distance themselves from the menstrual product industry and some of its toxic, unsafe products (106).[4]

A unique facet of menstrual activism is the use of menses to create art. This use exists in a broader timeline of artists who use bodily fluids in their art-making. Whether it is the use of urine, vomit, or excrement, artists have long used their bodies as material.[5] Emboldened by the rallying cry of the 1970s that the personal is political, feminist, women-identified performance artists began creating art to interrogate and challenge normative representations of their bodies and their gender. Forte (1988, 217) argues that within this specific subgenre of feminist performance art, performance artists engaged with feminist theory, creating a lens that allowed for a critique of androcentrism. As Dekel (2013, 3) explains, feminist performance artists began using their bodies as artistic and politicized tools.

In 1971, for example, artist Judy Chicago created a handmade lithograph entitled *Red Flag*, a piece said to be "most responsible for the breaking of the menstrual taboo in modern art" (Delaney, Lupton, and Toth 1988, 275). In *Red Flag*, Chicago's left thigh is visible and her right hand covers her right thigh; she is in the process of pulling a bloodied tampon out of her body. The piece is radical for visually capturing an act that repetitively occurs without acknowledgement. Chicago wrote to the authors of *The Curse: A Cultural History of Menstruation* (1988) that her goal with *Red Flag* was to "validate overt female subject matter in the art community and [she] chose to do so by making 'Red Flag' as a handmade litho, which is a high art process, usually confined to much more neutralized subject matter. By using such overt content in this form, [she] was attempting to introduce a new level of permission for women artists" (Delaney, Lupton, and Toth 1988, 275).

Red Flag birthed validation, visibility, and permission. By so bluntly presenting her bleeding body, particularly in the form of a lithograph, Chicago legitimized feminine subject matter. In her 1972 installation *Menstruation Bathroom*, a wastebasket overflows with used maxi pads in the corner of a white, spotless bathroom. Soaked and bloodied rags hang overhead and boxes of maxi pads and tampons are piled over the wastebasket. This installation similarly extends the argument that we must examine, not ignore, the social stigmas surrounding bleeding bodies. After Chicago, many other artists in the 1970s explored similar themes: Ana Mendieta painted with her menstrual blood; Barbara Hammer directed the short film *Menses*; and Emily Erwin Culpepper created the film *Period Piece*. Artists in the twenty-first century also continue to engage with menstrual blood in their work. From Zanele Muholi, Isa Sanz, Samera Paz, and Lani Beloso, to Sarah Levy and her most recent portrait of Donald Trump using menstrual blood, women continue to use menses as a way to de-stigmatize their cycles. These examples of menstrual art-making are a part of the larger menstrala movement.

Menstrala is a term coined by artist Vanessa Tiegs to name the eighty-eight mandala-like paintings she created in 2013 with her menses. Since then, other artists who use their menses as their medium to challenge the repulsion and shame that follows menstruation have adopted the word menstrala to describe their own work.[6] Menstrual art-making empowers artists to move past the socially constructed taboo that menstruation is equivalent to humiliation and disgust. Here, art-makers who identify themselves as a part of the menstrala movement self-craft their bleeding bodies into legitimacy.

Despite the decades of menstrual activism and art-making, disgust still overwhelmingly dominates the conversations we have about menstruation. Advertisements in the menstrual product industry maintain a strong influence in sculpting these conversations (Johnston-Robledo and Chrisler 2013; Merskin 1999). Johnston-Robledo and Chrisler (2013, 11) observe that in menstrual product advertising, "Allegorical images, such as flowers and hearts, and blue rather than reddish liquid, have been used euphemistically to promote secrecy and delicacy." The choice to use blue fluid in advertisements is a simple yet profound decision. Always was one of the first brands to use this trope in 1997. Since then, a bright, sky-blue liquid has been the sanitized and culturally appropriate color of menstruation. The closest representation of blood in an advertisement arrived in 2011, when Always printed an image of a maxi pad with a small red dot in the center. This decision was deemed so radical that advertising blogger Copyranter called it a "historical advertising move" (quoted in Stampler 2011). Perhaps the visual indicator of blood disturbs the regimented, clean, and ordered image of normative femininity. Perhaps this is why maxi pads and tampons are categorized as feminine *hygiene* products. Perhaps this is why they are scented: they are meant to push an unruly physiology into the realm of the tolerable and orderly. The industry's depiction of women dancing, playing sports, and otherwise looking comfortable and happy while on their cycles addresses the collective comfort that arises from moving menstruation as far away from reality as possible (Houppert 1999, 84).

The contemporary photography of Jen Lewis and Rupi Kaur enters into this culture by resisting the narrative of sanitation and hygiene. In fact, their works exist in direct tension with the socially constructed belief that menstruation must be a hidden and embarrassing bodily function.

Beauty in Blood: Jen Lewis

Jen Lewis began her photography project *Beauty in Blood* in 2012. As a self-proclaimed conceptual artist and "Menstrual Designer," Lewis uses a menstrual cup to collect her blood and slowly "dump, drizzle, and drip the bloody matter into a clean toilet bowl or other clear vessel . . . to render 'beautiful' or 'interesting' designs." She chose the name Menstrual Designer to speak to her "role in the art-making process . . . [as someone who works] in front of the camera rather than behind it" (Lewis n.d.). Originally, she was inspired by the medical "renderings showing bone, blood cells, [and] neurons" (quoted in Frank 2015) on the walls of a research building at the University of Michigan. Using macrophotography, she and Rob Lewis, her partner and collaborator, create stunning pictures of her menses in motion. For *Beauty in Blood*, Lewis pours and manipulates the blood while her partner uses a Canon 5D Mark II with a 100mm 2.8/FL macro lens (Frank 2015). Originally, Lewis chose to photograph the blood as she poured it into a toilet bowl; however, to allow for more fluidity in movement, they soon began shooting the blood in an aquarium filled with salt water. In an interview with *Huffington Post*'s Priscilla Frank, Lewis said, "I also work with more tools than just a cup now. . . . I like to experiment with different blood delivery systems, i.e., pipette (awesome), turkey baster (terrible), chopsticks (excellent), travel shampoo bottle (also excellent)" (quoted in Frank 2015).

Because *Beauty in Blood* is a series of close-up, abstract images with overwhelming shocks of color, one forgets that the medium is blood, and menses at that. With powerful subtlety, Lewis strips away the belief that abjection and disgust describe menses. With names for the photographs like *The Ribbon Rose*, *Tree*, and *Spiral Slow-mo*, viewers are instead in awe of the curves of color, the contrast of deep reds and plum pinks.

As a self-identified radical menstrual activist, Lewis shares her first reactions of seeing the "undeniable attractiveness" of her blood and clots as they poured into her toilet bowl: "The socially constructed 'ew' response was instantly and wholly drowned out by the vibrant design. Other people, especially women, need to see this . . . need to bear witness to the beauty their bodies create monthly. . . . Ultimately the *Beauty in Blood* project challenges the long-standing cultural taboo of women's menstrual cycles" (Lewis n.d.).

Similar to the way other radical menstrual activists' call to reverse the rhetoric of shame, Lewis empowers menstruators by expanding the ways they perceive menstruation and the concept of leakage. *Beauty in Blood* urges viewers to reckon with and untangle the connotations of menstrual blood. By offering these intimate yet out-of-context images, she creates a gap, a space for us to enter where our understandings of menstruation can move past the shameful and obscene. Lewis crafts a visual discourse of possibility by photographing these images of blood floating, sinking, and scattering in water. Her lens is an alternative one through which we can see menses, one that reconceptualizes blood as narrative, as time passage; blood so beautiful in its complexity that it becomes difficult to look away.

Along with the expansive and revisionary discourse that Lewis's art promotes, there have also been negative reactions to her work. She shared with *Lip Magazine*, "Many commenters will say my work is disgusting . . . but I would challenge those people to think deeper about why they think this way" (quoted in Conway 2015). The comments she has received on the *Huffington Post* article and on Facebook range from "This is awesome!" (comment on Jen Lewis's Facebook page, May 8, 2015, by Kelly M. Renn) to "Sick really sick!!" (comment on Mamamia's Facebook page, June 7, 2015, by Julie Sherry), and "Think I'll skip lunch. Lost my appetite" (comment on *Huffington Post*, May 5, 2015, by Don Comer). The reviews garnered from culture

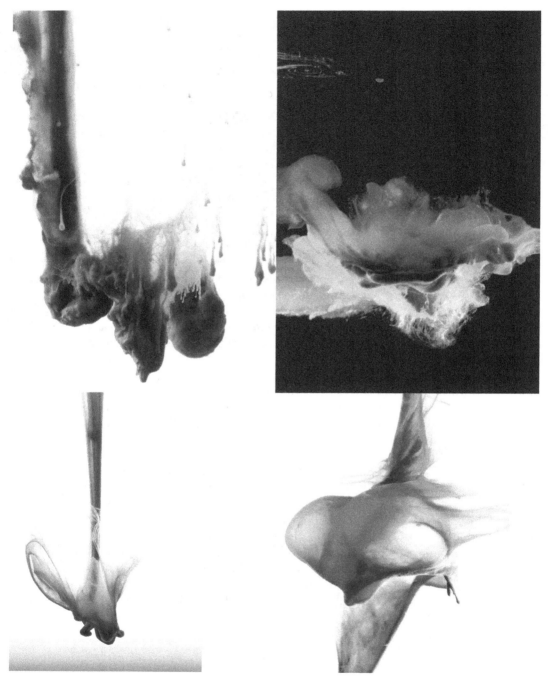

Menstrual Designer, Jen Lewis; Photographer, Rob Lewis. Top left: *Avalanche* (2013); top right: *A Break in the Clouds* (2013); bottom left: *Untitled #23* (2013); bottom right: *Bursting Through* (2015). Reprinted with artist's permission.

and photography magazines like *Feature Shoot* and *Lip Magazine* as well as popular online sites like *Jezebel* and *Buzzfeed* all actively challenge the reading of *Beauty in Blood* as vomit inducing; the reviews instead remind viewers that Lewis has provided them with an alternative framework.

To understand why visual depictions of menstruation are so repulsive and feared, it is helpful to turn to psychoanalyst and feminist theorist Julia Kristeva. In her book, *Powers of Horror: An Essay on Abjection* (1982), Kristeva names the abject as that which is "ejected beyond the scope of the possible, the tolerable, the thinkable. . . . It beseeches, worries, and fascinates desire" (1). Critics point out that abjectivity is gendered for Kristeva and that she identifies rotting food, human excrement, and menstrual blood as abject (Gilleard and Higgs 2011, 136). What is key for Kristeva (1982, 4) is not simply that these items are "improper" or "unclean." Rather it is what they represent: "It is thus not a lack of cleanliness or health that causes abjection but what disturbs identity, system, order. It refuses to be contained." In exploring the seepage of women's bodies, Elizabeth Grosz (1994) also urges that what is most repulsive about menses and its *potential* for leaks is its unruliness. To apply her language, menstruation renders a woman's body "leaking," "uncontrollable," and "seeping" (200); menstrual blood does not respect borders or boundaries (203). According to Kristeva's and Grosz's frameworks, menstrual blood, then, signifies disorder and chaos. The reading of menstruation as the abject is why, for example, so many teen magazines have sections devoted to revealing the shame and embarrassments that arise from the unruly chaos of menstruation (Houppert 1999, 86). *Seventeen Magazine*, for instance, continues the tradition of memorializing menstrual horror stories. In an online article entitled "10 Mortifying Period Horror Stories You're SO Glad Didn't Happen to You" (Orenstein 2017), *Seventeen* exposes stories that are, on the one hand, mortifying and publicly shaming around menstrual leaks and disasters. This is partially why confusion and disgust are the public reaction to Lewis's work. On the other hand, these stories also create a collective space for young girls to learn about menstruation. Fingerson (2006, 7) argues that adolescents "learn and form opinions about the mechanics and experience of menstruation from each other through storytelling and jokes." In this way, *Seventeen's* stories serve to complicate Kristeva's discussion of menstruation by creating a community where young women can use storytelling to unearth complex understandings of their bodies.

As it challenges the public perception of abjection, Lewis's project is also mindful of menstrual activists' call to move away from conventional menstrual products like tampons and single-use maxi pads to more sustainable products like cups and cloth pads. Upon her doctor's recommendation, Lewis began using a menstrual cup in 2012, a moment that allowed her to be more "hands-on" with her body. In her interview with *Huffington Post*, Lewis recalls "My relationship with my body began changing immediately following the first use. One day, when I had some blood on my fingers after emptying my cup, I started to wonder about why society framed up menstruation as something disgusting" (quoted in Frank 2015).

Traditional menstrual products, in many ways, distance us from our bodies. As assumed "sanitary" barriers, these items represent menses as abject. Lewis advocates with her photographs that perhaps we need to look again at our blood and sever the automatic, sterile cycle of inserting a tampon applicator and pulling on a piece of thread. This is very much aligned with the belief of some menstrual activists that menses are positive and should be celebrated (Patterson 2014, 106). *Beauty in Blood* is a part of this motivation to naturalize menstruation and re-empower the bleeding body.

Finally, the public display of Lewis's photographs allows for more expansive and communal conversations about menstruation. Lewis honors a critical goal of menstrual activists to "call on all women to reclaim their bleeding bodies" (Patterson 2014, 106). To promote the belief that we must dislodge shame, Lewis curated an exhibit for the biennial conference of the Society for Menstrual Cycle Research (SMCR). As an organization that positions menstruation as a human right and as a reproductive justice and gender equality issue, Lewis brought together juried art by thirty-eight artists from ten countries "to disrupt the current cultural narrative [of menstruation] and replace it with one that reflects the real thoughts, emotions and experiences of menstruators" (Lewis 2013). Entitled *Widening the Cycle*, this curated collection brings gender equality and reproductive justice to the foreground while furthering Lewis's commitment to shifting the shame and secrecy that so forcefully envelop a person's cycle. In privileging blood as the focal point of her artistic lens, Lewis's public display of menstrual blood and of menstrual narratives demands we look and not turn away.

Confronting Instagram: Rupi Kaur

Toronto-based spoken-word poet Rupi Kaur became involved with the tenets of menstrual activism and gender equality with a photo series she created with her sister Prabh Kaur in 2015 entitled *period*. The photographs are housed on Kaur's website, *rupikaur.com/period*.

This photo series includes six images exploring the rhetoric of menstruation. In the first photograph, Kaur lies on a bed facing away from the camera. She wears a white tank top and light gray sweatpants; a pale, yellow comforter covers her right thigh. As she faces the wall, we can see a small, round bloodstain on her and on the light gray sheet below her. This image evokes the exhaustion and pain that some experience with their menstrual cycles; it is the curled departure many of us undertake each month. In the second, the camera captures the lower half of Kaur's body sitting on a toilet. Her sweatpants gather by her ankles and her knees are exposed. Her left hand lowers a bloodied tampon into the wastebasket. The third presents a close-up of blood resting in a white toilet bowl. Bloodstained clothes spill out of a washing machine in the fourth photograph, while in the fifth, Kaur stands in a white tiled shower, a small amount of blood centered between her pigeon-toed feet. In the final photograph, Kaur rests on a bed, a hot pink hot water bottle pressed against her abdomen. Aside from Kaur herself, the pink water bottle, and her menstrual blood, the colors in the photographs are muted. The color scheme creates a contrast, allowing Kaur's tan skin and the boldness of her blood to overwhelm the frame. Additionally, in *period*, we never see Kaur's face. In these visual representations of her menstrual journey, Kaur becomes a symbol for every person who bleeds.

Kaur shared that her own experiences with the stigmas of menstruation served as inspiration for her project, an assignment for a visual rhetoric course she was taking at the University of Waterloo. She said "I wondered why I scurry to hide my tampons and pads from the world and why I'm too ashamed to tell people I'm in pain because of my period at times I may not be able to do certain things like come in to work" (*sic*; quoted in Gray 2015). Her photographs negotiate the tightrope walk between acknowledging the pain associated with menstruation and the desire to no longer engage in the concealment of maxi pads and tampons that young menstruators are so frequently taught (Fingerson 2006, 15).

Along with the photo series, Kaur (2015) included the following artistic statement on Instagram, a social networking site:

> i bleed each month to help make humankind a possibility. my womb is home to the divine. a source of life for our species. . . . but very few times it is seen that way. in older civilizations this blood was considered holy. in some it still is. . . . we menstruate and they see it as dirty. attention seeking. sick. a burden. as if this process is less natural than breathing. as if it is not a bridge between this universe and the last. as if this process is not love. labour. life. selfless and strikingly beautiful.

This statement, paired with her photography, powerfully demonstrates both radical menstrual and feminist spiritualist activism. Contrary to the rhetoric of abjection and pathology, Kaur names the womb and the act of menstruation as "divine," "holy," and "natural." Her framing of menstruation is akin to the feminist spiritualist belief that menstruation is a natural and empowering bodily experience. Kaur's artistic decision to depict menstruation as commonplace, as normative rather than dirty, also exemplifies radical menstrual activism. Her suggestion, however, that menstruation is "natural" exists in opposition with radical menstrual activism's call for a gender non-conforming politics. With her intentional use of words and imagery, she calls forth both lineages.

Critical to her repositioning of context here is the comparison she draws between menstruation, violence, and hypersexuality. Kaur (2015) reminds readers that we live in a culture where Western hegemony promotes the "violence and degradation of women" while demonizing menstruation. By placing how we culturally treat women in comparison to the act of monthly bleeding, she presents the absurdity of our cultural ideals, the absurdity of what we normalize and what we stigmatize. With this shift, Kaur also displays her feminist politics.[7] For Kaur, it "is the vehicle by which she can . . . challenge patriarchy, misogyny, and social taboos especially related to women" ("Poet & Activist" 2016). *period* embraces Kaur's feminist politics by refusing the gendered expectation that she remain silent about her body. By engaging in the politics of visibility, *period* instead combats the shame associated with menstruation.

Upon completing this project, Kaur posted her artistic statement and the first photo in the series—her sleeping body with blood staining her sweatpants and bed sheets—on Instagram. The series of events that followed were not only surprising for Kaur, they also troublingly demonstrated the regressive ways hegemonic culture frames menstruation even decades after the beginning of menstrual activism. On March 25, 2015, Instagram removed the post, messaging Kaur: "@rupikaur_ We removed your post because it doesn't follow our Community Guidelines. Please read our Community Guidelines to learn what kinds of posts are *allowed* and how you can help keep Instagram *safe*" (emphasis mine; comment on Kaur's Instagram page). Kaur's images do not challenge Instagram's Community Guidelines. According to their terms of use, effective as of January 19, 2013, "You may not post violent, nude, partially nude, discriminatory, unlawful, infringing, hateful, pornographic or sexually suggestive photos or other content via the Service" (Instagram 2013). Since her photograph did not violate any terms, Kaur reposted the image after March 25, only to have Instagram remove it again.

The language that Instagram used when referencing Kaur's work is critical. The photograph of her curled, sleeping, fully clothed body was deemed "unsafe" for the Instagram community specifically because it displayed visual evidence that she was menstruating. Kristeva's (1982, 4) urging that the abject is "what disturbs identity, system, order. What does not respect borders, positions, rules" is called forth here. Although this photograph contains no nude, violent, hateful, or pornographic content, the mere presence of menses is intolerable and disruptive. The sight of seepage unsettled Instagram to the point of censorship. The cultural discourse of menstruation as something to fear comes to mind here. By censoring Kaur's photography, Instagram reifies these reactions of abjection as normal.

As activism, in a moment of powerful push back, Kaur subsequently documented the blatant censoring on her Facebook and Instagram accounts; these posts were then shared "over 11,000 times" (Gray 2015). Kaur (2015) began by writing,

> thank you Instagram for providing me with the exact response my work was created to critique . . . i will not apologize for not feeding the ego and pride of misogynist society that will have my body in an underwear but not be okay with a small leak. when your pages are filled with countless photos/accounts where women (so many who are underage) are objectified. pornified. and treated less than human. thank you.

Kaur's statement references the hierarchical imbalance between genders when she identifies misogyny as the root of Instagram's censoring. In this way, her response functions as a bold counterargument to the perpetual shaming and objectification of women by social media and mass media. Kaur demands that we question why a menstruating body threatens and disturbs. Why does it render Instagram unsafe? Returning to the themes of her artistic statement, she asks why we allow misogyny to normalize images that objectify women but refuse to show a small bodily leakage.

She writes, "that's what this work is supposed to do. make you uncomfortable as you should feel when you watch others get abused and objectified. This just goes to show who is sitting behind the desk. And whose controlling the show. Whose controlling the media and who is censoring us . . . Their patriarchy is leaking. Their misogyny is leaking. We will not be censored" (*sic*).

Kaur's language here summons radical menstrual activists. With her documented protest, with her refusal to be silent and invisible, she brings to light the workings of Instagram as a patriarchal institution. Similar to Lewis's public renderings of the very intimate, Kaur's visibility evokes the menarchist goal that menstruators must reclaim their bodies from androcentric principles (Patterson 2013, 105). For Kaur, taking back power means visibly and loudly pointing to social media's censorship.

Once her protest began, Kaur received a message from Instagram stating that they had "accidently removed" the photograph. She shared the news on her page, writing, "we did it. you did this. your belief in the work. it's message. and your movement to not quiet down" (Kaur 2015). Her photo series and her artistic statement, as well as the posts that followed the censorship, demonstrate what menstrual activism online can look like. Kaur and those who reposted her work and words refused to subject their bodies and their cycles to the stigma of a culture that names the menstruator and their body as feared, bloody, and beyond rules. Her work reveals that menstruation is not inherently shameful; rather it is the ways we sanitize it and remove it from public spaces that renders it such.

Conclusion: The Movement Forward

What is dynamic about Lewis and Kaur is the way their works politicize the body and publicize the private. Their work reminds us that the taboo surrounding menstruation persists. We are still taught that our bleeding bodies should be hidden and spoken about in euphemisms. By centering images of a body that bleeds and on menses itself, these photographers offer narratives of menstruation that at once familiarize, normalize, and beautify.

Most unique to their works, particularly to Kaur's, are the ways their photographs open the conversation about menstrual activism in social media. I first began this journey of exploration into menstrual activism when I found Kaur's visual and written protests from Instagram on my Facebook feed. The visual resonance, the grammar, the familiar pull to my own body resulted in the research that led me into a history of activism with which I had been previously unfamiliar. Lewis's and Kaur's candid, visual activism reconnected me with a part of my body that was rooted in adolescent messages of anxiety and fear. This is what menstrual art-making can do: it can offer us a new vocabulary, a new lens through which we can reconsider the stories we have been taught about our own bodies.

NOTES

1. Also known as the menstrual hygiene industry, the menstrual product industry is a powerful, multibillion dollar conglomerate of "product manufacturers, medical and pharmaceutical companies, and advertising firms" (Docherty 2010, 2).

2. Menstrual activism in the 1970s was centrally comprised of white women. Bobel (2010, 11) also notes that a "disproportionate number of queer-identified activists" were a part of the community.

3. It is important to remember that although the feminist spiritualist branch provides a lens to view menstruation as positive, many menstruators suffer from extreme pain during their cycles. We must not overly romanticize menstruation.

4. Since the 1970s, feminists have advocated for the safety of menstrual products. The lack of safety was proven in higher absorbency tampons in 1980 when the Federal Centers for Disease Control connected them to over two thousand cases of toxic shock syndrome (TSS) resulting in more than thirty-five deaths. During this time, feminists and menstrual activists fought to bring awareness to the toxicity of menstrual products. Activists Esther Rome, Jill Wolhandler, and Nancy Reame created Public Citizen, a not-for-profit organization that "initiated a campaign to standardize absorbency ratings" (Bobel 2010, 333). In addition to grassroots and media campaigns, activists in the 1990s promoted safer alternative products like reusable pads, menstrual cups, and sea sponges.

5. For examples of this kind of art-making, see Andres Serrano's *Piss Christ*, Piero Manzoni's *Artist's Shit*, and Millie Brown's *Nexus Vomitus*.
6. Although I have pointed to the beginning of menstrual art-making and the current menstrala movement to demonstrate the longevity of this type of art-making, it is certainly not isolated to the decades of the 1970s or 2000s.
7. I was unable to find specific information about whether Kaur brings her racial and ethnic background to bear on her work *period*. It left me with questions: Does she want us to view *period* through a racialized lens, or does she want us to explore it in a more universalized sense? Are there any pitfalls to this decision? Although these questions cannot be answered, I believe we need to raise them.

REFERENCES

Bobel, Chris. 2010. *New Blood: Third-Wave Feminism and the Politics of Menstruation*. New Brunswick: Rutgers.

Conway, Bridget. 2015. "Beauty in Blood." *Lip Magazine*, July 5. lipmag.com/arts/beauty-in-blood.

De Beauvoir, Simone. 2009. *The Second Sex*. Translated by Constance Borde and Sheila Malovany-Chevallier. New York: Vintage Books. Originally published by Editions Gallimard, Paris, 1949.

Dekel, Tal. 2013. *Gendered: Art and Feminist Theory*. Cambridge: Cambridge Scholars Publishing.

Delaney, Janice, Mary Jane Lupton, and Emily Toth. 1988. *The Curse: A Cultural History of Menstruation*. Chicago: University of Illinois Press.

Docherty, Shannon. 2010. "Smear It on Your Face, Rub It on Your Body, It's Time to Start a Menstrual Party!" *Critical Theory and Social Justice: Journal of Undergraduate Research* 1, no. 1: 1–25. scholar.oxy.edu/ctsj/v011/iss1/12.

Fingerson, Laura. 2006. *Girls in Power: Gender, Body, and Menstruation in Adolescence*. Albany: State University of New York Press.

Forte, Jeanie. 1988. "Women's Performance Art: Feminism and Postmodernism." *Theatre Journal* 40, no. 2: 217–35. www.jstor.org/stable/3207658.

Frank, Priscilla. 2015. "Artist Explores the Unexpected Beauty of Menstrual Blood Using Macrophotography." *Huffington Post Arts & Culture*, March 5. www.huffingtonpost.com/2015/05/05/jen-lewis-beauty-in-blood_n_7205908.html.

Gilleard, Chris, and Paul Higgs. 2011. "Ageing Abjection and Embodiment in the Fourth Age." *Journal of Aging Studies* 25, no. 2: 135–42. doi: 10.1016/j.jaging.2010.08.018.

Gray, Emma. 2015. "The Removal of Rupi Kaur's Instagram Photos Shows How Terrified We Are of Periods." *Huffington Post Women*, March 27. www.huffingtonpost.com/2015/03/27/rupi-kaur-period-instagram_n_6954898.html.

Grosz, Elizabeth. 1994. *Volatile Bodies: Toward Corporeal Feminism*. Bloomington: Indiana University Press.

Houppert, Karen. 1999. *The Curse: Confronting the Last Unmentionable Taboo: Menstruation*. New York: Farrar, Straus and Giroux.

Instagram. 2013. "Instagram Privacy & Safety Center," last modified January 19, 2013. help.instagram.com/1188470931252371.

Johnston-Robledo, Ingrid, and Joan C. Chrisler. 2013. "The Menstrual Mark: Menstruation as Social Stigma." *Sex Roles* 68, no. 1-2: 9–18. doi: 10.1007/s11199-011-0052-z.

Kaur, Rupi. 2015. Instagram post, March 25. www.instagram.com/p/00vWwJHA6f/?hl=en.

Kissling, Elizabeth A. 2006. *Capitalizing on the Curse: The Business of Menstruation*. Boulder: Lynne Rienner Publishing.

Kristeva, Julia. 1982. *Powers of Horror: An Essay on Abjection*. Translated by Leon S. Roudiez. New York: Columbia University Press.

Lewis, Jen. n.d. "Beauty in Blood." *www.beautyinblood.com/about.html*.

———. 2013. "Widening the Cycle: A Menstrual Cycle & Reproductive Justice Art Show." *www.wideningthecycle.com*.

Merskin, Debra. 1999. "Adolescence, Advertising, and the Ideology of Menstruation." *Sex Roles* 40, no. 11: 941–57. doi: 10.1023/A: 1018881206965.

Novak, Emil. 1921. *Menstruation and Its Disorders*. New York: D. Appleton and Company.

Orenstein, Hannah. 2017. "10 Mortifying Period Horror Stories You're SO Glad Didn't Happen to You." *Seventeen Magazine*, July 10. *www.seventeen.com/health/sex-health/a39051/mortifying-period-stories-youre-so-glad-didnt-happen-to-you*.

Patterson, Ashly S. 2014. "The Social Construction and Resistance of Menstruation as a Public Spectacle." In *Illuminating How Identities, Stereotypes and Inequalities Matter through Gender Studies*, edited by D. Nicole Farris, Mary Ann Davis, and D'Lane R. Compton, 91–108. New York: Springer.

———. 2013. "The Menstrual Body." MA thesis, University of New Orleans.

"Poet & Activist Rupi Kaur on Pushing Social Boundaries for the Sake of Intersectional Feminism." 2016. *GirlTalkHQ*, July 12. *girltalkhq.com/poet-activist-rupi-kaur-on-pushing-social-boundaries-for-the-sake-of-intersectional-feminism*.

Stampler, Laura. 2011. "Always Runs First Feminine Hygiene Ad to Show Blood." *Huffington Post*, July 6. *www.huffingtonpost.com/2011/07/06/always-runs-first-feminin_n_891546.html*.

Vostral, Sharra Louise. 2008. *Under Wraps: A History of Menstrual Hygiene Technology*. Lanham: Lexington Books.

Whelan, Elizabeth M. 1975. "Attitudes toward Menstruation." *Studies in Family Planning* 6, no. 4: 106–8. *www.jstor.org/stable/1964817*.

5

Am I Pretty Enough for You Yet?

Resistance through Parody in the Pretty or Ugly YouTube Trend

Katherine Phelps

"It's my life, my body, my YouTube channel."

YouTuber az009601 sits in her bathroom in front of a laptop. She is making a You-Tube video. Cocking her head to one side and playing with her hair, she looks into the web camera and makes the above statement, asserting ownership over her body. But she then goes on to ask the question that hundreds of thousands of American girls are asking on YouTube: "Am I pretty or ugly?"

American girls are in trouble. Or do they just cause trouble? The current cultural purview of girlhood in the United States suggests it is both. Social, cultural, and political discourses have historically constructed the "girl" subject in dualistic terms: she is innocent and in need of protection, while also dangerous, erratic, and hypersexual (Driscoll 2002; Harris 2004a; McRobbie 1990; Thiel-Stern 2014). Collective social ideology may indicate that a girl can be anything she wants to be and do anything she wants to do, yet her worth remains deeply connected to physical appearance. Her body—as object of sexual desire, as social capital, as commodity—is a "project" to be constantly worked on, maintained, and improved (Bordo 1993; Brumberg 1997). American society at once presumes girls feeling dissatisfied with their bodies is a "normal" part of the adolescent female experience, and yet it fears girls' bodies for the potential they possess (Brumberg 1997; Driscoll 2002; Hesse-Biber 2006; Tolman 1994). Even in the so-called postfeminist age of "girl power," it is considered abnormal for a girl to exhibit body positivity, sexual assurance, and self-affirmation. Az009601's YouTube video effectively demonstrates this reality.

These incongruous expectations of girls, these "dueling dualisms," are readily recognizable in representations of girls in popular media (Willis 2008), which has catalyzed the sexualization of girls in the United States at ever-younger ages. In recent months, news media has been flooded with examples of girls being sent home from school for noncompliance with inherently sexist standards of dress, showing too much skin and "distracting" male counterparts. Alongside this sexualization of girls persists broad concern of girls as sexual beings, manifesting in uproar over matters such as premarital sex, sexually transmitted infections, teen pregnancy, and the newer social phenomenon of "sexting" (Ringrose et al. 2013). The evidence is mounting. Clearly, being a "girl" is precarious and loaded with contradictions; girls are both "trouble" and "in trouble," virtuous and threatening, capable and "don't know any better." So what is a girl to do?

Enter, the internet. Though the internet is often constructed as hostile and predatory, for girls in particular (Banet-Weiser 2014; Kearney 2011; Sales 2016), it can also be used as a democratizing and empowering space. From its inception, girls have found ways to carve out online territory and make it their own through blogs and websites, various social media accounts, and personal channels on web platforms (boyd 2007; Brown and Thomas 2014; Chittenden 2010; Davis 2010; Mazzarella 2010; Takayoshi 1999). As American girls are spending more time online, they actively play a role in discovering new avenues by which to resist and challenge the contradictory narratives of girlhood, most notably through creative enterprises of media production on platforms such as YouTube. As a digital public domain, YouTube has readily become one of the most popular sites to ever grace the Web, with more than five hundred hours of video uploaded to the site every minute (Robertson 2015). And because female adolescents are currently the top users of visually oriented web platforms, they are very much making their presence on YouTube known (Banet-Weiser 2011; Sales 2016).

A salient example of girls' resistance is evident in the Pretty or Ugly YouTube trend, which began, as best can be told, in 2011, when a handful of adolescent females between the approximate ages of ten and fourteen started posting brief, individual videos to the popular online platform asking their viewers to assess their appearances and "comment" on whether they are "pretty or ugly." By 2013, some media sources reported that more than 750,000 videos had amassed on YouTube by this demographic asking this same highly gendered question (Gallo 2013; Perle 2013).

Initial media reaction to the trend mirrored notions of girlhood deeply embedded in the American imagination and reflected the "unfortunate" reality of body dissatisfaction as a girlhood rite of passage. People were disturbed by the existence of the trend, though focused primarily on how sad they felt it was, and lambasted the "attention-seeking" nature of the videos or blamed the parents. Few seemed to challenge the actual social conditions surrounding the trend or sought to understand why girls were asking this question (on a global platform) in the first place. For American girls, asking "Am I pretty or ugly?" is not new, but how they are asking the question is. Exceedingly limited critical commentary and scholarly research currently exists on the Pretty or Ugly trend (Banet-Weiser 2014; Nurka 2014; Rossie 2015), and as a whole it warrants further in-depth empirical investigation.

This chapter's focus is on a trend that has arisen within the trend. Because online platforms like YouTube operate as public space where girls can readily achieve visibility, there comes significant opportunity and necessity to pay attention to the political possibilities of the adolescent female body in resisting constricting and conventional narratives of American girlhood. A notable number of the Pretty or Ugly YouTube videos made by this demographic of tween girls can be readily categorized as *parody*, because these girls blatantly exaggerate their performances in comedic mockery of the pretty or ugly question.[1] I argue that the parody faction of the Pretty or

Ugly YouTube trend is a powerful example of how tween girls are using their bodies in digital spaces to resist narrow, bifurcated constructions of girlhood and to challenge inherently contradictory expectations and ideals of girlhood bodies, beauty, and sexualities.

Background and Significance

Unless a young person has an entire lack of access to social media (which has in itself become another dimension of inequality), online participation has become a ubiquitous and compulsory part of identity development for "digital natives" (Buckingham 2008; Prensky 2001). Because youth no longer make the distinction between offline and online "selves," making the body visible has become a fundamental aspect of girlhood development in digital space (Palfrey and Gasser 2016; Sales 2016; Thiel-Stern 2014). Web and phone cameras now function as "mirrors"—providing literal reflections of the self as well as reflections that others can see and assess. The most popular and widely used social media sites among youth—Instagram, Snapchat, YouTube, and Musical.ly (Statista 2017), for example—all rely heavily on the visual. Participation on these sites contributes to the blurring of public and private because girls are essentially inviting public viewers into private spaces (e.g., bedrooms where videos are recorded). Research suggests that girls in particular employ these sites in pursuit of social capital, with the "selfie" being the most recognized form of currency (Banet-Weiser 2014; Simmons 2014; Sales 2016). The bodies of American girls are now vastly visible in online space.

The body has been theorized as a useful tool in the negotiation of public life as well as a site of political resistance (Bartky 1988; Bordo 1993; Reischer and Koo 2004). Women have long used their bodies in enterprises of resistance to and rejection of traditional understandings of femininity—performing their bodies through parody as grotesque, monstrous, hypersexual; as spectacle; and as excess (Evans Braziel and LeBesco 2001; Russo 1995). Parody is both imitation and subversion, and comedy patently plays a crucial role in parody as a feminist strategy (Butler 1990; Hutcheon 2000). There is a significant body of work surrounding feminist theories of performance, body politics, and parody; interdisciplinary scholarship that emphasizes the complexities of exploiting feminine appearance in service of humor and the feminist political project (Kent 2001; Kuppers 2001; Merrill 1988; Mizejewski 2014; Rowe 1995). Comedy performed by female bodies that critiques ideal femininity, that muddles societal understandings of "pretty," is both transgressive and resistant.

Far less is understood about how female adolescents, how *girls*, are employing these same strategies. This research contributes to understandings of the female body and parody by examining how tween girls are doing the challenging work of feminism in an era of "qualified liberation" (Franks 1997, 100). The Pretty or Ugly trend and the parody faction within it represent a dual mode of resistance—girls are parodying and mocking each other, while making social commentary on the cultural hegemony of constrained girlhood (Butler 1990). The traditional videos in the trend echo societal standards of body and beauty for girls, while the parody faction serves as the resistant voice of rebellion. This interplay between conformity and resistance through parody has largely been seen and used in literature and film (Hutcheon 2000), but the cultural material of today is the digital media that girls are creating.

Methods

This study employs a qualitative content analysis of a sample of 260 videos considered part of the Pretty or Ugly YouTube trend. YouTube videos are not generated randomly; rather, specific search terms are required in order to view desired content (Paek, Kim, and Lynn 2010). Because there is a large volume of videos in the trend, I was able to generate a sample of videos with diverse representation through the application of four configurations of YouTube search terms: (1) "Am I pretty or ugly?" (2) "Am I ugly or pretty?" (3) "Am I pretty?" and (4) "Am I ugly?" Sixty-five videos were then selected from the results of each search term.[2]

During sampling, videos were reviewed once in full to determine relevance and ensure that they met the following criteria: the video must be generated by one of the four specified search terms; the title must include the words "pretty," "ugly," or some combination thereof; the subject(s) must identify as female or have an assumed sex category of female (West and Zimmerman 1987); and the subject(s) must have an estimated age of fourteen years old or younger. Several factors were considered in developing a codebook for analysis including subjects' perceived racial identities; registered emotion in the video (e.g., anger, sadness); demeanor (e.g., apathy, uncertainty); elements of performance in how girls used their bodies (e.g., posing, gestures, dress); and perceived motivation for posting the video (e.g., genuine concern, boredom, parody).

From the 260 videos in the total sample, 26 were coded as contestation or parody, operating directly against or in total mockery of the larger trend. Contestation and parody were assigned as codes when video subjects either outwardly rejected the question through verbal language (e.g., "it doesn't matter if you are pretty or ugly, stop asking") or body language, with subjects overtly using their bodies in exaggerated comedic performance. In this analysis, I focus on how girls are performing their bodies in the videos as well as their motivation for posting, looking specifically at a select sample of videos that were coded as "parody." I examine how the subjects in these videos demonstrate resistance to embedded cultural narratives of girlhood through the use of their bodies in performing comedic spectacle and mimicry of the larger Pretty or Ugly trend. What follows is an exploration of performing parody online, the application of digital knowledge among these subjects, and the interaction of video subjects with their viewers in the practice of continued resistance to restrictive and harmful notions of girlhood.

Body Performance and Parody in Digital Space

YouTuber Beth White uses her body casually in her parody video, filmed in a bedroom obviously occupied by a tween girl. She is white and approximately twelve or thirteen years old. In her sing-song voice she says to viewers, "I was just wondering if you think I'm pretty. . . . [Because] I feel really pretty dead inside, and if you don't think I'm pretty outside, no harsh feelings. So comment down below and *tell me I'm pretty.*" The final few emphasized words are spoken in a harsh, deep voice, one completely set apart from the voice she uses in the start of the video. The obvious shift is meant to invoke laughter. She playfully threatens her viewers; she is not *asking* if she is pretty or ugly, rather she is demanding that her viewers *tell* her that she is pretty.

The performance is exaggerated; she is clearly having fun in front of the camera. She does not make the video in hopes of securing some objective understanding of her appearance; she makes it to be seen and to play with digital space and perceptions of girlhood. In doing so, she changes the narrative of "pretty or ugly" from one of uncertainty and docility to one of agency and dynamism.

In another video, YouTuber Bailey Mae, also white and around twelve or thirteen years old, masterfully sets up her parody: "So this whole video is about what I think guys like in a girl." Her performance turns manic and demented as she proceeds to rub makeup all over her face, messily putting on powder and smearing lipstick around her mouth and under her nose. She teases her hair and douses herself in perfume, comically coughing as she sprays it in her face. As she gets closer to the camera, her eyes begin twitching and she laughs wildly. At one point she puts on sunglasses and lifts up her shirt while yelling, "Facebook picture!" She mimics the peace sign gesture, found nearly universally in other more "traditional" videos in the trend, and makes a purposefully unattractive face in a final close up of the camera. Through clenched teeth, she banefully mutters, "So now am I pretty enough yet? Do I look like a clown? . . . [Do] I smell good enough for you yet? Is my hair pretty enough for you yet? I'm going to go out and get tanned, right? Am I pretty enough for you yet?"

This parody both encapsulates and dismantles the cultural expectations surrounding girlhood. She mocks all at once other girls in the Pretty or Ugly trend as well as recognized girlhood body narratives. Bailey Mae is calling foul on these expectations: be sexual but not too sexual, be pretty but modest, and consume products meant for aesthetic improvement, all with the intent of securing attention from adolescent males. Her bodily performance demonstrates the latent contradiction of society valuing the innocence of the adolescent female body while also fearing it. Through self-possessed humor, mania, and spectacle, Bailey Mae makes a political statement.

In a video made by YouTube user yourjellyofmyswag, two subjects, both white and approximately fourteen years old, emphasize Valley-girl voices contrasted with loud belches and displays of obscenity in their video, playing up a grotesqueness not associated with "pretty girls." One of the primary tropes in the larger Pretty or Ugly trend is the subject ostensibly seeking attention, or the "attention whore." These girls are clearly offering a parody of the attention-whore trope through both the language in the video and the performance of their bodies. Talking over each other, they make comments such as, "[We] think [we're] gorgeous . . . but just let us know," "[We're] pretty sure that you guys are going to compliment us," and "I mean, we both know we're [pretty], but like, we want your opinion." They lift up their shirts, show off their stomachs, grind up against each other, and feign orgasms. At the end of the video, they sink out of view of the camera, grunting and groaning and giggling with abandon. This video is transparent in its motivation to mock the Pretty or Ugly trend. Well aware of what it means to be "feminine" or "ladylike" and to behave in line with those heteronormative expectations, these two girls roundly reject them in favor of hilarious spectacle, their bodies the central mechanism of resistance.

It is crucial to note the racialization of the Pretty or Ugly trend. Girls of color are drastically underrepresented in the trend as a whole, and none of the twenty-six videos coded as contestation or parody feature a subject of color. The whiteness of the trend is significant. Social media has been theorized as a site of empowerment for girls of color, particularly Black girls and/or those girls who are more likely deemed "at-risk" (Harris

2004b; Lindsey 2013; Stokes 2007), but it has also been interpreted as a more perilous place, given historically bound stereotypes of Black women as hypersexual (Hill Collins 2000; hooks 1992). Visibility of girls' bodies is fundamentally political, yet this politicization is not homogenous across racial categories. A girl of color may risk more in simply asking if she is pretty or ugly, and beyond this, in creating parody of the question by exposing her body and presenting herself in a sexualized way, as Bailey Mae and the yourjellyofmyswag girls do. The language of "pretty" is loaded in terms of what it means to perform girlhood, and race and class status matter considerably in the construction of the "ideal" American girl. The whiteness of the Pretty or Ugly trend, and the politics of resistance tied up with this, merits further exploration. There is still risk involved in posting these videos, regardless of race, but the white girls participating seem to mitigate some of this risk by involving friends and making their parodies a social experience.

Distinct from the larger trend, in which the vast majority of the videos appear to have only one subject, the videos in the parody trend often feature more than one subject, with other girls either filming or participating directly. The social nature of the parody trend bolsters the possibilities for resistance. In the case of Beth White, a friend films the video. Though a second subject is never seen directly, this can be understood as something the girls have chosen to take part in together. At the end of Bailey Mae's video, another girl enters the bedroom and emphatically asks what Bailey Mae is doing. The moment is clearly premeditated and brings the performance full circle as this second subject "polices" Bailey Mae, reinforcing the mania and spectacle of the parody. The parody has stronger impact in this moment, as Bailey Mae is caught behaving in a way unbefitting of conventional femininity. The yourjellyofmyswag girls perform the parody together, each emphasizing the performance of the other. As a social experience, creating parodies of normative girlhood in digital space can operate as a form of consciousness-raising, with multiple girls "getting in on the joke."

The videos produced by these subjects indicate how comedy can be a feminist endeavor with clear critical power. Drawing out laughter makes an impact—a viewer is called to question *why* they are laughing. The hilarity of each of these videos rests in farce; subjects use their bodies ironically, serving the purpose of resisting social and cultural standards to which they are held. By blatantly rejecting notions of femininity in favor of comedy and parody of the larger trend, these subjects point out those stereotypes of girlhood, forcing viewers to confront the status quo of a harmful values system. As Merrill (1988, 272) asserts: "Because humor depends upon a perception of events or behavior as unexpected or incongruous, the individual who publicly points up such inconsistencies risks making a statement about the status quo. Consequently, satire, irony, and comedy pointedly directed can wield enormous social and political power." In these videos, parody operates as an aggressive practice meant to make a political point about how society values girls and their bodies. From their own bedrooms, these subjects can do political work in mocking oppressive contexts and restrictive narratives of girlhood.

Digital Knowledge in Practice

Through bodily performance, these girls show pronounced resistance to the social invention of female adolescents "naturally" feeling bad about their bodies and their selves, and what's more, they use a global online platform to do it. The site of this resistance matters. YouTube participation impacts sense of self, and the digital knowledge these girls are developing works in tandem with the creativity of parody performance to generate unique opportunity for girls to occupy online space in ways that are truly their own (Palfrey and Gasser 2016; Prensky 2001; Shields Dobson 2015).

YouTuber madepenn's parody video puts this digital knowledge into practice. She is white and approximately fourteen years old. In the start of the video, she wears very heavy eye makeup, blush, and lipstick; colorful bows in her short, brown hair; and a plain black t-shirt. She shoots the video under the covers of her bed, lying on her stomach with her face close to the camera. Using an exaggerated Valley-girl voice, madepenn tells her viewers that she is "feeling kind of un-amazing" and is asking if "you thought I was pretty or ugly." The scene then cuts to madepenn in the same position under the covers, but she is now stripped of makeup completely, sans bows, wearing thick-framed glasses, and using her normal voice, which is low and resonant. At first she uses her body in parody of the trend, and then very strategically reclaims it, with both body performances working collectively to serve as resistance. The video begins as a parody performance and then becomes a manifesto of empowerment and the value of inner beauty. She states, "A beautiful face is totally ruined by a rotten personality. . . . [If] you're a horrible person [and] no one likes you, then your beauty is worth absolutely nothing." It is the stark contrast in her appearance from the start to the finish and the seamless transition that give the video its impact as parody of the trend, and this is only achieved through the application of madepenn's digital skills.

Rather than shooting her video in real time, YouTuber Shannon McDonald, also white and twelve or thirteen years old, opts to present an image of herself with text that reads, "Please tell me if I am pretty or ugly! All my friends in real life call me beautiful, and I believe them, but what do you think?" At the outset, this video appears to be more in line with the trend itself, setting up the pretty or ugly question with apparent sincerity. The initial image viewers see has text that reads, "Me without make up." Then the video flawlessly morphs into the same image of Shannon McDonald, only now it has been heavily photo-shopped and played with as parody. With the text now reading, "Me with a little bit of makeup on," her hair has become starkly bleach blond, cheeks comically exaggerated with deep red blush, her lips coated in shockingly pink lipstick, and eyes surrounded with heavy makeup. She presents this second image with obvious humor and sarcasm. Shannon McDonald's video stands out because the parody is performed and made successful through her digital knowledge and ability to skillfully tamper with a photo and edit a video for desired effect. She is playing with her audience and using her knowledge to create a spectacle that resists expectations of normative girlhood.

Continued Resistance

The numbers of views these videos receive says a great deal. The public nature of them, and the fact that they exist within a much larger trend, means they have an increased chance of being seen. Bailey Mae's video has more than 16,400 views. Madepenn has more than 2,000. Beth White clocks in at over 600, and Shannon McDonald with more than 300. Yourjellyofmyswag may only have just over 90 views, but even this is impressive in terms of reach when one considers the dizzying amount of content uploaded to YouTube each minute.

In many instances, once these parody videos are made public, subjects continue interaction with viewers within the comment section that accompanies YouTube video posts. A quick scan of the comments sections in these parody videos reveals not only many of the aesthetic and behavioral pressures that female adolescents face in contemporary society (Rossie 2015), but also that a fair number of viewers do not watch the videos in full. Often viewers take it upon themselves to answer the pretty or ugly question even though the subjects themselves have clearly indicated that they do not care to know the answer. Many people miss the point, thus these subjects engage in continued resistance by redirecting viewers' attention, policing comments, and working to continue the dialogue.

Bailey Mae responds to multiple viewers on her comment board, reinforcing her performance of parody and asserting agency in her choice to post the video. She writes, "I Am 13. I Made This Video, Because I Was Making Fun Of Another Video I Had Seen On Facebook A Couple Weeks Ago. And My Bestfriend Was Over So We Decided To Do This." She presents the video in a context of parody and as a social experience she shared with a friend. To another viewer who chastises her for "copying" another video she responds, "Yes, I copied it. It says that right in the description dumbass. Didn't your momma ever teach you, that, if you don't have anything nice to say, don't say it at all? Obviously not. But here's the thing. I'm me, and you're hating on a video that you didn't even have to watch. So, do me a favor and fuck the fuck off. Thank you and have a nice day." Bailey Mae takes the time to respond to these viewers and continue the process of resistance to clarify her message. Beyond this, she exhibits a great deal of ownership over her content and agency in her choice to post it. The latter comment works to claim that space of her YouTube channel—it is part of her identity, a stage on which she can make herself visible in ways that she chooses.

Madepenn also interacts with her viewers, but gives her audience a distinct sense of what she is doing from the outset as well. She writes, "watch past the first minute before you comment. i'm not actually looking for ratings, guys," in the description of the video. Though she titles the video "AM I PRETTY OR UGLY?" she clues her viewers in, incentivizing them to watch past the beginning, to engage with her full purpose in posting.

Beth White carries on in the comments as she does in the video, with quick humor and biting sarcasm in her responses. She quips to one viewer, "I mean it is pretty obvious I'm way prettier then you . . . and it's ok to be jelious millions of people are:) oh btw don't even try and say your not jelious /insecure because we can all tell u are:)." In response to another viewer she writes, "Idk my friends say I'm ugly and I was probes born on the highway because that's where most mistakes happen." Beth White continues to assert herself in terms of confidence and self-possessed humor. She is able to laugh at herself while also disciplining other commenters.

Through continued interaction on comment threads, the girls in the parody trend reaffirm their sense of self and make apparent their lack of desire to be assessed by YouTube viewers in any kind of sincerity (Shields Dobson 2015). The videos are wholly their own, and YouTube channels operate as spaces in which to produce and publicize creative content, as well as offer cultural commentary on the limiting constructions of girlhood that inform their lives.

Girls Doing the Work

The overall Pretty or Ugly trend is perhaps disturbing, but not necessarily surprising. A girl wonders if she is pretty or ugly because she has been reminded through multiple avenues (media, peers, industry, and consumerism) that this is what matters when it comes to being a girl. Achieving girlhood is most certainly related to an aesthetically driven values system of pretty or ugly (West and Zimmerman 1987). This makes the parody faction of the trend all the more compelling and crucial, because even though the girls posting these parody videos are still asking this question, they are doing so in a way that proclaims they are not actually seeking an answer because they understand it does not matter in determining who they are and the value they have. What's more, they see the trend as an opportunity to make a political point, and elect parody and body performance as mechanisms to do so on a global online platform.

These digital native girls are cutting through the contradictions of girlhood via bodily performances and flipping grand narratives of body dissatisfaction and passive sexuality on their heads. The Pretty or Ugly parody trend necessarily demonstrates that in the current epoch of online participation, "Girls can engage and utilize media and technology to transform being 'worked over' by media to working media over—disrupting negative messages and seizing power through media production and digital literacy" (Preston-Sidler 2015, 195). And the trend is just one example of this engagement. It is becoming increasingly important to investigate how girls use and make media online, as American girlhood is now freely played out in digital space. Moreover, the need to understand girls' use of their bodies online is paramount because social media is effectively where a body politics of contemporary girlhood is now found—and girls are playing an active role in shaping these politics in ways they never have before.

The "pretty or ugly" question is indeed an old one for girls in the United States (and no doubt, beyond) (Brumberg 1997; Driscoll 2002). There is a great deal of work left to do in changing the values system that dictates how female adolescents are meant to behave in regards to their bodies and sexualities. That said, there is already significant work being done to incite this change. Antiquated understandings of girlhood *are* transforming in the midst of the increasingly digitized development of youth. Tween girls are now applying digital knowledge in digital space as means of making their bodies visible, and parodying dangerous ideals in the process. Though recognized notions of American girlhood are still very much tied to cultural ideas about innocence, purity, and passivity (Willis 2008), this renders perfectly clear the significance of the Pretty or Ugly parody trend, the timeliness of it, and the continued need to investigate how digital participation and development are influencing contemporary girlhood in the United States.

NOTES

1. The terminology of "tween" indicates a specific cultural category and set of behaviors related to the pre-adolescent to early adolescent life stage, particularly between the ages of ten and fourteen (Gill 2012; Vares, Jackson, and Gill 2011).
2. Videos were selected through a process of convenience sampling, in which a list of videos was generated through each of the search terms, and videos were watched individu-

ally to determine eligibility for inclusion. Videos were then catalogued by date of upload beginning with the earliest, and viewed several times. Observations and transcripts were recorded and subsequently analyzed using a codebook developed by the researcher through inductive content analysis (Hsieh and Shannon 2005).

REFERENCES

Banet-Weiser, Sarah. 2011. "Branding the Post-feminist Self: Girls' Video Production and YouTube." In *Mediated Girlhoods: New Explorations of Girls' Media Culture,* edited by Mary Celeste Kearney, 277–94. New York: Peter Lang Publishing.

———. 2014. "Am I Pretty or Ugly?: Girls and the Market for Self-Esteem." *Girlhood Studies* 7, no. 1: 83–101.

Bartky, Sandra L. 1988. "Foucault, Femininity and the Modernization of Patriarchal Power." In *Feminism and Foucault: Reflections on Resistance*, edited by Irene Diamond and Lee Quinby, 45–77. Boston: Northeastern University Press.

Bordo, Susan. 1993. *Unbearable Weight: Feminism, Western Culture, and the Body*. Berkeley: University of California Press.

boyd, danah. 2007. "Why Youth (Heart) Social Network Sites: The Role of Networked Publics in Teenage Social Life." In *Youth, Identity, and Digital Media*, edited by David Buckingham, 119–42. Cambridge, MA: MIT Press.

Brown, Adriene, and Mary E. Thomas. 2014. "'i just like knowing they can look at it and relize who i really am': Recognition and the Limits of Girlhood Agency on MySpace." *Signs: Journal of Women in Culture and Society* 39, no. 4: 949–72.

Brumberg, Joan Jacobs. 1997. *The Body Project: An Intimate History of American Girls*. New York: Vintage.

Butler, Judith. 1990. *Gender Trouble.* New York: Routledge.

Buckingham, David. 2008. *Youth, Identity, and Digital Media.* Boston: MIT Press.

Chittenden, Tara. 2010. "Digital Dressing Up: Modeling Female Teen Identity in the Discursive Spaces of the Fashion Blogosphere." *Journal of Youth Studies* 13, no. 4: 505–20.

Davis, Katie. 2010. "Coming of Age Online: The Developmental Underpinnings of Girls' Blogs." *Journal of Adolescent Research* 25, no. 1: 145–71.

Driscoll, Catherine. 2002. *Girls: Feminine Adolescence in Popular Culture and Cultural Theory.* New York: Columbia University Press.

Evans Braziel, Jana, and Kathleen LeBesco, eds. 2001. *Bodies out of Bounds: Fatness and Transgression.* Berkeley: University of California Press.

Franks, Jill. 1997. "Jesting Within: Voices of Irony and Parody as Expressions of Feminism." In *The Writing of Margaret Laurence Challenging Territory,* edited by Christian Riegel, 99–117. Alberta: University of Alberta Press.

Gallo, Amanda. 2013. "Am I Pretty or Ugly?" *The Argus*, December 9. *thesheaf. com/2013/12/09/am-i-pretty-or-ugly*.

Gill, Rosalind. 2012. "Media, Empowerment and the 'Sexualization of Culture' Debates." *Sex Roles* 66, no. 11/12: 736–45.

Harris, Anita. 2004a. *All About the Girl: Culture, Power, and Identity.* New York: Routledge.

———. 2004b. *Future Girl: Young Women in the Twenty-First Century.* New York: Routledge.

Hesse-Biber, Sharlene N. 2006. *The Cult of Thinness.* New York: Oxford University Press.

Hill Collins, Patricia. 2000. *Black Feminist Thought.* New York: Routledge.

Hsieh, H. F., and S. E. Shannon. 2005. "Three Approaches to Qualitative Content Analysis." *Qualitative Health Research* 15, no. 9: 1277–88.

hooks, bell. 1992. *Black Looks: Race and Representation.* Cambridge, MA: South End Press.

Hutcheon, Linda. 2000. *A Theory of Parody*. Chicago: University of Illinois Press.

Kearney, Mary Celeste. 2011. *Mediated Girlhoods: New Explorations of Girls' Media Culture*. New York: Peter Lang Publishing.

Kent, Le'a. 2001. "Fighting Abjection: Representing Fat Women." In *Bodies Out of Bounds: Fatness and Transgression,* edited by Jana Evans Braziel and Kathleen LeBesco, 130–45. Los Angeles: University of California Press.

Kuppers, Petra. 2001. "Fatties on Stage: Feminist Performances." In *Bodies Out of Bounds: Fatness and Transgression*, edited by Jana Evans Braziel and Kathleen LeBesco, 277–91. Los Angeles: University of California Press.

Lindsey, Treva. 2013. "One Time for My Girls: African American Girlhood, Empowerment, and Popular Visual Culture." *Journal of African American Studies* 17: 22–34.

Mazzarella, Sharon R. 2010. *Girl Wide Web 2.0: Revisiting Girls, the Internet, and the Negotiation of Identity*. New York: Peter Lang Publishing.

McRobbie, Angela. 1990. *Feminism and Youth Culture: From* Jackie *to* Just Seventeen. New York: Routledge.

Merrill, Lisa. 1988. "Feminist Humor: Rebellious and Self-Affirming." *Women's Studies* 15: 271–80.

Mizejewski, Linda. 2014. *Pretty/Funny: Women Comedians and Body Politics*. Austin: University of Texas Press.

Nurka, Camille. 2014. "Public Bodies." *Feminist Media Studies* 14, no. 3: 485–99.

Paek, H. J., K. Kim, and J. Lynn. 2010. "A Content Analysis of Smoking Fetish Videos on YouTube: Regulatory Implications for Tobacco Control." *Health Communication* 25, no. 2: 97–106.

Palfrey, John, and Urs Gasser. 2016. *Born Digital: Understanding the First Generation of Digital Natives*. New York: Basic Books.

Perle, Elizabeth. 2013. "What the 'Am I Pretty?' YouTube Trend is REALLY Saying." *Huffington Post*, November 11. *www.huffingtonpost.com/elizabeth-perle/what-the-am-i-prettyyout_b_4222947.html*.

Prensky, Marc. 2001. "Digital Natives, Digital Immigrants." *On the Horizon* 9, no. 5: 1–6.

Preston-Sidler, Leandra. 2015. "From Cyborgs to Cybergrrls: Redefining 'Girl Power' through Digital Literacy." In *Difficult Dialogues about Twenty-First Century Girls*, edited by Donna Marie Johnson and Alice E. Ginsberg, 195–206. Albany: State University of New York Press.

Reischer, Erica, and Kathryn S. Koo. 2004. "The Body Beautiful: Symbolism and Agency in the Social World." *Annual Review of Anthropology* 33: 297–317.

Ringrose, Jessica, Laura Harvey, Rosalind Gill, and Sonia Livingstone. 2013. "Teen Girls, Sexual Double Standards and 'Sexting': Gendered Value in Digital Image Exchange." *Feminist Theory* 14, no. 3: 305–23.

Robertson, Mark R. 2015. "500 Hours of Video Uploaded to YouTube Every Minute [Forecast]." *Tubular Insights*, November 13. *tubularinsights.com/hours-minute-uploaded-youtube*.

Rossie, Amanda. 2015. "Moving Beyond 'Am I pretty or ugly?': Disciplining Girls through YouTube Feedback." *Continuum* 29, no. 2: 230–40.

Rowe, Kathleen. 1995. *The Unruly Woman: Gender and the Genres of Laughter*. Austin: University of Texas Press.

Russo, Mary. 1995. *The Female Grotesque: Risk, Excess, and Modernity*. New York: Routledge.

Sales, Nancy Jo. 2016. *American Girls: Social Media and the Secret Lives of Teenagers*. New York: Knopf.

Shields Dobson, Amy. 2015. *Postfeminist Digital Cultures: Femininity, Social Media, and Self-Representation*. New York: Palgrave Macmillan.

Simmons, Rachel. 2014. "The Secret Life of Girls on Instagram." *TIME Magazine,* November 10. *time.com/3559340/instagram-tween-girls.*

Statista. 2017. "Reach of Leading Social Media and Networking Sites Used by Teenagers and Young Adults in the United States as of February 2017." Accessed August 7, 2017. *www.statista.com/statistics/199242/social-media-and-networking-sites-used-by-us-teenagers.*

Stokes, Carla E. 2007. "Representin' in Cyberspace: Sexual Scripts, Self-Definition, and Hip-Hop Culture in Black American Adolescent Girls' Home Pages." *Culture, Health, and Sexuality* 9, no. 2: 169–84.

Takayoshi, Pamela. 1999. "No Boys Allowed: The World Wide Web as Clubhouse for Girls." *Computers and Composition* 16, no. 1: 89–106.

Thiel-Stern, Shayla M. 2014. *From the Dance Hall to Facebook: Teen Girls, Mass Media, and Moral Panic in the United States, 1905-2010.* Boston: University of Massachusetts Press.

Tolman, Deborah. 1994. "Doing Desire: Adolescent Girls' Struggles for/with Sexuality." *Gender and Society* 8, no. 3: 324–42.

Vares, T., S. Jackson, and R. Gill. 2011. "Preteen Girls Read 'Tween' Popular Culture: Diversity, Complexity, and Contradiction." *International Journal of Media and Cultural Politics* 7, no. 2: 139–54.

West, Candace, and Don Zimmerman. 1987. "Doing Gender." *Gender and Society* 1, no. 2: 125–151.

Willis, Jessica L. 2008. "Sexual Subjectivity: A Semiotic Analysis of Girlhood, Sex and Sexuality in the Film *Juno*." *Sexuality and Culture* 12: 240–56.

YOUTUBE VIDEOS

az009601. 2014. "Be honest am I ugly or pretty update did I change." YouTube, November 11. *www.youtube.com/watch?v=ytCx7ESMXDw.*

Bailey Mae. 2013. "Am I Pretty Enough Yet?!" YouTube, January 2. *www.youtube.com/watch?v=WCoCRSStpUk.*

Beth White. 2012. "Am I pretty or ugly." YouTube, May 20. *www.youtube.com/watch?v=UpIoTNsQeZE.*

madepenn. 2012. "AM I PRETTY OR UGLY?" YouTube, January 23. *www.youtube.com/watch?v=Y6Yj2sFhMeY.*

Shannon McDonald. 2012. "Am I pretty or ugly? :)" YouTube, July 2. *www.youtube.com/watch?v=HOqL29j9JL4.*

yourjellyofmyswag. 2012. "are we pretty or ugly?" YouTube. December 30. *www.youtube.com/watch?v=nWTNHSblkVo.*

6

The Infidel in the Mirror

Mormon Women's Oppositional Embodiment

Kelly Grove and Doug Schrock

Embodying Mormonism

Each year thousands of Mormon women seek entrance into The Church of Jesus Christ of Latter-Day Saints (LDS) Temple. Although the Church does not publicize what happens inside of the Temple and the devout remain silent, in recent years some women— including the first author of this essay—have spoken publicly about it and key documents have been leaked (see, for example, The LDS Endowment, *www.ldsendowment. org*). The rituals center on making a series of sacred covenants, or promises imbued with holy meaning. In the Temple's Endowment Ordinance, women are first reminded that God made Eve from Adam's rib and gave Adam control over Eve and the Garden of Eden. Women are then instructed to bow their heads and dedicate their lives to the Church and promise to forever obey their righteous husbands. In the Temple's Sealing Ceremony, women *give* themselves to their husbands and husbands *receive* their wives. The rituals thus define Mormon women as subordinate to their husbands.

A key Temple ritual involves being clothed with the "holy garment"—a cap-sleeved undershirt and long undershorts resembling Spanx. Women learn the under-clothes represent all covenants made in the Temple (e.g., pledging oneself to God and husband). Women promise to wear the garment the rest of their lives, except when bathing, swimming, or having sex with their husbands. This garment is not to be seen in public and thus requires women to wear clothing that covers it. Bodily modesty is thus required of righteous LDS women. Although men must also wear similarly designed holy garments, it is important to point out that the underclothes represent promises made in the Temple, including the religious mandate of women's subservi-ence to men.

Because those who enter the Temple promise to God to keep the covenants secret, Mormon women—including participants in this study—who enter the Temple for the first time are often shocked to learn their religion requires them to commit to their own subordination. Although women preparing to enter the Temple in theory can now find out about such rituals on the internet, none in this study indicated they had, perhaps because it is strictly forbidden. Mormons are instructed never to talk about the rituals outside the Temple because they are too sacred. Many Mormon women look forward to entering the Temple their whole lives, and some feel betrayed when they discover that being granted religious prestige in the community and opening a pathway to the most desired afterlife depends on, essentially, handing over their bodily sovereignty. They often feel compelled to go along with the rituals because they are surrounded by friends, family, and religious leaders who are eager to bestow acceptance and praise. Many women say it was during these Temple rituals that they first felt they had lost control over their bodies.

Feminist sociologists use the term "patriarchy" to describe a social system that is male-dominated, male-centered, and male-identified (Johnson 2005). Because women are denied priesthood leadership positions in the LDS Church and are defined as subservient to their husbands, it is reasonable to say that male domination is woven into Mormon social relations. To say a culture is male-identified means that the key beliefs about what is desirable or normal reflects ideas about men and manhood. Because LDS women's subservience and modesty rests on the belief that males are natural leaders and struggle to control their sexual urges and behavior, male-identification seems to underlie their religious doctrine. To be male-centered means that a culture valorizes men and assumes men's experiences reflect everyone's. Founded by a male advocate of polygamy in the early 1800s, long before women had legal rights, it should not be controversial to say that the Church is male-centered. The Mormon Church is in many ways patriarchal, though the degree of patriarchy in the Church—or any institution—can fluctuate.

Like any culture, patriarchal culture is embodied. There are rules about how one should inhabit and control one's body, what one should put in it, and how one should decorate and talk about it. As Pharr (1997) points out, heterosexism is intertwined with patriarchy and is often a "weapon of sexism." The Mormon Church, for example, not only has rules about bodily modesty, it also states that only heterosexually married couples should have sex and no one should masturbate ("Chastity and Fidelity" 21.4.5). Mormon women are also not allowed to be sterilized, have an abortion (except in the case of rape or maternal endangerment), or be a surrogate ("Abortion" 21.4.1; "Surgical Sterilization" 21.4.15; "Surrogate Motherhood" 21.4.6). It is also forbidden to adopt a gender identity that does not correspond to one's biological sex ("Church Discipline and Name Removal" 6.7.2). Like many other religions (Barton 2012), the Mormon Church's embodiment culture thus not only subjugates women, but also differentiates men and women and is sexually repressive.

Mormon feminists have increasingly called into question the Church's patriarchal codes in publications, online forums, and public events (Beaman 2001; Brooks 2014; Hanks 1992; Peterfeso 2011). The group Ordain Women, for example, gained national attention for their large demonstrations demanding the priesthood be extended to women (Goodstein 2014). Although Mormon feminists are critical of and frustrated with the Church's gender politics, most continue to participate as believers and seek a difficult balance between autonomy and patriarchy (Beaman 2001; Ross 2014). Little is known, however, about how Mormon feminists engage in embodied resistance.

In this chapter, we analyze how women in two online forums express such resistance by sharing photographs of and reflections about themselves violating the Church's patriarchal embodiment codes. In addition to explaining how their photos defy Mormon doctrine, we investigate how the women critique the Church's embodiment rules as muting their "true selves" and contributing to their subordination. We also examine how these women valorize their opposition as fostering emotional liberation. We conclude by discussing how their methods of embodied resistance may in some ways limit and in other ways foment organized efforts to transform the Church into a more egalitarian institution.

Methods

We explored how women represent resistant embodiment by analyzing two online spaces feminists created to express opposition to the Mormon Church's embodied regulations. The Mormon Women Bare Project is a public website that displays nude photographs of twelve women engaged in various types of everyday activities.[1] Accompanying these photographs are each woman's reflections about their photos and, more generally, about their bodies and the Church. We also examined a Reclaiming Selfies thread on a Mormon feminist Facebook page, in which twenty-seven women shared photos demonstrating how they had "reclaimed" their bodies from the Mormon Church and posted commentary about what the photos meant to them. All of the women in our sample are white; this is not surprising given the LDS Church's history of racial discrimination (early Mormon Prophets argued Blacks were less righteous than whites and the Church banned Blacks from attending the Temple until the late 1970s [Shipps 2000]).

The first author of this essay, a former member of the LDS Church, learned about the online forums when she was exploring feminism for personal and educational reasons. She had been active in Mormon women's social movement groups and several Mormon feminist social media forums. Her engagement made her aware of the Mormon Women Bare project and the Mormon Feminist Facebook group, of which she became a member.

Both authors analyzed the photographs and accompanying text as embodied oppositions. Rather than examining the photos as individual or artistic expressions, we analyzed how they resonated with or contradicted the Church's embodiment rules. We conceptualized this process as "displaying embodied resistance." When we analyzed the participants' written reflections, we noticed two main themes: (1) how the Church's embodiment codes induce suffering and (2) how participants' resistance to the gendered rules felt liberating. We framed these themes as "problematizing embodied doctrine" and "valorizing embodied resistance." We argue that these public messages have the potential to emotionally motivate other Mormon women to resist the Church's embodiment culture.

Displaying Embodied Resistance

The participants of the Mormon Woman Bare project and the Reclaiming Selfies Facebook thread resist the Church's embodiment norms by sharing photographs of themselves breaking theocratic rules. These representations display opposition to the Church's guidelines and aim to empower others to do the same. In the opening words of the website: "Mormon Women Bare is about reclaiming. It is about women reclaiming our bodies from a culture that teaches us that we belong to men, to God, to the society that objectifies us. It is about reclaiming the female body as more than just

(1) Subverting Modesty.
Photograph by Jessica Jones

an object of lust. . . . These women show incredible bravery and vulnerability to share their stories through their words and their bodies" (Anderson 2013). Here we see how the director of the project suggests participation is resistant to the patriarchal culture of the Church and larger society. As we show, the women who participate in this project display this resistance by visually violating the Church's embodiment codes.

The Mormon Church's modesty doctrine emphasizes covering women's skin and curves so as not to evoke men's (hetero)sexual desires: "Revealing and sexually suggestive clothing, which includes short shorts and skirts, tight clothing and shirts that do not cover the stomach, can stimulate desires and actions that violate the Lord's law of chastity" ("Modesty" 2018). These rules are reinforced by the holy garment, which covers the shoulders, stomach, and thighs and must never be visible and thus always covered by clothing.

In the Reclaiming Selfies forum, most women posted "selfies" of themselves violating the Church's holy garment and modesty standards. By displaying their shoulders, thighs, and cleavage, women signify that they had removed the holy garment, broken their covenants of subservience, and reclaimed ownership of their bodies. Observant Mormons would consider these images highly inappropriate and sinful. The official modesty standards declare that women who disobey lose the presence of the Holy Spirit, meaning they have severed their connection to God and are not protected from the Devil's temptations ("Modesty" 2018).

In a picture similar to other posted selfies, the Mormon woman in Figure 1 flaunts modesty standards by wearing a shirt that shows her shoulders, cleavage, and bra. By dressing "immodestly," the women convey they do not feel it is their responsibility to dress in ways aimed at controlling men's alleged sexual natures, and by not

(2) Uncovering the Self.
Photograph by Katrina Barker
Anderson, Mormon Women Bare

wearing the holy garment, they imply they are no longer committed to patriarchal Temple covenants.

Mormon teachings often refer to women's bodies as the Temple of their spirits (Packer 2000). Prophets tell women to keep their bodies pure like the Temple, and women are not allowed to "pollute" their bodies with tattoos or multiple piercings, although one set of ear piercings is allowed ("Doctrine and Covenants" 89). Displaying tattoos and piercings, however, is common in the Reclaiming Selfies forum. The woman pictured in Figure 1, for example, reveals tattoos on both arms and thus signifies that she—not the Church—is in control of her body.

Church leaders take their modesty standards so seriously that they have altered great works of art presented in their publications (Stack 2012). The Church's magazine *The Ensign* added capped sleeves to the originally sleeveless angels portrayed in Carl Heinrich Bloch's famous nineteenth-century painting *The Resurrection* (1873). Women participating in the Mormon Women Bare project, however, took off more than their capped-sleeved undershirts. They expressed their resistance to Church standards by posing nude and sharing the pictures online.

By baring it all, these women—religiously speaking—risk it all. The Mormon Prophet Howard W. Hunter (1997) has stated that women who dress immodestly deserve disrespect. The Church's embodiment doctrine states it is women's responsibility to protect themselves and men's morality by covering themselves up (Seaward-Hiatt 2013).

The Mormon Women Bare webpage acknowledges that while "photographing a person turns their image into an 'object' . . . this project makes every attempt to hu-

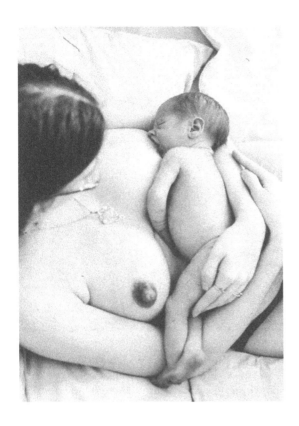

(3) Celebrating Reproduction. Photograph by Katrina Barker Anderson, Mormon Women Bare

manize the models rather than sexualize them" (Anderson 2013). The photographer did not pose the women sensually; instead, the women were photographed in environments they deemed meaningful. The unaltered photos prominently display stretch marks, cellulite, and rolls. As such, the women are not only resisting the Church's embodiment codes, but also saying to the world they are not ashamed, even if their bodies do not confirm to cultural beauty standards.

Pregnancy and fertility are noticeable themes in the images and words of women in the Reclaiming Selfies and the Mormon Women Bare project. Women displayed stretch marks, C-section scars, stretched out post-pregnancy stomachs, round pregnant bellies, and nursing breasts. Although motherhood is celebrated in the Mormon faith (*The Family: A Proclamation to the World* 1995), the fertile body is hidden. Women are discouraged from publicly breastfeeding and chapels have private nursing lounges. Women have even lost the ability to attend the Temple for publicly breastfeeding in church (Tumulty 2018). Many participants in the online forums displayed resistance to these body norms by publicly showing their fertile bodies.

The woman in Figure 3 displays her fertile body by cradling her newborn to her nursing breasts. By doing so, she celebrates the life her body gives and refuses to cover up or hide in a back room. These images not only reflect a reclaiming of the women's bodies but an embracing of motherhood.

LDS doctrine states: "Gender is an essential characteristic of individual pre-mortal, mortal, and eternal identity and purpose" (*The Family: A Proclamation to the World* 1995). Mormon dogma thus contradicts social science understandings of gender as

(4) Transgressing
Essentialism. Photograph
by Bobbie Angel

a malleable social construction; rather, Mormons define gender as being so fixed that it is determined before conception and continues on after death. There is no room in Mormon ideology for transgender people. In fact, official doctrine says if a Mormon chooses to identify as a gender that does not correspond to their birth sex, they are excommunicated. Upon excommunication they cannot hold official positions, pray in public, participate in ordinances, work with children, or join God in heaven.

Two transgender participants in the Reclaiming Selfies project display their resistance to these embodiment norms. Their pictures reflect traditional femininity: wearing makeup, jewelry, and tilting their heads in a demure pose (fig. 4). Although these images might appear to fit feminine cultural norms, it is a major resistance as the LDS Church refuses to recognize these women's gender. According to the LDS faith, these transwomen are men who are violating Church doctrine.

Problematizing Embodied Doctrine

The women's written reflections and posts in both Mormon Women Bare and the Mormon Feminist Facebook page often emphasize they felt coerced to embody subordination. They face an emotional double bind: if they do not conform they could be publicly shamed, yet conforming could evoke feelings of shameful subservience. Their narratives rhetorically use emotion to problematize the Church's embodiment doctrine.

About three-fourths of those posting on the Mormon Women Bare website wrote about feeling confined, restricted, and owned by the Church. One woman, Bridget, expressed this poetically, framing the male leadership of the Church as using moral language— "words from a pulpit / . . . / separating good from bad / virgin from whore"— and the holy garment—"building towering moral enclosures / held together with a wrapping of thin white cotton"—to coerce her to embody subordination—"sit / listen / obey / clench with guilt." Echoing other women in the Reclaiming Selfies forum, she suggested the Church's embodiment culture invoked guilt and shame, which led to "hiding the essence of my Self."

Participants in the Facebook forum often wrote about feeling a lack of self-ownership; as one simply put it, "My body wasn't my own before." Another emphasized her religion taught her that her body was "simply a gift for a matrimonial man, a means to bear and raise children for the delight of God [and] was only for serving, working, and nothing more." The women thus suggested that Mormon culture stole their bodily sovereignty and handed it over to the patriarch.

The women also suggested that the Church's embodiment culture caught them in heterosexual double binds that evoked self-hatred. Writing about her body, one expressed, "It spent years berating itself for being enticing, for being excited, for simply existing. It was supposed to be pretty but not too pretty." Another wrote, "I always disliked myself, especially my body, growing up in the LDS Church. It was like every day was wasted just hating myself. I hated it when I felt ugly and I hated it when I felt attractive. You have to be hot but not too hot to tempt the future priesthood holders." Mormon women are expected to present themselves as heterosexually desirable, yet not sexually tempting to young men. By emphasizing how the double binds gouged their self-worth, they critique the Church's gendered embodiment codes as psychologically damaging.

Some women in the online forums further problematize the Mormon's embodiment culture by stating Church members blamed them for men's unwanted attention and transgressions. One woman recalls struggling and being "very confused" about the Gospel because others viewed her physical body as indicating something about her sexual morality:

> [M]y apparent "sexuality," curvy figure, and robust bust line was a constant cause for discussion and concern. . . . If ever there was a sexual struggle between me and a boyfriend or I was looked at inappropriately, I always felt responsible in part because, as a woman, I was taught I had more control over my thoughts and expression of affection, but mostly because I was "blessed" with such a feminine body (by the time I was a freshman in high school, I was bordering on a DD with a tiny waist and wide hips). It's been engrained in my head that because of my features, I would never be seen as anything more than an object and I hated every physical aspect of myself.

Her narrative problematizes the embodied doctrine by suggesting believers unjustifiably judged her sexual morality and objectified her. The implication was that the Church's embodiment codes target women as a result of not only their sexual or fashion choices, but whether their physical bodies happened to align with secular beauty ideals. Here we can see how the patriarchal culture of the larger society reinforces the Church's patriarchy.

One woman posted about how a coach molested her when she was a child, how other Mormons blamed her for it, and how she in turn blamed herself. Her story implies Mormon patriarchal embodiment norms were used to justify the assault and caused long-term emotional suffering.

You slut, said my teammates when I told the police that our gymnastics coach was a pedophile. *She must have asked for it*, said my friends' parents. Our coach was one of the best we'd ever had, and at 9 years old, I harbored a private crush on him. But childish fancy turned to primal fear when he put his hand under my leotard. At that moment, a split occurred within me, born of an introduction into sexuality before I was ready and against my will. Shame followed me in the years before I spoke up. When no one but the police and my parents believed me, I figured my teammates were right. Puberty hit at about 13, and from that moment, I began an aggressive campaign to systematically destroy my sexuality.

Valorizing Embodied Resistance

In writing about their photographic resistance, most women do not emphasize targeting Church doctrine or patriarchal culture. Instead, they stress that their transgressive public self-representations restore control over their bodies, free their "true selves," and evoke feelings of authenticity and self-worth. Such valorizing thus draws heavily on a discourse of liberation psychotherapy, which defines freeing the "true-self" as liberatory (Rice 1996). In other words, they frame their oppositional embodiment as a self-improvement project.

One woman who posed for the Woman Bare project wrote what it was like to discard the holy garment and free herself from the Mormon Church's embodiment regulations. After standing in front of the mirror and watching herself "peel [her holy] garment off" for the last time, she put on some jeans and shirt and had a revelation: "Suddenly, she was me again. I was her. No longer unfamiliar with the infidel in the mirror, this girl without garments. . . . I lifted my t-shirt and saw a bellybutton and alabaster skin. They no longer belonged under a sheet or shroud. . . . This body belonged to me. I fell reflexively into rejoicing. God! I love this body." Another participant in the Mormon Bare project wrote: "This I now believe: my body is mine to worship, my body is mine to please. . . . My body is mine and no one else's, my body follows no rules. . . . My body is now completely free."

In these excerpts, the women describe the transformative experiences of reclaiming sovereignty over their bodies that "follow no rules." By publicizing their stories online, they publicly valorize bodily resistance as a means to emotional liberation. Mormon women harboring feelings of inauthenticity or a lack of agency may read these words and wonder if they, too, could feel better about themselves by rebelling against the Church's embodiment culture.

All participants in the Mormon Women Bare project suggest they felt a need to reclaim their bodies. They often write that their participation made them feel not only free but also appreciative of their bodies regardless of how much they conformed to the Church's or larger culture's standards. As one woman puts it, "I am no longer ashamed of my body." Another more elegantly writes, "All of the lessons, comments, and messages from my years as a Mormon woman have no place within this body. It's beautiful, it's powerful, and I refuse to feel ashamed of it anymore. . . . In that moment, I found my power, my sense of self, and I felt at one with my body, my struggles, my imperfections, and I accepted it all. This is who I am, and I love who I am." She describes how shaking off the theocratic embodiment doctrine enables her to appreciate her body as "beautiful" and "powerful" and to find her "sense of self." Her narrative reveals an emotional transformation that may lead readers to ask themselves if the emotional payoff might be worth the risks of oppositional embodiment.

Many of the women write about how resisting theocratic body norms enabled them to become more comfortable with their sexuality. One woman indicates that getting a tattoo "means that I can be confident and sexy and I am not responsible for what anyone else is thinking or feeling." As the woman who discussed surviving child sexual abuse puts it:

> I am not afraid to be naked anymore. I am not afraid to look like a woman, and I am not afraid to acknowledge the power that emanates from female sexuality. No wonder it is repressed; such a potent force threatens to change the world. I embrace the drive at the cost of my place within my religious community. I have disappointed my Savior. Right? *Slut.* This is what some people see. As for me, I can feel the split within me lessening, diminishing, whispering to me of a new life. I am not a slut. I am *whole.*

As these women feel more comfortable in their own skin, they begin to feel like powerful sexual agents who can decide what they want to do with their own bodies.

Feminist Movements in the LDS Church

Patriarchal culture is woven into the Mormon Church's embodiment doctrine. Its gendered and heterosexist embodiment codes usurp women's bodily sovereignty and reinforce their subordination. Both male leaders and male and female believers act as agents of social control in fostering women's conformity. The threat of excommunication and eternal damnation is enough to make many women think twice about resisting. But some Mormon women nonetheless resist.

Participants of the Mormon Women Bare project and the Reclaiming Selfies Facebook thread defy theocratic regulation of their bodies in three basic ways. First, they share images of themselves that directly counter rules surrounding modesty, body markings, and cisgender expectations. Second, they construct self-narratives that negatively frame the Mormon embodiment culture as fostering women's self-hatred, shame, abuse, and inauthenticity. Third, they valorize resistance by using secular self-help discourse to frame their opposition as a transformative emotional journey toward authenticity, empowerment, and pride.

Such defiance clearly resists patriarchal culture reflected in the Church's embodiment codes. Because they use online communities to accomplish oppositional embodiment, their work is somewhat akin to 1970s feminist consciousness raising groups in which members shared narratives linking their personal troubles to the patriarchal system (Kalcik 1975). Online participants can feel that they are not alone and can support each other in examining and reconstituting their embodied selves. Unlike 1970s groups, however, contemporary Mormon women can stumble upon and privately explore the online forums. If Mormon women reading these stories also feel stifled by the Church and desire to feel more authentic and worthy, they could be emotionally mobilized to participate (see, for example, Schrock, Holden, and Reid 2005).

Nevertheless, their methods of defying the Church's embodiment culture have limitations. Because their personal narratives draw so heavily on secular self-help culture emphasizing authentic "true selves," they risk depoliticizing resistance into a self-improvement project. Although their narratives critique the religious institution, they do not emphasize organizing to change Church doctrine. Instead, their stories emphasize liberating the self through embodied resistance. And if the end goal is limited to personal transformation, the male leadership of the Church might be let off the hook. The narratives could thus deflect energy away from efforts to transform Church policies and practices.

The online groups we examine, however, are a small sample of a larger feminist movement in the Mormon community. Many of the online participants are also part of Ordain Women, an international network of activists working diligently to pressure leadership to open the priesthood to women (Goodstein 2014). Other contributors express support for LDS Mama Dragons, which organizes parades, support groups, and advocates for LGBT inclusion (Stack 2015). Although they emphasize personal transformation when writing about embodiment, many also work to reform Church policies.

The Church's male leadership, however, has adamantly opposed reform efforts. After Ordain Women held a series of demonstrations and events, LDS leaders excommunicated the group's founder, human rights attorney Kate Kelly (Stack 2015). After Mormons increasingly supported sexual minorities and same-sex marriage was legalized in the United States, the leadership created a new policy that excommunicates all Mormons who marry someone of the same sex and declares that children of homosexual couples are not allowed to be baptized until they are eighteen years of age—if they disavow their parents' relationship. Excommunication means that one is no longer allowed to participate in the Church community and, according LDS theology, will never reach the highest level of heaven, which can also only happen if one is baptized.

Although we do not know if participants in the online forums have been disciplined for their embodied resistance, we do know it is common for Bishops to punish known violators. For example, small transgressions such as drinking coffee or wine might result in the Bishops barring members from taking the sacrament or praying in public. For larger "sins" that publicly defy the embodiment codes, such as wearing immodest clothing or sympathizing with resistant feminist groups, Bishops often remove the ability to attend Temple ceremonies and meetings. For violations viewed by Mormons as major "sins," such as sex outside of marriage or identifying outside of one's birth-assigned gender, the punishment is often excommunication. All of these punishments are socially stigmatizing and can negatively affect interpersonal relationships.

As Mormon women increasingly engage feminism and witness intransigent male leaders ignoring and sanctioning reform efforts, many become disillusioned and leave the Church. Leaving was initially a personal response, but it has developed into a social movement tactic. Many participants on feminist Mormon social media websites joined a 2015 mass resignation event to protest the new anti-LGBT policies. According to Mark Naugle (2016, pers. comm.), an attorney processing resignation paperwork, over 9,500 members have resigned their Church membership as part of this ongoing campaign. Because rules surrounding sexuality are essentially body regulations, the mass resignations constitute resistance to the Church's heterosexist embodiment culture.

While we have focused here on white Mormon women using online forums to express oppositional embodiment, they are not the only women engaging in such work.

Recently, a Facebook page was created in which 150 Iranian women posted pictures of themselves without their hijab, or headscarf (*www.facebook.com/StealthyFreedom*). Additionally, several Facebook groups such as "Natural Hair Rules!" have become popular places for Black women to post pictures of themselves wearing "natural" or "Afro" hairstyles as a way of resisting white-centric beauty ideals (*www.facebook.com/natural hairrules*). While such expressions are similar in that they resist embodiment norms, they likely carry different consequences. Resistant Mormon women may face severe social consequences (e.g., shunning by their family and Church), but many chose to leave the religion and relocate—enabling them to blend in with the dominant white American culture. Iranian women may face not only social consequences but severe legal penalties, and it may be difficult for them to relocate to more inclusive locales. Although Black women may not face severe social or legal consequences for wearing their hair "natural," they may face employment discrimination and find it impossible to escape white supremacy and its interrelated classist and sexist controlling images (Collins 2000).

While the body is often seen as personal, our chapter sheds light on how it is intertwined with institutions, culture, and relationships. Institutions may create policies for how one can inhabit, use, and adorn one's body, as well as what kinds of bodies are acceptable to love. Cultural beliefs can support these policies and provide moral incentive for conforming to body norms. The people that surround us often provide emotional incentives for conformity via pride-evoking affirmations and police deviant embodiment with shame-evoking sanctions. But as Mormon feminists have shown, non-conformity can be more than a fashion statement. Embodied resistance can challenge institutional authority, oppose patriarchy, and mobilize collaborative efforts to fight oppression.

NOTE

1. At the time of this research, the Mormon Women Bare Project's URL was *www .mormonwomenbare.com*. That URL has recently been taken over by an LDS missionary website, also called Mormon Women Bare. Additionally, at the time of this writing, the development website *mormonwomenbare.wordpress.com* is being taken over by the same LDS missionary website, one page at a time, though it still has some original pages remaining. The new website emphasizes LDS missionaries "baring" their faith.

REFERENCES

"Abortion." 2010. *LDS Church Handbook on Instructions II* (21.4.1).

Anderson, Katrina Barker. 2013. "Welcome." Mormon Women Bare, Nov. 5. *www .mormonwomenbare.wordpress.com*.

Barton, Bernadette. 2012. *Pray the Gay Away: The Extraordinary Lives of Bible Belt Gays*. New York: NYU Press.

Beaman, Lori G. 2001. "Molly Mormons, Mormon Feminists and Moderates: Religious Diversity and the Latter Day Saints Church." *Sociology of Religion* 62, no. 1: 65–86.

Brooks, J. 2014. "Mormon Feminism: The Next Forty Years." *Dialogue: A Journal of Mormon Thought* 47, no. 4: 1–18.

"Chastity and Fidelity." 2010. *LDS Handbook of Instructions II* (21.4.5).

"Church Discipline and Name Removal." 2010. *LDS Handbook of Instructions I: Stake Presidents and Bishops* (6.7.2).

Collins, Patricia Hill. 2000. *Black Feminist Thought: Knowledge, Consciousness, and the Politics of Empowerment.* New York: Routledge.

"Doctrine and Covenants" 89. *Book of Mormon.*

The Family: A Proclamation to the World. 1995. Church of Jesus Christ of Latter Day Saints. *www.lds.org/topics/family-proclamation.*

Goodstein, L. 2014. "Mormons Expel Founder of Group Seeking Priesthood for Women." *New York Times,* June 23, 2014. *www.nytimes.com/2014/06/24/us/Kate-Kelly-Mormon -Church-Excommunicates-Ordain-Women-Founder.html.*

Hanks, M. 1992. *Women and Authority: Re-emerging Mormon Feminism.* Salt Lake City, UT: Signature Books.

Hunter, Howard W. 1997. *Teachings of Howard W. Hunter.* Salt Lake City, UT: Deseret Book Company.

Johnson, A. G. 2005. *The Gender Knot: Unraveling Our Patriarchal Legacy.* Philadelphia: Temple University Press.

Kalčik, S. 1975. "'. . . like Ann's gynecologist or the time I was almost raped': Personal Narratives in Women's Rap Groups." *Journal of American Folklore* 88, no. 347: 3–11.

"Modesty." 2018. Church of Jesus Christ of Latter Day Saints. *www.lds.org/topics/modesty.*

Packer, B. K. 2000. "Ye Are The Temple of God." Church of Latter Day Saints, October. *www.lds.org/general-conference/2000/10/ye-are-the-temple-of-god.*

Peterfeso, J. 2011. "From Testimony to Seximony, from Script to Scripture: Revealing Mormon Women's Sexuality through the *Mormon Vagina Monologues.*" *Journal of Feminist Studies in Religion* 27, no. 2: 31–49.

Pharr, S. 1997. *Homophobia: A Weapon of Sexism.* Berkeley, CA: Chardon Press.

Rice, J. S. 1996. *A Disease of One's Own: Psychotherapy, Addiction, and the Emergence of Co- Dependency.* New Brunswick, NJ: Transaction.

Ross, J. F. 2014. "Mormon Feminist Perspectives on the Mormon Digital Awakening: A Study of Identity and Personal Narratives." *Dialogue: A Journal of Mormon Thought* 47, no. 4: 47–75.

Seaward-Hiatt, Erin. 2013. "Dirty Girl." In *Beyond Belief: The Secret Lives of Women in Extreme Religions,* edited by Susan Tive and Cami Ostman, 230–44. Berkeley, CA: Seal Press.

Schrock, Douglas, Daphne Holden, and Lori Reid. 2004. "Creating Emotional Resonance: Interpersonal Emotion Work and Motivational Framing in a Transgender Community." *Social Problems* 51, no. 1: 61–81.

Shipps, Jan. 2000. *Sojourner in the Promised Land: Forty Years among the Mormons.* Urbana: University of Illinois Press.

Stack, Peggy Fletcher. 2015. "Mama Dragons Lead the Fight for Their Gay Mormon Kids." *Salt Lake Tribune,* May 4. *archive.sltrib.com/article.php?id=2438383&itype=CMSID.*

———. 2012. "Mormons Alter Bloch's Angels so They're Wingless and Not Sleeveless." *Salt Lake Tribune,* May 18. *archive.sltrib.com/article.php?id=54142351&itype=cmsid.*

———. 2015. "Where Mormon Feminists Stand a Year after Kate Kelly's Excommunication." *Huffington Post,* June 27. *www.huffingtonpost.com/2015/06/27/mormon-feminists -excommunication_n_7647696.html.*

"Surgical Sterilization." 2010. *LDS Handbook of Instructions II* (21.4.15).

"Surrogate Motherhood." 2010. *LDS Handbook of Instructions II* (21.4.16).

Tumulty, Bronah. 2018 "LDS Mom Says She Lost Temple Recommend for Breastfeeding at Church." KUTV News, July 26. *kutv.com/news/local/ lds-mom-says-she-lost-temple-recommend-for-breastfeeding-at-church.*

LIVING RESISTANCE

A Cystor's Story

Polycystic Ovarian Syndrome and the Disruption of Normative Femininity

Ledah McKellar

For the first time since childhood, I put brush to canvas. It was 2014, and I was twenty-seven. To my surprise, the act of painting unleashed an energy that had accumulated through my experience of living with polycystic ovarian syndrome. The canvas offered a vehicle for the release of that energy and enabled me to find my voice.

I was diagnosed with polycystic ovarian syndrome (otherwise known as PCOS) as a teenager. PCOS is the most common endocrine disorder among female-bodied people, with estimates ranging between 5 to 20 percent of females affected.[1] The criteria for diagnosing PCOS are under continuous debate; there is no real consensus. Previously, a 2003 consensus workshop suggested that women must have two out of three of the following symptoms: polycystic ovaries, chronic anovulation, or hyperandrogenism (which, in a notably gendered way, is sometimes referred to as excess male hormones).[2] However, in 2012, a National Institutes of Health (NIH)–sponsored workshop panel suggested that the term "polycystic" be dropped from the name because it misleads the general public into thinking that polycystic ovaries are a necessary symptom.[3] Some health care professionals are now leading the way in changing the name from PCOS to metabolic reproductive syndrome. The NIH has argued in the past that chronic anovulation with clinical and/or biochemical hyperandrogenism should be the only criteria needed to diagnose PCOS in order to address the problem of over-diagnosis and mis-diagnosis.[4] However, there is still no consensus on how PCOS should be diagnosed, and some research suggests the diagnostic criteria remain inclusive of a broader spectrum of symptoms. It is possible that PCOS currently represents a variety of similar, but separate, disorders.

There are many sub-symptoms associated with PCOS, including but not limited to irregular menstruation or complete lack of menstrual periods, irregular ovulation or no ovulation at all, facial or body hair growth, hair loss, acne, weight gain, difficulty losing weight, depression, and mood changes.[5] Because PCOS diagnostic criteria is classified so broadly, a woman can have a couple of these symptoms, or all of them.[6] For this reason, individual experiences of PCOS can vary greatly.

In painting, I wanted to explore how I felt the symptoms of PCOS disrupted traditional normative femininity. I also wanted to explore how the medicalization of PCOS reinforces gender norms and stigmas.[7] For example, symptoms of PCOS like hair growth on the body and face, hair loss on the scalp, and weight gain, as well as

The author's painting. Photograph by Ledah McKellar

reduced fertility, directly conflict with culturally enforced notions of femininity, some-times to the point of causing some women to question their very identity as women.[8]

When I was seventeen, my doctor told me I could go on medication if I encoun-tered "excessive" hair growth. To me, the message from my doctor was clear: body and facial hair does not belong on women's bodies. I was afraid I would somehow become "manly." I did not understand why I should take medication for something as in-nocuous as hair. But I came to realize that while the hair *itself* might be harmless, the stigma associated with hair on a woman's body and face is *not*.

At the same time, I recognize that, until those stigmas are removed, medication for unwanted hair growth can significantly enhance a woman's quality of life. I under-stand that in rejecting the idea of medication for hair growth, I myself was denounc-ing a woman's personal choice to deal with the stigma of hair growth. This tension presents an untenable dilemma for those of us with PCOS. On the one hand, we desire to be what some may call feminist and body positive, accepting ourselves the way we are. But on the other hand, we also desire to be happy and accepted by others. We should not have to sacrifice our quality of life for what we may see as a greater feminist cause. We can't win, it seems. We may feel that we are either disappointing ourselves or others. In many ways, the painting allowed me to express these and other feelings that at the time I was afraid to express in words. It enabled me to resist hiding parts of myself and my body and my interior struggle.

My painting was hung in a university hallway art gallery. Within a couple of days, it generated some controversy. Several people felt it was a potential workplace hazard because, they asserted, some of its imagery may offend or agitate employees in the workplace and, indeed, some who viewed it did report a range of negative reactions to the painting including "shocked," "repulsed," "disgusted," "surprised," "uncomfort-able," "in-your-face," "frustrated," and "inappropriate." Some noted they were upset by the depiction of body hair and genitalia. To be fair, there are many complex reasons for these reactions and a large number of people who saw the painting offered positive feedback. Nonetheless, reactions to the painting revealed the cultural discomfort associated with bodies, and especially women's bodies, that fall far outside the confines of what is considered "normal." To be honest, I am implicated here. In spite of my deep reflections about these issues, I still feel shame about this painting. When it was hung, I avoided walking by it.

Following some debate about censorship, the painting was allowed to remain in the hall. Its presence became a way to put PCOS in the spotlight. But I recognize that while the painting was an outlet for my rebellion against normative femininity and social constructions of beauty, I understand that not all women with PCOS want the syndrome publicly aired. But some, like me, do want to feel seen and heard. As one woman put it, "[the painting] made my issues and concerns seem recognized and legitimized. So often PCOS is hidden away and inappropriate to talk about in social environments. I felt comfort in seeing this image in public, hanging on the wall. I felt less alone."

NOTES

1. Wendy A. March, Vivienne M. Moore, Kristyn J. Willson, David I. W. Phillips, Robert J. Norman, and Michael J. Davies, "The Prevalence of Polycystic Ovary Syndrome in a Community Sample Assessed under Contrasting Diagnostic Criteria." *Human Reproduction* 25, no. 2 (2010): 544–51.

2. Rotterdam ESHRE/ASRM–Sponsored PCOS Consensus Workshop Group, "Revised 2003 Consensus on Diagnostic Criteria and Long-Term Health Risks Related to Polycystic Ovary Syndrome." *Fertility and Sterility* 81, no. 1 (2004): 19–25.

3. *Evidence-based Methodology Workshop on Polycystic Ovary Syndrome December 3–5, 2012.* National Institutes of Health, 2012. *prevention.nih.gov/docs/programs/pcos/FinalReport.pdf.*

4. Ibid.

5. Ibid.

6. A group of signs and symptoms, when associated together, form a syndrome. In other words, a syndrome has more than one identifying feature or symptom. Unlike a disease, the underlying causation (or etiology) is not known.

7. Medicalization refers to the massive transformation in the last century of Western society to define life experiences in terms of health and illness. Increased medicalization is problematic because it blurs the line between "normal" and "disorder." This not only means that people are increasingly becoming consumers of a market culture focused on health and self-medicalizing in their daily lives, but the transformation of everyday life into pathologies is increasing the range of what is considered deviant or abnormal.

8. For my MEd thesis I conducted a research study on the self-perception, education, and medicalization of women living with PCOS. The voices of women living with PCOS in this narrative derive from these research findings. See Ledah McKellar, "Unveiling the 'Hidden Epidemic' with Stories of the Cystorhood: Exploring Women's Experiences with Polycystic Ovarian Syndrome." Master's thesis, Lakehead University, 2015.

Old Bags Take a Stand

A Face Off with Ageism in America

Faith Baum and Lori Petchers

It started with a conversation. We were two middle-aged female artists dealing with aging in a society that fetishes youthful beauty. There were so many questions. Have we become invisible? Are we devalued because we can't have children anymore? Are we hostages in our own bodies? Are we captives in an "anti-aging" culture we have bought into, both literally and figuratively? What is our place in society now that we are not young?

We wanted to know what other women thought so we reached out, interviewing friends, acquaintances, and strangers from all over the country. We discovered that many felt they were becoming irrelevant in a youth-fixated society at the exact time in their lives when they had achieved a true sense of who they were and what they wanted out of life. We believed this contradiction required a public discourse around the stereotypes of female aging that is more complex than the typical beauty issues often discussed. We wanted to creatively address this, and our *Old Bags Project* collaboration began. Our intention was to use conceptual art to confront conventional values and social concerns.

Our artistic decision was to turn the insult "old bag" on its head and create a visual idea that represented how many middle-aged women feel. Using both older women and old shopping bags, the OLD BAG, a post-menopausal woman in undergarments with a bag over her head, emerged. The feeling of being hostage to an ageist ethos was the genesis of this image. We chose to provoke awareness by mimicking a common media ploy that objectifies women by obscuring their faces. The bag over the head, an iconic representation of captivity, forces the viewer to look directly at the woman's aging body. Despite the tremendous amount of visual information in our society, middle-aged female bodies are rarely seen except in advertisements about lifting, incising, creaming, and hiding. The bag hides the face, rendering the woman invisible—nameless, faceless. The logos on the bags have identity, but the women do not. Standing in underwear, trying on shopping bags, the women in the photos beg the viewer to contemplate: Are we captive in an ageist society, only visible as potential consumers? Or are we unknowing collaborators, allowing ourselves to be invisible, by buying into the "anti-aging" culture?

Our project grew organically. First, friends were solicited as models and then, after each exhibition, other women, excited by what they saw and heard, jumped on board and joined in the next photo shoot. Women from diverse backgrounds stripped down to their underwear and posed in front of the camera with shopping bags over

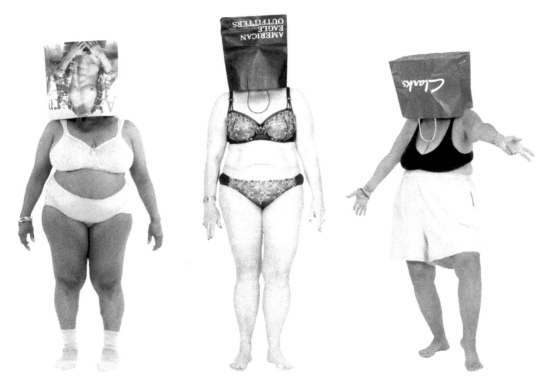

Some Old Bags taking a stand. Photograph by Liz Harvey for Old Bags Project

their heads, comfortably revealing their waist lines, hips, C-section scars, cellulite, appendectomy scars, blemishes, and whatever else life has dealt them. In the shoots, women were free to bring their own bags or choose one from the vast collection we procured by going store to store at suburban shopping malls. The women often gave careful consideration when picking bags. Everyone seemed to take much pleasure in choosing a bag. Sometimes it was because it was a favorite shop. Sometimes it was because it was the chance to identify with a luxury brand. Often it was to make a statement. Forever 21 was a favorite, as was Abercrombie with the half-naked male torso. One woman had read about the project in a local paper and strolled into a photo shoot carrying a bag that wasn't from a clothing store. It was a green STOP & SHOP bag. She had been working there as a checkout clerk for many, many years. Perhaps she brought that bag because she felt invisible both as a woman and as an employee. She posed with that bag and between the shots she danced around, having a grand time. Afterward she spoke about how freeing the experience was. She felt the bag provided her with a moment of respite from a daily onslaught of disrespect. The images of her are among our favorites.

The spontaneous chatter during a photo shoot or exhibition was also always astounding. It reinforced what we discovered through our interviews. And it was during those moments, listening to the conversations between women who refuse to be marginalized because of their age, that we understood how deeply this project resonated. Many women came in pairs, with a friend to give them courage to shed their inhibitions. The shoots gave some women a place to talk and reveal personal stories. One woman came with a journal entry about new beginnings that she had written as she was turning sixty. Another shared her story of finally overcoming abuse in midlife. Women bemoaned their aging bodies only to be pleasantly surprised by the beauty of their photos in the camera viewer playback. We always wondered if they were able to see their bodies objectively when their identity was not visible.

However, *Old Bags Project* is not a soap commercial about how everyone is beautiful, even older women. It is a statement about refusing to allow a youth-loving, commercialized, media-ridden culture to have the last word about who a woman becomes and her place in American society.

Working on *Old Bags Project* has been an enlightening experience. We have grown as artists and as individuals. We have come to a better understanding of our own responsibility as aging women, aware if we place too much value on the importance of youthful beauty, we are allowing ourselves to be marginalized.

Old Bags images have been in galleries and museums, even projected on buildings and storefronts. We published a book and have a social media presence reaching a global community. What started as a personal artistic statement has surprised us by the nature of its impact. Over time, hundreds of middle-aged women have proudly joined the *Old Bags Project*. Nameless and faceless, they are members of the baby-boom generation, like us, who are growing older and are boldly confronting the reality that old has become an insult in America.

Making Up with My Body

Applying Cosmetics to Resist Disembodiment

Haley Gentile

We sat on the back porch talking as the beginnings of a party stirred inside the house behind us. He prodded my skirt hem with his fingers to inquire about the goddess Athena tattooed on my upper thigh and expressed, "that's really sexy." As our relationship progressed I often revisited his words from that first night. The phrase "that's really sexy" penetrated my core and reverberated in my bones.

I heard its echoes when he suggested, in a period of mutually agreed upon non-exclusivity, that I did not love him unless I had painful, sore sex with him after having earlier had intercourse with someone else (which resulted in an excruciating kidney infection). I heard its echoes every time he forced me to participate in group sex with his other women partners. I heard its echoes when he instigated fights about sex acts I did not want to perform. I heard its echoes when, over time, he increasingly yelled at me for how infrequently we had sex. I heard its echoes when he convinced me to "allow" him to start sexual activity when I was asleep, and again when I tearfully rescinded my permission. I heard nothing but its echoes when I woke up to my pajamas askew and him raping me.

As a result of the sexual violence my partner subjected me to, I developed post-traumatic stress disorder (PTSD). My PTSD manifests as anxiety attacks, intrusive flashbacks, and, most frequently, disassociation. Episodes of disassociation can be understood as experiences of disembodiment. During disassociation I felt—and sometimes still feel—uncontrollably detached, as if my mind is floating away, untethered from my body. To combat disassociation, therapists suggest developing a grounding technique that requires attending to physical sensations, such as pinching one's arm. In order for this technique to be effective, my counselor told me it should be an action I can train myself to do the moment I feel a disconnect.

As I struggled to identify a grounding technique that aligned with my pre-existing routines, I eventually turned to cosmetics. Applying makeup, since puberty, has felt like a sacrament. In front of a mirror, under the halogen glow, there is a solitary stillness; this self-communion conferred grace. I thought of these sessions as independent explorations of my body. In the wake of my assault, given my attachment to makeup as a comforting form of self-expression, I thought applying makeup, which necessitated touching and engaging with my physical presence, might help. However, I found this coping mechanism newly constricted; how could makeup lessen my emotional distress when it felt like, at least partially, the origin of the problem? Could

The author using makeup as resistance. Photograph by Haley Gentile

cosmetics and careful self-presentation be the means to some end other than objectification and sexiness?

After some failed experimentation, I came to understand that I could not apply makeup in the same way I had in the past if it was to be a fruitful tool for fighting disassociation. To act as armor against my pain, my makeup application could not be domesticated. If I understood makeup before my rape as an effort to extend my natural beauty, now I needed to reject the "sexy" and repurpose my arsenal to manufacture ugliness.

Felt-tip-assisted winged eyeliner became increasingly complex and extravagant. I slathered black lipstick whose greasy constitution could not be confined by the feeble efforts of a liner so its slickness steeped onto the rest of my face. Other times I lined the outer boundaries of my lips in thick gold and left the rest of my face bare. Loose glitter and glue caked my eyebrows. I followed the curve of my cheekbones with green eye shadow reimagined as blush, aligning my appearance with how nauseous I felt. If achieving a contouring trend requires finesse, instead I went for brute force. I applied a glitzy body shimmer until my skin resembled the smooth metallic sheen of a robot; androids lack flesh. This was the effect I sought; my flesh felt like the locus of my suffering. Other times I smothered every inch, lips and all, with foundation so that each of my features was indistinguishable from the rest of my face. Red lipstick smeared along my bottom lashes externally realized my feeling that my eyes were bleeding from the months of incessant crying. Each stroke of the brush or swipe of gloss reminded me, "I am here. It is safe to be here."

Of course, my choice of makeup could not have saved me from my partner's harms. My choices are independent from his choice to abuse me. However, my novel approach aided me in my battle against the sensation of disembodiment and represented a transformation in my understanding of the audience of my gendered presentation. Cosmetics were no longer intended to help me look conventionally attractive; instead they became a form of expressing my resistance against my PTSD symptoms and the rape that caused them. Applying makeup to be grotesque, rather than beautiful, freed me from the concept of "sexy" that coerced and punished me, while it simultaneously forced me to acknowledge my physical presence in line with therapist-recommended grounding techniques. Through outrageous, zealous application of wild pigments I found a new way to relate to myself. The act of putting on cosmetics in this way yielded enough distance from "sexiness" that I could sometimes close the gap between my mind and body.

I Am a Person Now

Autism, Indistinguishability, and (Non)optimal Outcome

Alyssa Hillary

> You see, you start pretty much from scratch when you work with an Autistic child. You have a person in the physical sense—they have hair, a nose, and a mouth—but they are not people in the psychological sense. One way to look at the job of helping autistic kids is to see it as a matter of constructing a person. You have the raw materials, but you have to build the person.
>
> —Ivar Lovaas (1974), widely considered one of the first autism experts[1]

On December 12, 2015, I conspicuously and defiantly threw myself into a wall at a meeting of the American Academy of Arts and Sciences, with enough force that the vibrations could be felt at the podium.[2]

Thud.

While the conference was meant to question societal assumptions about autism and discuss the idea of "unique developmental trajectories" in autism, many presenters didn't (couldn't? wouldn't?) consider that a different trajectory would *lead somewhere different in adulthood.* The optimal outcome of equating "less autistic" with "better" and "more human" was taken as a given. That's the history (and present) I resist.

So there I was, an Autistic graduate student, math teacher, published author, and artist, fluent in two languages.[3] These "experts" were defining autistic people's optimal outcome, our best-case scenario, as losing the label I fought not to lose, but to claim. They did so without input from those whose best-case scenarios they defined. What else could I do? I stood up, found a flat bit of wall near the back of the auditorium, and began to throw myself into it.

Thud.

I am here.

Thud.

I am your best-case scenario in every way but one.

Thud.

I am Autistic and proud.

Thud.

Your ideals are not mine.

Thud.

I do not pretend to meet the goal you enforce upon us.

Thud.

I am a person *now*.

Thud.

And yes, I must remind you that I am a person *now*.

This is our history. Ivar Lovaas introduced Applied Behavioral Analysis (ABA) with the goal of making the children he worked with "indistinguishable from their peers," claiming a success rate of 47 percent.[4] He defined this as placement in typical classes and continued promotion through the next grades with their same-aged peers.[5] Today, ABA is considered the "gold standard" for autism treatment.

What therapists today don't like to talk about and are rarely taught anyways (besides the part where hitting and electric shock *totally are* part of the 47 percent successful ABA practice they so heavily cite), is that Lovaas pioneered these same methods on young boys considered to be "at risk" for being gay or transgender.[6] One of those "treated" was a young boy, Kirk Andrew Murphy, or Kraig, who, decades later, died by suicide. His mother believes the experimental therapy destroyed his life.[7] Autistic people are more likely to be suicidal than those without autism, even as children and teens,[8] making Kraig's story particularly chilling.

And what does all this have to do with me? I wasn't diagnosed young enough to be subjected to ABA. My interests in historically masculine fields like mathematics and engineering were accepted, not subject to behavior modification. I joined tenor bass choir with the boys when I was lucky enough to be a tenor rather than an alto or soprano. I even got away with asking, "For the purpose of this ensemble, what gender will I be at 7: 30 pm tomorrow?" and wearing the men's uniform for the next choral concert without comment or suspicion. (I am nonbinary, gendervague. They didn't know.)

Autism guides, typically addressed to parents and professionals, however, discuss gender and gender roles uncritically—it's generally assumed that autistic people lack the social awareness to *choose* to break gender roles or to be transgender. Two such guides, *Asperger's and Girls* and *Growing Up on the Spectrum*, tell parents they must make their daughters shave their underarms and legs, because our (American) society deems body hair on women unacceptable. An Autistic butch lesbian points out that the guides assume both that girls who don't shave fail to do so because of their autism, not because of any other aspects of their identities, and that choosing not to shave for disability-related reasons is unacceptable.[9]

I don't shave my armpits or my legs. I leave my (minimal, but extant) facial hair alone. I am asked when I plan to "start," to "do something about that." I laugh. I shaved my armpits for the last swim meet of the season, my senior year of high school. I was bad at it and disinclined to continue. Even the practical concern of swimming faster in a race could not induce me to shave my legs. I am not a woman, and I am bad at shaving.

We are told that children with autism cannot begin to learn until they (we) are "table ready." That is, these children must make eye contact and not flap or rock or fidget if they (we) are to be allowed in mainstream classes (be considered indistinguishable from our peers) and learn academic topics. I flap and rock and fidget as I write my final exam for a graduate mathematics course. I don't know what color my professor's eyes are.

We are expected to speak orally. Some professionals won't even teach other methods of communication or only consider them to be last resorts, because they might reduce the incentive to speak.[10] I can speak, sometimes. I have fluency and inconsistent speech in two languages. Rather than hide my missing speech under proper silence, I sit within reach of a whiteboard and carry a marker. I write.

Thud.

I am Autistic.

Thud.

I am nonbinary, gendervague.

Thud.

I am told my optimal outcome is to feign normalcy, forever.

Thud.

That lie is our history.

Thud.

The personal is political.

Thud.

Normal is not the best thing we can be.

Thud.

I am a person *now*.

Thud.

On December 12, 2015, I conspicuously and defiantly threw myself into a wall at the American Academy of Arts and Sciences, with enough force that the vibrations could be felt at the podium.

NOTES

1. Paul Chance, "A Conversation with Ivar Lovaas," *Psychology Today*, January 1974, 76–80, 82–84. Ivar Lovaas pioneered the use of Applied Behavioral Analysis (ABA) to "treat" autism. His studies are still cited as evidence that ABA "works," and he is widely considered one of the first autism experts. Today, many face barriers to therapies *other* than ABA. It is the only intervention insurance companies are specifically required to cover in some states, and people face coverage denials based on a service being provided by someone other than an ABA practitioner. It is frightful that someone who thought we weren't even people defined how we should be "helped" to appear more normal, and that he thought creating this appearance of normalcy was how you "build the person."

    Insurance coverage information is from: "Health Insurance and Medicaid Coverage for Autism Services: A Guide for Individuals and Families," Autistic Self Advocacy Network, last modified July 2015, *autisticadvocacy.org/wp-content/uploads/2015/07/Health-Insurance-and-Medicaid-Coverage-for-Autism-Services-A-Guide-for-Individuals-and-Families-7-9-15.pdf*; "Private Health Coverage for Autism Services: A Guide for Individuals and Families." Autistic Self Advocacy Network, last modified November 2016, *autisticadvocacy.org/wp-content/uploads/2016/11/Private-Health-Coverage-for-Autism-Services-A-Guide-for-Individuals-and-Families-1.pdf*; "Autism and Insurance Coverage: State Laws." National Conference of State Legislatures, last modified June 7, 2017, *www.ncsl.org/research/health/autism-and-insurance-coverage-state-laws.aspx*.

2. The American Academy of Arts and Sciences is one of the oldest learned societies in the United States.

3. Outside quotations, I capitalize Autistic when it is used as an identity in addition to a specific diagnosis. I leave it lowercase when it is used primarily as a diagnosis. This method of distinguishing community, culture, and identity from medical diagnosis alone is common in Autistic communities. Inside quotations, I use the original capitalization.

4. O. Ivar Lovaas, "Behavioral Treatment and Normal Educational and Intellectual Functioning in Young Autistic Children," *Journal of Consulting and Clinical Psychology* 55, no. 1 (1987): 3, 7.

5. Lovaas, "Behavioral treatment," 8.

6. George A. Rekers and O. Ivar Lovaas, "Behavioral Treatment of Deviant Sex-Role Behaviors in a Male Child," *Journal of Applied Behavior Analysis* 7, no. 2 (1974): 173–90.

7. Scott Bronstein and Jessi Joseph, "Therapy to Change 'Feminine' Boy Created a Troubled Man, Family Says," *CNN*, June 7, 2011, *www.cnn.com/2011/US/06/07/sissy.boy .experiment/index.html*.

8. Susan Dickerson Mayes, Angela A. Gorman, Jolene Hillwig-Garcia, and Ehsan Syed, "Suicide Ideation and Attempts in Children with Autism," *Research in Autism Spectrum Disorders* 7, no. 1 (2013): 109–19.

9. Caroline Narby, "Double Rainbow: Parent Guides, Part 1," *Bitch Media,* February 17, 2012, *www.bitchmedia.org/post/double-rainbow-parent-guides-part-1-feminism*.

10. MaryAnn Romski and Rose A. Sevcik, "Augmentative Communication and Early Intervention: Myths and Realities," *Infants & Young Children* 18, no. 3 (2005): 178–79.

PART III

Creating Community, Disrupting Assumptions

7

Yelling and Pushing on the Bus

The Complexity of Black Girls' Resistance

Stephanie D. Sears and Maxine Leeds Craig

It's 3: 30 pm on a Thursday afternoon, and a crowded bus full of noisy middle school students makes it way up Fillmore Street in San Francisco. Two voices rise above the din. A Black boy taunts a girl by calling her "Peaches," saying Peaches is her "stripper name." The girl, a tall and boisterous Black girl named Kayla yells "I'm not a stripper!"[1] The boy replies, "You should've been!"

Kayla moves to the back of the bus, which is filled with Black and Latinx youth.[2] Several of the youth are engaged in a play fight and she joins in the action. A white woman, who appears to be in her thirties, gets caught in the middle of the youth's play and suddenly yells, "Stop it! Stop it! You hit me!" She targets Kayla for hitting her. Kayla, matching her intensity, responds, "Don't get in my face!" The conflict stops briefly, but the kids become excited again and one of them bumps into the woman. She shouts at them, "If you want to be on this bus, you'll stop it!" Kayla announces to the rest of the kids, "This old ass woman talking to me like she my mama!" After an unsuccessful attempt to get the bus driver's attention, the woman turns to Kayla saying, "You do NOT act like this on the bus!" Without missing a beat, Kayla replies, "Get off the bus then!" The youth continue to push each other and they sideswipe a twenty-year-old white female college student, who was a part of our research team. Two boys instantly apologize to her, and she says, "it's okay." Kayla also chimes in, "I'm sorry to YOU, though." The thirty-year-old white woman barks, "Would you act like this if your mom was here?" An African American girl who had been watching the events unfold responds, "Yes! You're on the bus with hella ratchet kids. You're a grown ass lady fighting with kids!"

This is a study of Black middle- and high-school girls' attempts to claim space on public buses. Our focus in this chapter is Kayla and girls like her, and the relationship between public transit, intersecting identities, and girls' behavior on the bus. Consider the rapidly shifting stances Kayla takes. When she yells "I'm not a stripper," she announces to the boy who taunted her, and everyone else within earshot, that she refuses to be labeled a deviant. Moments later she is a playful child, unconstrained by notions of feminine bodily comportment. Then Kayla changes from child to capricious authority. She rebuffs one adult but apologizes to another. Throughout these interactions Kayla takes up positions—respectable young woman, playful child, dominant authority, well-mannered girl—that are only partially available to her. She rests in none of them, but instead moves from place to place on a tightrope stretched between stereotypes of Black femininity on one side and normative notions of Black respectability on the other (Sears 2010, 6–8).

Drawn from a larger study, this chapter focuses on a subset of girls who perform what we term *transgressive Black femininity*. These girls push back against corporeal containment to claim the bus as their space within a momentary hierarchy sustained by other Black teens who read and categorize their bodies in ways that recognize their collective value. The place they claim is fragile. It is threatened by the intersecting misogyny, racism, and elitism that devalues poor Black girls.

Researching Black Girls on Buses

There is a clear distinction between what happens in the front and in the back of the bus. The youth that ride in the front mostly sit or stand quietly, pay the fare, and follow the rules. The back, however, finds different norms in operation. While Black and Latinx girls and boys ride in the back, Black girls are the stars of the show. While riding the bus after-school, one of the co-authors observed:

> Two Black boys exit and say they're taking the next bus because there's just "too much drama." Suddenly, I hear a young woman yell out, "I'll beat your ass." The threat sounds real, said with such force and conviction that I am sure a fight will erupt, yet none does. The drama continues. "Tyler just ate my pussy"—a collective laugh from the kids, a collective groan from the adults. I watch the adult passengers; some sit with their heads down, others twist to see. There is tension in the air. At Turk and Fillmore, most of the youth exit the bus. From here the vibe on the bus shifts: The noise level drops and the energy is calm. The students and adult passengers remaining on the bus appear to relax (myself included). The remaining girls, even those yelling just a few stops before, sit in their seats and talk in "normal" bus voices.

What is it about public transportation that facilitates such performances? How can we understand the content of such scenes, as well as the shift in behavior over the course of the route?

For many middle- and high-school students in Oakland and San Francisco, California public transportation is a significant and distinct part of their lives. In these cities, large numbers of students must rely on public buses to transport them between home and school. Public transit brings strangers together for extended periods across racial and class boundaries. The potential for boundary-crossing interaction has long made public transportation a crucial site for state control and resistance against such control. As Kelley (1994, 57) has described, public transportation can be understood as a "moving theatre of race relations." Informed by an intersectional perspective, we adapt Kelley's metaphor to view the bus as a moving theatre of gendered race relations (Crenshaw 1989; Collins 1991). Black girls face constraints and public interpretations of their behavior that are shaped simultaneously by race and gender. In the San Francisco Bay Area, a varied and shifting racial, gender, and class mix of adults and youth momentarily fill the same space, creating possibilities for shared experience, interaction, and conflict.

Two contexts shape interactions on the bus. The first is the race, class, gender, and age distribution of persons inside the bus. Jewett (2005) found that due to the constantly changing composition of passengers, buses are "betwixt and between," or "liminal," spaces in which the usual barriers to cross age, cross gender, cross class, as well as cross racial interaction are overridden (39, 49). Within this liminal space, power shifts over the course of the ride, and social hierarchies on the bus slip into indeterminacy. On public buses, power is mobile, and authority can be claimed temporarily by youth who transform the space of the bus into their place (LaBennett 2011, 69). When a Black girl claims the space inside the bus she can, for a moment, contest adult authority and white middle-class cultural norms.

The second context is constituted by the narratives that encircle and give meaning to passengers' bodies. In her study of youth on public transportation, Fleetwood (2004) found that Black youth who rode San Francisco's buses were marked in public discourse "as deviant and anti-authority" (33). Aware of how they were perceived, these youth "engage with adults' fears and with media representations" via social performances on the bus that both challenged and reproduced such constructions (35). In addition to being constructed as deviant and anti-authority, Black children and youth are also prematurely perceived as adults. While the transgressions of white middle-class youth may be regarded as experimentation or forgiven as the missteps of the immature, Black children and youth undergo a process Ferguson (2000, 83–84) has termed "adultification" and are more likely to be treated as fully culpable adults when they misbehave.

Our focus is on the interactional level, yet, as Jones (2009, 91) has argued, there are "recursive relationship[s]" among interpersonal interactions, identities, and "larger oppressive forces, which are shaped by various overlapping and intersecting-isms." The contexts that surround passengers on the bus, therefore, are not merely fellow riders and the meanings commonly inscribed on their bodies, but also the vastly different circumstances of their lives beyond the bus.

Black Girls and Embodied Resistance

Race, gender, and class are "features of a culture that are read onto bodies as personal dispositions" (Skeggs 2004, 1). Race, gender, and class can be discerned from bodies because they are written on bodies through social processes of inscription that tend to hold individuals in fixed places within social hierarchies. According to Skeggs, inscription is "the way value is transferred onto bodies and read off them, and the mechanisms by which it is retained, accumulated, lost or appropriated" (13). Intersecting racism, sexism, and elitism devalue working class Black girls. In a study of young Black women living in a homeless shelter, Cox (2015) noted that "normative codes of white femininity mark the boundary between valued and devalued. . . . [Poor Black women] confront several layers of corporeal containment in their daily lives, including the reading and categorizing of their bodies, the regulation of their bodies legislated by the state, and the use of their bodies as surplus labor" (42). Despite, or indeed because of, the force of corporeal containment, Black girls enact forms of resistance. This study addresses Black girls' resistance to the reading and categorizing of their bodies. We place Black girls at the center of the study because of the specificity of stereotypes they must navigate. Moreover, we place Black girls at the center of the study because Black girls placed themselves at the center of attention on the bus.

Black scholars have led the way in thinking about Black girls' resistance, especially as it relates to the performance of racialized femininities. For example, Evans (1988) found that, "Oh, those loud Black girls," was a common complaint heard from teachers in "response to a confrontation in which Black girls had threatened the teacher's sense of authority" (183). She suggests that these young women exhibited a "defiance and stubborn refusal to conform to standards of white middle-class definitions of good girl behavior" (183). Fordham (1993) also uses loudness as a "metaphor to describe Black girls' collective denial of, and resistance to, their socially proclaimed position of nothingness" (25). She found that "loud Black girls" refuse to become invisible: They refuse to "comply with the view that as women they must become silent" (10). In these examples, Black girls' resistance takes the form of enacting racialized femininities that stand in contrast to the expectations for passivity and silence often associated with normative white femininity. These girls are not just resisting white femininity; they are also drawing upon notions of Black femininity. Race- and class-specific conceptions of femininity circulate within Black communities. When Black girls boldly use their voices and refuse to back down in confrontations, they are drawing from community-specific norms of femininity, some of which value feminine assertiveness.

Black girls remain aware of white, middle-class norms, even when they do not adopt them as their own. Resistance forms within and deploys dominant discourse (Foucault [1978] 1990, 95). It often attempts to flip the meaning of a sign from negative to positive. That is a risky maneuver, especially when made by someone whose body is stigmatized. A young woman's embrace of sexuality may be framed as resistance to demands to be chaste, and her aggression as rebellion against expected feminine passivity. Yet either one of these stances presents problems for Black girls, whose acts of resistance are haunted by racialized, gendered specters. Collins (2004, 123) argues that popular culture abounds with controlling images of working class Black women as hypersexualized and "aggressive, loud, rude and pushy." Resistance is a demand for an alternative reading of one's body, one that confers value upon it. Yet losses await these girls regardless of whether they claim sexuality or innocence, assertiveness or passivity, strength or vulnerability. Consequently, these girls push back in contradictory ways, and on multiple fronts. We focus on the ways that Black girls perform transgressive Black femininity as they attempt to win positive recognition. In contexts in which their bodies are inscribed as bad, this femininity alternately resists and embraces the white middle-class norms of female comportment contained within Black respectability, as well as resists and embraces controlling images of Black girlhood. Transgressive Black femininity refuses to accept subordination and rejects the labeling of that refusal as deviant. It is a performance that does not settle in one place. It ultimately says to the observer, "you don't know me."

Methods

We rode with students as they traveled to and from school on public buses. Specifically, the authors, along with one graduate research assistant and a team of eight undergraduate research assistants, collected observations on over 150 bus rides in Oakland and San Francisco between 2012 and 2013. The research team included

Asian, Black, Latinx, and white researchers who rode alone or in pairs. We concentrated on bus routes that carried students to and from middle and high schools and timed our trips to ride with students immediately before and after school. During each ride, each member of the research team jotted down as many observations as possible, focusing on the actions and words of youth. While some researchers used a notepad, many of the undergraduates used cell phones as they were able to appear as if they were texting and not draw attention to themselves on the bus. Immediately after every ride, the researchers reviewed their observations and added in details to fill out the notes gathered in transit. We trained research assistants to be careful not to neglect students who were quiet. Such notes were common. For example: "There are a few African American girls in the front that seem quiet and watch the kids in the back. . . . They dress and act somewhat different than the kids in the back. They don't engage in any of the activity taking place among the African American kids in the back." This chapter focuses on a subset of our data that records the words and actions of transgressive Black girls.

Using a grounded theory approach (Glaser and Strauss 1967), the authors independently analyzed each field note, noting patterns and themes that emerged from the data. From here we developed key codes and re-analyzed the data using a qualitative data analysis program. In this chapter, we focus on instances when girls used their voices and bodies to command attention on the bus. Such instances were not unusual. Public buses conveying middle- and high-school students after school are filled with the loud voices of girls. When coding, we gave particular attention to the social context of action. Specifically, when examining the actions and words of young riders as described in the field notes, we coded the apparent identities of those seated around the actors, as well as their reactions to the words and behavior of the students.

The Complexity of Resisting while Being a Black Girl

Performance

Transgressive Black femininity is a self-aware and situated performance that takes center stage despite the risk of being disparaged by the controlling image of the "aggressive, loud, rude and pushy" Black woman (Collins 2004, 123). In the following two field notes, girls speak directly about their conscious performances:

> A Black girl told her white friend "I only act ghetto when I have to. Only in certain areas." The white girl nodded and said, "Yeah, I get it." Then the Black girl said, "But I don't when I don't have to."

> Maya, a middle-school-aged Black girl pulls Tapatío [a hot sauce] out of her backpack. Her friend says "That's ratchet and gives black people a bad name." . . . Maya brags about the hot sauce she drank. . . . By Hayes Street, most of the kids have exited and the bus becomes quiet. . . . In this silence, Maya announces, to no one in particular, that she does not drink hot sauce that would make her look "cray cray" and she is not, but everyone at the school is.

In these examples, girls address their situational use of transgressive performance. For some Black girls, a situation that invites a transgressive performance is an audience full of peers on a crowded bus. An undergraduate research assistant recorded the following field note:

> One girl wore a red beanie, skinny jeans, and a black jacket. . . . It seemed as if she was wilder on the bus than outside, which is ironic because the bus was crowded especially in the back where she sat. She reacted to what seemed more restricting by being loud and moving in her seat even if it disturbed others.

These shifts from one character to another make visible the self-aware, performative, and temporary nature of girls' actions on the bus. Controlling images hold Black women in fixed places within social hierarchies by associating their bodies with negative meanings. These girls assert their own sense of mobility by performing "cray cray" one moment and sitting quietly the next.

Voices

We observed girls deftly using their voices and their bodies to walk the tightrope between normative and transgressive femininities. One way to do this was to loudly criticize others for being loud:

> The Black girl next to me yells back at a particularly loud group, "you're hella loud!" At Broadway, a 30ish white woman boards and stands in the front, glancing around at the kids and looking perturbed. The girl yells again, "Could y'all shut up and stop talking so loud, you're being inconsiderate!" The rest of the kids get louder (some actually scream) in response.

Transgressive Black girls do not accept the terms aggressive, loud, rude, and pushy as inherently or always negative. Yelling, explicit sex talk, profanity, and fight talk are within a repertoire of behavior that can earn the respect of their peers and increase their status as girls. A student researcher noted the following dialogue on an after-school ride on a San Francisco bus:

> "I told her to stop rolling her eyes at me before I hit her so hard that they fell out and then Ms. Nichols said to 'stop threatening her.' So, she lucked the fuck out because I was about to knock her the fuck out!!" The other two laughed and said, "Yeah, you would knock her out!"

On another ride, a student researcher noted:

> A Black girl screams at a boy on the bus, "I heard you! You said you'd eat her out!" All the kids around her react by laughing. The boy shakes his head in denial and quietly laughs.

In the last two excerpts, the girls' performance elicits laughter. An audience is crucial for a transgressive performance. Peer laughter rewards the young women and encourages their continued performances. Willis (1977, 29) highlights the role of "having a laff" in male working class culture. Having fun while pushing the boundaries of authority is at the center of this peer culture.

Gender scholars have stressed the importance of attending to class, racial, and ethnic variation in the content of gender norms (Bettie 2014; Brown 1998; Halberstam 1997; Jones 2010). For example, Brown (1998, 69) found that working-class white girls drew upon alternative images of femininity that included expressions of "desire and sexuality, directness and toughness, a direct and unapologetic expression of anger, in combination with a deep capacity for love and nurturance." Similarly, Jones (2010, 155) has argued that local conceptions of femininity circulating within poor Black communities "allow girls to use physical aggression when appropriate without sacrificing any and all claims to a respectable feminine identity." In other words, Black girls and working-class white girls, excluded from middle-class ideals of womanhood, draw upon a legacy of self-definition to construct racialized and class-specific femininities that incorporate strength, aggression, and talking back (Collins 1991; hooks 1989, 9).

Bumping, Pushing, and Blocking

Fleetwood (2004, 43) found that young women often used their voices on buses, while young men used their bodies, primarily by claiming the back of the bus as their place and broadcasting their identities via fashion. We similarly observed that girls used their voices to claim space on the bus more often than boys or adults, but beyond that, we observed that girls were also more likely to use their bodies to bump, block, and push others. One of the co-authors recorded this field note on an Oakland bus after school:

> We board a bus. . . . The feeling of this bus is actually happy. . . . I am squished up next to two Black girls. . . . They are small and boisterous. They push. They pull each other and have exaggerated responses to the bus's motion. They knock into me. I do nothing. They hit a guy. The high-school-age Latina says in a friendly tone to them "you're too loud." They ignore her. They start asking people for tissues. They ask me. When I look like I am going to respond they explode into laughter and turn away from me.

These girls were undoubtedly having fun at others' expense. Though jostled by them, the passengers around them let them play.

Girls also used their bodies to control access to space on the bus. They put their legs or belongings on seats to prevent others from sitting next to them. Taking it further, some girls used their bodies to control access to the bus, most commonly by blocking the exit or opening the back doors. Researchers made the following two observations:

> [The girls] got on and didn't even look for seats, they just stood right on the back door steps blocking the door.

> The driver only opens the front door. Kayla walks to the back door and steps into the stairwell to open the door—despite the girl next to her literally yelling at her not to do it. Once the back door opens, the kids pile on without bus passes.

In these examples, Black girls use their bodies to defy bus norms and rules. In the first example, girls blocked the back door. In the last example, which took place right outside of the middle school as students were boarding to head home, Kayla used her body to allow fellow students to board without paying the fare. Here, Kayla and her peers draw upon a racialized and class-located femininity. Instead of shrinking and ceding space, these girls boldly take up and control space.

Relational Identities in Context

Adults generally did not engage with the youth on the bus. We do not have any documented instances of adult male passengers directly challenging youth, but on several rides Black and Latina women admonished youth for their unruly behavior. When this occurred, the youth acquiesced with minimal resistance. However, when we examined the few instances of confrontation between adults and youth, something interesting emerged: the most intense confrontations occurred between Black girls and young white women. Researchers made the following two observations:

> Kids were blocking the door. A white-looking woman (actually she was a USF student because I saw her flash her ID) tapped the boy on his shoulder and impatiently said, "Excuse me!" One of the Black girls said, "Ooooh, Rodney, you in the way! But look at her pushing you! She hella rude! Oh, look at the way she pushing you!" Then the USF student just nudged her way through because the kids were not moving, and another one of the Black girls screamed after her, "Damn Bitch! She hella ugly anyways!" "Ugly Ass!" another one of them screamed at the woman.

> At the Presidio stop, a college student, white, female wanted to get off the bus and she quietly said, "Excuse me," to the girl who was blocking the door the most. The young girl turned around and said, "You excused," and turned back to her friends but didn't move at all. So the college student sighed and pushed by trying to not touch her as much as possible and the younger girl said, "Rude! She so rude!" talking about the white college student.

These examples echo the intensity of this chapter's opening field note. Jones's (2009, 91) theorization of the "recursive relationships" among interpersonal interactions, identities, and structures of inequality may help to explain the vehemence of the encounters. Interactions on the bus are shaped by the girls' sense of themselves as Black in relation to their perceptions of what it means to be white. These identities and perceptions are informed by "structures of feeling" that arise in longstanding conditions of social inequality. Williams (1961, 48) theorized structure of feeling as a generational culture, learned informally yet "as firm and definite as 'structure' suggests," which is the "living result of all the elements in the [society's] general organization." Today's structure of feeling for African American youth is informed by what Alexander (2010) terms the "New Jim Crow." According to Alexander, mass incarceration, which is fueled by racially biased policing, arrest, and sentencing, criminalizes racial minorities. Though Black and Latinx students may sit anywhere on the bus, the stigma of criminalization follows them there. Black girls are aware of the racialized suspicion that trails them, and they resent it.

Criminalization and surveillance were both intermittent and daily realities of youth's experiences on the bus. Researchers observed school, city police, and bus system security officers monitoring and/or riding on the bus. Two field notes highlight these interactions:

> Two MUNI officials ensure everyone pays and is moving back. Students stay quiet and stare at officials. The male security guard monitors the front of the bus while the woman is at the back. He stays quiet and mostly just observes while she yells for students to move back and asks for proof of payment. The male guard makes a call and says "the bus is under control."

> Bus driver says she's going to call the police. One girl says, "Be quiet she's going to call the police." All students in the back ignore the girl and begin screaming back and forth asking where's the police station around here.

Buses are equipped with cameras that may or may not be working, and transit police sporadically board. Field notes recorded multiple examples of bus drivers, youth, and school officials discussing "reviewing the tapes." The unpredictable presence of state authority, which may at any moment intrude into and entirely alter a youth's life, is one of the ways youth feel racism in the form of the New Jim Crow. Fare evasion and other infractions that may be inconsequential on most days may suddenly lead to serious consequences.

There is also a specifically gendered aspect of these interactions and the structure of feeling that undergirds them. Black girls are in confrontations with white women. As Evelyn Nakano Glenn (1992, 34) has argued, "to represent race and gender as relationally constructed is to assert that the experiences of white women and women of color are not just different but connected in systematic ways." For many Black girls who live in segregated neighborhoods, a common face of whiteness is a white woman with institutional power over them. The following three field notes, which took place on different dates, captured instances when white women in positions of authority boarded the bus to maintain order:

> A guard woman (white), is at the bus stop. . . . She seems to have authority and talks to a group of students about being polite to adults. She has a walkie-talkie and is keeping order at the bus stop. Talking to all the kids about respect for themselves and others. As the bus comes up, she makes all the kids get on the front to make sure they pay. One African American boy tries to get on the back, she yells at him. One African American girl can't pay and talks to the bus driver, who slips her a transfer. The driver is also black.

> A teacher (white woman) boards the bus and says behave and she will be looking at [bus surveillance] film tomorrow.

> While waiting for the bus to leave, three girls are taken off the bus by a white woman the students refer to as Ms. Duggan (Principal/VP??). One girl starts crying. She has to pick up her sister and says she will get in trouble if she is late. Ms. Duggan doesn't budge. They are not allowed to ride this bus.

For many Black girls riding the routes we observed, white women are the security guards at the bus stop, the school administrator who took three girls off the bus, and the school official who notified the youth that she will be reviewing the bus's surveillance videos. Amid the confrontation between Kayla and the white woman on the bus that opened this chapter, one girl mockingly said, "She's trying to help us."

Structural and discursive contexts shape interactions on the bus. On the one hand, Black girls perceive white women as agents of institutional authority. On the other hand, white women also represent a privileged location within dominant discursive constructions of femininity. The insult that a Black girl yelled at the white college student was "ugly." The word speaks to the ways in which all women are held to standards of beauty and are vulnerable to public scrutiny regarding their appearance. Yet a Black girls' deployment of the hurtful discourse of ugliness takes place within a broader context of the symbolic position of white women as ideals of feminine beauty, or merely as the unmarked norm against which women of color are made to seem at best exotic, or at worst deficient.

Conclusion

> Luminosities of momentary visibility or short-lived celebrity are forces of change, forms of power which re-define the landscape of class and gender (McRobbie 2009, 125).

When we describe girls' actions as resistance, we make no claims about the effectiveness of these actions in recasting the ways in which the girls are perceived. Our claim is more modest. It is only that girls show a resilience in the face of denigration. Black girls feel unwelcome and devalued in many public spaces. The center of a bus, when it is filled after school with their peers, is a place that opens possibilities for feeling valued. We found that the bus provides an opportunity for girls to transgress cultural norms of bodily comportment and challenge authority by yelling, taking up physical space, and using their bodies to bump, block, and push others. In addition, it is an opportunity to challenge the adultification of Black girls.

When a Black girl is loud and pushy on the bus, is she practicing resistance, contributing to a vicious stereotype, or merely acting like a kid? The answer is all of the above. When she commands the center of attention, she pushes back at anyone who questions her value. As she moves from being loud, amusing, and intimidating to being quiet and polite, she demonstrates that nothing should be permanently inscribed on her body. She can be a good girl when she wishes to be. Black girls continue to confront images of themselves as sexually available, hypersexualized, unwed mothers, fighters, disrespectful, rude, and uneducated. Too often adults in positions of authority refuse to recognize that they are children.

While the individual or group may experience disruptive acts as powerful, the ways that they are read in our national collective imagination, which is immersed in stereotypes of Black womanhood, can render such acts problematic and even reproductive of the larger structures of oppression. Despite how their behavior may be interpreted by other passengers on the bus, loud Black girls refuse to be defined or contained by those who perceive them as deviant and threatening, and they refuse to make themselves small and silent. Their actions carve out some space for pleasure and solidarity. They claim a space, enjoy being the center of attention in front of an appreciative audience, and assert their right to play. In other words, they assert their right to be kids. In the context of controlling images that constrain Black girls, perhaps merely acting like a kid constitutes resistance.

NOTES

This work was supported by the University of California Center for New Racial Studies and the University of San Francisco's Faculty Development Fund.
1. All names used in this chapter are pseudonyms.
2. Latinx is a gender-neutral or nonbinary term used to refer to people of Latin American origin or descent.

REFERENCES

Alexander, Michelle. 2010. *The New Jim Crow: Mass Incarceration in the Age of Colorblindness.* New York: The New Press.

Bettie, Julie. 2014. *Women without Class*, 2nd ed. Berkeley: University of California Press.

Brown, Lyn Mikel. 1998. *Raising Their Voices: The Politics of Girls' Anger.* Cambridge, MA: Harvard University Press.

Collins, Patricia Hill. 1991. *Black Feminist Thought.* New York: Routledge.

———. 2004. *Black Sexual Politics.* New York: Routledge.

Cox, Aimee Meredith. 2015. *Shapeshifters: Black Girls and the Choreography of Citizenship.* Durham, NC: Duke University Press.

Crenshaw, Kimberlé Williams. 1989. "Demarginalizing the Intersection of Race and Sex: A Black Feminist Critique of Antidiscrimination Doctrine, Feminist Theory, and Antiracist Politics." *University of Chicago Legal Forum* 1989: 139–67.

Evans, Grace. 1988. "Those Loud Black Girls." In *Learning to Lose: Sexism and Education*, edited by D. Spender and E. Sarah, 183–90. London: The Women's Press.

Ferguson, Ann Arnett. 2000. *Bad Boys: Public Schools in the Making of Black Masculinity.* Ann Arbor: University of Michigan Press.

Fleetwood, Nicole. 2004. "'Busing It' in the City: Black Youth, Performance, and Public Transit." *TDR/The Drama Review* 48, no. 2: 33–48.

Fordham, Signithia. 1993. "'Those Loud Black Girls': Black Women, Silence, and Gender 'Passing' in the Academy." *Anthropology and Education Quarterly* 24, no. 1: 3–32.

Foucault, Michel. (1978) 1990. *The History of Sexuality: An Introduction.* Vol. 1. New York: Vintage.

Glaser, Barney, and Anselm L. Strauss. 1967. *The Discovery of Grounded Theory: Strategies for Qualitative Research.* Chicago: Aldine Publishing Company.

Glenn, Evelyn Nakano. 1992. "From Servitude to Service Work: Historical Continuities in the Racial Division of Paid Reproductive Labor." *Signs* 18, no. 1: 1–43.

Halberstam, Judith. 1997. "Mackdaddy, Superfly, Rapper: Gender, Race, and Masculinity in the Drag King Scene." *Social Text* 52/53: 104–31.

hooks, bell. 1989. *Talking Back: Thinking Feminist Thinking Black.* Boston: South End Press.

Jewett, Laura. 2005. "Powerbeads, Bodyglitter and Backseat Badasses: Girls on the Bus." In *Geographies of Girlhood: Identity In-Between*, edited by Pamela Bettis and Natalie Adams, 35–52. Mahwah, NJ: Lawrence Erlbaum.

Jones, Nikki. 2009. "'I was aggressive for the streets, pretty for the pictures': Gender, Difference, and the Inner-City Girl." *Gender & Society* 23, no. 1: 89–93.

———. 2010. *Between Good and Ghetto: African American Girls and Inner-City Violence.* New Brunswick, NJ: Rutgers University Press.

Kelley, Robin D. G. 1994. *Race Rebels: Culture, Politics, and the Black Working Class.* New York: Free Press.

LaBennett, Oneka. 2011. *She's Mad Real: Popular Culture and West Indian Girls in Brooklyn.* New York: New York University Press.

McRobbie, Angela. 2009. *The Aftermath of Feminism: Gender, Culture and Social Change.* London: Sage Press.

Sears, Stephanie D. 2010. *Imagining Black Womanhood: The Negotiation of Power and Identity within the Girls Empowerment Project.* Albany: State University of New York Press.

Skeggs, Beverley. 2004. *Class, Self, Culture.* New York: Routledge.

Williams, Raymond. 1961. *The Long Revolution.* New York: Harper & Row.

Willis, Paul E. 1977. *Learning to Labour: How Working Class Kids Get Working Class Jobs.* Farnborough, England: Saxon House.

8

Big Gay Men's Performative Protest against Body Shaming

The Case of Girth and Mirth

Jason Whitesel

> Large gay men are as much in need (and are as worthy of) love and sex as anyone
> else. But in our world, never the twain shall meet. Gym rats, at the head of the
> food chain, hold a special place in our idealized culture, followed closely behind
> by hairless 18-25-year-old twinks, followed by [Bears] those virile, hirsute
> creatures, leftovers from the 1970s when having hair was the ideal and the norm
> not, in our super plastic surgery saturated world, the exception. Next come
> those of average stock, neither super good-looking nor toned but well within the
> American Medical Association's guidelines for height-and-weight proportionality.
> At the bottom, well, you know the rest. (Lee 2014)

Looksism is one of the organizing features of the gay male community in the United
States. It is "the societal belief in one ideal body type [that] contributes to poor self-
concept and body image" (Dworkin and Kerr 1987, 140). Like women, gay men experience conflict with their appearance, physique, and relationship to food more than
heterosexual men do (Foster-Gimbel and Engeln 2016). Therefore, big gay men have
an added exclusion, besides being gay—a topic that is increasingly receiving intense
and often critical media and scholarly attention (Gleeson 2016; Gremore 2016; Lang
2016). They not only encounter exclusion that all queer people experience, but also
within-group prejudice due to their ample size. Thus, fat gay men are marginalized
both for their sexual orientation in heteronormative society and for their size in gay
society. In this chapter, I discuss big gay men's creative performances in response to
sizeism, which I refer to as "fat performative protest." I argue that rather than capitulating to the shame of fat stigma in everyday life, the big gay men I interviewed and
observed playfully disregard it, insisting on their right to "sexual citizenship" (Richardson 2000). This includes equal access to intimacy, the recognition of status as a
sensual being, and opportunities to express oneself erotically and indulge in sexual
consumption. Fat gay men, routinely denied sexual rights, often must transgress the
rules of corporeal conduct in order to experience the very pleasures that others in their
sexual identity group take for granted.

Conventional Understandings of Fat

Fat has conventionally been reconfigured as a disease or deviance, such as when doctors medicalize it as "obesity" (Boero 2012) or when people say someone is "overweight," meaning s/he has deviated from some ideal measurement (Wann 2009). Because fat has become pathologized as a disease, which, by definition, is thought to be treatable, then fat people are expected to normalize their bodies if they wish to become eligible to fully participate in society. If fat people "fail" to adopt what Goffman (1963b, 103) calls "the right line" of fad diets, exercise, or weight-loss surgery, they are not granted full citizenship; and if they ask for citizenship without making an effort to physically conform, they are seen as disrupting the social order. Sociologically speaking, fat assumes a master status, where its stigmatizing character becomes a controlling category. Following Goffman, Goode (2004) argues that "normals" tend to fixate on a particular stigmatizing trait like fatness. However, fat takes on a broadly perceived focus. As a stigmatizing trait, it is rarely the only characteristic people find fault with in someone; it also comes with the assumption that the fat person possesses other associated "defects." Thus, fat supersedes many other traits, and it becomes lumped together with a whole host of imperfections. One might also think of the merely descriptive term "fat" as being reified to the extent that if one is ascribed this status, then one is thought to possess all of its negative characteristics, which are socially appointed (Goode 2004, 2005). Thus, "normal"-weight people make negative assumptions about fat people: that they cannot perform in sports; that they are slobs; that they deserve to be snubbed "as if they were not there at all, as objects not worthy of a glance," being given the "'nonperson' treatment" (Goffman 1963a, 83); or that they are unsexy and deserve to be taken advantage of (Gailey and Prohaska 2006; Prohaska and Gailey 2009, 2010).

Fat Studies/Activism

The vast network of fat-studies scholars/activists challenge conventional understandings about the fat body. They offer a "counter public" (Warner 2005) in which to share fat-positive ideas and bring their constituents, as well as the uninitiated, up to speed on a more radical view of fat's not being the "four-letter word" that sizeist society has made it out to be (see, e.g., Solovay and Rothblum 2009). Moreover, they counter dominant beliefs about how people of size *ought to* act. Fat activists assert that they ought to reconfigure the larger system of which they are a part and change the premise on which the system is built. Thus, fat activists promote self-acceptance and call for a change in fat-phobic society, especially in a fat person's own outlook. Murray (2005, 270) explains that as she tried to embrace fat activism as originally prescribed, she felt ambiguous about "living [her] fat body." She writes, "the ways in which I live my fat body are always multiple, contradictory, and eminently ambiguous." Likewise, I liken today's fat activists/scholars to engaging in category work that reconfigures the shame of fat stigma by differentiating "myriad fat selves from hackneyed essentialist stereotypes" (Whitesel 2014, 139). In rejecting the medical model, fat studies/activism rejects the imperative of regarding fat as a "defect" to be eradicated Rather, fat-positive scholars/activists highlight historical and cross-cultural variations in attitudes toward fatness and promote "health at every size" (HAES), an alternative to weight- and size-based paradigms upon which much current public health policy rests. The HAES concept "supports homeostatic regulation and eating intuitively (i.e., in response to internal cues of hunger, satiety, and appetite)," rather than falling prey to yo-yo diets or resorting to risky weight-loss surgeries (Bacon et al. 2005, 929). In these ways, fat studies/activism has become a powerful, counterhegemonic voice in recent years, by examining the biological/scientific/medical data on obesity as a discourse that can be understood in connection with other relevant discourses, affording alternative reconfigurations of talk surrounding body shape and size.

This chapter is situated in the emerging field of fat studies, adding to the subsection of the literature that highlights the significance of performative protest as a transformational strategy (Pyle and Klein 2011). The ethnography of big gay men herein offers a different perspective on fat than the medicalized angle, by examining how these men playfully reclaim their sullied identities. Other scholars in the field have analyzed the emancipatory possibilities for (mostly white) fat women who engage in burlesque (Asbill 2009), synchronized swimming (Wyman 2005), and dance troupes (McAllister 2009). Fat women's engagement in these activities challenges conventional norms about what the fat body can do—melding fat studies/activism with embodied resistance through performance (see, e.g., Braziel and LeBesco 2001). Wann has also made a significant contribution to fat activism/studies with her influential book, *FAT! SO? Because You Don't Have to Apologize for Your Size* (1998). As Wann remarked in an interview, "Performance is huge—it has the power to shift people's feelings about looking at certain topics like fat people" (quoted in Mathews 2008). Wann (1998) praises big gay men's "wonderful . . . extensive network[s]." She considers these men "freedom fighters, in the sense that living well is the best revenge" (168): partying, "getting laid," having a good time; big men expressing sexuality and sensuality, just as other body types of gay men do. This "notion of 'playful subjectivity'/performativity" (8) is at the forefront of LeBesco's 2004 book, *Revolting Bodies*, as well. In this chapter, I seek to honor LeBesco's "hope to have initiated . . . a different theorization of fatness and fat politics. By queering corpulent bodies/politics, perhaps we can equally resist dominant discursive constructions of fatness, while opening new (and playful) sites for reconstructing fat bodies" (14). Sedgwick, like LeBesco, proposes going further than Goffman does in his book, *Stigma* (1963b). Sedgwick (1995) suggests it would be good to expand Goffman's subtitle, *Notes on the Management of Spoiled Identity*, to include more than just identity management, because, in queer fat politics, one also approaches one's spoiled identity in ways that are "experimental, creative, [and] performative" (210–11).

Girth & Mirth

Girth & Mirth started as a national social movement organization in the 1970s, in reaction to weight discrimination within the gay community (Whitesel 2014; Pyle and Loewy 2009; Hennen 2008; Textor 1999). The club provides a safe haven, allowing members to stake a claim to be ordinary in a world that sometimes regards them as misfits. Worldwide, the organization offers a friendship circle to bring big gay men out of social isolation as members help one another deal with their "wounded attachment" to the gay community (Brown 1993). The local Ohio chapter of Girth

& Mirth, the subject of my research, has an "active" membership of approximately twenty to twenty-five, not including a number of peripheral folks who sporadically show up to events. The group positions itself as a social club or family responding to the needs of its members. It organizes bar nights, café klatches, dinner outings, holiday bashes, pool parties, and game-and-movie nights. The activities it sponsors have to do with the ordinary—ordinary people attending ordinary events, like a potluck with friends. Elsewhere, some chapters additionally function as sexual venues.

Members also attend annual pan–Girth & Mirth weekend reunions. One of these is the Super Weekend, a regional event that takes place yearly at a gay motel in Oklahoma City. About 175 big gay men and their admirers from around the country descend upon the motel for carnal encounters. During this weekend, they engage in a variety of campy-queer behaviors, being mirthful and having a laugh at their own expense. The Super Weekend provides a fat-affirming sanctuary for the big men where they can express their sexuality without fear of ridicule or rejection. They view it as one precious weekend in which they can amp up their sexual selves and play around with transforming themselves into sex objects. At the Super Weekend, Girth & Mirthers engage in a variety of playful performances. Through their performative play, they trouble and interrogate the thin and muscular body ideal in the gay male community and redefine themselves as embodied, sexual beings, motivated by the desire for, and of, other men.

Methods

For nearly three years, I spent time with an Ohio chapter of Girth & Mirth and interacted with members at local events. I also attended two of the group's yearly convergences. In conducting my research, I negotiated my position as an ally "outsider within" (Collins 1986). Like the research participants, I am gay; but I benefit from a thin "dividend" (Connell 1996). Interestingly, during my time in the field I became aware that thinness is not necessarily a category of privilege in all settings. While I was an insider to gay society, I could not become a total insider to the big men's social gatherings. At times, while I mingled among the Girth & Mirthers as a participant observer, my thinness stood out as a polar opposite to the bigness of the men I was studying. As Probyn (2004, 328) explains, the shame of being fat "makes apparent the ways in which radically different positioned selves are [deemed] contagious." In fact, some members wondered whether I had gained weight simply from hanging out with them. To the big men, I looked like a thin chubby-chaser. My thinness limited my empathic experience of oneness with the big men. At the same time, it allowed me to access data to which the men might otherwise not be privy. Like a fly on the wall, I passed with my thin privilege during events where the group mixed it up in mainstream public venues. Critics of the group at times would negatively comment on the big men well within my earshot, unaware of my affiliation with the group.

I was open with local members about my study and identified myself as a gay man and enthusiast of the organization. As a performativity scholar, I was a participant observer in the group's traditions. Thus, I became a dues-paying member who was active in the local Girth & Mirth chapter and served functional roles for the club. For example, I sold Jell-O shots at the bar night the local chapter hosted to raise money for LGBTQ charities, and I served as a fill-in coordinator at the Super Weekend in Oklahoma. Participating in the group's activities in these ways allowed me to get to know the men well and get an insider's feel for their experiences.

My data comes from ten in-depth interviews and field-notes taken at over one hundred club events, including Gay Pride Parades. I took field-notes in particular on corporeal conduct, i.e., how the men used their bodies in certain social contexts. After attending seventy-five events, I typed my handwritten field-diary and elaborated on it with coding schemas and theoretical memos that became the basis for my analysis. In analyzing my data, I extended Goffman's (1963b) stigma theory by incorporating theories of camp, carnival, play, and performativity. Two years into data collection, I asked club members to clarify ideas in the passages I wrote. Occasionally, I dined with a key informant, a big man who served on the club's board as both longtime treasurer and later, webmaster. Finally, I read messages posted to the group's listserv.

Club members ranged in occupations from an artist who worked at a screen-printing shop, to a Taco Bell manager, to an escalated call-center rep for a bank, as well as including retirees. Many had some college; local members were advantaged by their race (mostly white) and in some cases, class (lower middle).[1] The big men were negatively marked by two categories (fat, gay), and in some cases stigmatized for their age (middle-aged, older). Racial demographics of the local participants were partly a function of this club's Midwestern location, with its metropolitan area being 82 percent white during my research (American Community Survey 2008). The big men's race and class backgrounds presumably gave them some luxury of not being hampered by pressing concerns like racism or poverty. At the same time, because youthful men are favored in gay communities, these big men's age was working against them (Simpson 2015; Slevin and Linneman 2010). The Super Weekend drew more racially and ethnically diverse guests from across the country other than White, including a Cherokee Native American man exploring his two-spirit status, many Hispanic/Latino men from Texas, and a number of African American men. Precise numbers are not available, as the organizers do not collect official statistics on the attendees' race/ethnicity.

Fat Performances

Double Marginalization and the Safe Space of Girth & Mirth

Due to the layers of social injury they experience, big gay men feel doubly marginalized. One Girth & Mirther shared his disappointment about Disney's Gay Days, which he feels uncomfortable attending. Unsanctioned by Disney, Gay Days began in the early nineties with someone creating a website and posting dates for LGBT folx to congregate at Disney in Orlando for gay visibility, wearing red shirts or rainbow/gay-themed apparel, similar to pride parade attire. Antigay protesters outside the park gates also contribute to the orienting experience (Cascio 2014). The Girth & Mirther who bemoaned his inability to attend Gay Days at Disney felt that even if he could finally be in an environment where he could freely hold hands with his boyfriend, he was deterred from going by his weight. Yet he also remembered that when he was married to a woman, his fatness was not a detriment to him.

I was never so uncomfortable in my life as when watching videos of Gay Day celebrations. Everybody there was toned or muscular in speedos, there was hardly anybody in a boxer-style swim-trunk; there were no bellies to be seen, no other fat guys. . . . If you're the only fat guy who goes to something like that, people are gonna stare. . . . Now that I've seen what the Gay Day thing is like, I don't think I could go.

This Girth & Mirther chronicled the layers of injury big gay men experience—first for being gay, and second, for being fat. He elaborated on the complexities of double marginalization: "In Disney World, where I would want to be able to hold hands with my partner, I would not because of the stigma of being gay; and during Gay Days at Disney, we could hold hands, but I wouldn't even go, because of being big." This double stigmatization is where Girth & Mirth comes in, offering remedy to big gay men. The club provides a physical and psychological space where big gay men can be friendly and can receive friendship in a normal way. One member shared that he simply goes "to make friends and hang out with them from time to time, instead of being at home all the time." Local events provide a sense of comfort, in contrast to exclusion and humiliation the men usually experience in other public settings.

In response to being asked what brought them to the club, some said they came for the first time after reading about the group online or in a gay paper or upon the insistence of a friend. Many shared stories of how they almost gave up on finding happiness as gay big men before they encountered the safe space of Girth & Mirth. One member said he came across the ad for the club when he was looking for a suicide hotline. In the interview, he told me the following:

> I had no friends. I was 11 years older after the breakup of my relationship, I wasn't in the same physical shape, I was a little bigger—the grey hair and all that stuff. And I kind of felt, I have to get out and socialize or I'm gonna go insane. I was having suicidal thoughts, because I thought no one would ever want to speak to me. That's how the bars work. You've gotta be thin, have the right clothes, the right hair, and the whole thing. And I was reading one of these gay newspapers, and looking for some kind of support group for suicide prevention, and came across Girth & Mirth. It saved my life, quite frankly.

Stories like this have become part of the repertoire of origin stories for many Girth & Mirthers; for the members, they are as important as the historical account of the founding of the group.

Strategies of Fat Performative Protest

Girth & Mirthers use a smorgasbord of strategies to address the shame of fat stigma, rather than internalizing it. These include creating an inverse world, flaunting one's right to sexual citizenship, performing masculinities, and playfully disregarding shame.

CREATING AN INVERSE WORLD

The year I collected data at the Super Weekend, I observed several "chubs" engaged in an improvised underwater swimming competition in which they created an inverse world. The big men lined up in the motel's pool and spread their legs. Meanwhile, a handful of "chasers," admirers with thinner builds, got ready for the swimming competition. The object of the game was for chasers to swim across the pool and pass through the chubs' legs, trying to dodge their leg-locks, with a few scrambling underwater to find their lost swim-trunks. I marveled at the chubs' ability to reverse the criterion of the "ideal" body in determining dominance in the gay hierarchy, as they placed the chasers literally beneath them, under their command.

Big men's parody of synchronized swimming provokes some sociological questions: How is dominance determined/defined in the gay world? How is it inverted in this aquatic sports parody? What does this inversion tell us about Girth & Mirthers' "play"? By portraying chasers as submissive to chubs, the swimmers create an inverse world, giving the chubs the upper hand. Babcock (1978) refers to such performances as "institutionalized clowning," a way to enable performers to let off steam (22). She describes such activity as "symbolic inversion," which contradicts and abrogates, creating the possibility of a "reversible world" (14). Likewise, the chub-and-chasers' playful performances trouble the gay hierarchy's commonly held social codes.

Girth & Mirthers also created an inverse world while selling raffle tickets at the Super Weekend, which involved wrapping ticket-tape around the buyer's waist, his girth determining the number of tickets he would get for the set price–the greater his girth, the more tickets he got, the more he was worth. "Tex," who volunteers every year to be one of the "waist or double-inseam" ticket-sellers, carries on this tradition. As a veteran Super Weekender, he is the go-to guy for learning the ropes. He runs a good old-fashioned carny game reminiscent of the weight-guessing booth at amusement parks. In his duties as ticket-seller, Tex mentored an apprentice. Shirtless and wearing a carnival costume of crotchless suspender shorts, his apprentice was "going commando," letting it all hang out. There are two ways to be fitted for raffle tickets, both of which cost the same. The first uses ticket-tape to measure the buyer's, or—if the buyer prefers—the seller's, waist. Similarly, at a Big Fat Queer Prom hosted by NOLOSE (formerly the National Organization for Lesbians of Size), members used body wraps to measure the attendees' waists or busts to sell tickets (Rogers 2007).

A second way of being fitted for raffle tickets is by measuring the double inseam: the seller runs ticket-tape up the buyer's trouser leg, across his crotch, and down to his other ankle. The trick is to also loop the ticket-tape around the buyer's scrotum. Tex performed a special double inseam for a shy first-timer. In his deep voice and southern drawl, he gave his opening shtick on getting fitted for tickets; his sidekick reassured the newbie that Tex could retract the tape without any paper cuts. Up the guest's pants he went, stopping to rub the blushing man's penis and giving a carnival callout: "I think we've got a wiener!" After pulling out the tickets, he held them up saying, "I bet you didn't know your inseam was this long." Truth be told, after all the rigmarole and with the ticket-sellers' sleight-of-hand, most of the big men got about the same number of tickets.

In these ways, in the carnivalesque atmosphere of the Super Weekend, Girth & Mirthers work through the stigma of being fat by inverting popular cultural forms, like synchronized swimming and raffle sales, into their most bastardized renditions. Thus, they perform a "queer deconstruction of the opposition between 'original' and 'copy'" (Cleto 2002, 8). One thinks of synchronized swimming as a water dance performed by graceful, thin women in dazzling swimsuits; yet, the big gay men turn it into a campy spectacle by merrily sloshing around. Likewise, the raffle ticket sales draw Girth & Mirthers into an inverse world. Measuring with ticket-tape serves as an opportunity to flip the script and positively resignify the men's girth. Rather than privileging petite waists, they favor ample ones, whereby being fat gives one greater odds at being a winner. In both examples, the men claim a sense of "normalcy," as outlandish as their behavior may appear to outsiders. Carnival stunts like these—when the chubs get to call the shots in the pool or as they are happily groped while being measured with raffle tickets—invert the gay big men's generally abject experiences of being desexualized outside of the protective environment of this special weekend, instead creating a positive experience of wielding and exploring their erotic capital.

FLAUNTING ONE'S RIGHT TO SEXUAL CITIZENSHIP

Another theme of performative protest that emerged from the Super Weekend was flaunting one's right to sexual citizenship through donning various rebellious outfits. Volunteering as bartender in the hospitality suite, I took in fat-revealing, sexually suggestive clothing. The big men displayed their goods, regardless—and precisely because of—their girth. Because it is unsanctioned for fat bodies to show skin and wear seductive clothing, and because they are generally uncomfortable flaunting their bodies, the men donned various outfits as their weapon for "freedom fighting."

A fun-loving, young-looking twenty-something with a round face and oval-shaped glasses that accentuated his chubby cheeks asserted his right to sexual citizenship with his provocative outfits. His body harness—a large center ring in the front, fastened by chunky black straps—drew attention to his belly. He showed off his plump derrière in leather chaps and a Stars-and-Stripes jockstrap, revealing, rather than camouflaging, his fat body. Later, he showed up shirtless, wearing white football pants, his black rubber jockstrap visible through skintight spandex, with a label in front saying, "Nasty Pig." He showed off his athletic uniform and play-gear, implying, "I am a real 'pig' who likes it dirty." In the Super Weekend's fat-affirming carnivalesque framework, the meaning of dress changed; his carefully selected adornment enabled him to express a rebellious attitude and reframe his self-image. In picking out his wardrobe, he engaged in reinventing his fat body unapologetically as an object of sexual desire, reclaiming his right to self-definition.

Generally, the big men's bodies are read as soft, fat, and effeminized. To counter feminization, the men try to parlay their bigger build into masculine capital. They actively reconstruct the swelling of their generous frames in ways that pay "homage to the phallic power" of masculinity (Hennen 2008, 85). For example, one big man brought tees reading "Big Daddy," "Bigger Is Better," and "Big Dog's Well-Hung Drywall Co., We Have Big Tools!"; he wore other tees with funny and intentionally offensive slogans that said, "Let's play army. I'll lie down . . . and you can blow the hell out of me." Another displayed a grizzly bear with the slogan "Come any closer, and I'll eat you up." With such slogans and evocative attire, the big men insinuate, tongue-in-cheek, that being big gives them bigger genitalia, rendering their sexuality larger-than-life. And in the context of the Super Weekend, as Bourdieu (1996) would remark, any discussion of "swelling" rather quickly degenerates into various analogies to male erection (196–97). Bourdieu interprets such insinuations as "symbolic remaking of anatomical differences" (195).

In the carnivalesque atmosphere of the Super Weekend, fat exhibitionism is welcome and supported, giving the big men an opportunity to feel like sexual citizens and allowing them to recalculate their allure. One coordinator told me, "At the Super Weekend, you can feel attractive; 362 days a year, people make jokes about you, but here you can go into the pool and an admirer may say, 'Look at that big guy,' as a compliment," not a put-down. It is flattering to be recognized as a sexual citizen; for these men, it feels especially wonderful to be acknowledged and treated as sexual beings and to experience the same pleasures other gay men do. Through creative activism, they boldly repackage themselves and reclaim their sexuality, some claiming it for the first time. However, theirs is a temporary liberation at this carnivalesque retreat (Bakhtin 1968). They exercise their power and celebrate their fat identities only within their safe network, which does not reach mainstream society, not even the gay community, both of which regulate and impose rigid body ideals. Such retreats are "identity coves"— temporary enclaves that allow for amplified presentation of self (Hennen 2008, 18).

Nonetheless, as the big men themselves report, they are glad this temporary respite exists. This weekend getaway with other big gay men opens up a realm of creative possibilities where the "process of dissent, refusal, and carnivalesque" mimicry cannot simply be reduced to what will happen the "morning after" (Halberstam 2012, 135). As Halberstam asserts, "carnivals are . . . protests that never envision a return to 'normal life,' but see normal life as . . . a fiction used to bludgeon the unruly back into resignation" (135). In my research, I witnessed distinct carryovers in the men's behaviors from weekend retreats to local events. Taking over the semi-private space of the gay motel for the duration of the Super Weekend and publicly hamming it up with other Girth & Mirthers during a local pride parade are prime examples of out-of-town retreats and local events mutually reinforcing one another, allowing the big men to dream up alternatives to mainstream gay life. These carnivalesque weekend acts also have the cumulative effect of giving big gay men the wherewithal, but more importantly fun strategies, to weather the shame of fat and gay stigma in their everyday lives.

PERFORMING MASCULINITIES

In the "Chub-and-Chaser Contest," the men poked fun at, and almost completely masculinized, the traditional beauty pageant, appropriating the male gaze to focus on the fat bodies of the big gay men. They also mocked "gay hot-body contests" for which they would not have been considered. Nine chub contestants "loosely" constructed a recognizable masculine persona, for example, a soldier, football player, biker. The winner, selected by the audience's volume of applause, was judged not only by his physical characteristics, but also by the image he portrayed, as he strutted his stuff during the dance-off to Missy Elliott's song, "Hot Boyz."

While some consensus exists on a contestant's physical characteristics, there is less agreement on their attitudes and personas. One beefy contestant had a shaved head and tattoo, flicked his tongue like Gene Simmons, and claimed he had had sex with nine men in a foxhole while serving in Desert Storm. Another contestant, a bearded chub, wore a Denver Broncos football jersey, later stripping it off. Twirling around like a diva complete with some breast-dancing action, he dropped his drawers and shook his behind. A stocky Silver-Daddy Bear with rosy cheeks, an older man resembling Ernest Hemingway, looked comfortable in his tie-dyed shirt. The audience shouted "Woof, woof!" in approval, a compliment among Bears. Suavely, Daddy Bear planted a kiss on the emcee's lips. Including older men signals Girth & Mirth's greater level of acceptance of, and admiration for, aging gay bodies, when in reality the gay world makes men feel older a lot sooner than in the heterosexual world (Slevin and Linneman 2010). Another big man wore a Harley Davidson hat and flannel shirt with cutoff sleeves, joking about cruising for sex in truck-stop bathrooms. He coolly dropped his drawers and wiggled his ample buttocks against the stage railing to increasing applause and cheers. This biker exuded the full package, both appearance and panache. When the emcee stood beside each contestant to determine the winner by the audience's applause, he was the clear champion. Chub contestants assumed some leeway in performing their gendered self-presentation. Rather than humping the stage railing, the biker rubbed his derriere against it, a submissive/recipient posture emulating heterosexual gender-role expectations. Other chubs pushed their "femme" identity further. When Denver Broncos took off his jersey, he drew attention to anatomy typically thought of as a female sex characteristic: he cupped his hands to emphasize the shape of his breasts with accompanying dance movements. His dance mimicked a female burlesque dancer rotating her breasts with tassels, sending a deliberate sexual signal. Thus, when it comes to gender presentation, the Super Weekend offers room to maneuver among a range of masculinities.

Girth & Mirthers perform size as sexuality and masculinity, accentuating and embracing the very physical features used to shame them. In his performance, Desert Storm plays with a homoerotic undercurrent in all-male settings, like the military. His presentation, informed by stereotypical masculinity, reinforces the idea of a "real" man being sexually adventurous with multiple sexual partners. And Silver-Daddy Bear's performance represents a softer side of masculinity, signaling a less sexualized identity than Desert Storm's—one that is less provocative, just a regular guy, down-to-earth, at ease with his body. The biker portrays the regular-guy look, as well. His Harley hat signals outlaw biker culture, from which these weekend runs originated. He is most likely middle-class if he could afford to go on a weekend retreat; yet, he probably took very little time for self-reflection before he chose to perform a working-class "bubba drag" (Hennen 2008, 113–14).

This bastardized "contest" is anything *but* a beauty pageant, not only because tiaras and satin sashes are absent, but also because if there *is* an "ideal" body, it is a *fat* body exposing a protruding belly and with accoutrements that signal the big men's desirability. Girth & Mirthers use the carnivalesque to engage in category work, in which they lightheartedly resignify fatness into a desirable category, not a stigmatized one. While the Chub-and-Chaser Contest appears to be mostly about performing tropes of hegemonic masculinity, it also allows creative license for deconstructing masculinity through campy performances of fat gay sexuality. Society feminizes fat men and gay men, yet some of the playful, campy-queer performances of fat gay sexuality at the Super Weekend do not fully seek to disavow effeminacy, as Bears are wont to do. Rather, a few chubs seem open to embracing a performative resignification of femininity as an integral component of an active fat (and gay) sexuality. Likewise, a Girth & Mirther I interviewed commented that the group provides a space where members do not have to put on the "butch" act. This signals that the club allows for a wider range of gender performances that go into producing legible forms of fat-gay subjectivity.[2]

Playfully Disregarding Shame

Yet another theme of performative protest that emerged from my data was playfully disregarding shame, which epitomized the Girth & Mirthers' creative responses to fat stigma.

This theme was illustrated through a Gay Pride Parade float, "Rub-a-Dub-Dub, Big Men in a Tub," for which they unexpectedly won "Best Float." It consisted of a larger-than-life bathtub with shower curtains blowing in the breeze, overflowing with big men, all blowing bubbles. The float served as remedy for the big men's having been overlooked during previous Pride Parades when they had only experienced either derision or mere applause from onlookers, but certainly not formal recognition from gay community leaders.

Even though "Rub-a-Dub-Dub" earned "Best Float," it probably did little to change the big men's standing in the gay community. It was an instance of the big men adopting the acceptable party line, purposely capitulating to stereotypes others have of them and playing a recognizable role for men of their size as jolly fat men. However, Girth & Mirthers' willingness to be typecast comes at a price–the stigma sticks, perpetuating the stereotype of them as funny fat guys.

Ostensibly, in Gay Pride's festive context, the flamboyant and over-the-top float was simply appreciated as grotesque, as queering everything, from a nursery rhyme to sexuality. Girth & Mirther's float was not only about desperately seeking normality, but also about insisting on playing with multiple meanings to refuse any single, over-simplified rejection of fat. It worked well with its multiple insinuations—the innocence of a familiar children's rhyme, the allusion to three naked men in *any* tub implying "gay," and the fun of being in a tub and rub-a-dub-dubbing—being transgressive. The big men's performance aligns with LeBesco's (2004) call for fat politics that engage constant playfulness.

Conclusion

A takeaway from this ethnographic study of Girth & Mirth is that one of the ways to combat sizeism is by flaunting its limits through joyful disregard. These big gay men find ways to flip the script and engage in playful identity reconstruction as they celebrate their differences in body shape and size. One big man recapped: "I think we as a group at Pride have tried to show that we're not all just the pretty-perfect, chiseled guys. We are who we are. We accept who we are. We know we're not society's ideal of physical perfection. We're big guys, we have fun, and we're okay with it."

This cultural study of Girth & Mirth examined the seeming contradictions among the big gay men's desire to be normal; to redefine and embrace fat stigma; and to play with, exaggerate, and accentuate the very things about themselves and their bodies that are stigmatized. My findings support some of the conclusions other researchers have reached about how marginalized groups manage stigma by redefining themselves. They show how Girth & Mirthers play with who they are, creating disorder as they shamelessly perform their fat bodies. Their performances help us recognize that while their defiant acts are shameful, they are, nonetheless, liberatory.

My findings cannot be overgeneralized to the experiences of *all* people of size in queer communities. Intersections of sizeism with other systems of oppression—racism, classism, sexism, heterosexism, ableism, ageism—remain for future research to engage more seriously. For instance, few have researched how size intersects with race, sexual orientation, and gender, as in the case of fat African American lesbian and bisexual women. Such women presumably would have lower levels of body dissatisfaction compared to white or heterosexual women (Wilson 2009). Intersectional research may yield findings that show more forgiving attitudes toward fat than those held by the (mostly white) gay men in this chapter.

Likewise, this chapter said little about the ways the big men's racial or ethnic identities mutually construct their fat gayness or position them differently within the Girth & Mirth subculture.[3] Elsewhere, I have written about race-based problems with representation in the big men's' communities (Whitesel 2017), which tend to overlook same-gender-loving big men of color in their event advertising and erotic imagery, instead catering to predominantly white men. In the past three to six years, this has pushed big men of color to create their own weekend runs like Heetizm Myami, Big Boy Pride Orlando, and Heavy Hitters Pride Houston. In response to other gay prides and circuit parties across the nation that reinforce the mainstream gay media's narrow focus on young, hairless, thin or muscular, white men, these annual gatherings place men of size *and* of color at the fore. For example, the 2017 theme for Heavy Hitters' weekend is "My Presence Matters." The group's webpage describes Heavy Hitters as "a place where EVERY pound has a story" and where attendees come to "celebrate the urban man of size, his admirers and allies" (www.heavyhitterspride. com). The group's Facebook page reads, "Become part of the movement and celebrate your beauty amongst those that empower you—NOT TOLERATE YOU." The online photography and marketing materials for all three groups make it clear that theirs are events where same-gender-loving black and brown bodies of size are welcome and encouraged to attend. None of the promotional materials read "whites excluded," but perhaps they are less likely to attend, as it would force them to become conscious of their whiteness. If imagery like that put out by Heetizm, Big Boy Pride, and Heavy Hitters did not exist, then same-gender-loving big men of color might find it difficult to recognize themselves in existing big gay men's imagery, and thus might internalize the message "You are not welcome" (Whitesel 2017).

At the recommendation of a few members of the local Girth & Mirth board, I also went to another big gay men's weekend reunion called "Convergence," which had a distinctly different flair than the Super Weekend. The two events differed in how they approach status differentiation. The Super Weekend revels in the "crude" aspect of carnival à la Bakhtin (1968), while the more sanitized Convergence offers mainstream cultural activities to elevate the big gay men's diminished status. These activities include seminars, themed dinners, a dance, sightseeing, and outings to local cultural events, all of which are about big gay men's seeking class validation and respectability through engaging in "conspicuous consumption" (Veblen 1899). Moreover, Convergence takes place in a mainstream luxury hotel. Contrast this to the Super Weekend at what most would consider a "seedy" motel, where a big man in "bubba drag," likely dressed beneath his social rank, "social slums" it, as it were.

In American society, size often intersects with a class-based assumption that being fat equals being lazy and poor; therefore, Convergence's class-elevating route toward the reduction of fat stigma is unsurprising. Seeking class distinction through cultural consumption differs from the uncouth Super Weekend that mostly makes a mockery out of status-seeking behavior. In my book *Fat Gay Men: Girth, Mirth and the Politics of Stigma* (2014), I chose to carefully (or depending on the reader's take, "infuriatingly") avoid directly privileging one strategy over another as a better means for reconfiguring fat-gay stigma, electing instead to present the ambivalent nature of both big men's events (White 2015). The two weekend events led me to ask whether mocking the system as is done during the Super Weekend or assimilating toward the system as is done at Convergence is more effective in stigma reduction. Certainly, Queer Theory has its own answer, leaning toward the former.

In addition, scant research takes up the intersection of fat with transgender, where one violates two forms of "normative" embodiment (White 2014). Fatness influences how trans bodies are viewed; it can affect how transgender people's gender self-presentation is honored or how others might misgender them. The way a transgender person's fat body might be affirmed depends greatly on whether one is "read" as a man or a woman (Bergman 2009) and is even more complicated for those fighting to transcend binary obligations to choose one gender identity and living as fat and non-binary. Future research should heed Pausé's (2014) clarion call, heralding a new dawn of fresh and remodeled thinking within the relatively new field of Fat Studies, whereby its scholars should move forward in fully embracing intersectionality.

NOTES

1. However, during my time with the local club, its president ethnically identified as Mexican American.
2. Francis Ray White (2015, 250) deserves a great deal of credit for the last three sentences, pushing me to conduct a "deeper analysis of the gendered dynamics of fat gay identity."
3. White (2015, 250) also urged me to pursue further research into the implications of race/ethnicity at "presumably predominately white events."

REFERENCES

American Community Survey. 2008. "ACS Three-Year Estimates, 2006–2008." *www.census.gov*.

Asbill, D. Lacy. 2009. "'I'm Allowed to Be a Sexual Being': The Distinctive Social Conditions of the Fat Burlesque Stage." In *The Fat Studies Reader*, edited by Esther Rothblum and Sondra Solovay, 299–304. New York: NYU Press.

Babcock, Barbara. 1978. *The Reversible World: Symbolic Inversion in Art and Society*. Ithaca: Cornell University Press.

Bacon, Linda, Judith Stern, Marta Van Loan, and Nancy Keim. 2005. "Size Acceptance and Intuitive Eating Improve Health for Obese, Female Chronic Dieters." *Journal of the American Dietetic Association* 105: 929–36.

Bakhtin, Mikhail. 1968. *Rabelais and His World*. Cambridge: MIT Press.

Bergman, S. Bear. 2009. "Part-Time Fatso." In *The Fat Studies Reader*, edited by Esther Rothblum and Sondra Solovay, 139–42. New York: NYU Press.

Boero, Natalie. 2012. *Killer Fat: Media, Medicine, and Morals in the American "Obesity Epidemic."* New Brunswick: Rutgers University Press.

Bourdieu, Pierre. 1996. "Masculine Domination Revisited." *Berkeley Journal of Sociology* 41: 189–203.

Braziel, Jana, and Kathleen LeBesco. 2001. *Bodies out of Bounds: Fatness and Transgression*. Berkeley: University of California Press.

Brown, Wendy. 1993. "Wounded Attachments." *Political Theory* 21: 390–410.

Cascio, Justin. 2014. "Why I Still Go to Pride Events." In *Recognize: The Voices of Bisexual Men*, edited by Robyn Ochs and H. Sharif Williams, 67–70. Boston: Bisexual Resource Center.

Cleto, Fabio. 2002. "Introduction: Queering the Camp." In *Camp: Queer Aesthetics and the Performing Subject: A Reader*, edited by Fabio Cleto, 1–42. Ann Arbor: University of Michigan Press.

Collins, Patricia. 1986. "Learning from the Outsider Within: The Sociological Significance of Black Feminist Thought." *Social Problems* 33: 14–32.

Connell, Raewyn. 1996. "Politics of Changing Men." *Australian Humanities Review*, December. *www.australianhumanitiesreview.org/archive/Issue-Dec-1996/connell.html*.

Dworkin, Sari, and Barbara Kerr. 1987. "Comparison of Interventions for Women Experiencing Body Image Problems." *Journal of Counseling Psychology* 34: 136–40.

Foster-Gimbel, Olivia, and Renee Engeln. 2016. "Fat Chance! Experiences and Expectations of Anti-fat Bias in the Gay Male Community." *Psychology of Sexual Orientation and Gender Diversity* 3: 63–70.

Gailey, Jeannine, and Ariane Prohaska. 2006. "'Knocking Off a Fat Girl': An Exploration of Hogging, Male Sexuality and Neutralizations." *Deviant Behavior* 27: 31–49.

Gleeson, Jill. 2016. "The Ugliness of Fat Shaming." Edge Media Network. *chicago. edgemedianetwork.com/entertainment/culture/news/200868/the_ugliness_of_fat_shaming*.

Goffman, Erving. 1963a. *Behavior in Public Places: Notes on the Social Organization of Gatherings*. New York: Free Press.

———. 1963b. *Stigma: Notes on the Management of Spoiled Identity*. Englewood Cliffs: Prentice-Hall.

Goode, Erich. 2004. "The Stigma of Obesity." In *Readings in Deviant Behavior*, edited by Alex Thio and Thomas C. Calhoun, 176–82. Boston: Pearson/Allyn & Bacon.

———. 2005 "Physical Characteristics as Deviance." In *Deviant Behavior*, edited by Erich Goode, 324–51. Upper Saddle River: Pearson Education.

Gremore, Graham. 2016. "Author Calls Out Gay Men for 'Fat-Shaming and Negative Body Talk.'" *Queerty*, February 13. *www.queerty.com/curb-your-fatism-author-talks-anti-fat -stigma-among-gay-men-and-what-we-can-do-about-it-20160213*.

Halberstam, J. Jack. 2012. *Gaga Feminism: Sex, Gender, and the End of Normal*. Boston: Beacon Press.

Hennen, Peter. 2008. *Faeries, Bears, and Leathermen: Men in Community Queering the Masculine*. Chicago: University of Chicago Press.

Lang, Nico. 2016. "Fat Shaming, Toxic Masculinity, and the Gay Male Beauty Myth." *The Daily Beast*, February 2. *www.thedailybeast.com/articles/2016/02/02/fat-shaming-toxic -masculinity-and-the-gay-male-beauty-myth.html*.

LeBesco, Kathleen. 2004. *Revolting Bodies? The Struggle to Redefine Fat Identity*. Amherst: University of Massachusetts Press.

Lee, Steve. 2014. "'Fat Gay Men: Girth, Mirth and the Politics of Stigma' Paints Mixed Picture of the Realities that Fat Gay Men Face." *LGBT Weekly*, August 25. *lgbtweekly. com/2014/08/25/fat-gay-men-girth-mirth-and-the-politics-of-stigma-paints-mixed-picture -of-the-realities-that-fat-gay-men-face*.

Mathews, Travis, dir. 2008. *Fat Activism Goes Big* (film). San Francisco (out of circulation).

McAllister, Heather. 2009. "Embodying Fat Liberation." In *The Fat Studies Reader*, edited by Esther Rothblum and Sondra Solovay, 305–11. New York: NYU Press.

Murray, Samantha. 2005. "Doing Politics or Selling Out? Living the Fat Body." *Women's Studies* 34: 265–77.

Pausé, Cat. 2014. "X-Static Process: Intersectionality within the Field of Fat Studies." *Fat Studies* 3: 80–85.

Probyn, Elspeth. 2004. "Everyday Shame." *Cultural Studies* 18: 329–49.

Prohaska, Ariane, and Jeannine A. Gailey. 2009. "Fat Women as 'Easy Targets': Achieving

Masculinity through Hogging." In *The Fat Studies Reader*, edited by Esther Rothblum and Sondra Solovay, 158–66. New York: NYU Press.

———. 2010. "Achieving Masculinity through Sexual Predation: The Case of Hogging." *Journal of Gender Studies* 19: 13–25.

Pyle, Nathaniel, and Noa Klein. 2011. "Fat. Hairy. Sexy: Contesting Standards of Beauty and Sexuality in the Gay Community." In *Embodied Resistance: Challenging the Norms, Breaking the Rules*, edited by Chris Bobel and Samantha Kwan, 78–87. Nashville: Vanderbilt University Press.

Pyle, Nathaniel, and Michael Loewy. 2009. "Double Stigma: Fat Men and Their Male Admirers." In *The Fat Studies Reader*, edited by Esther Rothblum and Sondra Solovay, 143–50. New York: NYU Press.

Richardson, Diane. 2000. "Constructing Sexual Citizenship: Theorizing Sexual Rights." *Critical Social Policy* 20: 105–35.

Rogers, Thomas. 2007. "Big Girls, Don't Cry: The Fight for the Right to Be Fat, Queer, and Proud." *Village Voice*, June 12. *www.villagevoice.com/2007-06-12/nyc-life/big-girls -don-t-cry/full*.

Sedgwick, Eve. 1995. "Shame and Performativity: Henry James's *New York Edition* Prefaces." In *Henry James's* New York Edition*: The Construction of Authorship*, edited by David Mc-Whirter, 206–39. Stanford: Stanford University Press.

Simpson, Paul. 2015. *Middle-Aged Gay Men, Ageing and Ageism: Over the Rainbow?* New York: Palgrave Macmillan.

Slevin, Kathleen, and Thomas Linneman. 2010. "Old Gay Men's Bodies and Masculinities." *Men and Masculinities* 12: 483–507.

Solovay, Sondra, and Esther Rothblum. 2009. "Introduction." In *The Fat Studies Reader*, edited by Esther Rothblum and Sondra Solovay, 1–7. New York: NYU Press.

Textor, Alex. 1999. "Organization, Specialization, and Desires in the Big Men's Movement: Preliminary Research in the Study of Subculture-Formation." *International Journal of Sexuality and Gender Studies* 4: 217–39.

Veblen, Thorstein. 1899. *The Theory of the Leisure Class*. London: Macmillan.

Wann, Marilyn. 1998. *FAT! SO? Because You Don't Have to Apologize for Your Size.* Berkeley: Ten Speed Press.

———. 2009. "Foreword: Fat Studies: An Invitation to a Revolution." In *The Fat Studies Reader*, edited by Esther Rothblum and Sondra Solovay, ix–xxv. New York: NYU Press.

Warner, Michael. 2005. *Publics and Counterpublics*. Cambridge: Zone Books.

White, Francis. 2014. "Fat/Trans: Queering the Activist Body." *Fat Studies* 3: 86–100.

———. 2015. "Book Review: *Fat Gay Men: Girth, Mirth and the Politics of Stigma*." *Journal of Gender Studies* 24: 248–50.

Whitesel, Jason. 2014. *Fat Gay Men: Girth, Mirth, and the Politics of Stigma*. New York: NYU Press.

———. 2017. "Same-Gender-Loving Big Men of Color." *From the Square / NYU Press Blog*, June 30. *www.fromthesquare.org/same-gender-loving-big-men-color*.

Wilson, Bianca. 2009. "Widening the Dialogue to Narrow the Gap in Health Disparities: Approaches to Fat Black Lesbian and Bisexual Women's Health Promotion." In *The Fat Studies Reader*, edited by Esther Rothblum and Sondra Solovay, 54–64. New York: NYU Press.

Wyman, Julie, dir. 2005. *Buoyant* (film). New York: Women Make Movies, Inc. *www.wmm. com/filmcatalog/pages/c652.shtml*.

9

"What's Love Got to Do with It?"

The Embodied Activism of Domestic Violence Survivors on Welfare

Sheila M. Katz

In San Francisco on Valentine's Day 2004, ten welfare-rights activists staged a mock wedding outside city hall. The diverse group of women wore wedding veils, black or white dresses, and carried protest signs. "What's Love Got to Do with It? No Welfare to Weddings," one said. Others read: "Welfare to Weddings, George W. Bush Says . . . Til Death Do Us Part?," "No Welfare Weddings for Dollars," "Battered Women are Battered by Welfare Reform," and "We're a CalWORKs Family, But My Husband is in Jail for Domestic Violence, Do I Still Get My Cash Bonus?" But even more atten-tion grabbing than the protest signs was that each woman used makeup to simulate black eyes to signify personal experiences with domestic violence, including bruises that men they trusted put on their pregnant bodies. Two of the activists, in particular, were escaping severely abusive marriages and one had recently moved several states away to escape an abusive boyfriend. Local print media and two local television sta-tions covered the event.

The activists' aim was to raise awareness about the experiences of domestic vio-lence survivors who received welfare; they were "welfare mothers" or, in other words, participants in the Temporary Assistance for Needy Families (TANF) program called CalWORKs in California. They were protesting the hypocrisy of the George W. Bush administration's marriage promotion agenda for poor women. Under the marriage promotion proposal, the Bush administration focused on "traditional marriage," spe-cifically between a man and a woman, through the allocation of "federal money [to be] used for specific activities like advertising campaigns to publicize the value of mar-riage, instruction in marriage skills and mentoring programs that use married couples as role models" (Pear and Kirkpatrick 2004). In addition, money was specifically allo-cated to fund "fatherhood initiatives" that concentrated on men's parenting and "role" in relationships, including the generation of family finances. In 2004, as part of his federal welfare reauthorization plan, then US president Bush proposed apportioning $1.5 billion for such programs for poor couples. However, his proposition included nothing for domestic violence prevention or services for survivors, even though do-mestic violence is a strikingly common denominator for women on welfare. National estimates suggest that between half and two-thirds of mothers on welfare have expe-rienced domestic violence at some point in their lives, and, for many, partner abuse is what set in motion their need for welfare assistance (Tolman and Raphael 2000). The federal marriage-incentive policy suggests that marriage is a solution to the problem of poverty, a "solution" that ignores that many marriages are unsafe and women should not feel pressured to partner or remain partnered with men who are abusive.

As a result of the Valentine's Day protest, state and local agencies, such as the county of San Francisco's welfare department, invited the grassroots activists to have a voice in "policy working groups" for welfare and domestic violence. As that year progressed, these activists also led a coalition of grassroots welfare-rights groups across the country to plan larger national actions. Instead of internalizing the shame of surviving domestic violence, the activists leveraged their most powerful resource—the bodies that survived the abuse—to resist welfare reform policies that touted marriage promotion initiatives over services for domestic violence survivors. In other words, the mothers' activism functioned as embodied resistance to welfare reauthorization proposals. Their agenda was a direct challenge to the stigma of surviving domestic violence, and, through their collective efforts, they raised awareness of poor women's experiences with domestic violence. This chapter asks how these women rejected the assumptions of politicians and the general public about what poor women's bodies should "look like" and the shame associated with being a victim of domestic violence. Furthermore, it explores how the activists used their bodies and the "shirts off their backs" through grassroots activism to resist welfare policy.

Internalizing Shame: The Health Consequences of Partner Violence for Poor Women

Approximately half of women in the United States experience some type of domestic or sexual violence at some point in their lives (Breiding, Chen, and Black 2014).[1] This number is consistently higher for low-income women or those who receive assistance from the welfare system, with estimates closer to two-thirds (Tolman and Raphael 2000). While women of all economic statuses and classes experience intimate partner violence (IPV) and domestic violence, women who are lower-income need more economic help from public assistance to escape the violence, thus triggering more reports than from those of victims from other social classes. The Centers for Disease Control (CDC) defines IPV, which is the broader term for what we commonly refer to as domestic violence, as violence between people that "includes physical violence, sexual violence, stalking and psychological aggression (including coercive tactics) by a current or former intimate partner (i.e., spouse, boyfriend/girlfriend, dating partner, or ongoing sexual partner)" (Breiding et al. 2015, 11). The National Coalition Against Domestic Violence (on their website) defines domestic violence as "the willful intimidation, physical assault, battery, sexual assault, and/or other abusive behavior as part of a systematic pattern of power and control perpetrated by one intimate partner against another. It includes physical violence, sexual violence, psychological violence, and emotional abuse" (NCADV 2017). Domestic violence has five central forms: physical, sexual, verbal, emotional, and financial. Further, feminists connect the issues of control present in domestic violence to broader issues of gender inequality, patriarchy, and systems of oppression (Katz and McGuire 2018). Therefore, domestic violence is not just violence between individuals who know each other or are in a relationship. Rather, it is a form of violence embedded in systems of power and privilege that enables certain groups to wield control over others—such as men over women, whites over nonwhites, upper socioeconomic classes over lower ones, and so on.

Domestic violence produces numerous "negative consequences on health and well-being, including physical injury, depression, low self-esteem, and anxiety disorders" (Kaukinen 2014, 284), and these impacts are exacerbated by poverty for poor victims. Mothers on welfare who experienced domestic violence are almost twice as likely to report a physical limitation or rate their health as poor as those who have never been abused (Allard, Tolman, and Rosen 2003). The CDC reports that domestic-violence survivors report more health problems such as headaches, poor physical and mental health, trouble sleeping, and increased chronic pain than those who have never experienced IPV (Black et al. 2011). After leaving abusive relationships, people can experience multiple mental health problems including post-traumatic stress disorder (PTSD), depression, low self-esteem, or increased anxiety (Brewster 2002). Higher rates of depression and PTSD are found among mothers on welfare who experienced abuse than those who have not (Lyon 2000).

The reasons IPV causes such severe health consequences, especially those pertaining to mental health, are largely societal. Sexist attitudes toward women stigmatize those who experience abuse and encourage them to internalize or minimize their experiences with IPV (Davidson and Gervais 2015; McBride and Perry 2016). Because domestic violence occurs in the "private sphere" of the home, away from public view, social expectations dictate that women should deal with "private" troubles privately, even though IPV is illegal. When women, and especially poor women, report domestic violence, they are dismissed, disbelieved, doubted, or discounted. As a result, many victims do not report the crime. In fact, domestic violence is one of the least reported violent crimes (Breiding et al. 2015).

Women are stigmatized and shamed by society and social institutions for experiencing abuse, not unlike low-income women who experience a similar shaming and stigma about being poor. Adair (2002, 452), in her research about poor women's bodies and social control, found that "systems of power produce and patrol poverty through the reproduction of both social and bodily markers." Low-income domestic-violence survivors feel social pressure to conceal their experiences with IPV. This leads to women trying to cover up the bodily evidence of abuse such as bruises and scratches with clothing, scarves, makeup, or sunglasses (Katz 2019). In addition to concealing the evidence of domestic violence on the body, compounded by institutional obfuscation by the legal and criminal justice system, women also mask their experiences when they internalize the shame associated with domestic violence (Overstreet and Quinn 2013). Women are socialized to feel shame about their experiences with domestic violence, which discourages poor women from seeking help from the welfare system. Both issues—domestic violence and poverty—are viewed by society as individual failings instead of as the social problems they are, which have arisen from entrenched gender and class inequalities.

Economic status and financial dependence also makes it more difficult for anyone, but especially low-income women, to leave abusive relationships (Davis 1999). Escaping domestic violence as well as coping with its everyday effects is very expensive. Costs, such as moving expenses; legal fees associated with divorce, custody battles, or fighting for child support; and health care bills, add up quickly. Thus, women who need financial assistance to leave abusive relationships often turn to their families, shelter or advocacy groups, or the welfare system to provide the emotional and financial support necessary to leave (Davis 1999).

Controlling Women's Bodies at the Intersection of Welfare Reform and Partner Violence

In August 1996, President Bill Clinton signed the Personal Responsibility and Work Opportunity Reconciliation Act (PRWORA), which ended federal welfare for low-income families as an entitlement program and "reformed" the US welfare system. The TANF program gave states block grants to create new state-implemented welfare programs. This social policy was commonly referred to as "welfare reform" and it emphasized work for participants, time limits on public assistance, and punitive sanctions for noncompliance with regulations. Half of adult welfare participants were required to engage in work activities under the TANF program. The goal of "welfare reform" was to get participants quickly off welfare and to end dependence on government aid.

Public sentiment and assumptions about who receives welfare has always mischaracterized the welfare population and made a distinction between the deserving poor—or those we "should" help with public assistance—and the undeserving poor—or those who should not receive assistance. This distinction is based on racist and sexist stereotypes, specifically of Black women, despite the fact that white women are the predominate population on welfare (Katz 2019). In the US during the 1970s and 1980s, growing middle class resentment, misconception, and racism directed toward welfare benefit recipients affected the construction of welfare reform policies (Katz 2012). During this time period the "welfare queen" caricature was deployed by politicians and the media, as well as presidential candidate and later president Ronald Reagan, as a derogatory term for poor women who received benefits from the welfare system. This trope demonized Black single mothers in particular as lazy and guilty of defrauding the government to access welfare benefits. This caricature was consistently proven inaccurate by extensive social science research on low-income mothers; however, it continues to affect policymaking and public opinion around welfare and poverty issues.[2] As Adair and Dahlberg adeptly note, "poor women are feared, blamed, mocked, ridiculed, and punished in US media and society, and hence in public policy" (Adair and Dahlberg 2003, 4). And about the welfare reforms of 1996, Luna (2009) explains, "because of the negative social constructions associated with welfare, to many, the punitive nature of the policy seems justified" (442). Kelly (2010) agrees, finding "the controlling image of welfare mothers consists of racist stereotypes that represent women on public assistance as childlike, hyperfertile, lazy, and bad mothers. The construction of this controlling image sexist and racist stereotypes, myths, and moral judgments served to publicly justify the dismantling of public assistance programs and institute increased regulations on recipients" (77).

Social science research, such as Kaplan's *Not Our Kind of Girl* (1997), illustrates how Black single mothers, more generally, are stigmatized, demonized, and scapegoated for a variety of contemporary social problems. Racist and sexist stereotypes merge with public disdain for welfare recipients and are projected onto the bodies of poor Black mothers. Therefore, welfare reform became an opportunity to enact policies that sought to control poor, especially nonwhite, women's bodies. For example, the "family cap" policy played into the racist myth that Black women on welfare have more babies just to get a bigger welfare check. Therefore, the new welfare reform provision stipulated that a woman would not receive any benefits for any new children she had while receiving welfare. This provision thereby controlled poor women's reproductive freedom based on racist myths of Black women's childbearing. Further, welfare reform, like society in general, ignored the reality that most women on welfare have experienced domestic violence, and, in fact, through sanctions for noncompliance of work requirements, served to amplify women's trauma by making it more difficult to receive government support while escaping and recovering from abuse.

Domestic violence is one of the most commonly mentioned barriers to higher education and employment among low-income women (Katz 2008). It can derail a woman's efforts to obtain self-sufficiency through employment that enables her to move out of poverty. What's more, domestic violence frequently intensifies when mothers seek education, training, or work (Tolman and Raphael 2000; Lyon 2000). Batterers often sabotage women's efforts to work or study by making threats, inflicting injuries before tests or interviews, preventing women from sleeping or studying, stalking women on campus or at work, or refusing at the last minute to provide promised childcare that women need to work or attend school (Beechey and Payne 2002; Davis 1999; Kramer and Beutel 2014; Raphael 1999). A study of women on welfare in Wisconsin immediately after welfare reform was implemented found that 63 percent were fired or forced to quit their jobs due to domestic violence (Moore and Selkowe 1999). Furthermore, a study of Colorado women on welfare after the reforms found that 44 percent were prevented from working by abusive ex-partners (Pearson, Theonnes, and Griswold 1999). Domestic violence also limits employment in terms of options, quality and pay, and it renders sustained employment more difficult (Davis 1999; Lyon 2000).

Despite overwhelming research that illustrates the link between women's experiences with domestic violence and the need for welfare assistance to help them escape and rebuild their lives, the 1996 US welfare reforms neglected to include *mandatory* domestic violence safeguards such as screening, services, or waivers, all important to helping a woman recover from domestic violence. Under welfare reform, services to domestic violence survivors or waivers of the program's requirements are covered by the "Family Violence Option" (FVO). The FVO was merely an "option" in the legislation that states could implement to provide resources for participants who were experiencing or escaping domestic violence. Caseworkers can give participants waivers from the weekly work hour requirements while they are receiving domestic violence mental health services, living in a domestic violence shelter, or working on domestic violence–related legal issues. Without a waiver, if welfare participants do not meet their weekly welfare work hours, they are "sanctioned off" welfare and lose their benefits. However, not all states implemented the FVO, and even in states that did, such as California, the policy was inconsistently implemented county by county and welfare office by welfare office. In counties with higher caseloads of white clients, the FVO was more consistently used to help women escaping abuse through the provision of mental health services and waivers from welfare-to-work requirements (Spatz and Katz 2005). One of the organizations conducting research about access to and utilization of domestic violence services for mothers on welfare and raising public awareness on these issues was LIFETIME, a nonprofit grassroots community group in Oakland, California.

LIFETIME: Fighting for Rights for Women on Welfare

Low-Income Families' Empowerment through Education, LIFETIME, was founded in 1996 by Diana Spatz, a mother on welfare and student. While a student at various community colleges and later at the University of California, Berkeley, Spatz became an activist and grassroots organizer as she networked with other student parents, formed support groups, designed and conducted student-led classes, and created student parent resource centers on various local college campuses. She graduated from UC Berkeley the same year national welfare reform passed. Spatz founded LIFETIME to focus on fighting welfare reform policies that were demeaning and based on disparaging stereotypes of poor women and that restricted access to higher education. The organization focused on developing participants' activism by building leadership skills, teaching the structural aspects of welfare reform policy, and empowering political participation. The organization held parent leadership trainings to provide information about welfare policy and upcoming policy changes and about how to become involved in political advocacy. LIFETIME's organizing strategy was to empower parents to fight for rights in the welfare system and to work collectively to change punitive policies through a three-step system. Step one helped parents through immediate personal crisis with advocacy services empowering them to resolve their individual problems with the welfare system. Step two engaged them in leadership development and political issue training to enable participants to work collectively on grassroots campaigns to challenge welfare policies. And step three mobilized the participants in grassroots political action to change policies that caused the crisis. To achieve these three steps, LIFETIME provided peer-advocacy for welfare participants pursuing higher education. The organization conducted outreach workshops at community colleges and universities, as well as at the welfare offices, in the Bay Area designed to teach welfare participants how to advocate for themselves, how (or when) to reach out to LIFETIME or other advocacy organizations for support, and when to file a state appeal. Those who participated in LIFETIME's leadership trainings were designated "Parent Leaders" and were the most active in LIFETIME's grassroots political work and actions.

Methods

From 2003 to 2011, I conducted ethnographic research in the San Francisco Bay Area of California through in-depth qualitative interviews, focus groups, and participant observation with single mothers pursuing higher education while participating in the CalWORKs welfare program (Katz 2019). I recruited research participants through Bay Area community colleges and universities and through LIFETIME. My initial volunteer work with LIFETIME eventually developed into a part-time paid staff position helping the directors with research and grant writing. During the period of November 2003 through December 2006 I was engaged in both paid work in the office and observation of events and activities outside of my paid time. During this time, I observed or participated in most of LIFETIME's grassroots protests, parent leadership meetings, special events, and policy briefings.

I also interviewed forty-five women from November 2005 until December 2006, conducted three focus groups in June 2007 with eighteen additional women, and conducted second interviews with twenty-five of the forty-five interview participants in August and September 2008. In spring 2011, I conducted follow-up interviews with thirty-five of the forty-five participants (at a 78 percent retention rate). In 2006, just over half of the interview participants were involved in LIFETIME's activism (twenty-four) and the rest had no or minimal involvement (twenty-one). In 2006, interview participants in my study ranged in age from eighteen to fifty-one, with median age of thirty-three. Participants' racial and ethnic backgrounds reflected the diversity of single mothers on welfare in San Francisco and Alameda Counties: 21 percent (n=13) identified as white, 48 percent (n=30) identified as Black or African American, 21 percent (n=13) identified as Latina, 6 percent (n=4) identified as Asian Pacific Islander, and 4 percent (n=3) identified as other or multiracial. The median number of children interview participants had in 2006 was two.

Interviews and focus groups were recorded, transcribed verbatim, and entered into ATLAS.ti qualitative data software for analysis. Using longitudinal and ethnographic methods working with a marginalized population, I used a constructivist grounded theory approach to recruitment, data collection, coding, and analysis (Charmaz 2006; Charmaz and Katz 2017). I used constructivist grounded theory particularly because the population was suspicious of outsiders—especially bureaucrats or academics—asking invasive personal questions insensitive to people's stories or how they framed their experiences. Using constructivist grounded theory allowed me to conduct a few interviews or field observations, analyze them and reflect on the process, and then adjust questions or methods to be more sensitive, inclusive, and understanding of the narratives and complex experiences of participants.

Grassroots Resistance to Assumptions about Poor Women's Bodies

In my research, I heard the words "We don't talk about it" or "I can't tell anybody" or "No one will believe me" over and over again. Adair finds that "poor women learn at a young age that their stories are dangerous and obscene" (Adair and Dahlberg 2003, 4) and my participants echoed that sentiment. The women I encountered struggled with how poverty sometimes showed on their bodies through their clothes, shoes, accessories (such as their jewelry or purses), tattoos, and other signifiers such as the condition of their teeth, weight, hair, and skin. Relatedly, the women grappled with how to discuss the ways the stress of living with poverty and domestic violence exacerbated health problems and affected their bodies. However, those who were active with LIFETIME were less likely than those outside the organization to internalize the shame of poverty or surviving domestic violence. LIFETIME mothers were more likely to *externalize* the shame of poverty and surviving domestic violence. Purposely, the activists used their scant resources to resist demeaning welfare policies, especially their most powerful resource: the bodies that survived the abuse. Collectively, they organized grassroots actions aimed at reducing the stigma of surviving domestic violence and raising awareness of poor women's experiences with domestic violence. The activists expressed their belief that the welfare system intentionally judged them and targeted their bodies and their children's bodies through its reformed policies. The LIFETIME participants in this research recognized, resisted, and then embodied their activism to challenge welfare reform policies. In the following section, I explore how these women first recognized then rejected the assumptions of caseworkers, their communities, politicians, and the general public about what poor women's bodies should "look like." Then I explore how LIFETIME participants used their bodies and the "shirts off their backs" in embodied grassroots activism to resist welfare policy.

Recognizing and Resisting Assumptions about Poverty on their Bodies

First, in some of LIFETIME's advocacy work, the activists used the stereotypes about how poor mothers "should" look—and flipped the scripts. Poverty is very hard on a body. The women in this study struggled with their appearance, which was impacted by minor to severe health issues exacerbated by domestic violence, poor access to health care, substandard nutrition, and a lifetime of manual labor jobs that wear bodies out. As MMM, a Latina mother of three, thirty-one years old in 2006, said:[3]

> We had gang members who lived across the street, and I didn't look at them like, "oh, you dirty gang members," like how could I? I mean, I have the tattoos to prove that I . . . I understand [their lives in gangs and poverty], but I also understood that look. I'm thirty years old, and that [look] gets old after a while, and they hadn't really realized that they were older too. And they would look at me, and say, "Oh, you forgot where you came from" and I would say, "How can I forget? I live here (laughs), I don't forget my way home (laughs)." I have the tattoos, the scars, the emotional scars, the physical—the headaches, the whole thing, I didn't forget, but I just know that—when do you get beyond that? When do you get to move on from that?

MMM continued, sharing with me how she struggles with her "look"—specifically her gang and prison tattoos—as she tries to move out of poverty. She felt judged by those who are still "of the neighborhood" who criticized her for not acting or dressing the same as she did when she was in the gang. At the same time, she also felt judged for her look by her upper middle-class university classmates. She was acutely aware of their stares at her tattoos, her clothing, and the way she carried her body. She felt rejected and judged by both groups. Participants discussed how they felt judged both for "looking poor" and for not looking poor enough by dressing "too nice." They struggled to find a fine balance between the two.

The theme of women on welfare being judged for dressing "too nice" or "too poor" came up repeatedly. Welfare caseworkers and even the general public have ideas and conceptions about how poor people, and specifically women on welfare, are "supposed" to look. The women discussed how they felt judged daily for their clothing, tattoos, painted nails, and hairstyles. For example, when women meet with welfare caseworkers, many carefully "dress the part"—looking clean and simply put together but not "too nice." As Misha, a twenty-nine-year-old Black mother of one and community college student, explained: "If you come in there and you are dressed nice, and you are telling them that you are on aid they are going to look at you up and down, like how did you get all of that, if you know you are on aid. I think that they have a picture what a person on welfare supposed to look like." Women had to carefully represent themselves in order to access vital resources such as welfare benefits. Similar to West and Zimmerman's (1987) conception of "doing gender," these women were "doing poverty" or "doing middle class" through social class markers. The stakes are high. If they were not "believed," then their access to resources is in jeopardy.

Several women discussed losing welfare benefits while experiencing domestic violence because they didn't "look abused." One mother, Twitch, explained that her caseworker would not believe that she left her abusive boyfriend in the middle of the night with her infant son and moved to California, several states away. Twitch, as coached by the domestic violence advocates, requested domestic violence services and a waiver from the welfare-to-work requirements while she put her life back together—both of which were available under California's welfare policy. She said the caseworker looked her up and down, and said "I'll give you a domestic violence waiver when you come in here with a black eye, a police report, and a restraining order. Until then, you get a job." Needless to say, the advocates helped her appeal this, but this comment illustrates the broader problem—caseworkers were neither trained nor required to conduct domestic violence screenings. Therefore, they often resorted to the same stereotypes of poverty or domestic violence that are commonly heard in public discourse.

Through LIFETIME's empowerment and activist trainings, the mothers first learned to reject internalized shame about being in poverty or surviving domestic violence and instead view their experiences through a structural lens that explained partner violence as a systemic problem with personal consequences. The feminist expression "the personal is political" best summarizes this analysis. LIFETIME helped mothers on welfare understand and connect their personal experiences of poverty, welfare, and domestic violence with larger forces of oppression in society. Through LIFETIME's empowerment trainings, women recognized the stereotypes and caricatures of welfare mothers and domestic violence victims, and collectively worked to resist the societal shame imposed upon them. They discussed how to externalize shame, and how social institutions and systems created to "help" actually contributed to the problem. Upon this critical foundation, they worked to raise public awareness of social policy issues.

LIFETIME frequently organized women to testify in local, state, and federal hearings or to meet with politicians about poverty policy. When the activists testified about their experiences in poverty, on welfare, and with domestic violence, they took great care to "dress the part" of people who were going to business or political meetings by conforming to upper-middle-class business attire standards of business suits and conservative dresses. They exploited the normative expectation of business attire in legal settings to resist the stereotypes they regularly encountered. Sometimes, while planning legislative visits, they shopped together at local thrift stores or used a local nonprofit's "career closet" to access the necessary professional clothing. Some women had never dressed this way before while others did not feel comfortable wearing business attire. Issues of body insecurity developed during their difficult lives led some of the women to feel that they didn't deserve to wear such clothing. Together they worked through these issues, found clothing the women felt confident in, and talked about why this strategy was an important part of their message. And it worked. Often politicians or legislative staffers told the women, "Well, you don't look like welfare recipients," or, more bluntly, "you don't look poor."

This strategy both challenged normative expectations of what poor women should "look" like and built their credibility in the politicians' eyes. However, it does carry risk as it may partially reinforce the stereotypes of poor women who weren't organized enough to meet with the politicians, thus further stigmatizing "other" women on welfare and leaving assumptions about most poor women's appearance untroubled. Nevertheless, it was successful in arresting attention. For example, consultants to several state officials and aides to legislators told LIFETIME's directors that LIFETIME participants made welfare policy "personal" for the politicians. The policymakers also remarked to their staff that hearing from welfare mothers directly made it harder for them to vote against certain policies. This feedback fostered the women's confidence that they deserved to have a presence and a voice in the policymaking process.

Resisting Shame through Grassroots Activism

As described in the opening vignette, the activists also used assumptions about poverty and poor women's bodies to challenge welfare reform policies. They used their bodies in street theater to act out resistance to welfare policies. They planned protests that transformed oppression into resistance. They used their experiences as domestic violence survivors to give them strength to fight a system that victimized them a second time. In one protest, they gave themselves black eyes with makeup, they dressed up in black with handmade wedding veils, and hoisted protest signs to show resistance to the punitive policies of welfare reform.

In addition to the Valentine's Day mock wedding protest, the activists planned additional political protest actions to raise awareness about their experiences in poverty, on welfare, and surviving domestic violence. The women built on the idea that, when many of them fled their abusive situations, they left with little more than the shirts on their backs. They used this idea to launch three escalating actions using a simple object—the common t-shirt—to stage protest.

The first two actions used commercially printed t-shirts designed by the grassroots activists. The first set of t-shirts used a play on the WWJD (what would Jesus do?) shirt worn by Christians. The shirts said "Would Jesus Cut Welfare?" and included a relevant quotation from the Bible. The mothers wore the shirts when meeting with California state legislators at the capitol building in Sacramento. Their testimonies got the attention of many California politicians.

The second set of commercially printed t-shirts were designed by a research interview participant named Jasmine. She also designed signs and a long banner for use in the protests to raise awareness about domestic violence survivors on welfare. The protest signs used an image of a baby wearing a diaper with a bull's eye drawn on it. The sign read "Don't target our children." The t-shirts pictured children holding hands in the middle of a target, and also read "Don't target our children." These images were aimed at the governor of California, Arnold Schwarzenegger, who, during his first year in office, released a state budget that included drastic cuts to the state welfare program. Activists donned the shirts and hoisted the signs in a protest in April 2005 in San Francisco while Gov. Schwarzenegger attended an expensive fundraiser at a hotel. LIFETIME activists together with representatives from various organizations and unions surrounded the hotel and protested on all four streets surrounding the building, making it very difficult for the governor and attendees to enter the event. Recounting this protest, Jasmine explains the importance of her activism: "one of my slogans in the big t-shirt campaign I did at LIFETIME, which was very, very

LIFETIME activists staging mock weddings at San Francisco City Hall protesting welfare marriage promotion policies and raising awareness of domestic violence survivors' experiences on welfare. Photograph by Sheila Katz

emotional and extremely intriguing experience for me, and I wrote on the back of one of the t-shirts a slogan that said 'education is emancipation out of poverty' and it is."

The Shirts Off Our Backs

These smaller protests and actions were building to a larger, national action in collaboration with groups from around the country. California activists coordinated with their peers in several states to stage a national protest in front of the US Department of Health and Human Services (HHS) in Washington, DC. The event was called the "Shirts Off Our Backs" campaign, invoking how many mothers escaped abusive situations with little more than "the shirts on our backs." The women made t-shirts that told their personal stories and included pictures of their families, similar to the Clothesline Project developed to raise awareness about sexual violence. LIFETIME worked with welfare rights and domestic violence organizations across the country to have low-income domestic violence survivors create t-shirts with their pictures, stories, and a coordinated message to policymakers to drive home the message "Family Violence is *NOT* an Option," a clever play on the Family Violence Option (FVO) written into the 1996 welfare reform legislations. Jasmine also designed a ten-foot banner with the same text running along an image of a woman's face with a black eye. Over one hundred t-shirts were sent to LIFETIME or made locally by survivors. The plan was to deliver

Would Jesus
Cut Welfare?

Destruction is certain for the unjust
judges, for those who issue unfair laws.
They deprive the poor, the widows,
and the orphans of justice. Yes, they rob
widows and fatherless children!
What will you do when I send desolation
upon you from a distant land?

Isaiah 10:1-3

LIFETIME parent leader Dawn Love posing with one of the organization's activist t-shirts. Photograph by Sheila Katz

the shirts to Dr. Wade Horn, the Assistant Secretary of Children and Families for the Department of Health and Human Services, the agency that administered TANF.

In June 2005, low-income domestic violence survivors from across the country assembled under an overpass a block from the federal HHS offices. They constructed a portable Clothesline Project–style exhibit by quickly clipping t-shirts to clotheslines attached to six eight-foot-tall wooden poles. The group chanted "Family Violence is Not an Option" as they marched, intent on delivering the t-shirts and LIFETIME's research brief about domestic violence and welfare reform to HHS administration. On the sidewalk in front of HHS, activists chanted and marched for an hour, with LIFETIME's executive director, Diana Spatz, shouting the group's demands.

The activists were loud and visible on an otherwise calm street filled with sedate federal office buildings. After an hour of protests, a top aide to Dr. Wade Horn came down to meet the group. He had a brief conversation with the activists, but he declined to allow anyone, even a smaller group, to enter the building. He did, however, agree to take a copy of the research report and a couple of the t-shirts. At the protest, the women literally took the shirts off their backs and handed them over. One activist powerfully proclaimed, "We left our abusers with nothing more than the shirts on our backs. We give you these shirts to tell our stories and protest Bush's marriage promotion policies. We need help from welfare not marriage promises from dangerous men." Stunned, he took the shirts and quickly went back into the building.

Conclusion

A group of poor women survived domestic violence only to be further victimized by the welfare system. To resist this unfair treatment by the system they had turned to for help, they used their bodies and the "shirts off their backs." Their abused and healed bodies became the medium through which they expressed their frustration with policies that blamed them for their situations. Instead of internalizing the shame of domestic violence or being poor, these women collectively refused that shame by using their experiences to change the policy conversation. They shifted the narrative about "marriage promotion" and focused on their lived realities. The activists, many of them women of color, challenged the racist and sexist stereotypes and assumptions about welfare mothers, especially the caricature of the "welfare queen" through grassroots protests, public storytelling, and engaging the media and politicians to see them as whole persons instead of mere embodiments of stereotypes. Further, the mothers resisted dominant racist and sexist assumptions about welfare mothers through the language they used on their protest signs and t-shirts, in their personal narratives and marching chants.

The HHS marriage promotion proposals for the reauthorization of TANF and requirements for programs who received HHS funding evolved in 2005 and 2006 as a result of their and other activists' work on this issue. Diana Spatz, the founder of LIFETIME, and I were invited as experts to give workshops on our research on welfare mothers' experiences in domestic violence at a national meeting for organizations funded by HHS in support of the fatherhood initiatives that were part of the marriage promotion policies in fall 2006. Change was realized. The marriage promotion policies included language regarding "healthy families," and HHS required training in domestic violence awareness for groups that received funding from the initiative. The women's embodied resistance contributed to these policy revisions.

During the period of this research, the activists were protesting political decisions and policy changes during a previous presidency. Yet their experiences and more recent political protests and social justice events, such as those after the 2016 presidential elections, are strikingly similar. In recent political protests, marches, actions, and events, we see people organizing around some of the same issues, such as racism, sexism, and economic inequalities. People who have never been "activists" before are taking to the streets, organizing on social media, working in community groups, and calling or visiting their elected officials to raise awareness about social justice issues. In addition to broad issues of social inequality, issues around police brutality against minorities, access to health care, LGBTQ rights, reproductive rights, immigrants' rights, and gun control are being addressed by public protest. Through movements such as Black Lives Matter, Say Her Name, the Women's Marches, March for Our Lives, and others, people are organizing collectively, raising awareness of the issues, and pushing for social change. Many of these protests include embodied activism, such as the wearing of "pussy" hats or specially designed t-shirts, making the body a human protest sign, as well as the staging of "die-ins" at politicians' offices on Capitol Hill. Activists are using their bodies, their voices, and their presence to change the policy conversation. In the last few years, brand new and experienced activists alike are collectively organizing to challenge the oppressive status quo.

NOTES

1. This chapter uses both the terms *domestic violence* and *intimate partner violence*. When the research was conducted, the activists used the term domestic violence in their work. However, IPV is now the more commonly used term in academic writing. These terms are slightly different in meaning, which is why both are defined in the text. Specifically, IPV is the broader term covering most types of relationships and relationship violence. Domestic violence, especially as it is discussed in this chapter, more commonly refers narrowly to IPV in ongoing, in-person, romantic relationships, usually between men and women. I avoid interchangeable use of the terms to preserve their unique meanings.

2. For example, in 2013, the largest share (42 percent) of non-elderly Medicaid enrollees in 2013 were white (Kaiser Family Foundation 2013) and whites were the largest participating group receiving SNAP benefits (Gray 2014). However, it is important to note that that in many ways, regardless of who receives welfare benefits, assumptions are made that Black women need government assistance because they "behave badly" and therefore do not merit support.

3. The names used for the women are pseudonyms. Participants in this research selected their own pseudonyms at the first interview, and I asked them at subsequent interviews if they wanted to keep or change them.

REFERENCES

Adair, Vivian. 2002. "Branded with Infamy: Inscriptions of Poverty and Class in the United States." *Signs* 27, no. 2: 451–71.

Adair, Vivian, and Dahlberg, Sandra. 2003. "Introduction" in *Reclaiming Class: Women, Poverty, and the Promise of Higher Education* edited by Vivian Adair and Sandra Dahlberg. Philadelphia: Temple University Press.

Allard, Scott, Richard Tolman, and Daniel Rosen. 2003. "Access to Mental Health and Substance Abuse Services among Women Receiving Welfare in Detroit." *Urban Affairs Review* 38: 787–807.

Beechey, Susanne, and Jacqueline Payne. 2002. *Surviving Violence and Poverty: A Focus on the Link between Domestic and Sexual Violence, Women's Poverty, and Welfare*. Washington, DC: Legal Momentum.

Black, Michele C., Kathleen C. Basile, Matthew Breiding, Sharon G. Smith, Mikel L. Walters, Melissa T. Merrick, Jieru Chen, Mark R. Stevens. 2011. *The National Intimate Partner and Sexual Violence Survey (NISVS): 2010 Summary Report*. Atlanta, GA: National Center for Injury Prevention and Control, Centers for Disease Control and Prevention.

Breiding, Matthew, Kathleen C. Basile, Sharon G. Smith, Michele C. Black, and Reshma Mahendra. 2015. *Intimate Partner Violence Surveillance: Uniform Definitions and Recommended Data Elements, version 2.0*. Atlanta, GA: National Center for Injury Prevention and Control, Centers for Disease Control and Prevention.

Breiding, Matthew, Jieru Chen, and Michele C. Black. 2014. *Intimate Partner Violence in the United States—2010*. Atlanta, GA: National Center for Injury Prevention and Control, Centers for Disease Control and Prevention.

Brewster, Mary P. 2002. "Domestic Violence Theories, Research, and Practice Implications." In *Handbook of Domestic Violence Intervention Strategies: Policies, Programs, and Legal Remedies,* edited by Albert Roberts, 23–48. New York: Oxford University Press.

Charmaz, Kathy. 2006. *Constructing Grounded Theory*. London: Sage Publications.

Charmaz, Kathy, and Sheila Katz. 2017. "Subjective Stories and Social Issues: Strategies for Making Connections." *Qualitative Methods in Psychology Bulletin* 23 (Spring 2017): 8–14.

Davidson, M. Meghan, and Sarah J. Gervais. 2015. "Violence against Women through the Lens of Objectification Theory." *Violence Against Women* 21, no. 3: 330–54.

Davis, Martha. 1999. "Economics of Abuse: How Violence Perpetuates Women's Poverty." In *Battered Women, Children, and Welfare Reform*, edited by Ruth A. Brandwein, 17–30. Thousand Oaks: Sage Publications.

Gray, Kelsey Farson. 2014. *Characteristics of Supplemental Nutrition Assistance Program Households: Fiscal Year 2013*. Nutrition Assistance Program Report Series. Alexandria, VA: US Department of Agriculture, Food and Nutrition Service

Kaiser Family Foundation. 2013. "Medicaid Enrollment by Race/Ethnicity." *www.kff.org/medicaid/state-indicator/medicaid-enrollment-by-raceethnicity*.

Kaplan, Elaine Bell. 1997. *Not Our Kind of Girl: Unraveling the Myths of Black Teenage Motherhood*. Berkeley: University of California Press.

Katz, Sheila. 2008. "Pursuing a 'Reformed' Dream: CalWORKs Mothers in Higher Education after 'Ending Welfare as We Know It.'" PhD diss., Vanderbilt University.

———. 2012. "TANF's 15th Anniversary: Are Low-Income Mothers Celebrating Upward Economic Mobility?" *Sociology Compass* 6/8: 657–70.

———. (2019). *Reformed American Dreams: Welfare Mothers, Higher Education, and Activism*. New Brunswick, NJ: Rutgers University Press.

Katz, Sheila, and Laura McGuire. 2018. "Intimate Partner Violence in Higher Education: Integrated Approaches for Reducing Domestic Violence and Sexual Assault on Campus." *The Wiley Handbook on Violence in Education: Forms, Factors, and Preventions*, edited by Harvey Shapiro, 417–32. Hoboken, NJ: Wiley.

Kaukinen, Catherine. 2014. "Dating Violence among College Students: The Risk and Protective Factors." *Trauma, Violence, & Abuse* 15, no. 4: 283–96.

Kelly, Maura. 2010. "Regulating the Reproduction and Mothering of Poor Women: The Controlling Image of the Welfare Mother in Television News Coverage of Welfare Reform." *Journal of Poverty* 14: 76–96.

Kramer, Laura, and Ann Beutel. 2014. *Sociology of Gender: A Brief Introduction*. New York: Oxford University Press.

Luna, Yvonne. 2009. "Single Welfare Mothers' Resistance." *Journal of Poverty* 13: 441–61.

Lyon, Eleanor. 2000. *Welfare, Poverty, and Abused Women: New Research and Its Implications*. Building Comprehensive Solutions to Domestic Violence #10. Harrisburg, PA: Pennsylvania Coalition Against Domestic Violence, National Resource Center on Domestic Violence.

McBride, Dorothy, and Janine Perry. 2016. *Women's Rights in the USA: Policy Debates and Gender Roles*, 5th ed. New York: Routledge.

Moore, Thomas, and Vicky Selkowe. 1999. *Domestic Violence Victims in Transition from Welfare to Work: Barriers to Self-Sufficiency and the W-2 Response*. Milwaukee: Institute for Wisconsin's Future.

NCADV (National Coalition Against Domestic Violence). n.d. "Learn More: What Is Domestic Violence," *www.ncadv.org*. Accessed January 5, 2017.

Overstreet, Nicole, and Diane Quinn. 2013. "The Intimate Partner Violence Stigmatization Model and Barriers to Help Seeking." *Basic Applied Social Psychology* 35, no. 1 (January): 109–22.

Pear, Robert, and David Kirkpatrick. 2004. "Bush Plans $1.5 Billion Drive for Promotion of Marriage." *New York Times*, January 14.

Pearson, Jessica, Nancy Theonnes, and Easter A. Griswold. 1999. "Child Support and Domestic Violence: The Victims Speak Out." *Violence Against Women* 5: 427–48.

Raphael, Jody. 1999. "Keeping Women Poor: How Domestic Violence Prevents Women from Leaving Welfare and Entering the World of Work." In *Battered Women, Children, and Welfare Reform*, edited by Ruth A. Brandwein, 31–43. Thousand Oaks, CA: Sage Publications.

Spatz, Diana, and Sheila Katz. 2005. "Family Violence Is Not an Option: The Failure of CalWORKs to Serve Battered Women with Children." Research report. Oakland, CA: Low-Income Families' Empowerment through Education.

Tolman, Richard, and Jody Raphael. 2000. "A Review of Research on Welfare and Domestic Violence." *Journal of Social Issues* 56: 655–82.

West, Candace, and Don Zimmerman. 1987. "Doing Gender." *Gender and Society* 1, no. 2: 125–51.

"Your Signing Is So Beautiful!"

The Radical Invisibility of ASL Interpreters in Public

Rachel Kolb

A few years ago, while attending a Christmas carol concert to mark the start of Advent, I turned to my American Sign Language (ASL) interpreter and teased, "Remember, put forth your most beautiful signing when you're up there. All the hearing people are watching you."

"You want to bet how many people will come up to me afterwards and tell me that ASL is such a beautiful language?" she shot back.

Indeed, after the concert, several hearing people did what hearing people usually do: they filed past us on their way out of the auditorium and thanked my interpreter profusely for her beautiful signing. It had been a wonder to behold the intricate motions of her hands, they said, or something of that sort. A few older women beamed at me as they left, without saying anything more. They may as well have patted my head and thanked me, too, for enabling their visual enjoyment. There our interaction ended.

My interpreter and I looked at each other. "Oh, what a beautiful language!" we laughed.

But bringing ASL to this space was not as simple as it may have looked. Arranging an ASL interpreter did not merely enable a visual feast to materialize for my or anyone else's consumption, but initiated a complex communicative interchange that these hearing people missed when they marveled at its beauty and then walked back into their heedless lives. Here, for instance, is the gist of some impressions and commentary my interpreter and I exchanged about translation during the performance itself.

"Oh, now the program says it's the *Ave Maria*. Hold on, that's Latin. They're sing-ing in Latin. How do you sign that?"

"Fields and floods, rocks, hills, and plains repeat the sounding joy—wait, the *sounding* joy? This is such a non-deaf song."

"I missed it! What was that verse? Now they're harmonizing."

"I think they're singing in another language again. I can't sign it, but it sounds pretty."

"Glooooo-ooooooo-oooooooria, in excelsis Deo. Oh my. How long can your hands keep signing *gloria*?"

We engaged in other forms of signing wordplay, too, including the joy of joining in and signing *O Come, All Ye Faithful* with the congregation, replete with different spins on the refrain "O come, let us adore him." In ways that are not frequently recognized, ASL can enable one to play with visual and linguistic nuances in a way that spoken English does not allow.

I will be the first to say that American Sign Language *is* a beautiful language, and that it facilitates a rich form of communication distinct from spoken language. Signing Christmas carols—not just *O Come, All Ye Faithful*—does feel more joyous to me than singing alone. My entire body engages in my act of self-expression. I know this is why hearing people find signing so mesmerizing—and, truly, the more people who can share in this physically connected form of communication, the better. Nonetheless, others' appreciation would feel more sincere and less trite if it involved more direct engagement with the realities of signing, deaf experience, and ASL interpretation.

The process of working with interpreters can be an intricate business. Of course, with adequate preparation a sign language interpreter can deliver a spectacular rendition of any spoken performance. But even with a highly skilled interpreter, this does not always happen. The best interpreters mishear things, as everyone does. Language is messy, and translation even more so. Constant discussions occur about such issues as the meaning of words, acoustics, whether the interpreter accurately caught what the speaker said, and whether the deaf person has a different preferred way of signing a particular word. There is no such thing as a perfect interpretation, but there is such a thing as an excellent one— and this is the result of ongoing rigorous collaboration between interpreters and the Deaf community.[1] The camaraderie and partnership between d/Deaf people and interpreters is something hearing onlookers can miss when they remark only on "beauty." They may see the product, but they miss the process.

Another thing these well-meaning onlookers miss goes deeper: they miss me, the deaf person, and they miss my active role in making communication *happen* in this space. For me, ASL is not *just* a beautiful language, a mere aesthetic adornment. It is also a language that has given me access to a world otherwise governed by assumptions of sound and hearing. It is a core gateway to another sensory experience of the world that is rich and fascinating in its own right. People who approach my interpreters to say "Thank you for interpreting, that was lovely," rarely speak to me or engage with me at all. In these moments, I feel their uncertainty about how to connect. I am there, I am breathing and thinking and engaging, my presence has enabled this front-and-center visual spectacle of ASL interpretation—yet I am set aside. I feel myself becoming separate from them and their world at the same time as they gravitate toward the beauty of my language. They sometimes smile at me, but they often do not reach any further. We both have an opportunity to communicate, facilitated by an interpreter, and yet we miss it.

When I attend a concert or lecture or any other large event, I am aware simultaneously of how visible I am and of how my visibility can enable alienation and disconnection. Because I use interpreters, it is very difficult for me to attend any public event without drawing notice. Acquaintances have often emailed or texted me after an event: *Saw you there with your interpreters! Hope you are well!* Well, of course they saw me. Blending into the crowd has never been my forte. I feel my radical visibility encroaching upon me when well-meaning spectators approach my interpreter to remark on her beautiful signing, but at the same time I feel radically invisible. "Your signing is so beautiful": with this expression, followed by nothing else, my communicative process, history, and richer sense of self all disappear.

Hence my interpreter and I smile at each other at this choral concert—we share an understanding—and jest, "*Silent Night* in sign language is so beautiful!" Our joke parodies the distance that arises when any rich human experience is reduced to a mere aesthetic. We have freed ourselves to play with the idea of being spectacles rather than unobtrusive concertgoers. We take ownership of the disconnect that can arise from being up front and center, and in this moment we encounter a sense, however small, of resistance and camaraderie.

NOTES

1. The word Deaf, with a capital D, refers to individuals who use ASL as their primary language and who self-identify as part of a unique Deaf cultural and linguistic minority, as compared to lower-d "deaf," which refers only to having a physical hearing loss.

LIVING RESISTANCE

Two Shakes

Rev. Adam Lawrence Dyer

When I shook Dr. Cornel West's hand, I knew I had met a kindred spirit. But it went much farther than that; his handshake was a homecoming and an affirmation. His hands were not large, but they held the vastness of his years and experience, all of which I could feel in how he welcomed my touch. Dr. West, who is most familiar to older generations through his writing in books like *Race Matters* and familiar to younger generations through television shows like *30 Rock* and his involvement with Black Lives Matter protests, was speaking at a local event where I had the pleasure of introducing him. I was thrilled. His talk, though wide ranging, returned to themes that I know intimately and that shape my everyday existence as a black man. Specifically, he spoke of how white and predominantly male supremacy presents in American empire as three things: the pursuit of wealth, "smartness," and access to power. He gave voice to what most every black person in this country lives. Although deeply entrenched in the academy of the empire, he spoke as someone who also challenges that same academy and empire as part of the parade of other great black scholars, activists, and musicians before him. In his talk, James Baldwin, Fannie Lou Hamer, W. E. B DuBois, Marvin Gaye, John Coltrane, Billie Holiday and even Ashford and Simpson were all invoked as part of the dynamic challenge that blacks bring to white supremacy. But for me, the touch of Dr. West's hands communicated so much more before he even uttered a word. In one handshake, I not only felt the legacy, but I trusted it and I was fully affirmed. In his hands, I was acknowledged and *whole*.

I grew up in a white suburb in the 1970s. This situation presented many challenges for me as a black child, yet the most far-reaching difficulty was *literally* in my hands. From a very early age, I was aware that my hands looked and felt different from those of the white children. My hands have always had a deeply grained texture both on the palms and on the back. In school, I remember being asked to hold hands, as children are often asked to do, and thinking that the hands of the little pink-faced, blond girl, or the skinny redheaded boy, were deathly cool and clammy and slippery-smooth, with no strength or shape. I said nothing about this awareness and just held on as we crossed streets or moved from class to class walking two-by-two. I accepted their touch for what it was. But the little white children made a game out of teasing me about *my* hands saying that they were "old man" hands and that they were "gross." I experienced children reacting to my touch by saying, "eew." Receiving the disgust of white children over an aspect of my body became a crucial part of my early introduction to the mechanism of white supremacy. I wasn't yet ten years old.

Influenced by this experience, I grew to be almost completely hand shy in my teenage and young adult years. In greeting someone, I would only shake a person's hand briefly and I was terrified to think of touching someone's skin (arm, shoulder, face) directly with my hands. As I matured, sexual situations began to cause me extreme distress, particularly after a few white partners reacted badly to the feeling of my hands.

My perception of my hands only began to change when I enrolled in a brief introductory course on massage therapy. On the surface, I told myself that I was looking for an easy way to supplement my income, but on a deeper level, I believe I was actually yearning for an excuse to touch and be touched. My first breakthrough came when I shared with the class my paranoia about my hands and how reluctance lurked behind my touch. I said to the class that I had learned from an early age that my hands were "ugly" and that the feeling of my touch was unpleasant. My instructor then held my hands and responded, "But you have the most *beautiful* hands!" In my whole life I had never heard the word "beautiful" connected to my hands. I was never the same after shedding the tears that were prompted by those words.

Several years later, I did a more extensive certification in massage therapy and earned a professional license as both a therapist and Reiki practitioner. My practice focused on athletes and trauma healing, and it was this work that led directly to the ministry I serve today. The more I touched people, the more I learned that there is a vast language of "being" that uses no words yet is integral to the human experience. This was the beginning of my understanding that what human beings are capable of experiencing and communicating through touch has the potential to change our narrative of hatred, objectification, and marginalization. Touch is the universal donor.

At the end of the evening of the talk with Dr. West, I again shook his hand while we embraced. His touch stayed with me. Pondering that lingering sensation, I realized that I have never had another black man recoil from my touch; I have never had a black woman tell me my hands were ugly. Throughout my formative years I was robbed of a basic human connection—touch—by the ignorant racism of white children who knew no better than to place me outside of their circle of belonging because of the way they experienced my body as different. Thankfully, I have had the last laugh on those childish taunts. I was eventually able to make an entire career out of touch and to bring healing and a sense of wholeness and peace to people regardless of their race with my "beautiful" hands. I don't believe touch has a race, but I do believe the experience of race can be reconciled through touch. In the end, what matters is not that my touch is black but rather that my being black informs a uniquely precious and compassionate touch.

On the street later that night, after Dr. West spoke, I was approached by a young black man. He pointed over his shoulder toward another young black man who was in a heated conversation with an angry white man. He said that the white man was egging them both on with a lot of racist talk. The young man asked me, "Should I just hit him?" With Dr. West's words still in my ear and his touch still in my hand, I said, "No . . . you are better than that. No racist deserves the gift of your touch." He smiled and agreed and blessed me. We shook hands. In two shakes, the circle was complete.

LIVING RESISTANCE

"Showing Our Muslim"

Embracing the Hijab in the Era of Paradox

Sara Rehman

Drenched in Dr Pepper in a Walmart parking lot, I lean back against the headrest staring out the window. I look in my rearview mirror, fix my hijab, and take a deep breath. I recall the moments before I retreated into my car. I was walking out of Walmart carrying plastic bags filled with school supplies. The June sun radiated through the white fabric around my head. A man drives past in one of those trucks that are a little too big for just about anyone. Turning his big, red, angry, scrunched-up face toward me, he yells out his window: "Go back to your country you ter-rorist!" Then he throws his Whataburger cup directly in my trembling direction. Moments after being doused in soda, I slowly got into my car thinking, "So this is what happens the first time I wear hijab in public!" As I sit in my car, the sticky brown liquid drying on my skin and clothes, I recall what led me to wear the hijab and why harassment like this cements my commitment to do so.

I constantly live with a paradox: the hijabi paradox. This is a debate I have with myself whether or not to wear hijab—a decision that shifts under the ebbs and flows of the influence of my parents over my life. The hijab is something a girl dons between ages ten to twelve. It is a veil covering her head that reflects the "Muslim modesty code" and represents connection to God in a physical sense. But let me back up for a moment.

I grew up in pre-9/11 New York City. I always understood that my parents' push for hijab came from their deep love for our Muslim faith and culture, and for me, their daughter. Our faith expects my sisters, Farrah and Iman, and myself to wear the hijab proudly.

Around college, and to our surprise, Farrah started wearing the hijab. She was the first in our family to wear the hijab outside the home, both at college and at work. She wore it well and with pride. Farrah wasn't afraid to be herself as she walked about pre-9/11 New York City. My big sister set the precedent for me.

While 9/11 was a difficult time for everyone in New York City and across the nation, it was an especially daunting time for Muslims. Muslim women were at-tacked for their hijabs. Threats of violence made it too risky to publicly show our Muslim pride. At night my Muslim sisters wept as they made the difficult decision to take off their hijabs. But Farrah continued to wear the hijab, in spite of being constantly told by close friends, distant family members, our parents, and strangers to remove it.

It was a terrifying time to be a little Muslim girl. I lost some of my teacher's smiles in the mornings. I lost my freedom to walk to my best friend's house. I lost the security

The author. Photograph
by Nabihah Vaid

of my identity as my Muslim faith became the source of controversy served up on television screens across America. To protect us, my parents encouraged my little sister Iman and me to avoid "showing our Muslim." We complied and continued our lives, now more quietly and solemnly, in New York City. Five years after 9/11, my dad decided to move the family to Houston.

Moving to Houston was quite a relief, even though I initially resented my parents for the upheaval. (What fifth grader wouldn't?) It was a breath of fresh air to be far from the charged site of 9/11. I felt the emotional weight and fear of living in post-9/11 New York lift. The move enabled me to grow up and truly realize my Muslim identity. We moved to Katy, a part of Houston with a blossoming Muslim community. Finding kinship was a powerful experience. Here, I created amazing bonds with other Muslim girls and began to connect with my Muslim faith through activism and community outreach. I became a youth leader in my mosque.

As I developed my identity as a young Muslim activist, I made choices that rattled my parents. They started pointing out the little ways I defied tradition. I wore my pants cuffed and showing my ankles. I wore clothing that showed a little too much of my curves, such as shirts that sat right on my hips. I showed too much of my hair. To them, I was practically doing everything wrong! I understood their growing concern grew out of love for me and a fear of God, but in my "teenage rebellion" I insisted on doing things *my* way. I left the house with my hair up in a ponytail or in a loose bun, but even before I sat down on the school bus, I untied it and let it cascade down my backpack. I wore a jacket to cover my t-shirts until I arrived at school, where I took it off to show my school pride on my short-sleeved spirit wear. I vividly remember the sweet relief I got from defying my parents in these ways.

I resisted the expectations my parents *and* society had of me as a Muslim youth. I opposed the norms of being a proper Muslim; this was *my* freedom from the restraints of religious society. I would hear my mother whisper to my father about how I looked "too big" or "too Western." They were telling me to dress more modestly and to cover my body, but I refused. I wanted to be a liberated girl. I wanted to be Muslim on my own terms.

This struggle with my parents persisted for five years—through high school and my first year of college. Finally, in January 2016, my mom finally gave up and told me, in her soft Indian accent, that I was entitled to my choices; it was *my* responsibility to be a good Muslim girl. At last alone with my thoughts and freed from parental pressure, my path became clearer. In the current Islamphobic political climate, I felt strongly that it was important to be a good role model for the girls at my mosque. I felt an obligation to express my Muslim identity. I wanted to wear hijab as an obligation to my community, even more than to my parents. And so I did.

When I first wore the hijab, I defined it as a political symbol on my body and resistance to the notion that uncovered equated "liberated." But having just been on the receiving end of intense Islamophobia in the form of a hostile insult and a Dr Pepper bath, I remind myself of other reasons I choose to wear the hijab. I am a strong Muslim—an activist and a leader—and I embody my political resistance. The way the 2016 US presidential election played out against Muslims sharpens my resolve to claim my Muslim identity with pride. On the first day I wore the hijab outside the mosque, dazed by the vitriol of a complete stranger, I realized the power and the peril of one's embodied choices. While "showing my Muslim" is not without risk, I am proud to announce to the world who I am.

LIVING RESISTANCE

"Doing Out"

A Black Dandy Defies Gender Norms in the Bronx

Mark Broomfield

It is the summer of 2005, and for the last decade I have been living outside my hometown of the Bronx. I return, after this long absence, to conduct ethnographic fieldwork at the Alvin Ailey Dance Foundation in New York City. For my stay, I reside at my sister's house in the Northeast Bronx, an area heavily populated by many West Indians. I am Black British and Jamaican. I am also gay. For my queer black body, play and creativity define my fashion choices. Outside of the Bronx, I do not typically second-guess how I dress, but here, unsettling questions linger: Will I fit in? Can I walk around the predominantly West Indian neighborhood disguised enough to "pass" my fellow brothas on the street? In previous trips downtown, I intentionally wore loose fitting clothes and played down wearing anything that might lead people to construe my body as "gay," and therefore pass as "straight." Because I intimately know the homophobic attitudes held by many Jamaicans, I ask myself, "How can I avoid looking feminine?" I am careful about what I wear—avoiding anything that signals "gay." I now wonder, "Why did I live here when I can't even feel safe walking down the street?" At the same time, I wonder, "Am I too sensitive?"

These worries compel me to obsess over what to wear today, as I prepare to work in Manhattan. After much tortured deliberation, I choose my clothes for what promises to be a radiant day. Normally I would travel by car and avoid this hassle. When I previously lived in New York, my car protected me from the gaze of others and shielded me from possible harassment. But this summer, I have to rely on public transportation—a turn of events that forces me to reconsider the vulnerability of my body wearing the "wrong" clothes.

In the end, I choose to wear an outfit that displays my dancer's body: straight leg pants that accentuate my long, elegant lines, a bright-colored, close-fitting tank top, and black Oxford shoes, topping it all off with a messenger cap. Though I was proud of my snatched and pulled dancer's body, my choices instigated an interior dialogue:

Oh no! Is this outfit too "gay"?

It's okay. Fashion choices shouldn't matter, right?

Sigh. If I were in Greenwich Village or Chelsea, I wouldn't be worrying about my dandified look.

Before leaving the house, I asked my sister what she thought of my ensemble. With my sister's smile and approval (although she did throw in an "are you sure?"

look), I began my journey to the No. 2 train station. As I set off walking confidently, in spite of my internal struggle, I remain vigilantly aware of my surroundings—those ahead of me and those behind me. Perhaps my dancer's sensibility and street-smart training as a native New Yorker brings out a heightened awareness of my environment. The conservative nature of the residential black middle-class neighborhood adds to the attentiveness. As I walk, all men look suspicious to me. I probably should not have these thoughts, but I do have them. And with a commitment to truth-telling, I wish I did not feel this way.

I know. I know. Everyone should be judged individually and freed from stereotypes, but my experience of living in the Bronx, amongst "my own," as they say, bears another truth. I do not feel at home here anymore, and, quite frankly, I never really did. I grow tired of rhetoric extolling black people to love each other and keep our communities intact. Whose community? I must ask. I don't feel welcome here. I can't even walk down the street without feeling threatened with a homophobic attack. I have wondered many times, where do I belong? Which community will claim me? Jamaican? Black British? African American? Gay?

My unease subsides once I arrive at 59th Street at Columbus Circle—a multicultural milieu representing the diversity of New York City. My self-consciousness vanishes into the throngs as I make my way to the resplendent new home of the Alvin Ailey American Dance Theatre at the Joan Weill Center for Dance. But after a productive day of research at Ailey, my anxiety returns as I head home. I again become acutely aware of how I am dressed as I make my way to the No. 2 train. During the rush hour commute, thoughts of safety begin to consume me. Will I make it back to the Bronx without any verbal harassment or a physical assault?

And then it happens. Four blocks from my sister's house, a car dashes by as I cross a main intersection. It is filled with several gleeful black men whose words inflict a cruel reality on me. They call me "batty bwoy," a common gay slur used by Jamaicans. Now suspended between fight or flight, I wonder if they will return for more verbal insults or possibly worse—an attack? I had desperately hoped I would make it home without a verbal assault that day. I was devastated that I could not.

Imagine. A few rambunctious homophobes tried to curtail my self-expression. My "flamboyance," it seems, posed a threat to their ideas of masculinity and societal expectations of gender. Moving with quickness and determination, I arrive at my sister's house safely. Later that evening while listening to calls for community on a black Caribbean radio station in New York City, the host exhorted the need for the black community to come together. I stopped to think, "Was he talking to me, too? Am I a part of this black community-building project?" And then my focus turned toward the experience of being harassed earlier that day, suggesting that I was not.

This exhortation of the black community amid the punishment directed against me—one of its own—felt incongruent. Finding community amid the tensions of being a black gay man continues to be a source of peril and pleasure. My experiences on the streets of the Bronx details such perils, yet there are also pleasures to black gay men's community-building, including gay vernacular—for example, the recent creation and widespread circulation of "*yaaasss*" in popular culture, and other terms that have permeated American culture such as *reading*, *shade*, and *fierce* captured in the film *Paris is Burning*.[1] This language of intimacy and the continual imaginative potential to create and re-create ourselves in fashion and gender expression reveals power over our own bodies. Engaging gender performance in this way resists the marginalization of gay men of color in multiple communities: black culture, white culture, heterosexual culture, and gay culture. That day I chose to embrace playful fashion choices. The freedom to express myself signaled my embodied resistance to the policing of masculinity and gender norms.

Pleasures arise in the familiarity of the sights and sounds in this largely Caribbean neighborhood. White Plains Road, infamous for its five-and-dime stores, the Korean produce shops, the overhead noise of No. 2 train passing by, and the frequent bus stops of the Bronx 39, makes me feel at home. Pleasures arise in seeing the working-class take-out Jamaican restaurants on almost every corner it seems, and the Kingston Tropical Bakery, the first place I stop on any return to the Bronx and arguably the best patty shop in New York City. The familiarity of these sights and sounds felt jarring against my perilous homophobic experience. My encounter with hatred rekindled thoughts on just exactly why I left the predominantly West Indian section of the Northeast Bronx. Listen, I don't need any permission to stay in a neighborhood where I feel threatened to be who I am. My queer black body will continue to resist and play with all forms of gender expression.

NOTES

1. The emergence and proliferation of the expression "yaaasss," newly added to dictionary .com, is attributed to Lady Gaga's fans. For example, see *www.youtube.com/watch?v=5Pn 0JKmy5-M*; *www.latimes.com/books/jacketcopy/la-et-jc-dictionary-com-new-definitions-on -fleek-20151110-story.html*, and *www.theatlantic.com/technology/archive/2015/04/how-to -say-yes-by-not-saying-yes/390129*. Earlier terms such as "reading" and "shade" are most famously captured and defined in Jennie Livingston's *Paris Is Burning* (1990) by Dorian Corey, the "mother" figure in the film. A landmark documentary, the film features African American and Latino LGBTQ people who created ballroom culture. "Fierce" connotes defiance and the use of style in the face of oppression. See Joseph Beam's "Making Ourselves from Scratch," in *Brother to Brother: New Writings by Black Gay Men,* ed. Essex Hemphill (Boston: Alyson Publications, 1991), 262.

Everybody

Making Fat Radio for All of Us

Cat Pausé

It all began with a few posts on Facebook. A friend of a friend approached me after seeing some of my posts a mutual friend had liked. "Hey," he said, "wanna do a radio show on this fat stuff?" Turns out, he was the station manager at a local station, Access Manawatu. I remember trying to assure him that he didn't want me to do a show— "This is not the show you're looking for," I told him. It wouldn't be about diets, or weight loss, or apologizing for taking up space. If I did a show, it would be unapologetically fat positive. And it was bound to garner hostile attention from ~~trolls~~ people concerned about my health. You know the ones: "You are glorifying obesity, which is killing people!" "You are disgusting; just get off the couch!" "You are costing our health system millions!" He assured me that he didn't care about any backlash, and he wanted me to do the kind of show I'd be proud of. With his reassurance, I then had to reflect on a range of other questions that I had for myself. Did I want to do a radio show? Was I interested in having my voice out there—did I have anything interesting to say? Did anyone listen to the radio these days?!

I wasn't the first to consider making fat radio; Bostonians Judith Stein and Meredith Lawrence made *Plain Talk about Fat* in 1984 and *30 Big Minutes with Fat Liberation* in 1985. From 2004 to 2005, Marilyn Wann and Heather McCalister co-hosted a pirate radio show in San Francisco called *Fat-A-Tat-Tat—Soundtrack for a/the Fat Revolution*. And more recent fat podcasts include *Two Whole Cakes Fatcast* (2010– 2011) from Lesley Kinzel and Marianne Kirby, and *Bad Fat Broads!* (2015–) from KC Slack and Ariel Woodson.

Without a doubt, *Fatcast* has been the most influential in my own work, both as an activist and as a podcaster. This was the first fat-acceptance podcast I subscribed to, and I have fond memories of listening to that show. Especially in public—there was something that felt so subversive when surrounded by the fat-hating culture to have two fat-positive women in my ear. One particular memory of listening to an episode while enjoying high tea alone at The Tea Room QVB in Sydney rises to the fore; Marianne and Lesley had me cackling over my chubby scones and finger sandwiches.

After agreement that the station would podcast the show onto iTunes, I signed up for a weekly show entitled *Friend of Marilyn*. I decided quickly that I wanted to have a guest on each show; to date I've had more than two hundred activists/artists/scholars/ dancers/designers/rad fatties share a bit of their lives with me and my listeners.

Choosing a guest is one of my favorite parts; I usually make contact after reading, watching, or seeing something online from a fat activist or fat studies scholar.

The author prepares to record her show at Access Manawatu 999AM. Photograph by Fraser Greig

It's important that my show is a space for fat voices, something that is often missing from the mainstream conversations around obesity. I love and appreciate all of the guests who join me on *Friend of Marilyn*; a recurring favorite is London-based fat activist and para-academic, Charlotte Cooper. In 2012, she shared highlights from the recently concluded Fattylympics in London, an event organized to satirize the Olympics. Those participating pushed back against the ways that sport is leveraged as a weapon against obesity, engaging in games such as rolling, twirling, and "Spitting on the BMI." Charlotte, like many fat activists, avoids engaging with mainstream media about her work. Often times as fat activists, we find ourselves exploited by the media, who wish to present us in much the same way that the "Fat Lady" or "Bearded Lady" were paraded around in freak shows in travelling circuses. Mainstream media is also notorious for introducing red herrings, such as health, into any conversation around fatness. While fat activists want to talk about living a life free from shame and stigma, mainstream media outlets derail the conversation into one of health and a debate of whether or not fat people should ever be represented as anything other than diseased, ashamed, unhappy, undesirable, bodies.

The response to *Friend of Marilyn* has been overwhelmingly positive, and it has been interesting to see how the audience composition has shifted over the years. When the show began, most of those who would send in questions or feedback were actively involved in fat activism themselves. Then I began hearing from individuals who had no background, or possibly even interest, in fat politics, but who had been introduced to my show by a friend or family member. I've heard from men who have thanked me for the show, sharing that their wives are no longer miserable with their physical appearance and are much more confident in themselves as a result. I've received questions from thin people who wish to be allies for fat people, asking for ways they can support the fat people in their lives and join the fight against fat shaming and fat hatred.

When I looked back at the start of the fifth year, I realized that most of my guests are primarily from white Western countries (Australia, United States, UK, etc.), which is not okay. I do not want my show to reproduce white supremacy or to only engage with fat people and issues from a part of the world. To celebrate my fifth year, the show began a (virtual) world tour. Beginning in Auckland, New Zealand, in 2016, I have thus far travelled across Oceania, Asia, the Middle East, and Africa. The show is currently airing episodes across Europe; I imagine that will take the show to the end of the year, and then it is on to the Americas. I hope to talk to those engaged in fat activism across the entire world and on every continent, with the exception of Antarctica.

I started my show because the world wants to take away any claim fat people have to agency, or to an authentic life or experience. But the truth is this: Fat people are the ones who know best about their lives, their behaviors, and their experiences. Fat people are knowers, and fat people know. Fat people produce knowledge. *Friend of Marilyn* has become a great way for fat people to share their truths, their lives, and their resources in resisting body norms and asserting themselves as people who deserve the same rights and dignity as nonfat people.

PART IV

Transforming Institutions and Ideologies

10

Embodying Nonexistence

Encountering Mono- and Cisnormativities in Everyday Life

J. E. Sumerau

On the morning of June 12, 2016, I pulled off of the road in rural Florida to use the restroom and regain my composure at a gas station. During the night, a few hours earlier, the Pulse nightclub in Orlando had endured the deadliest mass attack in the country since 9/11, and the email and messenger applications on my phone were chirping incessantly as friends and colleagues who knew I sometimes went to that club sought to find out if I was there that night, if I was alive, or if I had lost people. Touched by the concern in people's messages and overwhelmed by fear wondering if any of my friends were there last night, I needed to get out of my car and breathe for a minute. I stopped at the gas station to respond to the messages and walked to the restroom marked "Men."

I had just finished crying at the mirror in the corner of the room, saddened and scared by the attack and simultaneously relieved that I hadn't been there that night, when I heard a gruff voice behind me, "Whoa lady, you're not supposed to be in here." I figured my long hair and/or the pink headband I was wearing had confused the speaker when they saw me from behind, and too upset to be cautious in the moment, I simply turned around, stroked my beard to draw attention to this aspect of my appearance, and stared at a male-appearing person in a camouflage jacket. "Oh," he said moving his hand between his legs, opening a nearby stall, and muttering "Faggot" as he situated himself inside. All too familiar with this type of situation, especially from other restroom stops in rural areas, I quickly rinsed off my face and headed back out to my car just in case he decided muttering a slur wasn't enough of a reaction.

Echoing many experiences in my own life and the lives of other bisexual, transgender, lesbian, and gay (BTLG) people I have met and interviewed over the years, this example reflects societal patterns of marginalization experienced by BTLG people when they become visible to heterosexual and cisgender others (Adams 2010; Barton 2012; Worthen 2013).[1] Similar to Lucal's (1999) use of daily experience to demonstrate the operation of gender in daily life, I focus here on the ways bi and trans everyday experiences illustrate the ways monosexual and cisgender people enforce binary sexual and gender norms (Moss 2012; Mathers 2017). I focus on the ways everyday interactions marginalize BT people (as well as many LG people), even when people do not go to violent extremes (Eisner 2013; Serano 2007), by focusing specifically on lessons about daily life people may learn from bi and trans people.[2]

Although most media and scholarly attention tends to focus almost entirely on the experiences of cisgender lesbian and gay people (Moss 2012; Worthen 2013), recent studies reveal BT populations face many of the same issues and, at times, at even higher rates than their cisgender LG peers (Harrison, Grant, and Herman 2011; Herek 2002). Recent studies show, for example, that transgender (binary- and nonbinary- identified) and bisexual (across the bi spectrum) people face significant rates of domestic violence; violence in public; negative health outcomes associated with harassment, stress, and violence; and higher incarceration and homeless rates than most populations in America (Beemyn and Rankin 2011; Goldberg and Meyer 2013; Mathers 2017). However, since BT people are almost never included or explicitly noted in media coverage (aside from occasional coverage of transgender people in relation to laws and murders in the past few years), scientific survey instruments (Nowakowski, Sumerau, and Mathers 2016), or published qualitative studies (Scherrer, Kazyak, and Schmitz 2015), we know far less about these experiences, their rates of occurrence, or the ways they impact the daily and overall life course of BT people.

A Primer on Normativities

The absence of BT people from scholarship and mainstream media coverage, as well as the experiences noted above in my own case and more broadly in society, reflect what social theorists call "heteronormativity." Put simply, heteronormativity refers to an ideology that requires all people to be sorted into mutually exclusive, hierarchical, and oppositional sexual (i.e., straight/gay/lesbian only) and gender (i.e., masculine/ feminine only) categories (Butler 1999; Warner 1999). Over the past twenty-five years, researchers have noted the operation and influence of heteronormativity throughout contemporary settings including but not limited to families, relationships, religions, schools, universities, occupational markets, workplaces, legal systems, political systems, medicine, and public space (see Schrock, Sumerau, and Ueno 2014 for a detailed review). Such studies reveal that heteronormativity relies upon both the separation of people into identifiable heterosexual and homosexual forms (Pfeffer 2014) and man and woman types (Schilt 2010) for its continued existence. The ideology works by allowing people to interpret everything they see as either straight or gay/lesbian and man or woman and align their behavior toward the specific person as a result of this initial interpretation.

Although rarely mentioned in social science to date (Eisner 2013; Sumerau, Cragun, and Mathers 2016), these findings reveal that heteronormativity itself is built upon what social theorists call "mononormativity" (Moss 2012) and "cisnormativity" (Schilt and Westbrook 2009). Mononormativity refers to an ideology that requires all people to belong to only one sexual category (i.e., monosexuality expressed as only either homosexual or heterosexual) and to seek only one sexual partner at a time (i.e., monogamy expressed as relationships with one person at a time or for life). Adopting mononormativity allows people to witness affection between others and categorize them within the sexual binary allowed by heteronormative frameworks and assumptions (i.e., if they show affection to someone who appears the same sex, they must be gay/lesbian only because same sex affection must be their only relationship).[3] It further allows people to dismiss the possibility of respectable life outside of hetero-normative requirements (i.e., everyone must be gay/straight/lesbian only). While this ideology allows people to "do heteronormativity" (Schilt and Westbrook 2009) for themselves and others, it results in the marginalization of sexually fluid people and possibilities in society (Eisner 2013).

Like heteronormativity, however, mononormative sexual assumptions and prac-tices also rely upon the ongoing construction of cisnormativity (Eisner 2013). Cis-normativity refers to an ideology that requires all people to conform to only one gender identity (i.e., masculine/male/man or feminine/female/woman) throughout their lives. Adopting cisnormativity allows people to observe behaviors and appear-ances defined as masculine or feminine and categorize these gendered interpretations within hetero- and mononormative frameworks (e.g., if they look like a woman, I can treat them the way women should be treated and expect them to have the genitals I have been told women will have, or if they look like a woman and show affection to someone that looks like a man, I can treat them as a heterosexual and expect them to always act that way). Like mononormative practice, believing in cisnormativity allows people to dismiss people who reject masculine- or feminine-only appearance or iden-tification (i.e., everything must be man/woman). While this ideology allows people to "do gender" (West and Zimmerman 1987) for themselves and others, it results in the marginalization of gender fluid people and possibilities in society (Westbrook and Schilt 2014).

As noted above, recent years have witnessed limited gains by cisgender LG people in society and an explosion of studies of heteronormativity (Schrock, Sumerau, and Ueno 2014). However, researchers have noted that such gains have not translated into more attention or better treatment for BT people even as occasional studies have begun—as they did with heteronormativity in the 1990s (Warner 1999)—to men-tion mono- and cisnormativity (Eisner 2013). In fact, recent legal victories, such as acquisition of same sex marriage rights after forty years of court cases, have been met with efforts to reinforce mono- and cisnormativities in the law (see, e.g., North Caro-lina's Senate Bill 2 / S.L. 2015-75 attacking the rights of transgender people to use the restroom safely and blocking nondiscrimination ordinances that would benefit all BTLG people). Within this climate, it may be past time for turning our attention to the ways mononormativity (Moss 2012) and cisnormativity (Westbrook and Schilt 2014) shape contemporary American social relations.

In this chapter, I utilize my own experiences as a bisexual (on the pansexual end of the bi spectrum) and transgender (still considering transition, but currently identifying as a nonbinary transwoman) person to illustrate some ways mono- and cisnormativities play out in everyday life. To this end, I focus on illustrative examples (i.e., moments and situations that repeat regularly in my daily life, see Blumer 1969) to demonstrate some ways BT people must manage the enforcement of mono- and cisnormativities in their day-to-day endeavors and interactions with others. Importantly, some of the examples contained herein also demonstrate issues monosexual (i.e., lesbian and gay) and cisgender (i.e., ciswomen) minorities face navigating heteronormative notions of gender and sexuality in their lives. In so doing, I illustrate connections between het-ero-, mono-, and cisnormativities that may be systematically examined by incorporat-ing awareness of and responses to mono- and cisnormativity into existing research, teaching, and activism related to heteronormativity in society. At the same time, I demonstrate the ways occupying sexual and gender identities beyond mono- and cisnormative expectations involves ongoing resistance of others' attempts to enforce these assumptions throughout my daily life.

Before turning to my analyses, it is important to note that other social locations influence my experiences. I am, for example, legally white and I appear white to others the vast majority of the time,[4] which means reactions to my gender and sexual fluidity are likely less extreme, on average, than those faced by bi and trans people of color (Harrison, Grant, and Herman 2011). Even though I have experienced significant violence related to biphobia and transphobia, research and my experiences require us to keep in mind that such reactions are even more common and can be even more violent for BT people of color. Similarly, I have experienced shifts in class status throughout my life that mirror research noting the much more difficult circumstances BTLG people in poverty face than those, as I have been in the last five years, in higher class groups in society (see also Sumerau 2017). In fact, I witnessed some aspects of my life get easier—while others, especially in public or intimate interactions, remained similar—as my class status increased over the past ten years. It is thus important to keep in mind that, while the experiences offered in this chapter may happen to any BT (and some LG) people at present, racial and class marginalization can exacerbate these patterns in powerful ways.

Methods

To examine the ways I am rendered nonexistent by mono- and cisnormative assumptions in daily life, I utilize autoethnography (Crawley 2012). As a method, autoethnography combines autobiography and ethnography. Whereas autobiography requires selectively and retrospectively writing about one's experience, ethnography involves participation and observation of cultural phenomena to facilitate understanding of the experiences of said phenomena. Autoethnography integrates these practices by retrospectively capturing common experiences of a given group one belongs to and situating these experiences into broader cultural patterns. Rather than simply telling one's story, autoethnography relies upon stepping back from one's life to reflect upon the social patterns such experiences illustrate in the world (Cragun and Sumerau 2017).

Autoethnography is especially useful in relation to topics that receive less attention from mainstream media and scholarship because it allows examination of what goes on in social life under the nose of people unaffected by given circumstances (Blumer 1969). Stated another way, it allows a researcher occupying a marginalized or lesser known social position to alert others to missing aspects of social life within existing theoretical and methodological traditions (Adams 2010). For the purposes of this analysis, I utilize re-occurring moments in my life where others remind me that bi and trans experience is unexpected, unwelcome, and/or undesirable in their view of the world. I illustrate how people may, intentionally or otherwise, maintain mono- and cisnormativities—and ultimately heteronormativity as well—by erasing sexual and gender fluidity from existence.

Encountering Cis- and Mononormativities in Everyday Life

What follows is an analysis of the ways others render my sexual and gender fluidity nonexistent by defining me in cisnormative and mononormative terms. First, I show how people cisgender their realities—or create a world devoid of transgender and otherwise gender fluid existence (Sumerau, Cragun, and Mathers 2016)—by reading my embodiment as evidence that I may only be a man *or* a woman. Then, I illustrate how people monosexualize their realities—or create a world devoid of bisexual or other sexually fluid existence—by reading my embodiment and association with other people as evidence that I must be only homosexual or heterosexual.

Cisgendering Reality

Examining the experiences of transgender Mormons, my colleagues and I outlined a generic process—or common way of achieving a shared goal—whereby religious leaders and lay people may create a worldview that does not include transgender people (see, e.g., Sumerau, Cragun, and Mathers 2016; Sumerau and Cragun 2015). In so doing, we revealed examples wherein people—intentionally or otherwise—erase, demonize, and punish transgender existence to establish a cisgender reality where everyone is always only male men or female women from birth to death (see also Nowakowski, Sumerau, and Mathers 2016). In this section, I outline some ways my own embodied experiences reveal similar processes of cisgendering reality whereby people read or interpret my appearance to place me in only one or the other option offered by their cisnormative worldview.

While I experience efforts of others to cisgender me—and by extension their visions of how the world works—throughout my interactions, there are times where such efforts become especially visible. On a Thursday evening in early 2017, for example, I was walking home from work with my long hair flowing, dancing on the sidewalk to the Beyoncé song playing in my headphones, and wearing a simple jeans and t-shirt ensemble when a car passing by began blaring its horn at what felt like full volume. As I cringed at the sound of the horn, the masculine appearing person in the passenger seat of the dark green sedan leaned out the window and screamed: "Hey Baby! Shake that ass for me! Oh what I could do to your sweet ass pussy!" I barely had time to react, but I remember feeling relieved that it was too dark for them to see my beard and experiencing an automatic sense of panic when they stopped at the light just ahead of me.

For these passengers, my long hair, my dancing body on the sidewalk, or the combination of the two suggested I was not only acting feminine, but also female. As a result, they assumed I had a "pussy" and directed forms of catcalling at me, which feminine-appearing people experience regularly in contemporary society (see Schrock and Schwalbe 2009). Further, illustrating societal patterns of masculine-appearing people's assumption of access to feminine bodies, they interpreted my dancing as for their benefit. While they appeared to enjoy this interaction, I experienced automatic terror drawn from the knowledge that transgender women (both those who are biologically and/or socially transitioning and those who simply wish to appear feminine at times) are often murdered in our country simply for not possessing the body parts (e.g., a "sweet ass pussy") others assume they will have (Schilt and Westbrook 2009).

Although the above illustration represents a fairly extreme case of cisgendering reality through interpretation of another's body, such moments become all the more clear when one experiences more subtle, everyday examples. Three days after the interaction described above, for example, I was outside a coffee shop with a cisgender friend, and we were talking about people who desire to transition from one sex to another. In the midst of the conversation, my friend casually noted, "I just don't think I could ever see you as a woman." While such comments are not unusual in my life and not likely to bother me much after hearing them repeatedly, I could not help but automatically think of what happened a few nights before when people did "see" me "as a woman." An hour later, this point was further driven home when I stopped at a gas station to use the restroom and startled a masculine-appearing person in the doorway. Looking up and seeing my long hair and favorite pink headband, the stranger remarked, "Hey, this is the men's . . . oh, sorry buddy, I thought you was a girl."

While each of these examples differ in content, magnitude, and danger, what they have in common are people's attempts to use my physical appearance in combination with their own expectations of gendered bodies to sort me into a cisgender reality. A few years ago, for example, I was drinking and reading in a dark bar when a server came upon me from behind and said, "May I get you anything ma'am?" As the server came around from behind and caught sight of my bearded face, they began looking back and forth between my skirt and my beard while exclaiming, "What are you?" before they could stop themselves. While the manager of the establishment kindly let me drink free for the rest of the night, the simple fact that my own embodiment did not fit into the expectations of our current social world caused a server to explicitly insult me two seconds after approaching me as just another customer.

As many transgender people of varied identifications have learned and experienced over the years (Mathers 2017), others' attempts to cisgender reality may have dangerous consequences that leave us regularly living in fear. Put simply, nonbinary and binary transgender people are assaulted, murdered, and arrested at much higher rates than cisgender people (Harrison, Grant, and Herman 2011).[5] When I decided to wear a skirt, makeup, and a "woman's" headband paired with a "man's" dress shirt, jeans, and a full beard in public one afternoon, for example, I was terrified when a police officer stopped me to "ask a few questions." At the time, I was simply walking through the neighborhood looking for a cisgender friend who had invited me to a party nearby, but even something so simple can become complicated when one doesn't look like what others expect. Luckily, the cisgender friend I was meeting knew many members of the police force; her brother was a cop and she saw me right as I encountered the police. She, thankfully, demanded to know why I was stopped, but all the officer could say was that I "looked suspicious," and that they stopped me—with their hand on their gun the whole time—in case I was "dangerous." When my friend, who the officer in question knew by name, tried to find out what was "suspicious" about me, the officer refused to elaborate, but kept staring at my makeup- and beard-covered face without ever letting go of their gun. My violation of cisnormativity through the use of *both* makeup (i.e., only for women in a cisgender reality) *and* a beard (i.e., only for men in a cisgender reality) was bad enough that it warranted at least the threat of violence from the officer, which only dissipated because I happened to be meeting someone the officer already knew and understood.

It is important to note that throughout this section I have intentionally only offered illustrations of everyday bodily experiences with cisgender people. Like every other transgender person I have met thus far—whether or not they sought full social and/or biological transition—I have experienced much worse (especially from masculine-appearing people who expressed sexual interest in me) reactions. I have focused on everyday interactions, however, to demonstrate that even when people do not go to violent extremes, their efforts to cisgender the world—intentionally or otherwise—effectively erase transgender people from existence, turn our world into one of constant threats and danger, and require us to consistently manage false assumptions. Whether utilizing overt violence, everyday interpretations like those noted above, or even something as simple as cisgender language and pronouns, cisgender people regularly act in ways that marginalize even the possibility of gender fluidity and/or change.

Monosexualizing Reality

Although rarely mentioned in scholarship to date, emerging studies of bisexual experience (McLean 2007; Scherrer, Kazyak, and Schmitz 2015) as well as my own embodied experience suggest people also seek to create a world devoid of bisexuality or other forms of sexual fluidity (Eisner 2013). People who conform to monosexual requirements (i.e., one is only lesbian/gay or straight/heterosexual and this remains true throughout the life course) often attempt to limit others to the same options. Here, I outline some ways monosexual people accomplish this in interaction, which I call "monosexualizing reality."

My life partners appear to be feminine much of the time. When I first showed pictures of me with one of them to old friends, most of these old friends asked me some variation of the following: "So, does this mean you're straight now?" Another important romantic relationship in my life was with an intersex person. To this day, I recall friends asking variations of the following questions: "Are you two gay or straight? I mean, you're both dudes, but neither of you are really always dudes, so which team are you on?" Another important relationship in my life was with a partner who appeared masculine and was assigned male. While we were dating, many of their monosexual friends told me—sometimes angrily—that I should, as one male man who identified as gay said over drinks one night, "Just start saying you're gay now that you're gay, I mean come on." In such cases, monosexual people sought to fit me and my ongoing attraction and desire for all types of bodies into their realities by encouraging me to—and sometimes demanding that I—conform to the monosexual rules they held dear and could understand.

Rather than doing so, I continue to embrace the fact that body type (whether in relation to size, to color, to genitals, or other factors) is—for whatever reason—not a part of my own development of attraction, desire, and/or love. However, I have often disrupted the assumptions of others with my embodied sexuality. Over the years, for example, I have had the same conversation with monosexual friends and acquaintances regarding these violations. While I could choose a pseudonym here to represent any one of them, instead I refer to them as "monosexual friend" because the conversation is basically the same whether I'm talking to a gay, lesbian, or straight person who seeks to monosexualize their reality.[6]

> Monosexual friend: So, I saw you dancing the other night, and you were kissing some guy. What was up with that, are you gay now?
>
> Me: Nope, I'm attracted to guys, girls, and everything else. I told you that when we were hanging out.
>
> Monosexual friend: But, okay, but you're older now, surely you have had time to choose. I mean, you can't just be with anyone—that makes no sense.
>
> Me: Sorry, that's how it is for me—I don't plan to pick a side.
>
> Monosexual friend: Okay, but is it like you like girls more when you're more girly or more like a boy, or the other way around? I mean, what are the rules?
>
> Me: The rules are simple—I like people and I don't care what kind of genitals or gender they have today, tomorrow, or ever. I want the person so what they are or will become doesn't really matter to me when I meet them.
>
> Monosexual friend: That's crazy!

I have further repeatedly had to explain to monosexual people that one can very easily be attracted to and find fulfillment with transgender and intersex people of varied body types, gender identifications, and backgrounds. In such cases, my embodied existence as one capable of attraction to various bodies, appearances, and especially genital configurations disrupts their expectation that (1) genitals determine sexual desire, (2) gender is necessary for attraction, and (3) one may not practice both homo- and heterosexualities throughout their lives without developing a need for only one or the other.

Similar to friends, acquaintances, and lovers, strangers also seek to sort me into monosexual assumptions. During a thirty-minute train ride with a bisexual gender-queer friend, for example, a passenger muttered, "damn dykes" under their breath before getting off at one stop, and another passenger said, "gay fag boys" before a separate train stop. In both cases, strangers saw people who blended masculine and feminine embodiment riding a train arm-in-arm, and interpreted us as necessarily lesbian or gay. When we got off the train, however, my companion removed their hat and revealed a hairstyle typically considered feminine, which encouraged another stranger to tell me, "Your wife looks lovely, sir," as we headed down the stairs.[7] Whether strangers assumed we were heterosexual or homosexual, they situated us within a mononormative framework, defined us in terms of only these two options, and interpreted our physical contact as evidence of a romantic sexual relationship we do not actually have or desire.

Another example arose one evening as I walked with a heterosexual masculine-appearing friend while their child was trick-or-treating. Their child, who also appears somewhere between feminine and masculine embodiment norms, generated confusion at three separate stops. Likewise, my friend and I were interpreted as a gay male couple taking our child to get candy on at least two occasions in different ways. In the first case, a couple of people walking together on the other side of the road smiled at us, and, as we passed, one of them said, "Aren't they just a darling little family." In the second case, however, a group of people walking together stared at us—which I felt and my companion did not notice—and one muttered, "That's disgusting. Why do we have to see couples like that?" Once again, comfortable bodily contact signified to others that we occupied a specific sexual position and relationship that we do not occupy or desire.

While the details in each of the aforementioned cases vary, each one reveals attempts to monosexualize reality. Whether read as homosexual or heterosexual, people expect—and at times demand—that others must be one or the other. Likewise, strangers interpret physical contact or demonstrated bodily comfort between people as indicators that such people must be sexually involved,[8] and then sort them into one of the expected types of sexuality within their mononormative worldviews (Pfeffer 2014). As a result, interactions with others continuously require bisexual people to confront their nonexistence in contemporary social expectations and to remain ready for the consequences of others' misdiagnosis of our embodied experiences.

Conclusion

As the above examples reveal, people may utilize their own assumptions about the bodies of others to cisgender and monosexualize their realities. While studies of gender and sexualities typically focus on heteronormativity (i.e., the experiences of cisgender women and men or gay/straight/lesbian people) (Butler 1999), this is only, at most, half the story. By embodying sexual and/or gender fluidity and the possibility of existing between or beyond mono- and cisnormative categorizations, bisexual and transgender people—as well as others who engage in sexual and/or gender fluidity—reveal the mononormative (Eisner 2013) and cisnormative (Westbrook and Schilt 2014) foundations that structure and preserve heteronormativity documented throughout contemporary American settings, relationships, and structures.

While researchers have shown how bisexual (Moss 2012) and transgender (Sumerau, Cragun, and Mathers 2016) people of varied types experience erasure in contemporary America, I demonstrate some ways cisgender and monosexual people accomplish erasure by selectively interpreting the bodies and actions of others. I also demonstrate some ways BT people experience erasure, and the ways it comes to represent a regular, ongoing, and systemic aspect of our everyday interactions (Scherrer, Kazyak, and Schmitz 2015; Schilt 2010). While many people may find comfort and meaning within existing systems, and such people should be affirmed, the ongoing marginalization of BT people—as well as the ways these patterns disadvantage cisgender heterosexual women and cisgender lesbian and gay people—occurs when such people seek to convert or force others into mono- and cisnormative realities. People seeking to avoid doing so may search their own everyday interactions for the ways they might—regardless of intention—cisgender and/or monosexualize reality at the expense of others' safety and wellbeing.

These observations also have implications for collective action. While most contemporary LG movements focus on assimilating to hetero-, cis-, and mononormative demands (Warner 1999), such tactics have been shown to only further institutionalize the marginalization of bi and trans people. Further, research often finds systemic patterns of biphobia and transphobia in many LG populations, organizations, and groups, which often means bi and trans people must face similar expressions of cis- and mononormativity even in supposedly nonheteronormative spaces (Eisner 2013).

As the influx of anti-BTLG legislation following the legalization of same-sex marriage suggests, assimilation strategies are not likely to facilitate equality on their own. It may thus be worthwhile for existing LG movements to recall the resistance-based strategies of the past and commit to the eradication of hetero-, mono-, and cisnormativities. In so doing, we may return to the pursuit of sexual and gender liberation for all.

Regardless of our intentions, we all act in ways that affirm and/or resist cisnormativity and mononormativity as well as systems that privilege masculine and heterosexual bodies and people. Whether we fit neatly into existing mononormative and cisnormative categories or exist outside the rules of such categorizations, we each have the power to make it easier for people who seek to engage in sexual and gender fluidity whether or not any given one of us wishes to do so. To this end, each of us can start by putting away hetero-, mono-, and cisnormative assumptions and seeking to actively interact with and affirm various embodiments of gender, sexualities, relationships, and physical contact. Doing so may help create safe spaces for all of us to freely use our bodies as tools of self-expression, shared existence, and collective engagement. Accomplishing this, however, will require people marshaling the necessary courage to send cisnormativity, mononormativity, and other ideological forces of inequality out of our own everyday interactions, assumptions, and bodily interpretations.

NOTES

1. While my use of this form of the acronym may seem odd to readers who have adopted a normative script for discussing sexual and gender minorities based on emphasizing LG experience, I do this intentionally to point out my focus on BT experience. Like many other people, I use BTLG, TBLG, LGBT, and GLBT in different contexts depending on the subject, and typically use BTLG and TBLG the most as they speak to my social position as a B and T person.
2. Although it may seem odd to some readers to discuss BT experiences together, both groups violate the sexual and/or gender binaries that structure cisgender and monosexual norms and assumptions, and both often face marginalization from gay/straight/lesbian monosexuals as well as cisgender women and men.
3. I utilize singular they/them as gender-neutral pronouns that may refer to anyone regardless of gender or sexual identity.
4. I use this specific language about racial identity and appearance because I am legally assigned white by the United States government and official record, but like many people, my ancestry and genetic makeup are more complicated. This becomes relevant in daily interactions at times because, while I am interpreted by others as white most of the time, I am also often interpreted as Mexican or more broadly as Hispanic by others in both positive and negative ways. This generally occurs more often in the summer months, and likely owes (as others have noted) to facial features and skin tone fluctuation due to ancestry. These situations have included, for example, people speaking Spanish to and with me in public about the (assumed at least) white people nearby; other people who appear white by American standards telling me to "go home," "get a job," or "learn the language" without having spoken to me or asked anything about me; and experiences where I am greeted with Spanish terms of endearment or commonality by strangers who appear to be Hispanic and/or greeted with slurs targeted at Hispanic populations by strangers who appear to be white.
5. As Beemyn and Rankin (2011) note, it is telling that researchers have difficulty locating

many nonbinary or binary trans people who have not experienced some form of violence or harassment at some point in their lives.

6. While this conversation may not seem unusual to people invested in a monosexual reality, it is incredibly difficult for a sexually nonbinary person because it feels like a missionary attempting to convert strangers to their chosen religion (i.e., I believe in monosexism and mononormativity so I must force you to fit my beliefs). Much like cisgender language (Sumerau, Cragun, and Mathers 2016), this type of conversation represents one of the many everyday occasions that create a context for the marginalization of and violence against bi+ people (Eisner 2013).

7. In this case, the stranger appeared to be offering a sincere compliment, but various companions and I have experienced this moment both in cases where it seemed like a sincere compliment and in cases where it seemed like a sarcastic or derogatory attack upon our presence and appearance.

8. It is noteworthy that such occasions may be read differently for people who appear masculine or appear feminine in varied settings, and that such interpretations are heavily dependent on context, culture, and setting.

REFERENCES

Adams, Tony E. 2010. "Paradoxes of Sexuality, Gay Identity, and the Closet." *Symbolic Interaction* 33: 234–56.

Barton, Bernadette. 2012. *Pray the Gay Away: The Extraordinary Lives of Bible Belt Gays.* New York: New York University Press.

Beemyn, Genny, and Susan Rankin. 2011. *The Lives of Transgender People.* New York: Columbia University Press.

Blumer, Herbert. 1969. *Symbolic Interactionism: Perspective and Method.* Berkeley: University of California Press.

Butler, Judith. 1999. *Gender Trouble: Feminism and the Subversion of Identity.* New York: Routledge.

Cragun, Ryan T., and J. E. Sumerau. 2017. "Losing Manhood Like a Man: A Collaborative Autoethnographic Examination of Masculinities and the Experience of a Vasectomy." *Men and Masculinities* 20, no. 1: 98–116.

Crawley, Sara L. 2012. "Autoethnography as Feminist Self-Interview." In *The Sage Handbook of Interview Research: The Complexity of the Craft,* 2nd Edition, edited by James A. Holstein, Jaber F. Gurbrium, Karyn D. McKinney, and Amir B. Marvasti, 143–60. Los Angeles: Sage.

Eisner, Shiri. 2013. *Bi: Notes for a Bisexual Revolution.* Berkeley, CA: Seal Press.

Goldberg, Naomi G., and Ilan H. Meyer. 2013. "Sexual Orientation Disparities in History of Intimate Partner Violence." *Journal of Interpersonal Violence* 28, no. 5: 1109–18.

Harrison, Jack, Jamie Grant, and Jody L. Herman. 2011. "A Gender Not Listed Here: Genderqueers, Gender Rebels, and Otherwise in the National Transgender Discrimination Survey." *LGBTQ Policy Journal at the Harvard Kennedy School* 2: 13–24.

Herek, Gregory H. 2002. "Heterosexual's Attitudes toward Bisexual Men and Women in the United States." *Journal of Sex Research* 39, no. 4: 264–74.

Lucal, Betsy. 1999. "What It Means to Be Gendered Me: Life on the Boundaries of a Dichotomous Gender System." *Gender & Society* 13, no. 6: 781–97.

Mathers, Lain A. B. 2017. "Bathrooms, Boundaries, and Emotional Burdens: Cisgendering Interactions through the Interpretation of Transgender Experience." *Symbolic Interaction* 40, no. 3: 295–316.

McLean, Kristen. 2007. "Hiding in the Closet?: Bisexuals, Coming Out and the Disclosure Imperative." *Journal of Sociology* 43, no. 2: 151–66.

Moss, Alison R. 2012. "Alternative Families, Alternative Lives: Married Women *Doing* Bisexuality." *Journal of GLBT Family Studies* 8, no. 5: 405–27.

Nowakowski, Alexandra C. H., J. E. Sumerau, and Lain A. B. Mathers. 2016. "None of the Above: Strategies for Inclusive Teaching with 'Representative' Data." *Teaching Sociology* 44, no. 2: 96–105.

Pfeffer, Carla A. 2014. "'I Don't Like Passing as a Straight Woman': Queer Negotiations of Identity and Social Group Membership." *American Journal of Sociology* 120. no. 1: 1–44.

Scherrer, Kristin S., Emily Kazyak, and Rachel Schmitz. 2015. "Getting 'Bi' in the Family: Bisexual People's Disclosure Experiences." *Journal of Marriage and Family* 77, no. 3: 680–96.

Schilt, Kristen. 2010. *Just One of the Guys?: Transgender Men and the Persistence of Gender Inequality.* Chicago: University of Chicago Press.

Schilt, Kristen, and Laurel Westbrook. 2009. "Doing Gender, Doing Heteronormativity: 'Gender Normals,' Transgender People, and the Social Maintenance of Heterosexuality." *Gender & Society* 23: 440–64.

Schrock, Douglas, and Michael Schwalbe. 2009. "Men, Masculinity, and Manhood Acts." *Annual Review of Sociology* 35: 277–95.

Schrock, Douglas, J. Edward Sumerau, and Koji Ueno. 2014. "Sexualities." In *Handbook of the Social Psychology of Inequality*, edited by Jane D. McLeod, Edward J. Lawler, and Michael Schwalbe, 627–54. New York: Springer.

Serano, Julia. 2007. *Whipping Girl: A Transsexual Woman on Sexism and the Scapegoating of Femininity.* Emeryville, CA: Seal Press.

Sumerau, J. E. 2017. *Cigarettes & Wine.* Boston, Massachusetts: Sense Publishers.

Sumerau, J. E., Ryan T. Cragun, and Lain A. B. Mathers. 2016. "Contemporary Religion and the Cisgendering of Reality." *Social Currents* 3, no. 3: 293–311.

Sumerau, J. E., and Ryan T. Cragun. 2015. "Trans-forming Mormonism: Transgender Perspectives on Priesthood, Ordination, and Gender." In *Voices for Equality: Ordain Women and Resurgent Mormon Feminism,* edited by Gordon Shepherd, Lavina Fielding Anderson, and Gary Shepherd, 115–32. Draper, UT: Kofford Books.

Warner, Michael. 1999. *The Trouble with Normal: Sex, Politics, and the Ethics of Queer Life.* New York: Free Press.

West, Candace, and Don Zimmerman. 1987. "Doing Gender." *Gender & Society* 1, no. 2: 125–51.

Westbrook, Laurel, and Kristen Schilt. 2014. "Doing Gender, Determining Gender: Transgender People, Gender Panics, and the Maintenance of the Sex/Gender/Sexuality System." *Gender & Society* 28, no. 1: 32–57.

Worthen, M. G. F. 2013. "An Argument for Separate Analyses of Attitudes toward Lesbian, Gay, Bisexual Men, Bisexual Women, MtF and FtM Transgender Individuals." *Sex Roles* 68, no. 11-12: 703–23.

11

Freeing the Nipple

Encoding the Heterosexual Male Gaze into Law

J. Shoshanna Ehrlich

In 1986, a small group of feminists in New York "made history at a topless picnic . . . staged for the sole purpose of getting arrested" (Merlan 2013). Gathered supporters carried signs with slogans such as, "Suppression Creates Obsession," "What is Indecent About Our Breasts," and "Keep Your Laws Off Our Bodies," and some "wore t-shirts bearing an image of a topfree Statute of Liberty emblazoned with the words, 'Equal Rights Now–Shirtless Equality in 1986'" (Pundras 1994–1995, 2). The women were arrested and charged with violating the state's indecent exposure law that made it a crime for women, but not men, to publicly expose their nipples.

The "Topfree Seven," as they came to be known, argued that the law violated their constitutional right to equal protection because it denied women the same freedom that men enjoyed to go topless in public. The court ultimately dismissed the charges against the Topfree Seven on a technicality. Disappointingly, this meant that it did not consider their claim that the law was discriminatory because men would not have been arrested had they similarly exposed their breasts during a picnic in a public park (*People v. Santorelli* 1992).

Indecent exposure laws, which make it a crime for women, but not men, to expose their nipples in public, subject to possible exceptions for breastfeeding and topless dancing, exist in many parts of the United States. These laws have traditionally been justified as both necessary to protect public morality and as simply reflecting a biologically based difference between men and women. These restrictions did not attract much opposition until the end of the twentieth century when "topfree" advocates, like the New York picnickers, began challenging them. Grounded in the belief that "breasts are not objects; they are part of subjects, women, who should be allowed to control when they are seen, why they are seen, how they are seen, and by whom" (Pundras 1994–1995, 21), these advocates argue that such measures discriminate against women. A number of celebrities, including Scout Willis, Miley Cyrus, and Rihanna, have also embraced the cause (O'Connell 2014).

Protests and legal challenges also have continued. For example, in 2015, members of Free the Nipple–Springfield Residents Promoting Equality gathered in Springfield, Missouri, to protest the city's indecent exposure ordinance permitting males, but not females, to show their nipples without fearing arrest or prosecution (Second Amended

Complaint 2016, 3). The women appeared topless, but covered their nipples to avoid arrest, while the men covered theirs in a sign of solidarity (4). The group has filed a lawsuit against the city asserting that the differential nipple exposure rule "perpetuate[s] traditional gender roles and the legal and social inferiority of women and girls" (12).

To date, however, most equal protection challenges to differential breast exposure rules have not been successful, as courts have typically concluded that they reflect a "real difference" between the sexes, thus making the distinction between male and female breasts legally permissible. Many courts have likewise concluded that the distinction is permissible because it promotes an important governmental interest in protecting, as the City of Springfield argued, "the moral sensibilities of that substantial segment of society that still does not want to be exposed willy-nilly to public displays of various portions of their fellow citizens' anatomies that traditionally have been regarded as erogenous zones" (Memorandum of Law 2015, 1).

The courts have accordingly been generally unresponsive to the argument presented by challengers that these laws both reflect and perpetuate "archaic . . . cultural stereotypes equating the female breast and women with sexual fantasies, irrespective of the wishes of women to treat their bodies with the same freedom available to men" (*Craft v. Hodel* 1988, 299). In turn, this unresponsiveness sends the message, as one court stated, that the "privilege sought here" does not involve "any serious interest" (*Seattle v. Buchanan* 1978, 921). However, as argued here, differential breast exposure laws are saturated with cultural meanings that inscribe a male-defined conception of eroticism on women's bodies in violation of constitutional guarantees of equality.

Female Breasts and the Encoding of the (Heterosexual) Male View of Their Eroticism

To better understand the problematic nature of the assumption that differential breast exposure rules are neutral expressions of real biological differences and moral sensibilities, it is instructive to consider the trajectory of the same-sex marital rights cases up through the recent Supreme Court decision in *Obergefell v. Hodges* in which the Court recognized the deep harms imposed by different marriage rules for same-sex and heterosexual couples. These cases offer a valuable framework within which to examine how once-presumed-natural differences were ultimately unmasked as socially constructed justifications for discriminatory treatment based on anti-gay animus.

"Natural Difference" and the Marriage Equality Cases

In the first wave of constitutional challenges to state laws prohibiting same-sex couples from marrying, courts were not at all sympathetic to the claims of parties who had been denied a marriage license because they sought to marry a same-sex partner. Although challengers had hoped the recent *Loving v. Virginia* decision in which the Supreme Court invalidated laws banning interracial marriage would support their position, their hopes were dashed by the unwillingness of courts to take their asserted right to marriage equality seriously.

This unwillingness was grounded in the oft-cited admonition that same-sex couples were not capable of marrying because when it came to the sine qua non of marriage—namely, procreative capacity—they were distinguishable from hetero-sexual couples and thus could be treated differently. Courts accordingly facilely con-cluded that the law "does not authorize the issuance of a marriage license [to same-sex couples] because what they propose is not a marriage" (*Jones v. Hallahan* 1973, 590). Framed by this naturalistic assumption regarding real differences, courts absolved states of responsibility for this discriminatory treatment, which was deemed to result "from the impossibility of reproduction rather than from an invidious discrimination" (*Singer v. Hara* 1974, 1195). In short, as seen by the courts, it was biology, rather than state laws, that made marriage between same-sex partners an impossibility.

However, in 2003, in the case of *Goodridge v. Department of Public Health*, the Supreme Judicial Court (SJC) of Massachusetts engaged in the kind of searching analysis regarding the marital rights of same-sex couples that courts had generally avoided until that point. Rather than simply assuming that a difference in procreative capacity justified a marriage ban, the SJC instead recognized that although "many, perhaps most, married couples have children together (assisted or unassisted) . . . if procreation were a necessary component of civil marriage, our statutes would draw a tighter circle around the permissible bounds of nonmarital child bearing and the crea-tion of families by noncoital means" (*Goodridge* 2003, 961–62). Accordingly, rather than placing procreation at the center of marriage, the Court instead gave place of pride to "the exclusive and permanent commitment of the marriage partners to one another" (961).

Challenging the traditional definition of marriage, the SJC made clear that the "marriage is procreation argument singles out the one unbridgeable difference between same-sex and opposite-sex couples, and transforms that difference into the essence of legal marriage," which, in turn, places "an official stamp of approval on the destructive stereotype that same-sex relationships are inherently unstable and inferior to opposite-sex relationships and are not worthy of respect" (*Goodridge* 2003, 962). Drawing upon *Loving,* the Court held that it was a form of invidious discrimination to bar people from marriage based on a "single trait"—be it race or sexual orientation (958).

A little more than a decade later, the United States Supreme Court likewise recog-nized in the landmark *Obergefell v. Hodges* decision that the "ability, desire, or promise to procreate is not and has not been a prerequisite for a valid marriage in any State," and that, while the "limitation of marriage to opposite-sex couples may long have seemed *natural and just*," the exclusion had "the effect of teaching that gays and les-bians are unequal in important respects" (*Obergefell* 2015, 2601–2, emphasis added). Accordingly, it concluded that same-sex couples must be afforded the same marital rights as heterosexual couples as the once-presumed naturally grounded and objective justification for differential treatment proved to be infused with harmful stereotypical assumptions about gay men and lesbians.

Application of the Marriage Equality Cases to Differential Breast Exposure Rules

As in the early marriage equality cases, most courts that have considered equal pro-tection challenges to differential breast exposure laws have concluded that the line-drawing between male and female bodies is permissible because it is based on real anatomical differences and is necessary to protect the public sensibilities. Paralleling the early unexamined assumption that nature, rather than discriminatory practices and laws, disqualified same-sex couples from marrying, they likewise have concluded that because "nature, not the legislative body created the distinction between that portion of a woman's body and that of a man's torso" (*J. A. Eckl v. Davis* 1975, 696–97), it is female biology, as inscribed by nature, that disqualifies women from enjoying the same freedoms as men.

However, assumptions about biological differences and community reactions to bared female breasts are not objective statements of a static biological and social reality. Rather, they represent a "regulatory practice that produces the bodies it governs" (Butler 2011, xi), which reflects normative understandings of the sexualized female body as constructed by the heterosexual male observer.

Encoding Male Sensibilities into Law

Although seemingly objectively grounded in real differences and the need to protect public/moral sensibilities, indecent exposure ordinances encode an implicit male bias into law in direct violation of the constitutional right to equality. I begin my discussion with three interrelated observations.

First, subject to the exception for their capacity to nurture the young, the anatomical structure of the male and female breasts are essentially the same. Particularly relevant, both "have the same erotic potential" (Glazer 1993, 130). Thus, anatomically speaking, "the female breast is no more or less a sexual organ than is the male equivalent" (*People v. Santorelli* 1992, 605).

Secondly, while "it seems obvious . . . that [heterosexual] men find women's breasts sexually stimulating" (Glazer 1993, 130), research shows that for many women, the chest is typically the most sexually arousing part of the male body (13), and it likewise holds erotic power for gay men. Their similar potential capacity to sexually stimulate the viewer is evidenced by the fact that "professionally erotic, bare-chested, male, adult dancing is marketable" to both homosexual and heterosexual patrons who find the dance routines stimulating (Cusak 2012, 209).

Third, as scholar Marilyn Yalom (1997) writes, "the sexualized view of the breast is by no means universal" and has varied across time and space (3). She stresses that "in a number of different cultures in Africa and the South Pacific, where women have gone around with the breasts uncovered since time immemorial, the breast has not taken on the predominantly erotic meaning it has in the West" (3). She further points out that throughout much of the West's early history "the milk-bearing function of the [female] breast was bathed in a sacred aura . . . and the nursing Madonna was the prototype of female divinity" (48). However, sometime during the fifteenth century, men succeeded in stripping the breast of "its relation to the sacred," and it "became the uncontested playground for male desire" (49). As a result, "in the graphic arts and literature, breasts were offered up for the pleasure of the male viewer, or reader, with the intent of arousing him, not her . . . [and] their sexual meaning began to overshadow their maternal meaning" (90).

In short, perceptions of the breast are not fixed or static. As one court put it, public response to female topless nudity is a "social concept," (*People v. Craft* 1986, 1010). Given this reality, courts should not be permitted to sidestep their responsibility to engage in a searching constitutional analysis of indecent exposure laws by facilely invoking the concepts of natural differences or the sensibilities of the community.

Instead, they have an obligation to carefully evaluate whether or not these laws are impermissibly saturated with outdated stereotypes

Taking as a starting point Yalom's (1997, 90) admonition that "historically speaking, the erotization of women's breasts has predominately been a male affair," it is clear that indecent exposure laws are both rooted in and further promote legally impermissible gender stereotypes. As developed below, these laws ignore the meaning that women attach to their own breasts and instead impose a limitation on female bodily autonomy based on the breasts' presumed impact on the heterosexual male viewer.

Rather than respecting a woman's own intentionality regarding her body, differential breast exposure rules constrain her choices based upon the potential impact her bared breasts may have upon her audience. In short, "it is the viewer's reaction to the viewed that determines what is too sexual for a given context," thereby giving the observer, namely the heterosexual male, "control over the observed object" (Whisner 1982, 112). Deeply problematic, it is readily apparent that these laws are a response to the male viewer's "erotization" of a woman's breast—it is his gaze, rather than her own subjectivity that defines the parameters of her bodily rights.

The case of *Buzzetti v. New York*, involving a challenge to a zoning ordinance that classified bars featuring bare-chested female dancers, but not bare-chested male dancers, as adult establishments is instructive. The case highlights how the "construction of the [female] breast is defined by the impact on the outside observer" (Arneil 2000, 248) rather than by the woman to whom the observed breast belongs. As the court explained, seemingly self-evidently, why differential breast exposure rules are not constitutionally suspect: "One does not need to be either a psychologist or a sociologist to recognize that, if it were widely known that ten topless women were walking down Park Avenue and ten topless men were walking down Madison Avenue, the effect on the traffic on Park Avenue would be substantially greater than on Madison" (*Buzzetti* 1997, 16). The court continued on to say that "even if we accept *arguendo* the view of plaintiffs' expert that the male and female breast are equally erotic, that does not change the fact that in our culture the public display of female breasts *will have different secondary effects* than the display of male breasts" (emphasis added; Buzzetti 1997, 16).

Agreeing with this approach, the appeals court subsequently stated that "given New York City's objective, which is not to oppress either gender's sexuality, but to *control effects* that flow from public reaction to the conduct involved, we must recognize that the *public reactions* to the exhibition of the female breast and the male breast are *highly different*" (emphasis added; *Buzzetti* 1998, 142–43). In short, as the Court makes clear, the desire of women to have the same freedom as men to stroll topless down a city street is irrelevant; rather, the only perspective that matters is that of the (heterosexual) male viewer and his eroticized vision of women's bodies.

Underscoring the androcentric nature of these laws, many contain a breast exposure exception for topless dancers. Women are thus free to expose their breasts in settings such as strip clubs that are intended for the pleasure of the heterosexual male viewer (Woswick-Correa and Jacobs 2008, 215). As Dahlia Schweitzer (2000, 68), who was herself a cabaret dancer, explains: "the stripper is a physical manifestation of an idea resident in the minds of men. The best strippers respond to the desires of their audience. . . .They become a feminine ideal in which natural sentience and fantasy have been replaced with a monolithic eroticism serving male fantasy." Characterized by one scholar as a "masculinizing practice," men who frequent clubs featuring topless dancers are provided with a space to indulge in the fantasy that the bare-breasted women they are viewing exist "outside of normative social constraints" where they enjoy tremendous "'sexual freedoms' and a kind of 'wild sexuality'" (Frank 2003, 67, 68). These settings accordingly provide them an opportunity to "enjoy the pleasure of a sexualized experience free from the pressures of sexual performance" (64).

This legal carve-out that allows women to fully expose their breasts within a "highly sexualized environment predicated upon male heterosexual fantasies and female subjectivity" (Woswick-Correa and Jacobs 2008, 215) underscores the fact that these laws embody the "notion of woman as object for a (heterosexual male) audience," with a clear lack of regard for "women's interests as *actors*" (Whisner 1982, 113). They accordingly encode the view that what "might arouse men can only be displayed when men want to be aroused," such as "at topless bars and clubs, in pornography, and in the bedroom" (Boso 2009, 147), thereby investing the viewer with power over the viewed.

Involving a "Serious Interest"

As discussed, upon closer examination the "real differences" and "public/moral sensibilities" rationales for differential breast exposure rules are rooted in outmoded assumptions about women's bodies. Nevertheless, when compared to other forms of gender injustices, the interests at stake here may appear to be of a less-pressing nature. However, these mandates are part of a long history of legal rules aimed at managing women's lives in ways that would not be acceptable if they were instead aimed at men. Accordingly, I now broaden my analytical lens to consider two historic examples of how the law has managed women's lives based on a social preoccupation with, in the first instance, their sexualized bodies and, in the second, their maternalized bodies. Situating differential breast exposure rules within this context further illuminates how they mark the female body as an appropriate regulatory subject in disregard of women's own understandings of their bodies.

Regulating the Sexual Body of Young Women

During the Progressive Era (roughly 1890–1920), states adopted a novel approach to "wayward" youth. Rather than being treated as adult criminals, they would instead be assigned to the newly created juvenile court where the focus was to be on rehabilitation and reform rather than on punishment. This novel approach reflected the emergent views of Progressive Era reformers that childhood was a uniquely fragile and impressionable phase of life during which youth should be shielded from the burdens of the adult world (Zelizer 1994).

The juvenile courts quickly became deeply gendered spaces. Boys were typically brought in for offenses against property, or, if charged with "being incorrigible or disorderly," the underlying conduct usually involved activities such as "loitering about the streets and using vulgar language, receiving money embezzled by another boy . . . going upon the roof of a building and throwing stones at passers-by, refusing to obey parents, and staying away from home" (Breckenridge and Abbott 1912, 30–31). In stark contrast, most girls were brought into juvenile court based on concerns about their "virtue"

(37–38). Moreover, if a girl was charged with "being incorrigible or disorderly," the underlying conduct almost always involved sexual "impropriety." Accordingly, as one prominent public official explained, when "we speak of the delinquent girl we usually have in mind the sex offender," whereas "we do not think of the problem of the delinquent boy as primarily related to sex as we do in the case of girls" (Johnson 1926, 385).

The conflation of female delinquency with sexual immorality did not, of course, mean that young men were more chaste than their female peers. Rather, this collapsing of categories was a clear signal that boys' sexual conduct was not considered sufficiently transgressive as to warrant subjecting their bodies to the supervisory control of the state. Astutely recognizing this double standard, one contemporary observer noted that, "If boys were brought to brook for sex delinquencies as girls are, their preponderant offenses would be found to lie in the same sphere also. But the boy who indulges in sex relations is seldom apprehended for that reason alone; the girl, if discovered, immediately comes under the social ban" (Richmond 1925, 113). Of course, the critical question is *why* was it that indulgence in sexual relations immediately placed girls, but not boys, under the "social ban?"

This differential treatment reflected the firm belief of Progressive Era reformers that, unlike the "boy who indulges in sex relations," the girl who does so is a disruptive force who must be managed for her own good and the well-being of society. Accordingly, as urban working-class and immigrant girls in particular began actively "experimenting with new cultural forms that articulated gender in terms of sexual expressiveness and social interactions with men" (Peiss 1986, 6), reformers feared that the firewall Victorian society had so carefully erected to distinguish the virtuous woman from the fallen would crumble, resulting in an unacceptable blurring of the boundaries between respectability and promiscuity. Vividly capturing this sense of fear, a noted sex educator exclaimed in a public lecture that "the great menace of the American City life was not the man who was going about trying to lure young people into horrible lives, but was the young girl . . . who was perfectly free to roam the streets morning, noon and night, who apparently had no moral outlook at all and who was constantly corrupting the young men and boys of large cities" (Mabel Ulrich 1915, quoted in Alexander 1995, 33).

Reformers sought to extinguish the "flamboyant assertion" of an emerging female identity that played with "notions of respectability, allure, independence and status" (Peiss 1986, 58, 63) in derogation of normative understandings of respectable womanhood by subjecting the youthful, sexualized female body to the supervisory authority of the juvenile courts. In contrast, given that, as the Newark Vice Commission put it, males have long been assumed to "have a right to the pleasure they can gain from their bodies" (Connelly 1980, 40–41), there was no similar push to wrap the law around the delinquent boy's body, as it was not marked as a dangerous site of personal and social dislocation.

Returning to bare breasts, as in the early days of the juvenile courts, indecent exposure laws target women and girls as appropriate and necessary regulatory subjects based on the dangers their bodies are thought to pose to public sensibilities without regard for their rights to bodily self-determination. Paralleling the steadfast refusal of Progressive Era reformers to read the changes they were seeing in the lives of young women as expressive of their desires rather than as a worrisome slide into immorality, differential breast exposure rules similarly erase the ability of women and girls to make choices about their own bodies due to externally imposed fears of an unregulated female sexuality. Invoking archaic and androcentric constructions of the female breast, they are linked to a long tradition of marking women's and girls' bodies as a site of disruptive sexual power that must be managed for the public good.

Regulating the Maternal Body

In the landmark 1908 case *Muller v. Oregon*, the United States Supreme Court upheld a protective labor law that limited the number of daily hours that women in designated industries could be required to work. Given that only three years earlier, in the infamous *Lochner v. New York* case, the Court had invalidated a similar law regulating the maximum hours of male bakers, one might reasonably assume that it would have also invalidated this law. However, in a radical departure from *Lochner*, the *Muller* Court concluded that in light of "woman's physical structure, and the functions she performs in consequence thereof," she was an appropriate subject of "special legislation restricting or qualifying the conditions under which she should be permitted to toil" (*Muller* 1908, 420). In short, as the Court explained, "real" differences between men and women empowered the state to manage women's lives regardless of their own desires or intentionality regarding the hours they wished (or, perhaps better, needed) to work.[1]

As far as men were concerned, the Supreme Court was resolute that the imposition of limitations on their autonomy would make them "wards of the State" (*Lochner* 1905, 57). As explained, there was "no contention that bakers as a class are not equal in intelligence and capacity to men in other trades or manual occupations, or that they are not able to assert their rights and care for themselves without the protecting arm of the State, interfering with their independence of judgment and of action" (57). In short, so long as there was no connection between the number of hours worked and the production of "clean and wholesome bread" (57), the state had no business restricting the autonomy of male bakers—it was up to them to manage for themselves any potential risks posed by their working conditions.

In stark contrast, the *Muller* decision clearly signaled that women were indeed "wards of the state" whose autonomy could be limited for their own good, as well as for the benefit of the public. In terms of their own welfare, the Court explained that, although in matters of "personal and contractual rights" women in Oregon stood "on the same plane as the other sex" (*Muller* 1908, 418), this did not alter the fundamental reality of woman's continued dependence on men. Accordingly, it was incumbent upon the state to step in and protect her from "the greed as well as the passion of man" (422). Relative to the public good, the *Muller* Court opined that because "healthy mothers are essential to vigorous offspring," the "physical well-being of woman becomes an object of public interest and care" (421). Having suffused her body with social meaning, the Court concluded that the state could restrict her working hours for the benefit of the public.

Looping back again to bare breasts, in *Muller*, as with differential breast exposure rules, women are denied the right to make their own decisions based on gendered assumptions about their bodies and place in the social order. Today, *Muller* is no longer good law, and women have the "power to decide" for themselves what kinds of "strenuous, dangerous, obnoxious, boring or unromantic tasks [are] worth the candle" (*Weeks v. Southern Bell* 1969, 236); nonetheless, differential breast exposure rules continue to selectively target women's bodies in order to protect the public good as determined by the heterosexual male viewer.

The Male Gaze and Self-Objectification

As discussed, differential breast exposure rules impermissibly mark women's bodies as socially disruptive based on an androcentric construction of the female breast. In addition to perpetuating outmoded stereotypes about female sexuality, as developed in this section, this marking is a form of sexual objectification that has serious negative implications for the well-being of women and girls.

Objectification theory begins with the observation that "the body is constructed from more than just biology" (Fredrickson and Roberts 1997, 194). Paralleling the above discussion about "real differences" within the equal protection context, it posits that "bodies exist within social and cultural contexts, and hence are also constructed through sociocultural practices and discourses" (194). Building upon this understanding of the body as socially and culturally constructed, as Fredrickson and Roberts explain in their seminal article, sexual objectification in particular occurs "whenever a woman's body, body parts, or sexual functions are separated out from her person, reduced to the status of mere instruments, or regarded as if they were capable of representing her" (175). Of particular relevance, "when objectified, women are treated *as bodies*—and in particular, as bodies that exist for the use and pleasure of others" (emphasis in original; 175).

Sexual objectification is not simply an abstract theory. Rather, it can lead to the damaging practice of "self-objectification,"—the "psychological process by which women [and girls] internalize observers' objectifying perspectives on their bodies" (Calogero, Davis, and Thompson 2005, 43). As a result of viewing "their own bodies through an objectified lens" (43), women and girls may engage in a constant self-monitoring and disciplining of the body in order to meet prevailing standards of female beauty. As many studies make clear, this can result in a cascade of negative outcomes including "increased opportunities for body shame, anxiety, negative attitudes towards menstruation, a disrupted flow of consciousness, diminished awareness of internal bodily states, depression, sexual dysfunction, and disordered eating" (43).

Of particular relevance in the present context, recent studies have shown that self-objectification may lead some women to view bodily functions associated with reproduction—most notably, menstruation and breastfeeding—with a sense of "shame or self-consciousness that arises from or is reinforced by restrictive and sexist cultural norms" (Johnston-Robledo et al. 2007, 436). Consequently, some may "worry that breastfeeding will render their breasts unattractive, that they will be perceived as maternal as opposed to sexual, and/or that they are engaging in an activity that is viewed as disgusting and inappropriate," while others may see "public breastfeeding as a display of sexual behavior" that may be regarded as "nasty" (430).

As a result, some women, particularly those who are "more prone to internalize or endorse the sexual objectification of the breast," may accordingly "avoid or have negative attitudes toward, breastfeeding, a bodily function that interferes with or complicates the view of women as sexually available or attractive" (Johnston-Robledo et al. 2007, 431). In what Roberts and Waters (2004, 10–11) have referred to as "a flight away from the corporeal body," the internalization of the viewer's objectifying gaze may thus lead women and girls to engage in efforts to disguise the messiness associated with normal reproductive functions, such as menstruation, in a vigilant attempt to "transform the physical body into the idealized body."

Conclusion

This chapter has sought to show how, rather than simply encoding real differences into law in order to protect community standards, differential breast exposure rules mark the female body as a site of dangerous erotic potential that must be managed for the public good. Accordingly, these restrictions have been challenged by activists who insist that the law must take account of women's own understanding of their bodies rather than ceding control to the heterosexual male viewer based on an androcentric conception of the erotic. This requires allowing women the same freedom that men currently enjoy to appear topless in public in accordance with their own sensibilities.

NOTES

1. For purposes of this discussion, contemporary understandings of the importance of workplace health and safety regulations have been put to the side as it is the gendering of the law that is of importance in the present context.

REFERENCES

Alexander, Ruth M. 1995. *The Girl Problem: Female Sexual Delinquency in New York, 1900-1930*. Ithaca, NY: Cornell University Press (quoting Mabel Ulrich, Lecture to Social Morality Institute, "The Child and the Young Girl," February 27, 1915).

Arneil, Barbara. 2000. "The Politics of the Breast." *Canadian Journal Women and Law* 12: 345–70.

Boso, Luke. 2009. "A (Trans)Gender-Inclusive Equal Protection Analysis of Public Female Toplessness." *Law & Sexuality* 18: 143–62.

Breckenridge, Sophonisba P., and Edith Abbott. 1912. *The Delinquent Child and the Home*. New York: Russell Sage Charities Publication Committee.

Butler, Judith. 2011. *Bodies That Matter: On the Discursive Limits of Sex*. London: Routledge.

Buzzetti v. New York. 96 Civ. 7764 (S.D., N.Y., 1997); affirmed, 140 F3d 134 (2nd Cir., 1998); cert den. 525 S. Ct. 816 (1998).

Calogero, Rachel, M. William, N. Davis, and J. Kevin Thompson. 2005. "The Role of Self-Objectification in the Experience of Women with Eating Disorders." *Sex Roles* 52: 43–50.

Connelly, Thomas M. 1980. *The Response to Prostitution in the Progressive Era*. Chapel Hill: University of North Carolina Press. Quoting the Newark Vice Commission, 1913–1914, *The Report of the Social Evil in Newark* (12–13).

Craft v. Hodel. 683 F. Supp. 289 (1988).

Cusak, Carmen M. 2012. "Boob Laws: An Analysis of Social Deviance within Gender, Families, or the Home (Etudes)." *Women's Rights Law Reporter* 33: 197–217.

Frank, Katherine. 2003. "'Just Trying to Relax': Masculinity, Masculinizing Practices and Strip Club Regulars." *Journal of Sex Research* 40: 61–75.

Fredrickson, Barbara L., and Roberts, Tomi-Ann. 1997. "Objectification Theory: Toward Understanding Women's Lived Experiences and Mental Health Risks." *Psychology of Women Quarterly* 21: 173–206.

Glazer, Reena N. 1993. "Women's Body Image and the Law." *Duke Law Journal* 43: 113-47.

Goodridge v. Department of Public Health. 798 N.E. 2d 941 (2003).

Johnson, Kay Burr. 1926. "Problems of Delinquency among Girls." *Journal of Social Hygiene* 12: 385–97.

Johnston-Robledo, Ingrid, Stephanie Wares, Jessica Fricker, and Leigh Pasek. 2007. "Indecent Exposure: Self-Objectification and Young Women's Attitudes toward Breastfeeding." *Sex Roles* 56: 429–37.

J. A. Eckl v. Davis. 124 Cal. Rptr. 685 (1975).

Jones v. Hallahan. 501 S.W. 2d 588, (1973).

Lochner v. New York. 198 U.S. 45 (1905).

Loving v. Virginia. 388 U.S. 1 (1967).

Memorandum of Law in Support of Defendant's Motion to Dismiss. 2015. *Free the Nipple – Springfield Residents Promoting Equality v. City of Springfield.*

Merlan, Anna. 2013. "New York's Topless Pioneers—and What They Gave Up for Your Right to Bare Breasts." *Village Voice*, December 11. *www.villagevoice.com/news/ new-yorks-topless-pioneers-and-what-they-gave-up-for-your-right-to-bare-breasts-644038.*

Muller v. Oregon. 208 U.S. 412 (1908).

Obergefell v. Hodges. 135 S. Ct. 2584, 576 U.S. _____ (2015).

O'Connell, Sean. 2014. "How Miley Cyrus is Supporting the Topless-Rights Movie *Free the Nipple*." *Cinema Blend. www.cinemablend.com/new/How-Miley-Cyrus-Supporting-Topless -Rights-Movie-Free-Nipple-68340.html.*

Peiss, Kathy. 1986. *Cheap Amusements: Working Women and Leisure in Turn-of-the-Century New York.* Philadelphia, PA: Temple University Press.

People v. Craft. 509 N.Y.S. 2d 1005 (1986)

People v. Santorelli. 600 N.E. 2d 232 (1992).

Pundras, Helen. 1994–1995. "Public Exposure of the Female Breast: Obscene and Immoral or Free and Equal?" *In the Public Interest* 14: 1–38.

Richmond, Winifred. 1925. *The Adolescent Girl: A Book for Parents and Teachers.* New York: Macmillan Company.

Roberts, Tomi-Ann, and Patricia L. Waters. 2004. "Self-Objectification and That 'Not so Fresh Feeling.'" *Women & Therapy* 27, no. 3-4: 5-21.

Schweitzer, Dahlia. 2000. "Striptease: The Art of Spectacle and Transgression." *Journal of Popular Culture* 34: 65–75.

Seattle v. Buchanan. 584 P. 2d 918 (1978).

Second Amended Complaint. 2016. *Free the Nipple – Springfield Residents Promoting Equality v. City of Springfield.*

Singer v. Hara. 522 P. 2d 1187 (1974).

Weeks v. Southern Bell. 408 F. 2d 228 (5th Cir. 1969)

Whisner, Mary. 1982. "Gender Specific Clothing Regulation: A Study in Patriarchy." *Harvard Women's Law Journal* 5: 73–119.

Woswick-Correa, Kassia R., and Laura J. Jacobs. 2008. "Sexy Ladies Sexing Ladies: Women as Consumers in Sex Clubs." *Journal of Sex Research* 45, no. 3: 201–16.

Yalom, Marilyn. 1997. *The History of the Breast.* New York: Ballantine Books.

Zelizer, Vivian A. 1994. *Pricing the Priceless Child: The Changing Social Value of Children.* Princeton, NJ: Princeton University Press.

12

Give Us a Twirl

Male Baton Twirlers' Embodied Resistance in a Feminized Terrain

Trenton M. Haltom

It is the final round of the National Twirling Championship. A nine-year-old contestant parts the folds of a thin blue curtain to reveal two judges waiting with fixed smiles for the next round of routines to begin. This is the culmination of a summer of gruesome daily practices full of sore muscles, lively pep talks, and jagged, broken nails from missed catches. Finding a spot under the lights on the gymnasium floor, the contestant strikes a pose indicating readiness. As music begins to blast out of the speakers at a steady tempo, in a flash of chrome, *he* winds up for *his* opening trick.

There is a persistent perception that baton twirling is only for girls. This insight is not unwarranted because more often than not, audiences only see girls twirling. Baton twirling, however, is *not* exclusive to girls; boys twirl too.

In this chapter, I explore how the participation of men and boys in the sport of baton twirling exemplifies forms of embodied resistance. In defiance of more masculine and male-dominated sports, men and boys who twirl exhibit embodied resistance in three key ways: through their participation in this feminized sport, by redefining components of twirling to downplay gender, and through choreography involving contentious body movements. Through their participation in a sport in which they are the minority, men and boys' presence in twirling works against more traditional notions of what sports they "should" play. Within competitive twirling, male twirlers reduce certain body movements in an attempt to "undo" their feminine nature (Deutsch 2007).[1] Finally, there is resistance in the ways the free hand (the hand not twirling a baton) is used, with twirlers rejecting judges' and coaches' suggestions to form a fist, a gesture associated with masculinity and power. The twirlers instead prefer to use the free hand for personal expression. Within these forms of embodied resistance, tension is ever present and surfaces in questions such as "What is too feminine?" "When is masculinity conformity?" and, "Can gender in twirling be 'undone'?"

Background on the Gendered Nature of Twirling

The origins of baton twirling can be easily traced through military drum majors leading marching bands. Eleven years after the first baton twirling contest at the Chicagoland Music Festival in 1935, the first major baton twirling organization, the National Board of Technical Advisors (later renamed the National Baton Twirling Association), was formed in 1946 and an official score sheet debuted in 1947 (Sartell 1965). The formation of other competitive baton twirling organizations quickly followed. Post WWII, known as the "Band Craze" era (Robison 1980), audiences became accustomed to seeing thousands of military bands around the United States. Today, countries around the globe compete in Olympic-style competitions.

As the sport of baton twirling evolved, so too did the gendered nature of the sport. There is some discussion about the redesign of the baton and females' entrance into baton twirling. Some speculate that as the batons got lighter during the 1930s and 1940s, they also became easier for females to wield (Miller, Smith, and Ardman 1980; Orr 1981; Sartell 1965). Up to the end of the 1940s, however, men made up the majority of baton twirlers (Sartell 1965). It is likely, in a phenomenon parallel to cheerleading, as men left for war, spaces previously considered too masculine for women opened up (Hansen 1995). Ultimately, as the popularity of the sport increased among young women, twirling became a symbol of feminine grace rather than the masculine leadership it had represented among drum majors.

The differences between the drum major, a leader of the marching band, and majorettes, the drum major's female counterpart, can be seen in the style of their movements. Drum majors retain a sharp, militaristic style and use their batons or maces in ways that would traditionally signal in which direction ranks of band members should move. Early majorettes, who learned their twirling skills from drum majors, added their own flowy, feminine grace—characteristic of an activity "appropriate" for young ladies.

As baton twirling became a competitive sport, however, routines became increasingly difficult, particularly as dance technique became a requirement. As men further culturally distanced themselves from dance (Craig 2014), baton twirling too fell out of favor among men. Additionally, as numbers of female twirlers grew, they became the faces of twirling, making it the effeminately stereotyped activity we know today. Thus, it is young women many people associate with baton twirling and whom new twirlers, whether male or female, model themselves after.

As a result, men's participation is stigmatized in much the same way it is for men in cheerleading (Grindstaff and West 2006), dance (Craig 2014), or figure skating (Adams 2011). In other words, it creates for participants "an attribute that is deeply discrediting" (Goffman 1963, 3), and, therefore, male twirlers today must use certain techniques of resistance and justification to justify their presence in a space that is now a feminized sport rather than in a masculine, "tough" "blood sport" (Drummond 2016) like football or basketball.

"Doing" Baton Twirling

On a daily basis, we make intentional decisions regarding how to perform gender in order to influence how others may determine our sex, thus informing how they treat will treat us. In this way, we are accountable for our sex category transmission and membership (West and Zimmerman 1987). Any uncertainty in interpreting sex or gender leaves some observers confused and unsure as to how to interact. Performance of gender is also related to sexual expression wherein the gendered body regulates the performativity of sexuality (Butler [1990] 2008). By not participating in sports deemed "masculine," like baseball or football, male twirlers challenge the roles set forth by their ascribed sex category and by the rules of heterosexuality, in turn challenging gendered power dynamics (Drummond 2016; Messner 1992). Indeed, men's bodies are not "blank slates," but are rather "arenas for the making of gender patterns" on which the goals of a hegemonic masculinity may be embodied (Connell 2002, 163–64). Alongside this traditional masculinity also comes heterosexuality, a valued practice of masculinity. By performing a sport now typically associated with women and femininity, boys and men in baton twirling are thrust into a category of sexuality (i.e., homosexuality) that may not be an accurate representation of their self-identified sexual orientation. It is at this intersection that male twirlers demonstrate a form of embodied resistance.

Following this idea, the notions of not only "doing," but also "undoing" gender arise (Butler 2004; Deutsch 2007; West and Zimmerman 1987). Deutsch (2007) is critical of the "doing" of gender, suggesting that the semiotics of "doing" construct difference; thus, she asks, if someone "undoes" gender, are they deconstructing it? By "undoing" gender, one behaves or exudes the characteristics of a gender opposite of that expected by their sex as a form of deconstruction and resistance. For example, drag queens' application of feminine behaviors, mannerisms, and dress to a male body is a helpful way to see how men perceive femininity. On the other hand, it is this "cross-contamination" of a gendered performance that challenges the social definition of what it means to be male (Butler [1990] 2008). Indeed, male twirlers are perceived as having created a conflicting gendered performance simply because they are twirling a baton (something that females more typically do). By twirling a baton, men and boys replace associations of power and dominance granted by traditionally masculine sports with weakness and femininity (Drummond 2016; Messner 1992; Whitson 2002).

As I describe in my findings, though the baton acts as a feminized symbol for baton twirling, the accompanying bodywork is also gendered. Here I use Gimlin's (2007) description of bodywork as the production of the body through work environments or, in this case, the sport of baton twirling. Williams (2002), for example, considers how adolescent girls "try on" gender in varying contexts based on the nature of local gender regimes. These gender regimes are patterns of gender relations, a concept borrowed from Connell (1987; 2006), within an institution in which they may be reproduced or deconstructed. To elaborate, Williams (2002) describes adolescent girls who experiment with gender regimes by testing the boundaries of femininity through resisting thinness norms, aspiring to be police officers, or asking boys to dance. Such actions, as predominately masculine practices, go against local gender regimes and are also forms of resistance. This ability to "try on" gender emphases the fluid nature of gender and bodywork based on social time and place.

In a similar vein, previous research suggests that men's ability to "take on" and "take off" certain forms of embodiment speaks to reflexivity (Adkins and Lury 2000; Gimlin 2007, 364; McDowell and Court 1994), a privilege of masculinity. Twirlers enact a form of bodywork in which they interpret the gender regime within baton twirling, negotiate meanings attached to bodywork, and assess their embodied experiences. It is in this discussion of the embodiment and undoing gender that I embed my analysis.

The production of bodywork can be seen among men in feminized sports as well. Men in sports like figure skating (e.g., Adams 2011), cheer (e.g., Grindstaff and West 2006), and dance (e.g., Haltom and Worthen 2014) emphasize the masculine components of certain movements, tricks, or other technical aspects to make them more "macho" (Fisher 2007). By highlighting the athleticism of higher jumps or leaps, pushing for more spins, and showcasing feats of strength, men in these second string, fringe, or marginal sports can better justify their involvement (Adams 2011; Craig 2014; Grindstaff and West 2006; Haltom and Worthen 2014). When dance is performed solo or for the sake of artistry (as is the case with twirling), however, men run the risk of feminization (Craig 2014). To avoid this process, male figure skaters use manly movements like hip thrusts, snapping their fingers, or putting their hands into fists (Adams 2011). Men in these feminized sports appropriate recognized forms of masculine embodiment (strength, toughness, aggressiveness, etc.) in attempt to distract from a soft label (Bordo 1999; Drummond 2016).

Race and class also act as distractions from feminization. In Pascoe's (2012) study of high school students, African American boys were allotted freedom to dance and dress well due to their lower social, economic, and institutional power. Indeed, belittled embodiments like dance are granted exemption for lower classes, women, people of color, and gay men—all of whom are often reduced to their bodies (Craig 2014). White, middle-class men "adopt stolidity and physical reserve as habitual forms of embodiment" in contrast to these disadvantaged groups (Craig 2014, 190). The masculine "physical reserve" of drum majors marks their difference from baton twirlers and their feminine movements. In this way, men who twirl undo gender by resisting cultural assumptions that emphasize difference through defining "socially appropriate bodies" (Gimlin 2007, 364).

Methods

Between August and September of 2014, I conducted and recorded thirty retrospective, semi-structured, in-depth interviews via phone, Skype, or FaceTime. The interviews lasted between a half hour to just over two hours. As a current competitor and coach, I was able to recruit through purposive sampling by contacting competitors, coaches, judges, and administrators via e-mail and social media using a recruitment advertisement and script. I transcribed and thematically coded the interviews using Atlas.ti and used line-by-line coding in order to extract pertinent themes. In the findings section below, I use pseudonyms to preserve participant confidentiality.

The male twirlers represent seventeen states and seven decades of baton twirling. Participants' ages at the time of interview ranged from nineteen to seventy-eight years with an average of forty-one years. Competitive ages ranged from starting at three and retiring at thirty-one years old with the average twirling career lasting fourteen years. On average, the males in my sample began twirling around nine years old. Most of the men were white (twenty-seven). Nineteen participants self-identified as gay, seven as heterosexual; four identified as bisexual or chose not to answer. The population of twirlers as a whole is difficult to estimate as only one American organization requires membership and not all twirlers compete (for instance, they might twirl recreationally or in clubs). Nevertheless, as of March 2016, fewer than 2 percent of the competitors,

Left to Right: Richie Terwilliger, Jeffrey Matiash, Jonathan Burkin, Matt Freeman, and Joel Claudio receive their awards. Photograph by Tim J. Glore

coaches, and judges registered by the United States Twirling Association (USTA) were men or boys (57 men in contrast to 2,923 women). I estimate that there is approximately one male twirler for every one hundred female twirlers.

Findings

Men and boys who twirl demonstrate embodied resistance in three ways: through an association with twirling, by undoing gender in descriptions of twirling, and by choreographing controversy. Mere participation in baton twirling goes against the expectation that boys play more traditionally masculine sports. As a result, male twirlers experience stigma for their association with twirling. To manage this stigma, male twirlers struggle with how to undo gender when it comes to bodywork and rationalize that certain movements are perhaps gender neutral or androgynous. Moreover, because the free hand, the hand not manipulating the baton, is a point of contention between twirlers and judges, formation of the free hand for self-expression permits another opportunity for resistance.

Coming Out of Left Field: Resisting Masculine Sports

In a culture dominated by rough-and-tough sports, men and boys who twirl resist by "coming out of left field." That is, they break expectations of masculinity by twirling. While several participants dabbled in more traditional sports early on, twirling ultimately became their sport of choice. A minority were made to twirl by "stage parents" who in some way lived vicariously through their children. Regardless of how these men and boys became involved in twirling, their participation exemplifies a form of embodied resistance which resulted in experiences of stigma for many. The stigmatized attribute, in this case baton twirling, is one that does not fall in line with the tenets set forth by either traditional sports or masculinity. Some were lucky enough to avert this discretization through associations with accepted sports or athleticism.

Masculine sports are so deeply embedded in American culture that the decision to focus solely on twirling rather than another sport is often met with resistance from family members, and particularly from fathers. While some were lucky enough to have their dad's support and encouragement, others were not. In many cases, fathers were silent wallets begrudgingly paying for lessons. Two dads went so far to make comments: "You know people are starting to talk," and "When are you going to quit that damn thing?" The twirlers not only challenge notions of masculine sports, but also avert the homosocial bonding and father/son time that accompanies them.

Iterations of other competitive team sports sneaked their way into the twirler's lives through an emphasis on athleticism, however. When in the presence of basketball players, Hayden felt he needed to frequently practice his "big" tricks in order to gain credibility as an athlete under the notion that if he impressed them, they would respect him in return. In college, Zeke got a scholarship for twirling and, as other athletes do, used it as a comeback when his fraternity brothers would try to put him down. "I had to brush it off and do my own thing. It was my meal ticket. It was like kiss my ass, I've got to go practice." In two rare cases, Brian's and Victor's fathers stepped in to help their sons' practice, saying if they were going to twirl, they had to be the best. Victor's father would analyze tricks to see why they were not working if Victor dropped the baton too much, and Brian's father put Brian on a strict practice and workout regimen. As if necessary because of the feminized reputation of twirling, components of traditional sports worked their way into baton twirling as mechanisms of legitimization. However, not all the twirlers were so lucky to receive such a pass.

Being forced to twirl was something that added fuel to an already tumultuous fire. That is, the reproach male twirlers experienced was made all the worse when they continued to twirl only due to their parents' influence. Consider Chuck, whose countercultural parents enjoyed seeing their names next to his accomplishments and, according to him, lived vicariously through him and his siblings who also twirled. Because of twirling, Chuck was teased and bullied extensively. For example, during one football game, fans dumped popcorn and soda on him while he twirled. Repeated negative experiences affected him to the extent that he delayed attending college until his thirties to avoid his high school peers. He also refused to walk in his high school graduation and quit three jobs because of his fear of being recognized as a twirler.

Similarly, Uri's mother pushed him to twirl despite teachers and students alike tormenting him with epithets such as "fag" or "fucking homo." In his senior year of high school, he quit twirling for a more traditional sport: wrestling. In his words, "I traded up [from] doing a completely effeminate sport [and] getting called a homo, to doing a sport where you wear like less costuming than you did twirling baton to wrestle guys in a heap. . . . [All] to prove that I'm not gay . . . I'm going to wrestle dudes."

Uri was cognizant that his association with twirling was a violation of masculinity and heteronormativity, yet he found irony in his new setting. Much like baton twirling, wrestling is another sport that is questionably sexualized not just because of the required uniforms (a form-fitting spandex singlet), but also due to the same-sex bodily contact.

Like Uri, Hayden was also subject to various forms of name-calling and torment. On several occasions, he found his locker taped shut or epithets scribbled on surfaces with permanent marker. These experiences are all exemplary of how men's association with the effeminate is met with intolerance and results in negative repercussions for those who step outside of the boundaries of stereotypically male sport norms. Interestingly, Uri now appreciates the life lessons twirling taught him and, as a performer, is able to find humor in his twirling past. Chuck, after an almost fifty-year hiatus from twirling, is now back as a judge.

In sum, all the twirlers I interviewed were aware they were going against the grain by twirling. In addition, they all experienced forms of stigma that manifested in physical bullying, name calling, and vandalizing. In twirling, the embodied gender practice of these men and boys is antithetical to notions of gendered sport and comes "out of left field" because twirling is a sport for girls, and boys' participation is unexpected. Some twirlers, however, were spared in limited ways through athletic association. Nevertheless, the strain many twirlers felt was a product of resistance to the expectation that they play traditionally masculine sports; because they did not, they were left to deal the consequences of that resistance. In competitive twirling, however, they deal with this stigma by attempting to undo gender in bodywork.

Running Interference: Resistance and Undoing Gender through Bodywork

For male twirlers, resistance did not end with participation. Indeed, in reaction to stigma, twirlers "run interference" by the ways they define and perform certain bodily movements and baton tricks. They attempt to undo gender in certain tricks and body movements, preferring instead to define them as "gender neutral" or "androgynous" in nature. In this way, the men reduce the movement so that it becomes less feminine, but still not masculine—a tactical redistribution of gender.

When asked if any baton twirling tricks are specific to men or women, few could come up with any that are exclusively masculine or feminine except one. Rather, they referred to embodiments of gender that revolved around the dance and bodywork that accompany the baton. Hayden removes gender in his explanation: "You know, I mean twirling a baton doesn't make you any less masculine than, you know, playing volleyball or playing ping-pong or wrestling with guys in spandex on a mat. I mean, let's put it in perspective. What's so feminine about twirling a baton? I don't see it, you know? . . . I never saw it in the same light that everyone else did." Here, Hayden grapples with justifications as to why the baton and baton twirling, both effeminate symbols, have been labeled as such by society. To him, twirling baton is no different than playing any other sport and the gender of the player should not matter.

Only in one instance was there agreement on the gendering of a certain "boy trick": the floor bounce—a trick that requires spinning the baton as fast as possible while angling it toward the ground as it is released. Upon hitting the ground, the baton then bounces back up toward the twirler to be caught. The trick requires a high speed of rotation in order to generate the rebound necessary for it to bounce off the ground high enough to catch (remember Newton's third law of motion: every action has an equal and opposite reaction).

While "boy tricks" may exist, male twirlers often resisted these labels. Nate's coach tried to teach him some of these "boy tricks," but he deemed them "stupid": "[My coach] was one of the major pioneers of twirling . . . he would try to teach me what I call the usual boy tricks; I always thought they were stupid. . . . I didn't want to use the same tricks that people had already done." Rather than worry about the gendered nature of a trick, Nate was more concerned with developing his own style within twirling; for him, gendered characteristics of tricks or movements did not matter. As I illustrate shortly, the claim of self-expression and personal style over the femininity of twirling is also a strategy that applies to the "free hand."

Even though some of these boy tricks "did not look good on girls" at the time Gary was twirling in the 1950s and early 1960s, he admits to teaching some of them to his female students more recently. For example, a split-leap pullout is when the twirler jumps into the air with his or her legs spread apart in a split and catches the baton under the legs. While originally categorized as a boy trick because of the athleticism involved and the "unladylike" jump, both females and males perform it now. This speaks to the reflexivity of tricks and how their gendered association can be undone over time.

Along with undoing gender by redefining specific tricks, many twirlers also em-phasized dance technique. When asked if he thought there were any tricks that were specific to men or women, Hayden instead mentioned dance and compared male twirlers to male dancers: "I don't think tricks are based on masculine or feminine [characteristics]. Like if you have an amazing sissonne [a type of leap], you'd be stupid not to put it in [your routine], you know? . . . I mean that's like saying male ballet dancers shouldn't leap. Well, then why are they ballet dancers? You know? So, no, I don't think tricks are gender-specific."

Isaac too mentions leaps as potentially gendered bodily movement when talking about the intersections of sexuality and gender presentation. "You're always supposed to have a fist. You're always supposed to be powerful. I don't think just being gay and having people know that you're gay would have an effect on how you twirl. Maybe you care a little bit less about being masculine or feminine so you may end up being more androgynous in it and if you're going to do a leap, do an awesome leap. Who cares?" Both Hayden and Isaac emphasize that, to them, none of these movements are particularly gendered, and in fact should probably be labeled gender neutral. Either way, both agree: Who cares?

Steven echoed this point and compared twirling to other feminized sports that stigmatize male participants by saying, "You look at figure skating or rhythmic gymnastics or gymnastics and whatnot, I think it's the same thing. . . . Even male gymnasts are required to do pirouettes and do them technically and on balance and whatnot." In this appraisal, Steven attempts to legitimize dance in other artistic sports similar to baton twirling as a way of further justifying its use and thus also redefining the gendered connotation. Gary put this notion to rest using the example of a tour jeté, a leap in which the dancer jumps off of one foot, turns in the air at least half a rotation, and lands on the other foot:

> Gary: Well, I think the role of dance now is great in baton twirling. It wasn't that much when I was twirling.
>
> Interviewer: And you don't have a problem with that even for the boys?
>
> Gary: Oh no, absolutely not. A tour jeté is a tour jeté . . .

For Steven and Gary, when dance technique like the tour jeté is incorporated into baton routines it is just that, a dance step without gendered connotation. Steven and Gary acknowledge both sides of the story: They admit to the feminization of dance and therefore try to downplay it through their detachment. But simultaneously they realize that an attempt to make dance very masculine is futile given the feminized context (a gender regime). In this way, the men attempt to undo gender when it comes to bodywork by reducing the threat of dance while also accepting that it is an essential part of twirling.

Faced with assumptions that baton twirling is a "girl's sport," male twirlers instead enlist the tactic of undoing gendered parts of twirling and dance elements. In doing so, they attempt to legitimize their participation in this otherwise effeminately stigmatized sport in which their presence is contested. This strategy, however, is not limited to dance technique, but is also reflected in the ways male twirlers position the free hand.

Hand Check: Management of the Free Hand

In a baton routine, a good portion of the time one hand is not in use. This hand is referred to as the "free hand" and incorrect formation of it results in an unofficial "hand check" foul. Among male twirlers, coaches, and judges, there is debate as to whether, in order to appear more masculine, a twirler should make a fist of their free hand or not. Female competitors almost never fist their free hand because it would be too masculine. Thus, for men, doing so aids in making their routines that much more "macho" (Fisher 2007); in other words, it's a matter of style and technique. This contentious negotiation of free hand formation—male twirlers' refutation of the fist—acts as a form of embodied resistance.

Paul, now a judge, is a huge proponent of the fisted free hand because it emphasizes the musculature of the male body:

> When you make a fist, it's going to make our bicep, girl or a guy, punch out, you know, pop out. When you do a soft hand, it's making the line and the muscle relax which is then having it appear softer, and so if a guy's twirling with more of a balletic hand without making the tension in the hand strong, it's not going to pop the muscle that makes it look very male or very masculine and so the feminine style of a guy twirler is more softer [sic].

Anatomy aside, in Paul's explanation, the tension created in the arm when the hand is in a fist and punched out is the epitome of the masculine free hand. If any part of the arm is relaxed, he sees it as too feminine or "soft." Paul goes on to say that a guy who uses a softer free hand might also do "a lot of tricks that the girls do that accentuate the strength of the female body type versus doing the tricks that will accentuate the male body type." To Paul, they go hand-in-hand: fists and boy tricks, soft hands and girl tricks. Not all twirlers share this ideology, however.

Aaron's knowledge of dance has influenced how he sees the use of the free hand. After he was given a comment on a score sheet to fist his free hand, his coach told him to ignore it. Aaron "cannot stand" the fisted free hand: "It bothers the crap out of me because if they were to go to a dance class you would never see a guy with a fist for a free hand. Ever." Victor agrees by calling the fist "ridiculous," stating that he prefers a dancer's style of movement of the arms and hands. Indeed, because of the infusion of dance into twirling, both Victor and Aaron see no use for the free hand as an identifier of masculinity. These twirlers undo gender because they see dance as an artistic form in which both men and women perform similar movements, despite feminized perceptions (see, for example, Craig 2014).

What is suggested in lieu of the fist? Certainly not a "limp wrist" (Steven, Tim, Walter, Zeke), a "break in the wrist" (Jason, Walter), a "flip" (Gary), or "flex" (Nate) of the wrist, nor what Jason calls "wings." All of these terms refer to a bend in the wrist (whether up or down), which has an effeminate connotation. Though a majority of the twirlers identified themselves as gay (63 percent), avoidance of these effeminate hand positions may additionally be linked to an avoidance of homosexuality, a devalued social identity. According to Jason, Quinton, Hunter, and Nate, their response was to place the free hand in a "blade" formation with fingers straight out and thumb tucked under. Overall it was important to these men was that the free hand be neither too masculine (a fist), nor too feminine (limp).

Nate and his mother finally decided that the fisted free hand, much like the "boy tricks" discussed earlier, was "stupid":

> We were so worried about, "Oh well you don't want him to look like a girl when he's twirling." So I always had to hold my free hand while I was twirling as a fist and so I did the fist thing for a while and I just didn't like doing it. I felt stupid so I eventually opened my palm up and I asked them . . . "Does that look too effeminate?" and they said, "No, it looks fine," and so from then on, I just kept my hand open.

In the end, the gendered association of the free hand was no big deal to Nate who instead chose to position his hand as a blade, palm up. Elaborating on his previous point, Nate was more interested in creating his own style and did not let criticism get in his way. Nate's insistence that he not use a fisted free hand is a clear form of resistance to the fist as a symbol of power, violence, and masculinity, but there remains the risk that the flipped free hand could be read as weakness, passivity, and femininity. The blade was a middle ground. His stance that the free hand be used to aid in the development of his twirling style coincides with others' opinions that the free hand today is much more emotive than ever before. Despite more variation in free hand formation, the fist remains hegemonic among judges and coaches: it stands to create difference between the girls who twirl and the boys who twirl.

In sum, even the smallest detail like a free hand can be a form of embodied resistance. Calling out the simplistic use of a hand, when the manipulation of the baton is the focus of the sport, emphasizes how critical even minute details become. Male twirlers become critically self-conscious because of their minority status and, as a result, feel they must undo certain gendered features as a form of resistance. By justifying undoing gender in free hand formations, the men lessen the risk of being associated with femininity, but also fall short of embodying masculinity.

Jonathan Burkin poses during a routine at the National Baton Twirling Association's national championship. Photograph by Tim J. Glore

Discussion and Conclusion

Throughout this chapter, I exemplify the ways in which male twirlers enact forms of embodied resistance. Men and boys' participation in baton twirling comes "out of left field" because twirling is counter to sports men and boys are *supposed* to play. By choosing baton twirling over other, more masculine sports these men and boys refute the idea that their gender identity requires that they play these sports. Moreover, the stigma they face as a result of their contested presence causes them to "run interference" by adapting and justifying their presence through forms of resistance. They do so by undoing gender within bodywork by attempting to label it as gender neutral and, at times, emphasizing technique over gender. Male baton twirlers are policed through "hand-checking" the free hand, making sure neither to make it too "macho" as a fist, nor too femme when it is flipped. It is also in establishing this middle ground that they undo gender.

These findings provide a look into the case of how embodiments of gender are negotiated and are ultimately undone through resistance among men and boys in a feminized terrain. Deutsch (2007) suggests that situations in which gender differences are reduced or deconstructed should be referred to as instances of "undoing" gender, and this is the model these twirlers follow. An archetype for men and boys in twirling is not only to resist the notion that the sport itself is a feminized gender regime, but also to resist embodiments of that femininity and, at times, masculinity. Simultaneously, the men attempt to distance themselves from body movements stigmatized as effeminate and therefore potentially "gay." In this environment, the ability to choose aspects of choreographed movement allows male twirlers to demonstrate forms of resistance. Despite the pushback, however, embodiments of hegemonic power structures, such as the fist, remain steadfast.

With this work, I use baton twirling as a case to demonstrate how men and boys strategically negotiate their place in a feminized terrain. As a limitation and area for future study, the largely white sample may speak to privileged intersections of race, class, and gender within baton twirling. In addition to being predominately white, a majority (83 percent) of the sample attained some education beyond high school, perhaps indicating a middle-class standing. Baton twirling is also not cheap when considering the cost of batons, costumes, lessons, contest entry fees, and travel expenses. Greater racial diversity may be better represented in groups of noncompetitive or club-based twirlers. Moreover, the limited representation of twirlers of color of any gender exemplifies how baton twirling is an elite sport that reifies larger race, class, and gender inequalities. The work of Craig (2014) and Pascoe (2012) also highlights the ways in which the body is policed such that middle-class, heterosexual white men have more to lose by twirling, whereas women, people of color, and gay men are already disadvantaged by their lower social statuses. In this case, the narratives of white, gay, middle-class men I present are examples of the maintenance required when both privileged and disadvantaged identities intersect. The lesson here is nevertheless clear. Though the twirlers enlist various strategies to justify their participation in twirling, notions of gender do not always predict what men and boys *should* do. Sometimes, resistance and deconstruction are necessary.

NOTES

1. I acknowledge the term "male" refers to a biological sex category rather than gender. However, in this chapter I use it when referring to men and boys who twirl for a number of reasons. First, it is language the participants use themselves (none identified as transgender). Second, these adult men are reflecting on their experiences as boys, and "male" encompasses both phases of life. And third, many understood sex and gender as interchangeable concepts and conflated the terms in interviews.

REFERENCES

Adams, Mary Louise. 2011. *Artistic Impressions: Figure Skating, Masculinity, and the Limits of Sport*. Toronto: University of Toronto Press.

Adkins, Lisa, and Celia Lury. 2000. "Making Bodies, Making People, Making Work." In *Organizing Bodies: Policy, Institutions and Work*, edited by Linda McKie and Nick Watson, 151–65. London: Macmillan.

Butler, Judith. (1990) 2008. *Gender Trouble: Feminism and the Subversion of Identity*. New York: Routledge.

———. 2004. *Undoing Gender*. New York: Routledge.

Bordo, Susan. 1999. *The Male Body: A New Look at Men in Public and Private*. New York: Farrar, Strauss and Giroux.

Connell, Raewyn. 1987. *Gender and Power: Society, the Person and Sexual Politics*. Stanford, CA: Stanford University Press.

———. 2002. "Debates about Men, New Research on Masculinities." In *Gender and Sport: A Reader*, edited by Sheila Scraton and Anne Flintoff, 161–68. New York: Routledge.

———. 2006. "Glass Ceilings or Gendered Institutions?: Mapping the Gender Regimes of Public Sector Worksites." *Public Administration Review* 66, no. 6: 837–49.

Craig, Maxine Leads. 2014. *Sorry I Don't Dance: Why Men Refuse to Move*. Oxford, UK: Oxford University Press.

Deutsch, Francine M. 2007. "Undoing Gender." *Gender & Society* 21, no. 1: 106–27. doi.org/10.1177/0891243206293577.

Drummond, Murray J. N. 2016. "The Voices of Boys on Sport, Health, and Physical Activity: The Beginning of Life through a Gendered Lens." In *Child's Play: Sport in Kids' Worlds,* edited by Michael A. Messner and Michela Musto, 144–64. New Brunswick, NJ: Rutgers University Press.

Fisher, Jennifer. 2007. "Make It Maverick: Rethinking the 'Make It Macho' Strategy for Men in Ballet." *Dance Chronicle* 30, no. 1: 45–66.

Gimlin, Debra. 2007. "What is 'Body Work'?: A Review of the Literature." *Sociology Compass* 1, no. 1: 353–70.

Goffman, Erving. 1963. *Stigma: Notes on the Management of Spoiled Identity*. New York: Simon and Schuster.

Grindstaff, Laura, and Emily West. 2006. "Cheerleading and the Gendered Politics of Sport." *Social Problems* 53, no. 4: 500–518.

Haltom, Trenton M., and Meredith. G. F. Worthen. 2014. "Male Ballet Dancers and Their Performances of Heteromasculinity." *Journal of College Student Development* 55, no. 8: 757–78.

Hanson, Mary Ellen. 1995. *Go! Fight! Win! Cheerleading in American Culture*. Bowling Green, OH: Bowling Green University Press.

McDowell, Linda, and Gill Court. 1994. "Performing Work: Bodily Representations in Merchant Banks." *Environment and Planning D: Society and Space* 12, no. 6: 727–50.

Messner, Michael A. 1992. *Power at Play: Sports and the Problem of Masculinity*. Boston: Beacon Press.

Miller, Fred, Gloria Smith, and Perri Ardman. 1980. *The Complete Book of Baton Twirling*. Garden City, NY: Doubleday and Company.

Orr, Susan Dailey. 1981. *Baton Twirling Unlimited*. Indianapolis, IN: Carl Hungness Publishing.

Pascoe, C. J. 2012. *Dude You're a Fag: Masculinity and Sexuality in High School*. Berkeley: University of California Press.

Robison, Nancy L. 1980. *Baton Twirling*. New York: Harvey House.

Sartell, Don. 1965. *Who's Who in Baton Twirling 1965*. Janesville, WI.

West, Candace, and Don H. Zimmerman. 1987. "Doing Gender." *Gender & Society* 1, no. 2: 125–51.

Whitson, David. 2002. "The Embodiment of Gender: Discipline, Domination, and Empowerment." In *Gender and Sport: A Reader,* edited by Sheila Scraton and Anne Flintoff, 227–40. New York: Routledge.

Williams, L. Susan. 2002. "Trying on Gender, Gender Regimes, and the Process of Becoming Women." *Gender & Society* 16, no. 1: 29–52.

13

"That Gentle Somebody"

Rethinking Black Female Same-Sex Practices and Heteronormativity in Contemporary South Africa

Taylor Riley

I hung my wet jeans up to dry on a laundry line in a small, freestanding room in the hilly greenery of Inanda township, just a half-hour ride inland from the coastal metropolis of Durban, South Africa. Thandeka did the same. She put on a pair of boxer shorts, and I retrieved the pajama bottoms I had in my damp backpack from staying at a friend's place in town the night before. As the rain came in through holes in the metal roof and began to fill buckets and plastic containers, Thandeka told me about her love life and her sense of self as a woman who loves other women. She relished her own masculinity, her butchness, and her gentleness, ideas which are often contrasted. "I am a woman," she said, "a woman who can do what men do!" She then added, "But I'm not a man. I don't feel like a man. I love wearing men's clothes, presenting myself as that gentle somebody." Gentleness is something Thandeka practiced intentionally, after having been abused for her sexuality and her presentation of gender since childhood. Her words are spoken against the backdrop of violence committed against, and projected onto, the lives of Black lesbians in South Africa.

After spending time with several women and gender-nonconforming persons in the Black LGBTI (lesbian, gay, bisexual, transgender, and intersex) communities of Pietermaritzburg and Durban in South Africa, many of whom were in loving same-sex relationships, I could not help but wonder how the following assumption could be challenged: Black lesbians in contemporary South Africa only either reject or reinforce heteronormative roles. My curiosity was fueled by noticing how both options were at times normatively valued as progressive, healthy, and/or good, or as backward, unhealthy, and/or bad. All the while, the autonomy and self-determinism of Black lesbians was overshadowed. Heteronormativity, a value system of distinct and complementary gender roles based on the male and female sex, is rejected and replaced with homonormativity, in this case a value system based on the active rejection of gender roles.

Because patriarchy and heteronormativity are seen as dominating social forces, nonnormative ways of being, including "lesbian existence" or female same-sex life, are constructed as going *with* or *against* those forces. This is misleading. For example, the totality of heteronormativity as a frame of reference relates to the totality of gender as a frame of reference. If everyday rituals, such as the way one dresses or the way one speaks to others in the street, are always analyzed in terms of gender conformity or nonconformity, other possibilities are erased. This is important particularly in the African and South African contexts, as the concept of gender has its roots in Euro-American sexology and feminism (Magnusson and Marecek 2018, 13–14). While gender is of course still relevant in contexts outside Europe, it may not be so in the same way, or in predictable ways.

Similarly, I argue that while the binary frame of either rejecting or reinforcing heteronormativity in lesbian relationships is plausible, the reality is much more multifaceted. Intentional practices of transgressive female masculinity, or "masculinity without men" (Halberstam 1998), can undermine this binary. In addition to acknowledging that hetero- and homonormativity can be inaccurately projected onto female same-sex life and relationships, female masculinity must be understood outside of that binary and through intentional practices of resistance.

In this chapter, I provide ethnographic data on Black female same-sex lives and relationships in contemporary South Africa to emphasize that, while lesbian relationships can both replicate and reject heteronormative gender roles, Black lesbians in this context also express their gender and sexuality as a unique constellation of constraints and choices. My focus on female masculinity as embodied resistance to dominant norms adds to critical literature on same-sex life in South Africa including, for example, Morgan and Wieringa 2005; Judge, Manion, and De Waal 2008; Steyn and van Zyl 2009; Gunkel 2010; Munro 2012; Swarr 2012a; and Reid 2013.

Background

Although its constitution served as the first in the world to enshrine gay rights (Massoud 2003, 301), the rape and murder of lesbians in South Africa has been called an epidemic (Human Rights Watch 2011). This is the context in which I am writing, and though I do not have the space to do it justice here, this violent reality is inseparable from the national contexts of colonialism, apartheid, and the continued marginalization of those deemed "others." Similarly, tensions between visions of modernity, exemplified by same-sex rights such as marriage, and tradition, based on Black African value systems which oppose same-sex visibility, iterate these histories.[1]

While women, and women of color in particular (Chan 1989; Greene 1994), were long left out of analyses of same-sexuality, work on female same-sex life and relationships has shown the diversity of female embodiments of gender and sexuality (Arnfred 2004; Morgan and Wieringa 2005; Wekker 2006; Dankwa 2009; Blackwood 2010; Engebretsen 2013; Moore 2011; Allen 2015).[2] In particular, the study of female masculinity (Halberstam 1998) has uniquely situated the female nonconforming body's threat to patriarchal social orders. However, analyses of female same-sex practices and relationships, and lesbian life more broadly, can fail to adequately unpack how norms interact with embodied selves and resistances.

For example, while doing fieldwork in South Africa, I found that what particularly illuminated the assumption that lesbians can only either reject or reinforce heteronormative roles was a research report on intimate partner violence (IPV) in female same-sex relationships in the Western Cape (Lynch and Sanger 2016). The report summarized its findings on heteronormative gender roles as follows:

> An overarching trend . . . relates to power disparities within relationships that are informed by normative, taken-for-granted understandings of gender roles. In this normative understanding of gender, women have specific roles that are tied to ideas of heterosexual femininity: providing care, being responsive to others' needs, and being gentle. Men, on the other hand, are associated with roles tied to normative heterosexual masculinity: expressions of power, control, assertiveness and aggression. Participants described how these heteronormative scripts are not limited to heterosexual relationships but also shape the context in which individual roles and relationship dynamics are negotiated within same-sex relationships—often cohering around masculine "butch" and feminine "femme" lesbian identities (12).

While I do not in any way seek to undermine the accuracy or importance of the report, the first of its kind in the country, or take its findings out of the context of IPV, it led me to consider the pervasiveness of the heteronormative gender scripts it identifies and the logical binary it infers: a "heteronormative" embracing of gender roles or a "homonormative" rejection of them.

An example of where the pressure to uphold tradition meets the pressure to challenge gender norms is the tradition of *lobola*, or bride price, usually paid by the husband to the family of the wife in the form of cattle and/or money. A spread in a KwaZulu-Natal newspaper with the headline "Gay and Proud" told Black African gay and lesbian stories of discrimination, perseverance, and love, including a short article on the first traditional Zulu lesbian wedding to occur in the province (Makhaye 2009). A week later, an activist wrote a critical response to those stories, singling out the mentioning of lesbians and lobola in particular. Steven Roche (2009), who was involved in lobbying for the sexual orientation clause to be included in the Constitution's Bill of Rights, which eventually led to the legalization of same-sex marriage via the Civil Union Act, said the following:

> Apart from wondering who owes whom lobola, the notion that two women are required to adhere to "husband" and "wife" roles to legitimate their union is anachronistic and reinforces stereotypes. Worse, however, is that this suggests that gay men and lesbians have gender identity disorders. . . . Lesbians do not want to be men . . . and they generally do not want to be forced into traditional gender roles. The tragic irony, and hence the frustration here, is if "we are (genuinely) tired of pretending to be straight" then why are we still buying into heteronormativity with our mimicry of straight rituals and ceremonies? (n.p.)

Roche's celebration of same-sex marriage in the article combined with his critique of the "mimicry of straight rituals" infers that all same-sex marriage ceremonies that do not involve these specific Black African traditions, such as the exchange of cows, are free from any ties to heteronormativity. This hypocritically fails to acknowledge that same-sex marriage ceremonies involving rings, gendered attire, and the taking of names would thus also be heteronormative. Roche's critique of specific gender roles in female same-sex relationships echoes tensions along lines of gender and race in South African same-sex activism.[3] The same critique also reflects a strain among feminists, specifically between women's liberation and lesbian/female masculinities, that may seem counter-intuitive or even paradoxical. While female masculinity has had an important place in both lesbian subcultures and feminist struggles, some argue that either its usefulness or its existence reaches a kind of political limit. For example, radical feminists have equated butch-femme culture with sexual dysfunction or a horrifying cultural and political backwardness. Halberstam (1998, 130) points to Sheila Jeffreys's logic that gender role-play is an expression of confused self-hatred, and to Julia Penelope's explanation of the misguided, nostalgic sexism of the butch façade. The notion, for example, that lesbians have a responsibility to, through their self-styling and relationships, challenge gender norms or roles is echoed by Ardill and O'Sullivan (1990): "'Gender play' is all the rage, but in all this, where is a feminist consciousness and challenge to gender divisions and inequalities?" (79).

That consciousness has been the subject of much debate, if not only because of the irony of policing female choices in the name of fighting for female autonomy to exercise choice. In the wake of (white, US American) feminism's third wave, many feminists in the United States still contest whether feminism is or is not about the existence of "good" and "bad" feminist choices (see, for example, Caputi 2013, 141; Crispin 2017, 44). Relatedly, the question as to whether a "good" lesbian can engage in gender role-play, historically gendered traditions, or female masculinity is thus like questions as to whether a "good" feminist can choose to be a submissive sexual partner or get a Brazilian wax. Meanwhile, as South African gay rights activists like Roche criticize a lack of feminist consciousness among Black lesbians, Black lesbian activists have, for example, criticized the lack of racial consciousness among white lesbian activists (Luphondwana 1996).

Methods

Situated in this contemporary context, this chapter is based on ethnographic fieldwork conducted in the province of KwaZulu-Natal in South Africa for a total of ten months in 2014 through 2016. Located on South Africa's eastern coast, KwaZulu-Natal has a diverse population of over ten million people, most of whom are of Black African descent. I conducted twenty-three semistructured interviews, some with experts such as LGBTI nongovernmental organization (NGO) practitioners and local academics who work on issues of same-sexuality. Most of my time, however, was spent interacting with women in same-sex relationships, listening to their stories of hardship, acceptance, and love, and tuning into their everyday realities. While participant observation took place primarily in NGO settings—at community workshops on gender and sexuality, for example—observation also took place at informal gatherings such as LGBTI picnics, parties, and hangouts. Key research participants were from KwaZulu-Natal, of Black African descent, between the ages of twenty-one and forty-three, and mainly living in and around the cities of Durban and Pietermaritzburg. To ensure anonymity, I have used pseudonyms. I sought a small number of research participants with whom I could go for depth rather than breadth through life story interviews, interviews that explored personal sexual subjectivities, and informal conversations. Some people I met and spoke with did not identify as women, and some did not identify as lesbians, though all the research participants were female and all engaged in same-sex relationships in some form. Thus, my broad focus was on Black female same-sexualities and Black lesbian relationships, though informants themselves did not uniformly use this language to self-identify.[4] I analyzed data by identifying common themes in participants' personal narratives and comparing experiences and self-perceptions of gender roles and other dynamics in relationships between participants. These results are organized into the following two complementary sections and come together to emphasize that embodiments of gender and sexuality in Black South African lesbian relationships are neither uniformly heteronormative nor uniformly homonormative.

Rituals, Gender Expressions, and Toxic Heteronormativity

There is a careful but tenuous separation between gender identities and roles and "toxic heteronormativity," a gendered imbalance of power which may lead to violence and control in lesbian relationships. This separation, reflected in the wider South African society, is made difficult in practice when traditions like lobola are associated with toxic heteronormativity. From both within and outside the Black LGBTI community, some might agree with Roche's critique of lobola as heteronormative and problematic, despite how he implies that women in same-sex relationships do not choose but are forced to adhere to such traditions. One informant, thirty-eight-year-old Nolwazi, living in Durban, noted in an informal conversation that she does not want to pay lobola for her partner, Lerato, when they marry, because she does not want to buy her. Still, she said she might wish to arrange an alternative and more mutual exchange to symbolize the tradition.

However, others spoke of the importance of paying lobola in same-sex unions. Khosi, a transgender man in his late thirties who had previously identified as a lesbian, had been in lobola negotiations with a female partner's family. Minenhle, a forty-three-year-old church leader and community organizer, was already a wife. Her female spouse had paid lobola to her family, and, in addition to their previous legal wedding, the two planned to have a large traditional wedding ceremony (*umabo*) to formally introduce one another to the ancestors of each family. Whether lobola is inherently heteronormative or problematic is thus subjective. Just as lobola could be considered "heteronormative," not performing lobola could in turn be considered "homonormative," when rejecting binary gender roles is valued as the only positive way of engaging in same-sex relationships.

Identification of "the profoundly patriarchal context in which normative gender identities and roles are constructed in South Africa" (Lynch and Sanger 2016, 12), can thus undermine lesbian agency. For female individuals in same-sex relationships, affirming masculinities, femininities, and differences to one another becomes difficult and problematic when assumptions about gender roles and violence are imprinted onto same-sex lives and relationships by members of wider society. As Nandi, a Black butch lesbian activist from a Pietermaritzburg township in her early thirties, expressed during a workshop on gender and religion: "My gender is being a woman, not a homosexual. It [sexuality] is twenty percent of me." Nandi's masculinity coincided with, rather than contradicted, her nonviolence and her womanhood.

As sexuality has become politically "visible" in South Africa since the Constitution and landmark marriage ruling, so too have individuals who are assumed to be LGBTI become iterated as part of a minority group. This has coincided with human rights organizations' identification of "corrective rape," or the rape of lesbians, as well as gay men and trans people, to "cure" them of their sexual and gender deviance. Twenty-one-year-old Phindi was "born free," or after apartheid, and lives in a peri-urban area of Pietermaritzburg, known somewhat locally for instances of corrective rape. Phindi had a female partner at the time of our interview and said she prefers exclusively to be with women, but neither sees herself, nor is seen by others, as a lesbian. She told me she was bisexual, as she would sometimes engage in brief casual relationships with local men to protect herself from stigma and violence.[5] She said, "I'm not interested, I just do it . . . because sometimes you end up getting raped because, like in this area . . . men, they see, they know that you dating women, and most of·them don't like it." However, there was a time when Phindi expressed a form of masculinity and wanted to be seen as a lesbian. She recalled when she first saw "out" lesbians when she went to high school: "They used to like, you know act like boys and all those things, and I was like oh, I wish I could be like that one day! And girls were so interested into them! . . . So . . . I started changing you see . . . because I had like, long hair. . . . So, I started doing . . . plaits in my hair, and I started to wear long skirts, and you know I started smoking . . . because I also wanted to be seen . . . that I'm interested in girls."

Phindi's gender identity is fluid, but others are not as willing or able to easily move into a space of performing femininity, and therefore assumed heterosexuality, as she has in her adulthood. Others, like Nolwazi, Thandeka, and Nandi, have felt masculine for as long as they can remember. Nolwazi said, "I grew up as a boy. Everything. Soccer, you name it." She added later, "I actually enjoyed when people mist[ook] me for a boy. Oh, I love[d] that!" Nandi too grew up like a boy. She was allowed to have close-cropped hair, and, like Nolwazi, engage in typically male homosocial activities and play. Both would eventually identify as butch lesbian women. Female masculinity among Black lesbians, like the claiming of positive African masculinity by Black South Africans in the wake of apartheid (Ratele 2014), has been an important aspect of the political and everyday struggle for freedom of expression and freedom from violence (Swarr 2012b, 964).

Instances where female masculinities become "toxic" are often linked to the racialized geographic marginalization of Black South Africans living in the townships, the residential areas engineered to maintain apartheid (Lynch and Sanger 2016, 12). This internal enforcement of normative heterosexuality, either through violence against lesbians or through IPV in female same-sex relationships, is a legacy of its external enforcement during apartheid, an era that maintained bans on sodomy and on interracial sexual relations. However, while the identification of toxic heteronormativity has been important to identifying IPV in female same-sex relationships, a very real issue in South Africa often left undiscussed, it has failed to disrupt the apartheid notion that Black masculinity, male or female, is inherently problematic. Phindi, for example, was in an abusive same-sex relationship at the time of our discussion. Gender dynamics played a significant role in her volatile relationship, but when toxic masculinity is seen as the culprit, possible underlying reasons for the violent disposition of Phindi's partner, such as orphanhood, poverty, crime, and a lack of familial support and economic opportunity, are erased.

"Gentle Butchness," "50/50," and Rewriting Gender Scripts

To destabilize the notion that Black lesbians only either reproduce or reject heteronormative gender roles, light must be shed on the ways that masculinities, femininities,

and difference are negotiated in female same-sex relationships. I argue that these negotiations occur not in adherence to or rebellion against heteronormative gender scripts,
but rather they operate in their own unique way, resulting in a distinctive form of cultural production. One example of this is Thandeka's performance of "gentle butchness."

Thandeka is twenty-one years old, the only working member of her immediate
family, and therefore the breadwinner. Her twenty-five-year-old partner, Nomfundo,
also works, so Thandeka sees her responsibility to provide care for her partner as more
than merely financial. Thandeka said that, though she is Nomfundo's first female lover,
she has only been with women. Though Nomfundo identifies as straight and her relationship with Thandeka as an exceptional case, Thandeka has seen a change in her.
Nomfundo would make comments about their sex life, such as she no longer knows
why she spent so long "dicking." Thandeka remarked that Nomfundo is "becoming like
her." To explain how, she gestured to her own boxer shorts, and said, "She loves this!"

The reference to "this" is at once figurative and literal, referring to the vulva, with
it the clitoris and vagina, and at the same time more broadly to the sexual life of those
organs: wetness, friction, touch, taste, and the physicality of pleasure. The statement
that her partner loves "this" implies Thandeka feels that were Nomfundo truly disin-
terested in women, she would only be on the "receiving" end when it came to sex; she
would not "love" (used here as an active verb) "this." But in her love for Thandeka's
female body and taking part in the "giving" of pleasure to her partner, she disrupts a
certain assumed narrative of female same-sex practice where butch/masculine partners
"give" and feminine partners "receive."

Thandeka explained, "I've noticed a lot 'my kind,' that mannish type, butch lesbian, they don't like being called girls. . . . They hate this 50/50 thing." "50/50"
refers to a sexual encounter where both female partners pleasure one another specifically through touch and/or other methods such as oral sex and penetration. Matebeni
(2011) describes it as "a language of mutual (sexual) pleasure, sharing and how sex
is organized" (271). In casual conversations, and at gender and sexuality workshops,
some raised the topic of 50/50 as an indication of gender expression. In this instance,
lesbians who do not practice 50/50 were seen as transgender men. These descriptions, however, were not uniform. As much as some women told me that butch or
masculine-identified lesbians do not like 50/50 because they prefer to pleasure their
partners and wish not to be touched themselves, none of the butch-identified people I
encountered in this research expressed that they do not or would not practice 50/50.

Female individuals in same-sex relationships define their intimate practices and
preferences in a number of ways, with various implications for their understandings of
gender and sexuality. For example, I spoke with Nandi about safe lesbian sex and the
use of female condoms as opposed to gloves. Though gloves are promoted by LGBTI
organizations as a form of protection, one that theoretically provides more range of
motion in sexual practice, Nandi expressed that the condom is sexier because of its
sexual universality. That is, the condom is synonymous with sex, while the glove is
clinical. Here, the phallic condomed dildo, or condomed hand, can be seen as a heteronormative representation of safe sex, where alternatives are relegated to the margins
of not only what is sexy, but also what is safe and healthy. However, this view also
presupposes that penetration with the phallic object or organ is monopolized by maleness or its lesser imitation.[6] While butches pleasure their partners using various techniques, it would be false to see those who primarily penetrate their partners as merely

replicating heteronormative sex. To assume that heterosexuality has sole ownership of differential penetration dynamics is itself a heteronormative assumption.

Still, Thandeka in particular believed that, for butches specifically, it is both pleasurable and important to engage in 50/50: "There's this thing when you are mannish like me . . . if you're having a sexual intercourse, you're not take off the jeans, you take off and like have a sport bra, that's all—men do not take off everything. And . . . I believe that if you're making love, you must connect . . . I connect with my girlfriend through my— [gesturing between her legs, laughing]." She sees the lack of reciprocity in a non-50/50 sexual relationship as problematic in more ways than one, saying, "They do not understand, they take . . . this thing as like—'no, I am a man, I have to show them that I can . . . keep a girl mesmerized,' and they have this attitude like 'no, I have had sex with you,' . . . In clubs, they have had sex with you so you're a whore."

While Thandeka argues that sexual inequality can be violent, and that same-sex practices, not unlike heterosexual encounters, can either reproduce or undermine that violence, she sees the latter task as integral to butchness. For her personally, that means engaging in 50/50. Thus, for Thandeka, rejecting heteronormative violence does not mean ridding herself or her relationship of her masculinity. On the contrary, part of being a "soft" butch is engaging in practices of care she perceives as a form of emotional labor and describes as "motherly" love. This is important for Thandeka because of her history. Her immediate family criticized her boyishness starting when she was a young schoolchild and, at one point, physically abused her for it and her assumed lesbian sexuality.

"As a butch lesbian," she said, "the meaning of me loving a woman is . . . taking care of them . . . understanding them . . . not rendering them powerless, and giving them unconditional love . . . love is all about understanding. It's all about communication, listening to each other." She elaborated, "It's not about being men, It's about that motherly love. That's what I was looking for—giving to another woman. Motherly, but . . . also [other things]." As an example, Thandeka would always put on and take off Nomfundo's socks and shoes. As Thandeka and others mentioned to me, female men and butch women in relationships are expected to care for their partners financially, as well as more intimately. One essential part of intimacy for Thandeka is providing that "motherly" love to her partner Nomfundo. Though Nomfundo is feminine, older than Thandeka, and a mother, Thandeka sees her role as in the relationship as a nurturing figure, a role that can thus be synonymous with masculinity and decoupled from femininity.

Thandeka sees herself as "a woman who could do what men do," but "not a man." She emphasized that her masculinity is "soft," and that she longs to be seen for the positive rather than negative aspects of her own butchness, and to display the positive rather than negative aspects of female masculinity. Reflecting on the abuse she faced from family, Thandeka said, "I have to separate myself from being an angry self . . . I have to try by my best to be good . . . maybe, the experience made me more gentle." Both gentleness and masculinity were essential to Thandeka's identity as a lesbian and as a person in a relationship.

This "queering" of female same-sex relationships and practices occurs within and against ideas, roles, and bodies invoked in discussions and images of lesbian sex/ sexuality. Perceived links here between lesbian sex and heterosexual ideas, roles, and embodiment fail to consider possibilities beyond the heteronormative imaginary, as does equating enjoyment of vaginal penetration with a desire for men or the male body or viewing butch-femme culture as a poor imitation of male and female social and sexual roles. As Halberstam (1998) notes, "female masculinities are framed as the rejected scraps of dominant masculinity in order that male masculinity may appear to be the real thing," in an environment where "masculinity and maleness are profoundly difficult to pry apart" (1–2).

In KwaZulu-Natal at least, that prying is facilitated by altering the gender scripts of traditional roles and rites, such as the paying of lobola. Because traditions are important, disrespect for those traditions can be a worse transgression than the existence of same-sex relationships and/or gender nonconforming people who engage in those traditions. Here, gender flexibility is thus possible as seen through the example of female individuals wearing masculine ceremonial attire, performing masculine traditional dances, and taking on masculine roles in same-sex traditional engagements and weddings. The widespread historical practice of economic marriage between women on the continent (see, for example, Nyanungo 2014) also provides an example of how the separation between maleness and masculinity may prove easier than many assume. Just as female same-sex relationships are not free from the reach of heteronormativity, diverse expressions of female masculinities cannot be so simply attributed to a striving for maleness.

While, as a butch woman, Thandeka enjoys being touched and engaging in a "50/50" relationship, she did not offer her opinion on penetration. But other women I met, like twenty-five-year-old Black bisexual activist Yvette, implied casually that women in same-sex relationships who enjoy penetration must at least be bisexual, as any men who enjoy anal penetration must be bisexual or gay. While the focus on penetration as a signifier for sexual orientation or preference is limiting in terms of how desire can be understood, it also seems to pose little or no problem to acknowledging the realities of sex between female individuals, even when one partner is considered "the" lesbian, and the other might not be, or not in the same way.

This understanding is not ubiquitous, as several female same-sex couples have blurred or shifting roles in their relationships, including but not limited to the ways in which they practice intimacy. Sometimes, this fluidity is unstated or subtle. Zama for instance, who is in her thirties and lives in Pietermaritzburg, embodies both masculine and feminine qualities. She said that she considers herself "the" butch or masculine partner in her relationship with Busi, though they have sometimes been asked about whether Busi might also be considered "the" singular butch in the relationship. Busi herself presents as masculine, and Zama would admit to her own casual femininity and feminine soul. Despite her feminine qualities, when asked about butch-femme or masculine-feminine relationship dynamics, Zama said that she possesses the masculine role in her relationship with Busi. It can be said that this result says something more about the question and the nature of dividing roles and traits in such a gendered way than it does about Zama and Busi's relationship. Nandi too enjoyed some of her own feminine qualities. While I noticed similar, blurred dynamics between Nandi and her partner, Nandi seemed to take up masculine roles. For instance, in the gendered setting of a holiday meal, Nandi would be served food by her partner, rather than serving her.

While Zama and Busi both identified as lesbians, others who did not, like Minenhle and Phindi, referred to themselves as women who *date* lesbians. When I asked whether she sees herself as a lesbian, Minenhle reluctantly identified as straight, even though she had been exclusively in relationships with women since her divorce from her husband many years prior and currently had a female spouse. Minenhle's role as a straight woman, a feminine partner, and as *umakoti* (bride) was relational to her spouse's role as a masculine lesbian and as her (female) husband. This was exemplified by her wearing of traditional feminine clothing and beads during a Heritage Day celebration. On the same day, her spouse wore men's trousers and the hide headband traditionally worn by married men. Minenhle's "heteronormative" femininity, like her spouse's "heteronormative" masculinity, is only made real by the poetics of contrast. Reflecting on the dynamics between Thandeka and Nomfundo, Busi and Zama, Nandi and her partner, and on the image of Minenhle and her spouse in their complementary clothing, relational expressions of "masculine" and "feminine" selves are intra- and interpersonal choices and far from mere imitations of heterosexual life. While some individuals in same-sex relationships may consciously idolize heteronorms, for those who took part in my research this was not the case.

Conclusion

The freedoms and constraints of expressing one's own gender and sexuality, within and outside of romantic relationships, disrupt hetero- and homonorms in powerful ways. Alterations, negotiations, and rejections of gender roles in lesbian relationships, and intentional practices of female masculinity (gentle butchness, for example), demonstrate that while Black female same-sex identities, relationships, and practices in South Africa can defer to both hetero- and homonormative narratives, they also engage in their own transgressive and creative forms of cultural production.

This queering of Black female same-sex relationships and sexual practices, namely understanding their potential outside of heteronormativity, and toxic heteronormativity in particular, is critical for rethinking and reframing gender and same-sex desire in contemporary South Africa. There is a difficulty that comes with understanding Black female masculinity in its own right, when Black masculinity is continually associated with violence. Even among lesbians, masculinity can still be associated with, in the case of the butch women I spoke to, size, strength, economic power, and other qualities viewed as not only positive but normative or even superior. However, there is a productive potential to the subtleties and self-descriptions here: for example, Thandeka's gentleness, and Nandi and Zama's feminine qualities, are a part of rather than distinct from their butch subjectivity.

Female same-sex relationships that embrace difference must not always be associated with heteronormativity, either through its supposed embrace or rejection. While intimate partner violence and other imbalances of power based on gendered ideologies are reprehensible in same- and opposite-sex relationships alike, understanding differences of expression between female same-sex partners, from care practices to personality and style to lovemaking, must be more nuanced, just as the role of tradition must not be underestimated. The gender-flexibility of marriage customs in this context is a testament to the instability of gender itself. The iteration of heteronormativity in same-sex relationships and practices involving gender-related roles reveals how female same-sex life is always seen as a secondary, reactionary, imitative, or rebellious condition. Instead, it should be seen in its own right.

NOTES

1. For example, the indirect rule of colonialism weakened civil society not necessarily by discrediting, but by bolstering, traditional structures. This led to the establishment of separate institutions, such as the Human Rights Commission and the House of Traditional Leaders, which serve as "two poles in society that work to solidify consciousness into one of two camps" (Hunter 2010, 9). The post-apartheid state reified this binary by complementing the Constitution's advances in gay and lesbian rights with the right to practice tradition, which allows for conscientious objection to those rights and the duties they come with, such as performing same-sex marriages as a civil servant (RSA 2006, 6). It is not these rights to practice tradition which are problematic so much as the positioning of tradition as antithetic to not only gay and lesbian rights, but also to the paradigm of human rights, which broadly equates rights, exclusively, with respect for human dignity.
2. I borrow Lindiwe Mkasi's (2016) use of the term "same-sexuality" as a brief and poignant way to get a notion of "same-sex sexualit(ies)" across.
3. Such tensions have been noted with regards to specific events, such as a Black lesbian protest at the 2012 Johannesburg Pride parade, during which protesters highlighting the rape and murder of Black lesbians were met with racist abuse (Davis 2012). Similar tactics by Black lesbian activists at Cape Town Pride were called militant and divisive by (white) *Out Africa Magazine* editor Tommy Patterson (2015).
4. I capitalize Black to signify the collective experience of Black identities and the social factors, including racism, which shape them (as in Yancy 2005, 282). My use of the word lesbian, which must be troubled for its problematic Westernized ubiquity, refers to those who identified with the term and to those female same-sex relationships that must sometimes be classed as lesbian relationships for brevity and to signify certain degrees of commonality. I also note that Black lesbian is an important political category in South Africa (Matebeni 2011), which is relevant to individuals who identify with it.
5. I call Phindi bisexual because this is often how she described herself, and, while her sexuality was also fluid, it was shifting and situational. Therefore, bisexuality being accurate or limiting as a description in a given context shows the contradictions and gray areas of identities and challenges the fixedness of sexual categories.
6. While the language I use here is phallocentric, the point is that phallic should not exclusively equal an iteration of, desire for, or imitation of maleness as opposed to femaleness.

REFERENCES

Allen, Andrea Stevenson. 2015. *Violence and Desire in Brazilian Lesbian Relationships*. New York: Springer.

Ardill, Susan, and Sue O'Sullivan. 1990. "Butch/Femme Obsessions." *Feminist Review,* no. 34 (spring): 79–85. *doi.org/10.2307/1395307.*

Arnfred, Signe. 2004. *Re-thinking Sexualities in Africa*. Uppsala: Nordic Africa Institute.

Blackwood, Evelyn. 2010. *Falling into the Lesbi World*. Honolulu: University of Hawaii Press.

Caputi, Mary. 2013. *Feminism and Power: The Need for Critical Theory*. Lanham, MD: Lexington Books.

Chan, Connie S. 1989. "Issues of Identity Development among Asian-American Lesbians and Gay Men." *Journal of Counseling & Development* 68, no. 1: 16–20. *doi.org/10.1002/j.1556-6676.1989.tb02485.x.*

Crispin, Jessa. 2017. *Why I Am Not a Feminist: A Feminist Manifesto*. Brooklyn, NY: Melville House.

Dankwa, Serena Owusua. 2009. "'It's a Silent Trade': Female Same-Sex Intimacies in Post-Colonial Ghana." *NORA - Nordic Journal of Feminist and Gender Research* 17, no. 3: 192–205. *doi.org/10.1080/08038740903117208.*

Davis, Rebecca. 2012. "Johannesburg Gay Pride Parade Pits Politics against Partying." *Guardian*, October 9. *www.theguardian.com/world/2012/oct/09/joburg-gay-pride-clash.*

Engebretsen, Elisabeth L. 2013. *Queer Women in Urban China: An Ethnography.* New York: Routledge.

Greene, Beverly. 1994. "Lesbian Women of Color: Triple Jeopardy." In *Women of Color: Integrating Ethnic and Gender Identities in Psychotherapy*, edited by Lillian Comas-Díaz and Beverly Greene, 389–427. New York: Guilford Press.

Gunkel, Henriette. 2010. *The Cultural Politics of Female Sexuality in South Africa.* New York: Routledge.

Halberstam, Judith. 1998. *Female Masculinity.* Durham, NC: Duke University Press.

Human Rights Watch. 2011. "'We'll Show You You're a Woman': Violence and Discrimination against Black Lesbians and Transgender Men in South Africa." December 5. *www.hrw.org/report/2011/12/05/well-show-you-youre-woman/violence-and-discrimination-against-black-lesbians-and.*

Hunter, Mark. 2010. *Love in the Time of AIDS: Inequality, Gender, and Rights in South Africa.* Bloomington: Indiana University Press.

Judge, Melanie, Anthony Manion, and Shaun De Waal. 2008. *To Have and to Hold: The Making of Same-Sex Marriage in South Africa.* Auckland Park, South Africa: Fanele.

Luphondwana, Nomfundo. 1996. "Race Relations in the Lesbian Movement." *Agenda: Empowering Women for Gender Equity*, no. 29: 72–78. *doi.org/10.2307/4065804.*

Lynch, Ingrid, and Nadia Sanger. 2016. "'I'm Your Maker': Power, Heteronormativity and Violence in Women's Same-Sex Relationships." Cape Town, South Africa: Triangle Project.

Magnusson, Eva, and Jeanne Marecek. 2018. "Setting the Stage: Gender, Sex, and Sexualities in Psychology." In *Gender, Sex, and Sexualities: Psychological Perspectives,* edited by Nancy Dess, Jeanne Marecek, and Leslie Bell, 3–28. New York: Oxford University Press.

Makhaye, Chris. 2009. "Gay and Proud." *Sunday Tribune* (KwaZulu-Natal, South Africa), May 23.

Massoud, Markd F. 2003. "The Evolution of Gay Rights in South Africa." *Peace Review* 15, no. 3: 301–7. *doi.org/10.1080/1040265032000130896.*

Matebeni, Zethu. 2011. "Exploring Black Lesbian Sexualities and Identities in Johannesburg." PhD thesis, University of the Witwatersrand. *wiredspace.wits.ac.za/handle/10539/10274.*

Mkasi, Lindiwe P. 2016. "African Same-Sexualities and Indigenous Knowledge: Creating a Space for Dialogue within Patriarchy." *Verbum et Ecclesia* 37, no. 2: 1–6. *doi.org/10.4102/ve.v37i2.1576.*

Moore, Mignon. 2011. *Invisible Families: Gay Identities, Relationships, and Motherhood among Black Women.* Berkeley: University of California Press.

Morgan, Ruth, and Saskia Wieringa. 2005. *Tommy Boys, Lesbian Men, and Ancestral Wives: Female Same-Sex Practices in Africa.* Johannesburg: Jacana Media.

Munro, Brenna M. 2012. *South Africa and the Dream of Love to Come: Queer Sexuality and the Struggle for Freedom.* Minneapolis: University of Minnesota Press.

Nyanungo, Hleziphi Naomie. 2014. "Female Husbands without Male Wives: Women, Culture and Marriage in Africa." *BUWA! A Journal on African Women's Experiences* 2, no. 2 (December): 61–66.

Patterson, Tommy. 2015. "Gay, Proud & Colour Blind." *Out Africa Magazine*, no. 23 (winter): 21.

Ratele, Kopano. 2014. "Masculinities without Tradition." In *Gender and Multiculturalism: North-South Perspectives*, edited by Amanda Gouws and Daiva Stasiulis, 133–56. New York: Routledge.

Reid, Graeme. 2013. *How to Be a Real Gay: Gay Identities in Small-Town South Africa*. Pietermaritzburg, South Africa: University of KwaZulu-Natal Press.

Roche, Steven. 2009. "Why Use Straightjacket to Define Being Gay?" *Sunday Tribune* (KwaZulu-Natal, South Africa), May 30.

RSA. 2006. *Civil Union Act*. No. 17 of 2006. November 30. Republic of South Africa.

Steyn, Melissa E., and Mikki van Zyl. 2009. *The Prize and the Price: Shaping Sexualities in South Africa*. Cape Town: HSRC Press.

Swarr, Amanda Lock. 2012a. *Sex in Transition: Remaking Gender and Race in South Africa*. New York: SUNY Press.

———. 2012b. "Paradoxes of Butchness: Lesbian Masculinities and Sexual Violence in Contemporary South Africa." *Signs: Journal of Women in Culture & Society* 37, no. 4: 961–88. *doi.org/10.1086/664476*.

Wekker, Gloria. 2006. *The Politics of Passion: Women's Sexual Culture in the Afro-Surinamese Diaspora*. New York: Columbia University Press.

Yancy, George. 2005. *White on White / Black on Black*. Lanham, MD; Oxford: Rowman and Littlefield.

Showing Up as Myself

Embodiment and Authenticity in the Classroom

Ryan Ambuter

The thing about bodies is that they're always there and they're always doing something, but we act like they're not. As a high school English teacher, I wasn't supposed to talk about my body; I was supposed to ignore it and teach. There are some people who are very good at pretending parts of themselves do not exist, but I am not one of them. I am a nonbinary, transmasculine person. My chest is flat, I have leg and armpit hair, a smooth face, a higher voice, and a hard time entering public bathrooms without being questioned. This is who I am. It didn't take me long to realize that if I was going to make it as an educator I'd have to show up as myself.

Three years into a job teaching ninth and tenth grade English, I knocked on my principal's door. He invited me in and I went for it in a rush of words. "I came to talk because I'm transgender. I can't come back to this school next year as Ms. Ambuter or Ms. Anything. I don't live as a woman in my life and I can't be one here."

There was a long pause. "Well, we're a last name school here. Do you want to go by Mr. Ambuter?"

I didn't.

"Can you think of another option?"

"How about just 'Ambuter'?"

That was okay with him.

I continued the conversation. "I know I don't need to tell you this, but I'm having top surgery this summer, basically a double mastectomy. I don't plan to bring it up with students, but if they ask me questions about my gender or transition I'm going to be honest." He nodded and I searched his face trying to see whether teaching out would be a struggle here. All in all, the conversation was better than I expected. He was supportive and I didn't need to find a new job.

September came, and I showed up on the first day dressed as always: cargo pants and a plaid, button-down shirt, tucked in. I was standing by my open door, which had a nameplate that just read AMBUTER in all caps. I was highly conscious of my newly flat chest, but I pulled my shoulders back and tried to exude confidence as I welcomed students back. Owning my body matters to me.

I greeted my students as a group. "Hi! I'm so excited to see you all! For those of you who don't know, my name is Ryan Ambuter. You can call me 'Ambuter.' I prefer that you don't call me Ms. or Mr. Ambuter, but I know that calling teachers Mr. or

Ms. is automatic in schools and I won't be angry with you if you slip up." There were a few nods and I saw one student mouth the word "cool." We did a quick round of introductions and then I continued: "Tenth grade English is a little different than ninth grade. Now that we've covered the basics we will focus on depth of analysis and critical thinking . . ." Before I knew it I was passing out the syllabus and explaining the course like I'd done for the past three years. I could do this.

My classroom was on the second floor, and I had four windows along the back wall that let in a lot of sunlight. There was no AC or temperature control in the building, and that fall it was hot. My room must have been close to 90 degrees. I taught with the lights off and three fans going. It was still too hot. One day I was wearing jeans and a v-neck t-shirt and had been walking around the room for hours, stopping by various students and engaging them with their writing. I paused, put my feet up on a chair one at a time, and rolled my pant legs up to the knee. I hadn't shaved my legs in years, but this was the first time I'd shown that to students and my heart was pounding. Class continued. I decided I would wear shorts tomorrow.

A few weeks later, a student came into my room and told me her classmates were talking about how weird I looked now that my chest was flat. Her response to me was something like, "I don't know what the big deal is. Same Ambuter, same plaid shirt," with a shrug and a smile. The exchange didn't make me feel uncomfortable, it just strengthened my awareness that students notice bodies, and they notice their teachers. They notice who is hiding. They notice our fear and shame. And they also notice our confidence and unapologeticness. I try to send the message that differences are something to embody, not something to fix.

Later that week I was standing in front of twenty sixteen-year-olds, part way through a lesson on identifying figurative language, a benchmark mandated by the Common Core. I was aware of my flat chest, higher voice, no-fitting-pronoun-or-title self at the front of the room, scribbling on a white board, trying to get them to unpack Thoreau's line about how "we do not ride on the railroad; it rides upon us" (*Walden*, 1908). There was a question. "Mister, I mean miss, I mean, uh . . ." I didn't correct my student, or tell her which one to use. I just said "yes?" and proceeded.

These experiences have shown me that bodies are pedagogical. As teachers, what we do and don't do, say and don't say, show and don't show, are all part of the discourse of the classroom. To proceed as though the only significant learning in a class is through the course content is reductive. It's false. There is deep and significant learning that comes from the ways our bodies speak us. When we refuse to assimilate our bodies, when we take up space with power-in-difference, we are resisting a system that mandates conformity and making room for all bodies to do the same.

Sitting and Resisting

How Using a Wheelchair Confronts Ideas of Normal

Margaret Stran

"What's wrong with you?" is a question I get with much-too-frequent regularity. "Nothing," is my response. Which is typically followed with, "Then why are you using that wheelchair?" I spend much of my life resisting this idea that because I use a wheelchair there is something wrong with me. Many people see my wheelchair and assume I need to be fixed in some way, that there is no way I can be happy because I do not walk. I think it is, in part, that I represent what can happen to anyone, at any point in life. People look at me, and it is clear that disability is as real as my wheelchair.

Others tell me, "You're so inspiring" or, "I can't even play basketball and I can use my legs." Both of which, from the person saying it, are meant to be compliments but instead are incredibly demeaning. To help my students understand this concept, I reframe these comments as a man telling a woman who has run a marathon, "You're so inspiring," or a white person telling a person of color, "I can't even play golf and I'm white." Suddenly, someone is patronizing you for doing what you do, for being who you are, simply because of your gender or skin color—or your wheelchair.

For others, my using a wheelchair reflects a lack of faith, an inability to pray, or an unwillingness to try and work hard. Complete strangers feel it is appropriate to tell me about the power of prayer and pray for, or over, me. When I was younger, I would simply listen to these people, nod, smile, and leave. Then I'd vent to friends about what they said. I realized they were negatively impacting my life, but I had no impact on theirs. I decided that I needed to speak up. One day at the park, my husband and I were walking the dog. A man came up and said hello. He then proceeded to tell me that he used to use a wheelchair and that through prayer he was able to walk and he was going to pray for me. I told him I didn't need his prayers, that he should pray for those who were hungry, homeless, and sick. I was feeling very pleased that I had actually spoken up and made him think. And then he informed me it was the Devil in me who was saying that and I needed his prayers more than ever.

What people who want to pray for my healing fail to understand is that I *am* healed. My spinal cord is severed, but my back is healed. My body functions perfectly, and I rarely get sick. People love to tell me their stories of when they used a wheelchair and how they worked hard and now they can walk. And, if I just tried harder—like they did—I could walk. No amount of faith, prayer, or hard work will change the fact that I cannot walk. And I'm okay with that.

The author at the Lincoln Memorial in Washington, DC. Photograph by Daniel Koenig

The author getting ready to row the Black Warrior River in Tuscaloosa, Alabama. Photograph by Daniel Koenig

Some people only see my wheelchair and, to them, a wheelchair signifies helplessness. Thus, I will be pushing down a sidewalk and someone will come up and just start pushing me, even though my wheelchair doesn't have push handles. Often I will drive somewhere by myself, get my wheelchair out of the car by myself, get in my wheelchair by myself, only to have someone come up as I'm headed to my destination and ask, "Do you need help?" My favorite offer of help comes when I go to the bathroom. I have always wanted to respond to someone's well-intentioned—but completely ridiculous—offer by saying, "Yes, will you wipe?" It's not really me they're asking to help, it's the idea that a person in a wheelchair must certainly need help. The fact is, some people who use a wheelchair do need help, but they are not relying on the kindness of strangers for it. Instead, they have likely made arrangements to get assistance from someone they know, most often a paid attendant but sometimes a friend or family member.

One of the reasons I resent the "what is wrong with you" questions and offers of help are because of what I do and where I work: I co-founded and am currently associate director of the University of Alabama's (UA) Adapted Athletics program. We have twenty-five elite athletes with ambulatory disabilities who train and study at UA. I work with and interact with students who, though younger, are like me in many ways: they are active, they will have a college degree, they either use a wheelchair full time or for sport, and they are happy and comfortable with whom they are (to the extent that any twenty-year-old is and can be). In this world, not being able to walk (or not being able to play stand-up sports) has given these students, as it gave me, a chance to go to school and play wheelchair basketball and get a degree. For many, as well as for me, using a wheelchair or losing a limb provides them with a chance to compete internationally for their country and play in the Paralympics.

Of course, life would be easier if I could walk. Just as life would be easier when I travel if I spoke the language of the country I was visiting. But just as I end up muddling through in a foreign country where English is not the native language, I also somehow seem to muddle through my amazing life, despite all the people I encounter who simply cannot believe it.

My life is not perfect, and sometimes using a wheelchair is a pain, but my disability is an important and meaningful part of my identity—just as being female, white, and left-handed are parts of my identity. And I would not change any part of who I am, including using a wheelchair. Which is why, when people ask, "What's wrong with you?" I tell them "Nothing."

LIVING RESISTANCE

Against Diabetic Numerology in a Black Body, or, Why I Cannot Live by the Numbers

Anthony Ryan Hatch

There aren't too many grown, Black cis-gendered men like me walking around with type 1 diabetes. To be clear, I don't have type 2 diabetes, the diabetes that's currently decimating and debilitating Black people at a horrifying rate. About 95 percent of all diabetics have type 2 diabetes; type 1 is rare and more prevalent in white ethnic groups.[1] I have the kind of diabetes that means lifelong insulin therapy, constant blood sugar testing, and close biomedical management. Having type 1 means that I spend a lot of my time with numbers—blood sugar values, grams of carbohydrates, insulin doses, dates of appointments. And those numbers mean *nearly* everything for my life as a diabetic person. My doctors certainly think those numbers are important—they seem to be practicing what I think of as diabetic numerology, an approach to clinical medicine that sees numbers as essential for the management of bodies. It is a strange feeling to simultaneously fixate on and try to ignore this diabetic numerology so that I can live my life outside the confines of what these numbers say about my body and my diabetes. My embodiment also means I have to go to the endocrinology clinic all the damned time.

My clinical encounters usually begin in the same way. I walk into the clinic and see the nurse technician, who takes my vitals: weight, height, blood pressure, temperature, pulse, and blood sugar. Then, the doctor comes in and performs their function—to fixate on numbers. Since the blockbuster *1993 Diabetes Control and Complications Trial*, I have been subjected to a well-evidenced regime of diabetic numerology that fixates on my quantifiable level of blood sugar control.[2] In that 1993 study, over 1,400 type 1 diabetics were assigned into two groups: the experimental "intensive insulin therapy" group who used three or more daily insulin injections or an insulin pump and frequent blood sugar monitoring, and the control "conventional therapy" group who only used one or two daily injections and less frequent monitoring. Not surprisingly, diabetics in the intensive therapy group had much lower risk of serious diabetes-related complications and had better health overall. This statistical fact has transformed the clinical treatment of diabetes since the study, but the numbers only narrate a small piece of the struggle that type 1 diabetics experience. In 1992, the year I was diagnosed, I went from taking two or three insulin injections a day and frequent blood sugar monitoring to hooking up to an external insulin pump and even more frequent blood sugar monitoring by 1995. This was a big shift for me. But the other piece of the struggle is *in* the fleshy lived experiences of diabetic subjects who have had to become patient-technician-experts.

Many of these experiences unfold in the clinic. I don't see a lot of middle-aged type 1 diabetic Black men patients in the clinic. Part of the reason for this might be epidemiological—there are few Black men with type 1 diabetes. The leading etiological theory is that type 1 diabetes is a genetic autoimmune disorder. While scientists don't know how genes, nutrients, and environments interact to make the body turn off the islet cells that make insulin in the pancreas, they do believe that people inherit the genes from their bio-parents. My own bio-parentage remains a mystery because 1) I am adopted and 2) I wear a racial look that defies instant visual classification. I look Classic Light-Skinned North American Negro, Latino, or Egyptian, depending on my facial hair and your assumptions. People are always walking up to me speaking Spanish; when I had a full beard, a few people spoke Arabic. Without a gene test, the ethno-national distribution of the genetics of type 1 can only be deduced, inferred, predicted by looking at patterns of disease distribution in living racially coded human populations.

I don't usually say much during clinic visits. As a young Negro raised in Georgia, I learned to code switch to a more friendly, talkative, and obviously educated version of my personality as a way to try to disarm white people in positions of power—to let them know *what kind of Black person* they were dealing with. But I don't code switch at the doctor's office anymore because it doesn't really work. So many of my clinical encounters feel like they are organized around assumptions about my blackness. First, there's always the assumption that either I have type 2 diabetes, or that I am somehow more morally culpable in my management of my type 1 like Black folks who have type 2. I must not be taking good care of myself; I must not be that interested in my diabetes care; I must be ignorant about diabetes, nutrition, insulin, and long-term risks. I must be one of those medicine-hating and unruly Negro patients. For years, I wouldn't even reveal to my clinicians that I was a doctoral student in medical sociology who was studying the histories of race, biotechnologies, and metabolic health. If I did, I'd be upgraded from your more basic Friendly Negro to the dangerous Uppity Negro. Most health care providers don't like to be questioned by any of their patients; they certainly don't like to be questioned by smarty-pants Black ones.

Back in 2003, this Uppity Negro had to break up with his endocrinologist, a much older white man who was obsessed with my cholesterol numbers, but who wasn't too happy about my challenges to his authority. My labs showed LDL cholesterol levels that were slightly above new standards set by the National Cholesterol Education Program in 2001. He desperately wanted me to take statins to lower the cholesterol numbers but refused to talk about things like my diet, which at the time included fast foods, lots of cholesterol-rich animal products, and alcohol. I told him about my fears of taking pharmaceuticals every day for the foreseeable future, especially starting at age twenty-seven. I raised concerns about the weakness of the statistical relationships between cholesterol levels and heart disease risk among Black type 1 diabetics. He seemed to be lumping me into the much larger group of Black people with type 2 diabetes, among whom cholesterol management has been shown to be more especially important for reducing the long-term complications associated with heart disease. Besides this error, I didn't want to live only by the numbers, but he wasn't trying to hear any of that. Our break up was over my refusal to always privilege the numbers in living my life and my profound disagreement with his race-based clinical recommendations that ignored my own experiences. So, I got up and bounced.

That encounter began a big, long-term transformation in my life. I began to experiment with vegetarianism and, later, veganism, and stopped eating fast food. I started paying closer attention to what I put in my body without the constant demoralization that too often accompanies eating nutritiously. It is not possible to perfect diabetes self-management through obsessive diabetic numerology, but it is possible to be at peace with the numbers at least some of the time. Today, I have little choice but to continue monitoring my blood sugar daily, and my other metabolic biomarkers, like cholesterol, when I go to the clinic. But I make it clear to my health care providers that I don't only care about the numbers—that can be their job. My job is to stay Black, take insulin as needed, and try to survive.

NOTES

1. Andy Menke, Trevor J. Orchard, Giuseppina Imperatore, Kai McKeever Bullard, Elizabeth Mayer-Davis, and Catherine C. Cowie, "The Prevalence of Type 1 Diabetes in the United States," *Epidemiology* 24, no. 5 (2013): 773–74; Centers for Disease Control and Prevention, *National Diabetes Statistics Report, 2017* (Atlanta, GA: Centers for Disease Control and Prevention, US Dept. of Health and Human Services, 2017).
2. Diabetes Complications and Control Trial Working Group, D. Nathan, S. Genuth, J. Lachin, P. Cleary, M. Davis, L. Rand, C. Siebert, "The Effect of Intensive Treatment of Diabetes on the Development and Progression of Long-Term Complications of Insulin-Dependent Diabetes Mellitus," *New England Journal of Medicine* 329, no. 14 (1993): 977–86.

My Women's Studies Professor Uses Botox?

Dana Berkowitz

I used to believe that women who used Botox were foolishly vain and narcissistic beauty-obsessed junkies who would do anything to hold onto their youth. This all changed a few years ago when I became one of *those women* while researching and writing a book about Botox.[1] I, not a foolishly obsessed beauty junkie, but a regular woman, and, more pertinently, a feminist woman, started using Botox.

I certainly did not set out planning to ever try Botox myself or, worse, to become a habitual user, but in the course of my research, something changed. During my interviews with facial cosmetic surgeons and dermatologists, I voluntarily subjected my face to agonizing close readings that called my attention to which of my wrinkles could benefit from Botox injections. My otherwise-healthy face became defined as faulty as medical and aesthetic "experts" repeatedly scrutinized my body.

During the five years I spent researching and writing my book, I watched—through the particular lens of the subjects of my research—as my skin lost its volume and elasticity, and I witnessed new wrinkles slowly creep up next to my eyes and into my brow, a process that profoundly impacted my sense of self. While I interviewed practitioners and customers and conducted content analysis of women's fashion and beauty magazines, I was repeatedly confronted with dominant discourses about femininity, youth, and beauty that made me increasingly sensitive to what these messages communicated about how my body should look. One woman I interviewed who was a few years younger than me called me "a fool" for not jumping on the Botox bandwagon, and another asked me outright, "How can you write an entire book about Botox without trying it yourself?"

I first tried Botox in 2012—an event that marked an unintentional and much more intimate immersion in my research than I had originally planned. Within a week of the procedure, I was in awe of the results. I was surprised at how refreshed and awake, and, yes, a little bit younger, I looked. When others began commenting on my appearance, not being able to place if it was a new haircut or perhaps a suntan that they were noticing, I could not help but feel at once secretly pleased and overcome with guilt about my decision. As a feminist sociologist, I was embarrassed that I had capitulated to the very patriarchal ideologies I was supposed to be critiquing. But, it was for the sake of research . . . or so I rationalized.

As I became acquainted with my newly Botoxed face during the early weeks of my adjustment period, I noticed that not only had the creases on my brow completely disappeared, but I also had this added space between my eyes and my eyebrows that made me look perpetually alert, even after a night of insomnia or too much red wine.

The author's face before Botox. Photograph by Dana Berkowitz

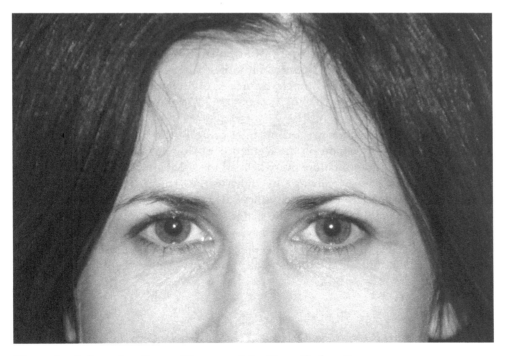
The author's face after Botox. Photograph by Dana Berkowitz

But my face also felt strange, and my range of facial motion was stunted. The entire top half of my face felt invaded and occupied by a foreign substance. Although I was still very much able to move my face and express emotion, I soon realized that I was only able to express certain emotions. The curious thing was how easy it was for me to look bright-eyed and happy but how rarely I looked upset, anxious, or perplexed. It wasn't long after the emotional high of my overarched brow and wide eyes subsided that I soon began to worry about how I was now going to give someone a disapproving look, crinkle my brow to express frustration at my students or colleagues, or signal to my partner that I was annoyed. It was then that I realized why Botox's effect on facial expression was so enticing to women who from early childhood are taught to project cheerfulness and to disguise unhappiness. Botox's erasure of the brow creases and frown lines that can cause women to look angry fits within a long-standing history of disciplining women's bodies to accommodate societal standards of feminine attractiveness.

Because Botox only promises a temporary cure for wrinkles, about four months after my first injections the effects began to wear off and the faint lines on my brow started gradually reappearing. I could rationalize trying Botox once as research, but becoming a habitual user was something entirely different. As I debated whether to inject my face again, my feminist ethics pulled me in one direction and my desire to look more youthful and attractive pushed me in a very different direction. Ultimately, two years later, when the deeply etched creases in my brow became too unpleasant to bear, I decided to try Botox again. A dedicated feminist committed to challenging gender inequality, I was also knowingly participating in an oppressive beauty culture that rewards a narrow visual display of feminine bodies.

My tensions around Botox reveal a great deal about the complexity of feminist debates around body modification. Although my decision to continue using Botox was shaped by conscious assessments about how to preserve my youth and beauty privilege, my decision was also constituted against a backdrop of structural gender inequality wherein medical and beauty authorities dictate and interpret what is appropriate body modification. Through the process of becoming a habitual Botox user, I learned firsthand how women's bodies could be *both* voluntarily cultivated *and* culturally objectified.

One day, not long after my second time using Botox, when I was leading an undergraduate class discussion on the regulation of women's bodies and beauty culture, a visceral sensation of failure overwhelmed me. I couldn't shake the feeling that I was a fraud, that I was deceiving my young women students who were only just sensing their budding feminist consciousness. But instead of coming out to them as a Botox user, as I should have done, the shame I felt for conforming to an oppressive beauty culture compelled my secrecy. I have vowed, the next time I teach any class on the topic of gender and bodies, I will come out as a Botox user, using my personal experience to communicate the contradictory and messy landscape of feminisms.

NOTES

1.   Dana Berkowitz, *Botox Nation: Changing the Face of America* (New York: New York University Press, 2017).

Afterword

Bodies of Resistance

Sonya Renee Taylor

It is Monday afternoon and Roberta watches her sons
spout laughter from their geyser throats;
sunchoked and full of joy when she brings them to the beach.
All six family members a sanctuary slightly out of reach,
a raft against the lash of constant waves.
But the undertow will be too savage for her to save them.
Today, the ocean is a tyrant appointed to swallow them all.
Until 80 Samaritans build a wall in the Gulf of Mexico,
single-mindedly summoned to ferry Roberta's drowning family to shore.
Humans who intuitively know that every wall needs at least one door.
Today, 80 disparate strangers became bodies of resistance
Today, 80 people rebelled against an apathetic ocean's insistence on a sacrifice.

And this is life y'all. In these bodies. Breathless and beleaguered,
we coax one another to survive. We are alive
despite even our bones' dissent. The slack-jawed mutter that says
these bodies were not meant for delight. Who are we to smile
as the world spins in entropy, a hula hoop at our feet?
What right have we to meet this day with anything but fear?
We are safe right now but out there . . .
wails the tiny bloom of child
we hush from inside. And I know
she is, he is, they are, you are afraid,
convinced we must beware and hide.
But what are we, if not survival personified?

Because at this very shake of second a queer kid
is unapologetically lucent in the lion's den
of a middle school cafeteria, just as a woman
takes a seat in a precinct steeling herself
to report the rape, defiant against the red tape
inclined to indict her skirt's failing reach,
only acquit the menace of toxic masculinity.
All while a fabulously fat woman on a plane

explains to the man who has spent four hours
dissecting her body in a series of tweets
that she has no intentions on vacating her seat
of dignity to make room for his hate.
A transwoman clutches the doorknob
of a women's bathroom at the exact second
a politician attempts to legislate her into invisibility.
A college student with cerebral palsy and 7000 signatures
petitions for accessibility in the office of a college dean.

Some days the invocation of simply being seen
in the body you have today is the chant,
is the march, is the picket sign.
There is no time in all of history when these bodies
have not resisted. Even as they tried
to gavel our silence
nevertheless, we persisted.
Each of us a link in the human chain.
Your shame has not slain even the lowliest
of beasts. But our collective transformation
has defeated entire empires. Ushered us intrepid
to capital city streets, 3 million grains of sand
forged under the heat of oppression until we
were fine as keen-edged glass. Made us
a buttress of bodies unafraid to ask
why Black lives should not matter?
We saw no "they" in we, knew solidarity
was a word that must spring like water
forever beside a standing rock. The clock of justice
will not tarry while you question
whether you are worthy of the fight.

Forget all you have been told.
Resistance is an everyday act,
the work of excavating each tiny artifact
of the oppressor that lives in you.
Your call to be a balm to every self-inflicted wound
is how movements are birthed.
In a world content to bid you endless slumber
waking unrepentant in your skin is a hero's journey.
The only way we collectively prevail. Only then can we celebrate
in the words of the great poet Lucille Clifton,
that every day something has tried to kill us
and has failed.
And has failed.
And will fail.

Contributors

Ryan Ambuter is a social justice educator, an English teacher, and a PhD student at the University of Massachusetts Amherst whose research focuses on visible otherness and embodiment in secondary education. Ryan teaches courses on college writing, methods in English education, and embodiment in education. Ryan's activism focuses on LGBTQ students in K12 schools, particularly transgender and gender-nonconforming youth.

Monica Basile holds a PhD in gender, women's, and sexuality studies from the University of Iowa. Her 2012 dissertation, "Reproductive Justice and Childbirth Reform: Doulas as Agents of Social Change," explores the intersections of doula work and reproductive justice. She is a certified professional midwife, certified doula, and childbirth educator, and has been an activist and birth worker for twenty years.

Faith Baum is founder and principal of Faith Baum Architects in Lexington, Massachusetts, and Senior Critic in the INTAR department at the Rhode Island School of Design. Her architecture and coursework explore human-centered design. She has created curriculum and degree programs for the Boston Architectural College, serves as guest critic at numerous universities, and presents and writes for industry conferences and journals. Her art practice includes the Old Bags Project, and she is co-author, with Lori Petchers, of *Old Bags Taking a Stand*.

Dana Berkowitz is an associate professor of sociology and women's and gender studies at Louisiana State University. Her broad research and teaching interests lie within the social construction of gender, sexuality, families, and, most recently, bodies. Her research has been published in *Symbolic Interaction*, *Qualitative Health Research*, *Journal of Marriage and Family*, *Journal of Contemporary Ethnography*, *Qualitative Sociology*, *Sociological Perspectives*, and *Teaching Sociology*. She is the author of *Botox Nation: Changing the Face of America* (New York University Press, 2017).

Chris Bobel is an associate professor of women's and gender studies at the University of Massachusetts Boston. Her scholarship lies at the intersection of social movements, gender, health, and embodiment, or how feminist thinking becomes feminist doing at the most intimate and immediate levels. She is the author of *The Paradox of Natural Mothering* (Temple University Press, 2001), *New Blood: Third Wave Feminism and the Politics of Menstruation* (Rutgers University Press, 2010), and co-editor of *Embodied Resistance: Challenging the Norms, Breaking the Rules* (Vanderbilt University Press, 2011). Her current project is an ethnographic study of menstrual health campaigns targeting schoolgirls in the Global South. In short, she finds bodies and their taboos endlessly fascinating.

Mark Broomfield is an assistant professor of dance studies and associate director of the Geneseo Dance Ensemble at SUNY Geneseo. Mark is a scholar-artist who has danced with Cleo Parker Robinson Dance, performing works by leading African American choreographers. Forthcoming publications include "Branding Ailey: The Embodied Resistance of the Queer Black Male Dancing Body" (*Oxford Handbooks*) and "So You Think You Are Masculine?: Dance Reality Television, Spectatorship, and Gender Nonconformity" (*Routledge Dance Studies Reader*, 3rd ed.). He is currently working on his book *Passing for Almost Straight: Dance, Race, and Gender after Alvin Ailey* and his documentary *Danced Out*. For more information about Mark, visit *www.markbroomfield.org*.

Maxine Leeds Craig is a professor in the Gender, Sexuality and Women's Studies Program and affiliated with the performance studies and sociology graduate groups at the University of California, Davis. She studies everyday embodied practices to investigate social formations of race, gender, and class. She received her doctorate in sociology from the University of California, Berkeley. She is the author of *Sorry I Don't Dance: Why Men Refuse to Move* (Oxford University Press, 2014) and *Ain't I a Beauty Queen?: Black Women, Beauty, and the Politics of Race* (Oxford University Press, 2002).

Rev. Adam Lawrence Dyer is the lead minister at First Parish in Cambridge, Unitarian Universalist, in Cambridge, Massachusetts. He is the author of *Love beyond God* (Skinner House Books, 2016), a collection of poetry and reflections focused on black identity and liberal religion. His blog, Spirituwellness (*spirituwellness.org*), explores the relationship between bodies, faith, and politics and has been featured in *UU World*. Adam has also worked with PolicyLink, the PICO Networks, and the UU Justice Ministry of California advocating for racial, economic, and health equity, as well as LGBTQ inclusion. He is a graduate of Princeton University and the Pacific School of Religion.

J. Shoshanna Ehrlich is a professor of women's and gender studies at the University of Massachusetts Boston. Her interdisciplinary scholarship focuses on the legal regulation of reproduction and sexuality. Her books include *Who Decides?: The Abortion Rights of Minors* (Praeger, 2006) and *Regulating Desire: From the Virtuous Maiden to the Purity Princess* (SUNY Press, 2014). She is currently engaged in a project focusing on the invocation of "abortion regret" as a means of controlling women's reproductive decisions. She also works with a variety of advocacy organizations that are committed to securing the reproductive and sexual rights of teens.

Anne Esacove is the associate director of the Alice Paul Center for Research on Gender, Sexuality and Women at the University of Pennsylvania. Her research explores how health promotion efforts and social movements attempt to create meaning about and control bodies, sexuality, and gender. She is the author of *Modernizing Sexuality: US HIV-Prevention in Sub-Saharan Africa* (Oxford University Press, 2016). Her current research examines the natural death movement, including death acceptance efforts, home funerals, and green burial.

Breanne Fahs is an associate professor of women and gender studies at Arizona State University, where she specializes in women's sexuality, critical embodiment studies, radical feminism, and political activism. She has published widely in feminist, social science, and humanities journals and has authored or edited four books: *Performing Sex* (SUNY Press, 2011), *The Moral Panics of Sexuality* (Palgrave, 2013), *Valerie Solanas* (Feminist Press, 2014), and *Out for Blood* (SUNY Press, 2016). She is the director of the rambunctious Feminist Research on Gender and Sexuality Group at Arizona State University, and she also works as a clinical psychologist in private practice where she specializes in sexuality, couples work, and trauma recovery.

Christina Fisanick is an associate professor of English at California University of Pennsylvania, where she teaches writing, literature, and digital storytelling. Her writing has appeared in many venues, including *Feminist Teacher*, *The Fat Studies Reader*, and the *Journal of Advanced Composition*. In addition, she has written more than thirty books, including her recent memoir, *The Optimistic Food Addict: Recovering from Binge Eating Disorder* (MSI Press, 2016).

Haley Gentile holds an MS in sociology from Florida State University. Her research interests include social movements, political sociology, stratification, and legal mobilization. She has co-authored articles that appeared in *Symbolic Interaction* and *Sociological Perspectives* and a chapter in *Letting Go: Feminist and Social Justice Insight and Activism* (Vanderbilt University Press, 2015). She is a dedicated reproductive justice activist.

Kelly Grove is a sociology PhD student at Florida State University. Her research interests include embodiment, religion, death, and sexual health. She is also a sexual health counselor for the Center for Health Advocacy and Wellness at FSU. She is a committed activist in the areas of disability, HIV, and comprehensive sex education.

Trenton M. Haltom is a PhD student in the Department of Sociology at the University of Nebraska-Lincoln, where he is also pursuing a graduate certificate in women's and gender studies. His research interests include men and masculinities, sexuality, health and the body, and work and occupations. Trenton's scholarship has been published in the *Journal of Men's Studies* and the *Journal of College Student Development*. In 2015, he represented Team USA at the inaugural International Grand Prix of baton twirling and was the feature twirler for both the University of Houston and University of Nebraska.

Anthony Ryan Hatch is an associate professor in the Science in Society Program, Sociology Department, and African American Studies Program at Wesleyan University. His research and teaching focus on the relationships between health sciences, biotechnologies, and social inequalities. He is the author of *Blood Sugar: Racial Pharmacology and Food Justice in Black America* (University of Minnesota Press, 2016) and has held fellowships from the American Sociological Association, the National Institute of Mental Health, and the Center for the Humanities at Wesleyan. His current project is a political history of psychotropic drugs in US society.

Alyssa Hillary is a PhD student in the University of Rhode Island's Interdisciplinary Neuroscience Program and holds a master's degree in mathematics. Alyssa is a Queer Autistic writer and activist, with work in *Criptiques*; *The Queen's Readers: A Collection of Essays on the Words and Worlds of Tamora Pierce*; *Typed Words, Loud Voices: A Collection*; *The Real Experts: Readings for Parents of Autistic Children*; and *The Spoon Knife Anthology: Thoughts on Defiance, Compliance, and Resistance*. Alyssa is interested in disability, neurodiversity, and representation, with a focus on young adult speculative fiction. Alyssa blogs at *yesthattoo.blogspot.com.*

Shayda Kafai is a lecturer at California State Polytechnic University, Pomona, in the Ethnic and Women Studies Department. She earned her PhD in cultural studies from Claremont Graduate University. Her dissertation, "Re-inscribing Disability: The Performance Activism of Sins Invalid," explores the performance art and disability justice work of Sins Invalid, a San Francisco Bay Area–based performance project. As a queer, disabled woman of color, she is committed to exploring the numerous ways we can reclaim our bodies from intersecting systems of oppression. Shayda lives in Los Angeles with her wife, Amy.

Sheila M. Katz is an assistant professor of sociology at the University of Houston and an affiliated faculty with UH's Women's, Gender, and Sexuality Studies Program. Her qualitative sociological research focuses on gender and poverty, specifically low-income women's experiences in domestic violence, grassroots activism, and higher education. Her first book, *Reformed American Dreams: Welfare Mothers, Higher Education, and Activism,* is forthcoming with Rutgers University Press. She serves on the boards of the National Center for Student Parent Programs and *Social Problems*. She also contributes research to the ACLU's Reproductive Freedom Project and Planned Parenthood.

Rachel Kolb is a PhD student in the Department of English at Emory University, where she is also pursuing a graduate certificate in bioethics. She has master's degrees in literature and higher education from Stanford University and the University of Oxford. Her research interests include twentieth-century American literature, disability and deaf studies, science and literature, the health humanities, and how cultural ideas form about communication and embodiment. She is committed to advancing public conversations about communication and accessibility, and her other written work includes publications in the *New York Times* and the *Atlantic*.

Samantha Kwan is an associate professor of sociology at the University of Houston. Her research focuses on the politics of embodiment, particularly how individuals embody, resist, and negotiate body norms and scripts. She is co-author of *Framing Fat: Competing Constructions in Contemporary Culture* (Rutgers University Press, 2013) and co-editor of *The Politics of Women's Bodies: Sexuality, Appearance, and Behavior*, 4th ed. (Oxford University Press, 2014) and *Embodied Resistance: Challenging the Norms, Breaking the Rules* (Vanderbilt University Press, 2011).

Praveena Lakshmanan is a PhD student in the Department of Sociology at Michigan State University, where she is also pursuing a graduate specialization in women's and gender studies. She received her bachelor's degree in political science and a master's degree in sociology from the University of Houston. Her research interests are in the areas of gender, migration, and development. Praveena is actively involved in social justice advocacy for women and children in Houston, as well as transnationally.

Ledah McKellar is a sustainability coordinator at Lakehead University, Thunder Bay, Canada. She recently completed her Master of Education, specializing in women's experiences with polycystic ovarian syndrome and the implications of these experiences for education, self-perception, and medicalization. Her research interests include polycystic ovarian syndrome, health and embodiment, and arts-informed research.

Cat Pausé is the lead editor of *Queering Fat Embodiment* (Routledge, 2014). A senior lecturer in human development and fat studies researcher at Massey University, her research focuses on the effects of spoiled identities on the health and well-being of fat individuals. She has published in journals such as *Human Development*, *Feminist Review*, *HERDSA*, and *Narrative Inquiries in Bioethics*. Cat hosted Fat Studies: Reflective Intersections in New Zealand in 2012, and Fat Studies: Identity, Agency, and Embodiment in 2016. Her fat-positive radio show, *Friend of Marilyn*, is travelling the world—listen in on iTunes!

Lori Petchers is an award-winning documentary filmmaker and visual artist. Her documentaries have been shown on PBS, as well as at numerous film festivals and venues throughout the world. A recipient of an Artist Fellowship Grant from the state of Connecticut, her work aspires to confront social norms and stereotypes through both traditional and nontraditional media. Lori is the co-creator of the Old Bags Project, a feminist response to aging in America. She holds a BA from Brandeis University and an MA from Emerson College.

Katherine Phelps is a doctoral candidate in sociology at the University of Massachusetts Boston and has a master's in gender and cultural studies from Simmons College. She has published in *Fat Studies: An Interdisciplinary Journal of Body Weight and Society* and is a contributor to the American Sociological Association's *ASA Section on Body & Embodiment* blog. Her research interests include body politics, girlhood studies, feminist theory and research methods, digital sociology, and fat studies. She is currently completing her dissertation research focusing on digital girlhood in the United States, specifically how girls present their bodies on social media and navigate body image and sexuality.

Joanna Rankin is an instructor in Community Rehabilitation and Disability Studies in the Cumming School of Medicine at the University of Calgary, Alberta, Canada. Her work has focused on narrative and story as a tool in the discussion and understanding of disability in public spaces.

Sara Rehman is a student at the University of Houston studying women's studies and political science. She is a senator in the University of Houston Student Government Association who plans to pursue a career in public service. Sarah is a social justice activist who fights for human rights and equality. She uses a transnational and intersectional feminist lens in her aim to reform policy and law in the United States. She is committed to opening a dialogue on her college campus about embodied resistance to patriarchal norms.

Taylor Riley is a junior fellow at Bayreuth International Graduate School of African Studies, University of Bayreuth, where she is currently completing her PhD in social anthropology on knowledge and female same-sexuality in KwaZulu-Natal, South Africa. She is also an adjunct instructor in gender studies at the Institute for Sociology, Ludwig-Maximilian University of Munich. She has a master's degree in gender, development, and globalization from the London School of Economics, and her areas of interest are feminist and queer anthropology, South Africa, critical theory, (hi)stories of sexuality, gender in popular culture, and creative ethnographic practices.

Doug Schrock is a professor of sociology at Florida State University. He explores how inequalities are reproduced and challenged from an interactionist perspective. Much of his work emphasizes gender and sexuality, with a focus on culture and identity, emotion and embodiment, and personal and social change.

Stephanie D. Sears is an associate professor of sociology at the University of San Francisco. She received her PhD from Yale University's joint program in African American studies and sociology. As an interdisciplinary scholar, her research examines how race, class, gender, sexuality, and generation intersect and interact in complex and contradictory ways, often simultaneously reproducing oppression and facilitating empowerment. These theoretical concerns and interdisciplinary approach formed the basis of her book *Imagining Black Womanhood* (SUNY Press, 2010), in which she examined how Black women and girls work with and against each other to create safe space, construct identities, and empower themselves.

Margaret Stran is the associate director and co-founder of Adapted Athletics at the University of Alabama. She teaches classes about disability and sport and works to create and expand opportunities for students, staff, and community members with disabilities to be active. She is a former wheelchair basketball player and coach with success on the national and international levels.

J. E. Sumerau is an assistant professor of sociology and the director of applied sociology at the University of Tampa. Their teaching and research examines intersections of sexualities, gender, religion, and health in the interpersonal and historical experiences of sexual, gender, and religious minorities. For more information and examples of their work, visit *www.jsumerau.com*.

Sonya Renee Taylor is a national- and international-award-winning writer, performer, and author, and the founder and Radical Executive Officer of The Body Is Not an Apology (TBINAA)—an international digital media and education company committed to radical self-love and body empowerment. Sonya has been seen, heard, or read on HBO, BET, MTV, NPR, PBS, the *New York Times*, *Huffington Post*, *Ms. Magazine*, and many more. In 2016 she was a guest of the Obama White House, where she spoke about TBINAA's work on intersectionality. She is an inaugural fellow of the Edmund Hilary Fellowship. To learn more about her radical self-love work, visit *www.sonyareneetaylor. com* and *www.thebodyisnotanapology.com*.

Cheryl Thompson holds a Banting Postdoctoral Fellowship (2016–2018) at the Centre for Drama, Theatre and Performance Studies, University of Toronto. Her research focuses on the intersections of race, gender, and media. She explores the function, impact, and aesthetics of media as embodied performances as well as visual culture. Her first book, *Beauty in a Box: Detangling the Roots of Black Beauty Culture in Canada* (Wilfrid Laurier Press, forthcoming), offers one of the first examinations of Canada's black beauty culture, exploring the historical, global flow of products, beauty imagery, and services between the United States and Canada since the nineteenth century. In 2018, she joined the Faculty of Communication and Design as an assistant professor in the School of Creative Industries at Ryerson University in Toronto, Canada.

Jason Whitesel holds a joint appointment in the Department of Sociology and Anthropology and the Women's and Gender Studies Program at Illinois State University. He teaches the core sequence of classes in the queer studies concentration: Sociology of Gender, Sociology of the Body, Introduction to LGBTQ Studies, and Queer and Transgender Theory. He researches, writes, and consults on intersecting categories of oppression, men and masculinities, gay men's experiences, fat studies, and social constructions of deviance, and has authored a critically acclaimed book, *Fat Gay Men: Girth, Mirth, and the Politics of Stigma* (NYU Press, 2014). He is currently writing on groups with a mission to support older gay and bisexual men, and he is researching the representation (and lack thereof) of same-gender-loving men of color and size in the queer community.

Index

CPSIA information can be obtained
at www.ICGtesting.com
Printed in the USA
LVHW021031151221
706264LV00005B/162

9 780826 522344